LITURGIAM AESTIMARE : APPRECIATING THE LITURGY

Series editors
James G. Leachman OSB – Daniel P. McCarthy OSB – Patrick Regan OSB

The « *DREI* » project was developed during the Summer of 2007 as a response to the felt need for a more comprehensive examination of the post-Vatican II liturgical texts, and was announced at the biennial congress of *Societas Liturgica* in August 2007 in Palermo, Sicily. The series *Liturgiam Aestimare : Appreciating the Liturgy*, just one part of the « *DREI* » project, presents a new methodology for interpreting liturgical texts that combines a clear analysis of the Latin language with the literary-critical methodology used at the Pontifical Institute of Liturgy, Sant'Anselmo, Rome.

A further stimulus and encouragement was the Holy Father's 2006 announcement that the Synod of Bishops to be held in October 2008 would reflect on the Word of God in the Life of the Church. As God's Word calls Christians to a deeper unity, we hope that this project, being both ecumenical and international, by promoting shared study and reflection may assist Christians in their desire for a deeper unity.

Far from polarizing positions, a detailed and delicate study of the renewed liturgical texts offers liturgical scholars the resources for deeper and more irenic study. Even as contributions from England, North America, Africa and Australia witness to an international consensus, so too contributions from both Roman Catholic and other ecclesial perspectives ensure that this gift is offered to the broader church.

It is intended that this series will comprise both monographs and edited collections, with appeal both to an academic community, and more broadly to all those who are engaged in liturgical study, research and teaching. This series is promoted by the research project *Documenta Rerum Ecclesiasticarum Instaurata* « *DREI* » in the spirit of its commitment to the renewal of the intellectual and liturgical apostolate of the Catholic Church.

Research libraries and seminaries will have an invaluable tool, and bishops will find in this series resources needed to fulfil their ministry of directing the future course of liturgical renewal.

Project

Documenta Rerum Ecclesiasticarum Instaurata
« *DREI* »

Project moderator

Ephrem Carr OSB

Project directors

James G Leachman OSB – Daniel P. McCarthy OSB

Endorsed by

The President's Council
The Pontifical Institute of Liturgy
Sant'Anselmo, Rome

Volume 1

APPRECIATING THE COLLECT
AN IRENIC METHODOLOGY

Volume editors

James G. Leachman OSB – Daniel P. McCarthy OSB

APPRECIATING THE COLLECT

AN IRENIC METHODOLOGY

James G. Leachman OSB – Daniel P. McCarthy OSB

The Authors have asserted their right under the Copyright,
Designs and Patents Act, 1988,
to be identified as the Authors of this Work.

Nihil obstat   Father Anton Cowan

Imprimatur   ✠ Abbot Martin Shipperlee OSB, Ealing Abbey
✠ Rt Rev. George Stack, V.G., Auxiliary Bishop in Westminster

Westminster, 30th September 2008, Feast of St Jerome

The Nihil obstat *and* Imprimatur *are a declaration that a book or pamphlet is considered to
be free from doctrinal or moral error. It is not implied that those who have granted the* Nihil
obstat *and* Imprimatur *agree with the contents, opinions or statements expressed.*

Cum superiorum permissu
✠ Barnabas Senecal, Sancti Benedicti monasterii apud Atchison in Kansas Abbas
✠ Martin Shipperlee, Sancti Benedicti monasterii apud Ealing in Anglia Abbas
✠ Cuthbert Brogan, Sancti Michaelis monasterii apud Farnborough in Anglia Abbas

British Library Cataloguing in Publication data

A catalogue record for this book is available
from the British Library

ISBN 978-0-907077-61-9

First published in 2008 by St Michael's Abbey Press
Saint Michael's Abbey
Farnborough, Hampshire, GU14 7NQ

www.farnboroughabbey.org
www.theabbeyshop.com

St Michael's Abbey Press is a division of
St Michael's Abbey Press Ltd (reg. no. 326241)

Printed and bound in Great Britain by
T J International Ltd

LITURGIAM AESTIMATURIS

CONTENTS

ABBREVIATIONS

AAS　　= *Acta Apostolica Sedis*, Rome 1909 ff.

BEL　　　= Bibliotheca Ephemerides Liturgicae, Rome.

CLV　　　= Centro Liturgico Vincenziano, Rome.

EL　　　= *Ephemerides Liturgicae* , Rome 1887.

EtL　　　= Études liturgiques, Paris – Louvain c. 1953.

GelasV　= *Liber sacramentorum romanae aeclesiae ordinis anni circuli* (*Cod. Vat. Reg. Lat. 316/Paris Bibl. Nat. 7193, 41/56*) (*Sacramentarium Gelasianum*), ed. L.C. Mohlberg – L. Eizenhöfer – P. Siffrin (Rerum ecclesiasticarum documenta. Series maior, Fontes 4), Herder, Rome ³1981.

GL　　　= GILDERSLEEVE, B.L, - G. LODGE, *Gildersleeve's Latin Grammar*, Bolchazy-Carducci, Wauconda IL 2003, reprint of ³1985.

Goth 1961 = *Missale gothicum* (*Cod. Vat. Reg. Lat. 317*), ed., L.C. Mohlberg (Rerum ecclesiasticarum documenta. Series maior, Fontes 5), Herder, Rome 1961.

Goth 2005 = *Missale gothicum e codice vaticano reginensi latino 317 editum*, ed., E. Rose (Corpus christianorum series latina 159 D), Brepols, Turnhout 2005.

Gregor　= "Hadrianum ex authentico", *Le Sacramentaire Grégorien: Ses principales formes d'après les plus anciens manuscrits*, 3 vol., ed. J. Deshusses (Spicilegium Friburgense 16), Éditions universitaires, Fribourg ³1992, 1, 83-348.

HBS　　　= Henry Bradshaw Society, London 1890 ff.

ICEL　　= International Commission for English in the Liturgy, Washington DC

MR　　　= *Missale Romanum*

MR ¹1970 = *Missale Romanum ex decreto Sacrosancti Oecumenici Concilii Vaticani II instauratum auctoritate Pauli PP. VI promulgatum, editio typica*, Typis polyglottis Vaticanis, Città del Vaticano ¹1970.

MR ²1975 = *Missale Romanum ex decreto Sacrosancti Oecumenici Concilii Vaticani II instauratum auctoritate Pauli PP. VI promulgatum*, Typis Vaticanis, Città del Vaticano ²1975.

MR ³2002 = *Missale Romanum ex decreto Sacrosancti Oecumenici Concilii Vaticani II instauratum auctoritate Pauli PP. VI promulgatum Ioannis Pauli PP. II cura recognitum, editio typica tertia*, Typis Vaticanis, Città del Vaticano ³2002.

OICA　　= *Rituale Romanum ex decreto Sacrosancti Oecumenici Concilii Vaticani II instauratum auctoritate Pauli PP. VI promulgatum, Ordo Initiationis Christianae Adultorum, Edito typica*, Typis polyglottis Vaticanis, Città del Vaticano 1972.

Pad 1992 = "Gregorianum paduense ad fidem codicis Paduensis D 47, Fragmentis collatis Salisburgensibus", *Le Sacramentaire Grégorien*, 3 vol., ed. J. Deshusses (Spicilegium Friburgense 16), Éditions universitaires, Fribourg ³1992, 1, 607-684 (*Pad* 1992).

Pad 2005 = *Liber sacramentorum paduensis (Padova, Biblioteca Capitolare, cod. D 47)*, ed. A. Catella – F. dell'Oro – A. Martini (Bibliotheca Ephemerides Liturgicae, Subsidia 131. Monumenta italiae liturgica 3), Centro Liturgico Vincenziano edizioni liturgiche, Rome 2005.

PL   = Patrologia cursus completa, Series latina, Garnier, Paris, 1844-1855.

RCIA   = *The Roman Ritual: Rite of Christian Initiation of Adults: approved for use in England and Wales, Scotland*, The International Commission on English in the Liturgy, Geoffrey Chapman, London 1987; *The Roman Ritual: Rite of Christian Initiation of Adults: Study Edition*, ICEL – US Bishops' Committee on the Liturgy, Liturgy Training Publications, Chicago IL 1988.

SCM   = Student Christian Movement

SCR   = Sacra Congregatio Rituum

RL   = *Rivista Liturgica*, Torino 1914 ff.

Leon   = *Sacramentarium Veronese (Cod. Bibl. Capit. Veron. LXXXV [80])*, ed. L.C. Mohlberg – L. Eizenhöfer – P. Siffrin (Rerum ecclesiasticarum documenta. Series maior, Fontes 1), Rome ¹1956, ³1978.

Engol   = *Liber sacramentorum engolismensis (Cod. B. N. Lat. 816)*, ed. P. Saint-Roch (Corpus christianorum series latina 159 C), Brepols, Turnhout 1987.

Suppl   = "Hadrianum revisum anianense cum supplemento ad fidem codicis augustodunensis 19", *Le Sacramentaire Grégorien: Ses principales formes d'après les plus anciens manuscrits*, 3 vol., ed. J. Deshusses (Spicilegium Friburgense 16), Éditions universitaires, Fribourg ³1992, 1, 349-605 n° 1019a-1805.

ACKNOWLEDGEMENTS

The inspiration for this first volume in the series *Appreciating the Liturgy* was generated during the Spring of 2007 while writing a paper to be presented at the biennial meeting of *Societas Liturgica* in Palermo, Sicily, the following August. In that paper James G. Leachman OSB and Daniel P. McCarthy OSB presented both a new model of liturgical renewal and a new methodology for interpreting post-Vatican II liturgical texts, which they named *Appreciating the Liturgy*. Encouraged by the paper's favourable acceptance at the conference, and its subsequent publication in *Studia Liturgica* in 2008, they proposed a series of volumes for publication to promote this new model of liturgical renewal and methodology of liturgical study.

As project directors, they invited others working in the field of textual studies to collaborate in this project, one as a project moderator, one as a series co-editor and twelve as permanent members; their positive responses were encouraging. The directors are grateful to the Council of the *Preside* of the Pontifical Institute of Liturgy for its endorsement of this project.

In developing the « *DREI* » project, the directors subsequently convened a one-day international colloquium on the theme "Appreciating the Collect: An Irenic Methodology" held on 31 May 2008, at Sant'Anselmo, Rome. The four papers presented and the day's discussion further helped to develop this volume.

The directors are most grateful to the *Preside* of the Pontifical Institute of Liturgy, Fr Juan Javier Flores Arcas OSB for his welcome and encouragement, to Fr Patrick Regan OSB for presiding at the colloquium, to Fr Ephrem Carr OSB for summarising the day's papers, to Fr Mark Sheridan OSB, Rector of Sant'Anselmo, for the hospitality provided by the Athenaeum and to Abbot Notker Wolf, Primate of the Benedictine Confederation, for his foreword to this volume and his valued ongoing support. We wish to thank all the speakers and participants for their cooperation in making this a well-organised, lively and serious event.

The volume editors would like to express their gratitude to those who helped produce this volume; especially to Abbots Martin Shipperlee of Ealing, and Barnabas Senecal of Atchison, who support us with kind words and financial help, to those who generously accepted the invitation to submit papers and to those who worked on the translating and editing. The contribution of Mgr Renato De Zan was translated from Italian by James G. Leachman OSB and Ephrem Carr OSB. Dom Maximilian Chambers OSB was so generous as to put the project directors in touch with Abbot Cuthbert Brogan of Farnborough Abbey, England, who graciously agreed to publish this volume.

Our thanks go also to Dr Ferdinando Cannicci of the staff of the liturgical periodical *Ecclesia Orans* at Sant'Anselmo for his gentle administrative and linguistic support and to Dom Sixtus Roslevich OSB of St Louis Abbey, Missouri, for his serious application to the indices. We could not have included several resources or perfected the notes without the much appreciated help of Miriam O'Hare and Jane Schuele, Librarians, of Benedictine College, Atchison, Kansas. Our thanks go to the external reader prof. Basilius Groen of the Institute of Liturgy, Christian Art and Hymnology at Graz University, Austria for his valuable insights and advice, and to the copy editor, Peter Harden.

Finally all the contributors to this volume are most grateful to Abbot Cuthbert Brogan OSB of Farnborough Abbey, not only for his help, patience and encouragement, but especially for accepting the volume for publication by St Michael's Abbey Press.

We trust that this volume will prove to be a perennial reference point and source of inspiration for those who have come to 'Appreciate the Liturgy'.

CONTRIBUTORS

Fr Ephrem Carr OSB is a monk of St Meinrad Archabbey, Indiana, and professor of eastern liturgies at the Pontifical Institute of Liturgy and at the Patristic Institute, the *Augustinianum*, Rome. He is editor of the review *Ecclesia Orans* and of the series *Analecta Liturgica*. He serves as consultor for the Liturgical Commission of the Vatican Congregation of Oriental Churches and as moderator of the *DREI* project and the series *Appreciating the Liturgy*.

Fr James G. Leachman OSB is a monk of St Benedict's Abbey, Ealing, London, who teaches and writes at the Pontifical Institute of Liturgy, Rome. He is assistant editor of *Ecclesia Orans*, co-director of the *DREI* project and co-editor of the series *Liturgiam Aestimare : Appreciating the Liturgy*. He writes on the Liturgy of the Church of England and the theology of Rite of Christian Initiation of Adults. He edited the volume *The Liturgical Subject: Subject, Subjectivity and the Human Person in Contemporary Liturgical Discussion and Critique.*[1]

Fr Reginaldus Thomas Foster OCD is for forty years a papal Latinist and professor of the Latin language renowned for his unique pedagogical style and presentation of the living Latin language. His patient and clear understanding of the Latin language provides the standard analysis of the language upon which the methodology of the series *Appreciating the Liturgy* is founded.

Fr Anthony Igbekele is a priest of the diocese of Ondo, Nigeria. He completed a Doctorate of Sacred Liturgy at the Pontifical Institute of Liturgy in 2006 writing on: "Eucharist as *oblatio* and *sacrificium* in the Latin Fathers". Apart from his on-going research into patristic eucharistic themes, he is now undertaking a complementary music course with special focus on composition and counterpoint at the Institute *Musica Sacra*, Rome.

Fr Daniel P. McCarthy OSB is a monk of St Benedict's Abbey, Atchison, Kansas. Having just completed his doctorate at the Pontifical Institute of Liturgy, he now teaches and writes in Rome. He is the author of two series of weekly commentaries published in *The Tablet*, one on the collects (2006-2007), the other on the prayers over the gifts (2007-2008). He is co-director of the *DREI* project and co-editor of the series *Liturgiam Aestimare : Appreciating the Liturgy*.

---

[1] SCM Press, London 2008, 172-200.

Dr Gerard Moore wrote the seminal doctoral dissertation *Vatican II and the Collects for Ordinary Time: A Study in the Roman Missal (1975)*.[2] He is assistant professor at the Sydney College of Divinity, Australia, and has just published volume *Understanding the General Instruction of the Roman Missal*.[3]

Dr Bridget Nichols completed her doctoral studies at Durham University, England, writing on *Liturgical Hermeneutics: Interpreting Liturgical Rites in Performance*.[4] She is Lay Chaplain to the Bishop of Ely and her publications include *Literature in Christian Perspective*[5] and contributions to *A Companion to Common Worship*.[6] Dr Nichols is the editor of *The Collect in the Churches of the Reformation*, to be published by SCM.

Fr Patrick Regan OSB was abbot of St Joseph Abbey, Louisiana, for almost twenty years. He served as President of the Swiss-American Congregation of Benedictines for twelve years. He currently teaches liturgy in the faculties of theology and of the Pontifical Institute of Liturgy both at Sant'Anselmo, Rome. He is co-editor of the series *Liturgiam Aestimare : Appreciating the Liturgy*, and has contributed many articles to *Worship*, Collegeville, MN.

Mgr Renato De Zan is the professor of liturgical hermeneutics at the Pontifical Institute of Liturgy, professor of Scripture and liturgy at the Institute of Pastoral Liturgy, Padua, and professor at the seminary of Pordenone, Italy. He is a liturgical consultant for the Italian Bishops' Conference. His literary-critical hermeneutics, as found in his contribution to this volume, is the standard methodology used in *Appreciating the Liturgy*.

---

[2] International Scholars Publications, Washington 1996.
[3] St Pauls, Strathfield, Australia 2007; Paulist Press, Mahwah, NJ 2007.
[4] Peter Lang, Frankfurt 1996.
[5] Darton, Longman, Todd, London 2001.
[6] Ed. P.F. Bradshaw SPCK vol. 1, 2001; vol. 2, 2006.

FOREWORD

by Notker Wolf, Abbot Primate of the Benedictine Confederation

Liturgy, or divine worship, according to the Constitution on the Sacred Liturgy *Sacrosanctum Concilium* of the Second Vatican Council is "an exercise of the priestly office of Christ ... an action of Christ the priest and of his Body which is the Church".[1] This priestly ministry of Christ is exercised in the liturgy in various ways, as if at the intersection of distinguishable yet interdependent celebrations at diverse altars:[2] primarily at the Christological altar of Jesus' body, for the Word "assumed our mortal humanity that we might share divine life"; at the architectural altar where we offer and receive the gifts; at the altar of Christian service in the world; and at the altar of our own transformation; all of these being diverse altars where gifts are exchanged between God and humanity.

Jesus Christ our Saviour, the same yesterday today and forever! While in every liturgical celebration we encounter his person, fully divine and fully human, we approach the liturgical encounter, nevertheless, with the understanding of our own time, culture and language. In order to understand and preserve the ancient faith of the Church that has been handed on to us in the liturgical texts, the liturgical scholar must first understand the language and culture of the Church's prayer and then seek to understand it from his or her own unique cultural perspective. Through the Church's celebration of the liturgy and her resulting ministry of humble service in the world, the Church proposes our faith in Jesus Christ in our age to every culture and people.

One of the tasks of the research liturgist today is to be like the wise teacher in the Gospel who takes from the treasure chest, that is the treasury of the rites and prayers of the Church, things both old and new (Matt 13:52), in order to nourish the faith and witness of Christians. In their project *Documenta Rerum Ecclesiasticarum Instaurata*, Dom James and Dom Daniel with their collaborators are doing just this. In this first volume they bring together different studies that first present the method and then apply it to the study of specific prayers. The first chapters on history, methodology and structure lead to three detailed studies of specific collects following the

---

[1] CONCILIUM OECUMENICUM VATICANUM II, Constitutio de sacra Liturgia *Sacrosanctum concilium*, 4 decembris 1963, n° 7, in *Acta Apostolicae Sedis* 56 (1964) 101.

[2] Cf. the prayer over the gifts of the Ninth Sunday in Ordinary Time: "In tua pietate confitentes, Domine, cum muneribus ad altaria veneranda concurrimus, ut, tua purificante nos gratia, iisdem quibus famulamur mysteriis emundemur" (*Missale Romanum ex decreto Sacrosancti Oecumenici Concilii Vaticani II instauratum auctoritate Pauli PP. VI promulgatum Ioannis Pauli PP. II cura recognitum, editio typica tertia*, Typis Vaticanis, Città del Vaticano ³2002, 459).

methodology of the Pontifical Institute of Liturgy. The final two chapters treat of the biblical sources and the presence of anamnesis and eschatology in the collects. A concluding synthesis splendidly summarizes the volume's contributions.

The Pontifical Institute of Liturgy was erected by the Holy See as a faculty of the Athenaeum of Sant'Anselmo for the promotion of the Sacred Liturgy through teaching and research. The Institute of Liturgy is the only faculty in the world dedicated solely to the study and research of the Liturgy, and we do so at the behest of the Holy Father himself. As Grand Chancellor of the Athenaeum, I am encouraged by this initiative which draws not only from the scientific methodology promoted by the Liturgical Institute, but also from the whole ethos which drives our Athenaeum.

In my travels, while promoting the welfare and growth of Benedictine monasteries throughout the world, I have often appreciated that the study of liturgy is a key element in the formation of young vocations and in the continuing formation of those already well established in the monastic life of their communities. No matter what their cultural expression, monks of every culture draw from the riches of the liturgy.

I have long been committed to promoting the spiritual life in China. To this end I have welcomed several priests from China to live and study with us at Sant'Anselmo. They too have shown how we all draw from a common tradition of Latin liturgical inheritance already planted in China by past generations.

This same Latin liturgical inheritance has also found a proper expression in the Anglican communion, and this too provides hope for our future reunion.

The editors have so structured this volume as to present both their methodology and several studies on collects with the intent that the collection be useful to bishops and liturgical commissions in their further work of translating the Latin *editiones typicae* into the vernacular. This first volume on the collect brings together studies which treat the fabric of the liturgy according to its proper content and expression: on the one hand the grammatical and lexical connections within the collects and on the other the semiological connections as they are proclaimed.

I hope that a greater appreciation of the liturgical encounter between our Creator and Redeemer and the people of all races, cultures and languages, will make Christ, who is the same yesterday, today and forever, better known, better followed and better imitated in our day.

EDITORS' PREFACE

We intend and hope that this, the first volume in the series *Liturgiam Aestimare : Appreciating the Liturgy*, stands in continuity with the developing tradition of liturgical research and renewal.

First, we see ourselves to be in continuity with Abbot Fernand Cabrol, Dom Marius Férotin and Dom Louis Gougaud of St Michael's Abbey, Farnborough, whose patient study and publications contributed so much to the liturgical movement and renewal at the beginning of the twentieth century. Second, we see ourselves to be in continuity with Doms Leo Cunibert Mohlberg, Leo Eizenhöfer, Peter Siffrin and Anselm Strittmatter of the former *Institutum Liturgicum* (1950-1967) at Sant'Anselmo, Rome, who prepared for the liturgical renewal that would be mandated by the Second Vatican Council through their corpus of critical editions of ancient liturgical documents published in the corpus *Rerum Ecclesiasticarum Documenta* (*RED*). Third, we see ourselves to be in continuity with the methodology developed and used at the Pontifical Institute of Liturgy established by Pope John XXIII at Sant'Anselmo on 15 June 1962.

In the forty years since the publication of the four Constitutions of the Second Vatican Council, naturally the first phase of work was that of producing new *editiones typicae*, a process that lasted from the establishment of the *Consilium* until the publication of the *Martyrologium Romanum*. Since the production of these editions, there has been a second phase of work, that of translating the *editiones typicae* into the vernacular languages and then of implementing the renewed liturgical books mandated by the Council in their vernacular translations.

In his essay "Agendas for Liturgical Reform", first published in *America*[1] in 1996 and then rewritten in 2004 as, "The Catholicity of the Liturgy: Shaping a New Agenda",[2] Francis M. Mannion helpfully lays out and clearly presents five different paradigms for liturgical renewal, which we present along the following spectrum:

a. Restore the pre-conciliar liturgy (the restoration model).

b. Reform the reform (revisit and change the initial direction of the liturgical reform).

c. Advance the reform (continue the official agenda).

d. Re-catholicize the reform (stop the reform; spiritualize or internalize the liturgy).

e. Inculturate the reform (continue the reform following *SC* 37-40).

---

[1] F.M. MANNION, "Agendas for Liturgical Reform", *America* 175 (1996) 9-16.
[2] F.M. MANNION, "The Catholicity of the Liturgy: Shaping a New Agenda", *Masterworks of God: Essays in Liturgical Theory and Practice*, Liturgy Training Publications (Hillenbrand Books), Chicago IL 2004, 202-235.

Mannion's further article on the models or paradigms of liturgical musical style[3] also illustrates another balance of emphases between the 'conventual model' of liturgy inspired by Dom Guéranger and the Solesmes renewal of monastic music and life in which ministry is professional and the participation of the faithful is primarily visual and auditory; and the 'participatory or ritual model' derived from the tradition founded by Dom Lambert Beauduin, wherein participation is seen to be ministerial.

We have noticed that little attention has been given to the detailed study of the renewed *editiones typicae*, because the effort shifted to translating and implementing them pastorally. The time is now opportune, we believe, to deepen the academic study and appreciation of the renewed *editiones typicae*. Accordingly, at the meeting of *Societas Liturgica* in Palermo, August 2007, we proposed a new model of liturgical renewal, which we call *Liturgiam Aestimare : Appreciating the Liturgy*, for, to the degree to which we deepen our appreciation of the current liturgical documents, will the Church discern the way forward.

Thus, we began to develop the project *Documenta Rerum Ecclesiasticarum Instaurata*, « *DREI* », which offers a hermeneutical analysis of the liturgical documents renewed (*Instaurata*) at the behest of the Council, that the Church may further discern the course of liturgical renewal. The « *DREI* » project employs a new methodology for interpreting liturgical texts that combines the clear and detailed understanding of the Latin language, as taught by Reginaldus Foster OCD, Rome, and the textual hermeneutic of Renato De Zan, a professor of the Pontifical Liturgical Institute, Rome. We have already employed the « *DREI* » methodology in our paper given at Palermo and in a chapter on the collects of the three scrutinies.[4]

More specifically, in the article by De Zan cited above,[5] eight keys are presented for interpreting liturgical texts. There, they are arranged according to four dimensions and four foundations.

---

[3] F.M. MANNION, "Paradigms in American Catholic Liturgical Music", *Masterworks of God: Essays in Liturgical Theory and Practice*, Liturgy Training Publications (Hillenbrand Books), Chicago IL 2004, 116-143.

[4] Of note in the weekly column on the Sunday collects by D.P. McCarthy that appeared in *The Tablet* from 2006-2007, see especially: "Self-transcending Gift", *The Tablet*, 10 February 2007, 18, and "Giving as One and as Many", *The Tablet*, 17 February 2007, 15. See also: J.G. LEACHMAN - D.P. McCARTHY, "Preparation for the Piazza: The Preface of the Second Scrutiny (the Fourth Sunday in Lent): The Mystagogical Formation of the Neophytes and the Assembly", Societas Liturgica Conference, 11 August 2007, *Studia Liturgica* 38 (2008) 114-133; J.G. LEACHMAN - D.P. McCARTHY, "The Formation of the Ecclesial Person through Baptismal Preparation and the Celebrations in the OICA: The Collects for the Scrutinies", *The Liturgical Subject: Subject, Subjectivity, and the Human Person in Contemporary Liturgical Discussion and Critique*, ed. J.G. Leachman, SCM - Notre Dame, London - South Bend IN 2008, 172-200.

[5] R. De Zan, "Criticism and Interpretation of Liturgical Texts", 344.

The four dimensions are:

- anamnesis
- epiclesis
- doxology
- koinonia

The four foundations are:

- theandric
- christological-pneumatological
- ecclesial
- symbolic

Having applied this new method of liturgical study, we have discerned a further interpretative key: Christian maturation by developmental steps. We present this new interpretative key in this and hopefully subsequent volumes, as we continue to investigate further aspects of the truth that, in the course of history, have been forgotten or overlooked, and which we now hope to recover.

We have come to perceive in the euchology a developmental process of Christian maturation. As Cyril of Jerusalem (c. 315-386) says that we are the offspring of that nuptial chamber who come to feast first as infants at the breast on the body and blood of Christ,[6] so we might add that as we are enabled by the recurring and sustaining gift of God's self to mature first into the freedom of the children of God and then to our full stature as adult daughters and sons of God, we are called once again to enter into the same bridal chamber as spouse and therefore to a new generativity. Thus, we are called to do the work of God, both through full conscious and active participation in the liturgy and through service in the world.

We have learned that in the liturgy those empowered by God, who have already given themselves to be immersed in baptism and received as God's own, now with the whole church present their offerings as representative of their ongoing self-gift to God and neighbour with the prayer that God receive the gifts, thereby perpetuating the mutual self-gift originally made in

---

[6] " Εἰς γάμου σωματικὸν κληθεὶς ταύτην ἐθαυματούργησε τὴν παραδοξοποΐαν, καὶ τοῖς τοῦ νυμφῶνος οὐ πολλῷ μᾶλλον τὴν ἀπό λαυσὶν τοῦ σώματος αὐτοῦ καὶ τοῦ αἵματος δωρησάμενος ὁμολογηθήσεται... " : "Appelé à des noces corporelles, il accomplit ce miracle merveilleux, et quand, aux compagnons de l'époux, il donne en présent la jouissance de son corps et de son sang, ne le confesserons-nous pas bien davantage?" : "Ad nuptias corporales vocatus, stupendum hoc miraculum effecit: et non eum multo magis filiis thalami nuptialis corpus suum et sanguinem fruenda donasse confitebimur?" (CYRILLUS HIEROSOLYMITANUS, Catéchèses mystagogiques 4, 2, ed. A. Piédagnel [Sources Chrétiennes 126 bis], Cerf, Paris, ²1988, 136-37. Latin text: PG 33, 1100)

baptism and praying both that this exchange of gifts may come to its fruition, and that they may pursue the happiness of mutual self-gift in this life and its fullness with God in the next.

It has been a pleasure to meet and work with this varied and distinguished group of contributors from such different theological and cultural perspectives; and an honour to be able to offer these papers on "Appreciating the Collect: An Irenic Methodology" to a wider audience of those who in study or in celebration wish to deepen their Appreciating the Liturgy.

James G. Leachman OSB and Daniel P. McCarthy OSB

CHAPTER 1

History of Collect Studies

James G. Leachman

Introduction

The title of this chapter belies the difficulties encountered in the undertaking. A mere diachronic treatment of all the material that has dealt with the history of collect studies over the centuries would be so enormous as to obscure the parallel development of different schools of textual study. A synchronic study of the material, on the other hand, would be able to trace the simultaneous development of different research movements and methods, yet would obscure how scientific research relies upon the research undertaken by previous generations. A full study would require both a diachronic and a synchronic treatment, and this is beyond the brief given for this article.

In order to limit the length of the article, we have decided therefore, to focus on the development of one methodology only; that used at the Pontifical Institute of Liturgy in Rome, and yet also to make reference to other schools. The background and history of the establishment of the Pontifical Institute of Liturgy in 1961 by Pope John XXIII[1] shows how the methodology used there is based upon previous studies, always approved by the Church.

The first course offered at the PIL was on the hermeneutics of liturgical texts, entitled *Lectio textuum liturgicorum antiquorum* and given in 1961 by

---

[1] A. J. CHUPUNGCO, "The Pontifical Liturgical Institute", *Sant'Anselmo: saggi storici e di attualità*, ed. G.J. Békés (Studia Anselmiana 97), Pontificium Athenaeum S. Anselmi de Urbe, Rome 1998, 193-226.

Dom Adrien Nocent.[2] Dom Salvatore Marsili began to define the scientific method in his report to the Congress of Abbots in 1966, "*intentus noster est alumnus* [sic] *potius ad scientificam ut dicunt investigationem introducere*".[3] Dom Anscar Chupungco, in his turn, commented subsequently, "Concretely this means that in the first place, the professors should teach the method of doing research work, so the students can carry on later by themselves".[4]

In the same article Chupungco averts to the debt owed to previous researchers, upon which the research work of the PIL is based. When Dom Augustin Meyer had been rector of Sant'Anselmo, he had decided already in 1950 to establish an *Institutum Liturgicum* at Sant'Anselmo, not for teaching liturgy but for advancing liturgical research through the editing of historically important liturgical sources. The first members were Dom Cunibert Mohlberg as Director, Dom Petrus Siffrin (Sion), Dom Anselm Strittmatter (Washington) and Dom Leo Eizenhöfer (Neuberg).[5]

This succession of events shows the successive stages of development in the history of collect studies, and as a result we have divided our study into seven sections, to reflect the different stages and periods of development. The first is the longest historically though with the thinnest scattering of studies and the last period is the shortest but with the largest number of studies per year. The stages and periods I have identified are the following:

1. Pre 1600:   Collecting and publishing the sources
2. 1600-1799:   Collections and commentaries
3. 1800-1899:   Beginning scientific studies. Anglican pre-eminence
4. 1900-1959:   Source criticism, critical editions,
                          diplomatic editions; the study of Christian Latin
5. 1960-1979:   Beginning a Scientific-Liturgical methodology
6. 1980-1999:   Developing hermeneutical studies
7. 2000 onwards: The two pillars of a new methodology

1. **Pre 1600**: Collecting and publishing the sources.

In this period leading up to and including the Protestant and Catholic Reformations the evolution of the liturgy proceeded relatively undisturbed by scientific principles and was based on centres of ecclesiastical power and influence, Rome, Paris, Mainz, Cologne and Vienna on the Continent and Canterbury, York and Westminster in England. Vogel writes, "By the XVI

---

[2] CHUPUNGCO, "The Pontifical Liturgical Institute", 203.

[3] CHUPUNGCO, "The Pontifical Liturgical Institute", 202.

[4] CHUPUNGCO, "The Pontifical Liturgical Institute", 202.

[5] P. ENGELBERT, *Geschichte des Benediktinerkollegs St. Anselm in Rom: von den Anfängen (1888) bis zur Gegenwart* (Studia Anselmiana 98), Pontificium Athenaeum S. Anselmi de Urbe, Rome 1998, 183, 189-192, 219.

century, the process of liturgical codification was over, ... [and] the documents liturgical scholars collected were to prove helpful for the [later] study of medieval liturgy".[6] It was not until after the publication of the Missal of Pius V that J. Pamelius (Jacques de Joigny de Pamèle) in 1571 published the two volumes of *Liturgicon Ecclesiae latinae*, in Cologne, containing the Codex *Capitulum metropolitanum n. 137* of the Gregorian Sacramentary.[7] Angelo Rocca, too, published the *Sancti Gregorii Magni Liber Sacramentorum* in Rome in 1593, containing *Codex Vaticanus Latinus 3806*.[8]

2. **1600-1799**: Collections and commentaries.

In this period many scholarly works appeared, remarkable both for the documents they assembled and for the learned commentaries which accompanied them.[9] Some of the more important, now certainly re-edited and used in the study of collects today, are listed in Vogel's volume.[10]

Cardinal J. M. Tomasi[11] published the *Codices Sacramentorum nongentis* [sic] *annis vetustiores*, in Rome in 1680, and this included texts of the Gelasian Sacramentary (*Vat. lat. Reg. 316*),[12] the *Missale Gothicum* (*Vat. lat. Reg. 317*),[13] *Missale Francorum* (*Vat. lat. Reg. 257*)[14] and *Missale Gallicanum Vetus* (*Palat. lat. 493*),[15] all four *editiones principes*. Tomasi's works, published in the editions of A.F. Vezzosi between 1747-1754, were long a source for liturgical scholars. In Paris in 1685 Dom Jean Mabillon published the first study on the liturgy in France, *De liturgia gallicana libri tres*, and Mabillon and Germain Morin together then went on to publish the *Museum italicum seu collectio veterum scriptorum ex bibliothecis italicis*, in 1687 and 1689. Of these, the first volume includes the Bobbio Missal under the title, *Liber Sacramentorum Ecclesiae*

---

[6] C. VOGEL, *Medieval Liturgy: An Introduction to the Sources*, tr., rev. W.G. Storey – N.K. Rasmussen, (National Association of Pastoral Musicians Studies in Church Music and Liturgy), Pastoral Press, Washington DC 1986 (of *Introduction aux sources de l'histoire du culte chrétien au moyen âge*, Centro italiano di studi sull'alto medioevo, Spoleto 1981), 17.

[7] I. SCICOLONE, *Il Cardinale Giuseppe Tomasi di Lampedusa e gli inizi della scienza liturgica* (Studia Anselmiana 82, Analecta Liturgica 5), Pontificium Athenaeum S. Anselmi de Urbe, Rome 1981, 79 n. 44.

[8] SCICOLONE, *Il Cardinale Giuseppe Tomasi*, 79, n. 45.

[9] VOGEL, *Medieval Liturgy*, 17-18.

[10] VOGEL, *Medieval Liturgy*, 18-20.

[11] J.D. CRICHTON, "The First Liturgical Saint, Giuseppe Tommasi (1649-1713)", *Lights in the Darkness: Forerunners of the Liturgical Movement*, Columba, Blackrock 1996, 11-13; SCICOLONE, *Il Cardinale Giuseppe Tomasi*, passim.

[12] SCICOLONE, *Il Cardinale Giuseppe Tomasi*, 70-75.

[13] SCICOLONE, *Il Cardinale Giuseppe Tomasi*, 75-76.

[14] SCICOLONE, *Il Cardinale Giuseppe Tomasi*, 76-77.

[15] SCICOLONE, *Il Cardinale Giuseppe Tomasi*, 77-78.

gallicanae. Then F. Bianchini's first edition of the *Verona Sacramentary* was published in Rome in 1735.[16] Thus were many first editions of key texts published within one hundred years after the end of the Council of Trent.

In Paris 1642 Dom Hugo Ménard published his *Divi Gregori papae I Liber sacramentorum*, containing the Codex *Paris, B. N. ms. Lat. 12051*,[17] which was in fact a mixed Gelasiano-Gregorian sacramentary. Dom Edmond Martène produced *De antiquis Ecclesiae ritibus libri tres* in Rouen 1700-1702. Pierre le Brun wrote a commentary on the prayers of the Mass, *Explication littérale, historique et dogmatique des prières et des cérémonies de la messe*, in four volumes in Paris between 1716 and 1726.

In 1748 L.A. Muratori[18] published under the title *Liturgia romana vetus*, in two volumes in Venice, editions of the Verona (so-called Leonine), Gelasian and Gregorian Sacramentaries as well as the *Missale Gothicum*, the *Missale Francorum*, two other Gallican missals and *Ordines* I and II, already published by J. Mabillon, with whom Muratori was in correspondence.

Nor should we forget the publication of a new edition of the *Missale parisiense* in 1685 by the Archbishop of Paris, followed by further editions in 1705, 1738 and 1776. The 1738 edition was probably of most importance because it was widely accepted throughout France.[19]

All of these discoveries and publications, and many others, revolutionised studies on the liturgy and led the way to a scientific treatment of the development of the texts in the following century.

3. **1800-1899**: Beginning the scientific study of the liturgy and Anglican pre-eminence.

In this period editions of medieval texts began to be produced all over Europe, and especially by Church of England authors who were assisted by the numerous Ecclesiastical Clubs dedicated to liturgical interests. These included the Caxton Society, the Wycliffe Society, the Camden Society (1839), which in 1848 became the Ecclesiological Society, and the English Historical Society, to name but a few.[20] The Parker Society was founded to the same end

---

[16] VOGEL, *Medieval Liturgy*, 38-39.

[17] SCICOLONE, *Il Cardinale Giuseppe Tomasi*, 79.

[18] J.D. CRICHTON, "Lodovico Antonio Muratori (1627-1750)", *Lights in the Darkness: Forerunners of the Liturgical Movement*, Columba, Blackrock 1996, 14-24.

[19] G. O'CONNOR, *The sources of the Orations of the* Missale Parisiense *of 1738: A study of the Concordances*, Pontificium Athenaeum S. Anselmi de Urbe (PIL exceptum ex diss. dott. 316), Rome 2004, 1-2.

[20] P. JAGGER, *The Alcuin Club and its Publications 1897-1987*, Alcuin Club, Norwich 1986, 3.

in Cambridge in 1841,[21] the Henry Bradshaw Society in London in 1890[22] and the Alcuin Club in London in 1897.[23] The Surtees Society, also useful in this field, had been founded in 1834 with the somewhat different aim of publishing manuscripts, including religious ones, of those parts of England and Scotland which once constituted the ancient Kingdom of Northumbria.[24]

F.H. Dickinson produced the first edition of the Sarum Missal, *Missale ad usum insignis et praeclarae ecclesiae Sarum*, in London in 1861. J. Wickham Legg[25] edited the volume, *The Westminster Missal: Missale ad usum Ecclesiae Westmonasteriensis* in three volumes for the Henry Bradshaw Society in Oxford 1891, 1893, 1897. C.L. Feltoe edited the *Sacramentarium Leonianum* in Cambridge somewhat later in 1896.

A study on the origin and history of the *Book of Common Prayer* was produced by W. Palmer, named *Origines liturgicae or Antiquities of the English ritual and a dissertation on primitive liturgies*, in two volumes at Oxford (vol. 1. 1836, 1845, vol. 2 1839). Francis Proctor[26] published *A History of the Book of Common Prayer*, in London and New York as early as 1855, to be revised early in the following century.

More importantly for us, the first studies on the collect were written in the nineteenth century by three Church of England liturgical scientists. J.M. Neale has a useful chapter, "The Collects of the Church", in *Essays on Liturgiology and Church History*, London 1863; and E.M. Goulburn's two important volumes *The Collects of the Day*, vol. 1, *Preliminary Essays and Collects from Advent to Whitsunday*, and vol. 2, *Trinity to All Saints*, both published in London in 1891, are still much consulted. John Dowden's *The Workmanship of the Prayer Book* published in London in 1899 contains some solid material on the Collects, as befits a Bishop of Edinburgh.

French Catholic research was not far behind that in the Church of England. Abbot Prosper Guéranger's *Institutions liturgiques*, in two volumes was published in Le Mans and Paris in 1840 and 1842. Louis Duchesne

---

[21] *The Parker Society for the Publication of the Works of the Fathers and Early Writers of the Reformed English Church*, Cambridge UP, Cambridge 1841-55. On-line at Pickler memorial Library, Truman State University, MI, retrieved 14 May 2008.
http://library.truman.edu/microforms/parker_society_publications.htm.
[22] A. WARD, *The Publications of the Henry Bradshaw Society* (Bibliotheca Ephemerides Liturgicae, Subsidia 131, Instrumenta Liturgica Quarreriensia 1), Centro Liturgico Vincenziano edizioni liturgiche, Rome 1992; "Henry Bradshaw Society", *Ephemerides Liturgicae* 122 (2008), 126-28.
[23] JAGGER, *The Alcuin Club*, 3.
[24] The Publications of the Surtees Society, retrieved 14 May 2008.
http://www.boydell.co.uk/pubocity.htm
[25] M. DUDLEY, "J. Wickham Legg", *They Shaped our Worship: Essays on Anglican Liturgists*, ed. C. Irvine (Alcuin Club Collections 75), SPCK, London 1998, 22-28.
[26] P. TOVEY, "Francis Procter", *They Shaped our Worship*, ed. Irvine, 7-13.

published *Origines du culte chrétien* in Paris in the last year of the century, and it was translated into English and first published in London before 1910.[27]

4. **1900-1959**: Source criticism, critical editions, diplomatic editions; the study of Christian Latin.

After the enormous output of editions and studies in the nineteenth century, the science of liturgy in this period came not only gradually to learn from scientific Biblical studies and to use source and form criticism, but also produced more accurate critical and diplomatic editions of source texts. In addition, the new discipline of the study of Christian Latin emerged and in this period became closely linked with textual studies.

Edmund Bishop, an oblate of Downside Abbey, produced the enormously influential *Liturgica Historica*, containing the foundational chapter "The Genius of the Roman Rite",[28] in 1918. Church of England liturgists were also still highly active at the beginning of the new century. W.H. Frere[29] edited the then nearly fifty-year old volume *A History of the Book of Common Prayer*, to produce *A New History of the Book of Common Prayer* in London in 1901. John Wickham Legg produced *The Sarum Missal* in Oxford in 1916[30]. As late as 1945 Dom Gregory Dix,[31] a monk of Nashdom Abbey, continued this productive stream of Church of England publications with *Shape of the Liturgy* in London. This liturgical classic attempted to trace the origins of liturgical texts to their sources and to give a structural analysis of large components of the liturgy.

The Henry Bradshaw Society was also busy, producing *The Stowe Missal*, edited by G.F. Warner, (HBS 31, 32) in 1906, *Missale Gothicum: A Gallican Sacramentary*, edited by H.M. Bannister (HBS 52, 54) in 1917 and 1919, *The Bobbio Missal: A Gallican Mass-Book*, edited by E.A. Lowe (HBS 53, 58, 59) in 1917, 1920, 1924. The third of these volumes, "Notes and Studies" was produced by Dom André Wilmart, E.A. Lowe and H.A. Wilson, the first book we have found showing ecumenical collaboration.

Michel Andrieu produced the first edition of *Les Ordines Romani du haut moyen âge*, in two volumes in this period (Spicilegium Sacrum Lovaniense 34, 23), at Louvain in 1959 and 1948, later to be re-edited in four volumes between 1961 and 1974.

---

[27] The reference to the first English edition of 1902 is given in: L. DUCHESNE, *Christian Worship*, tr. M.L. McClure SPCK, London ³1910 (of *Origines du culte chrétien*, Thorin, Paris ⁴1908), xi.

[28] P.C.F. GUNTER, *Edmund Bishop and the Genius of the Roman Rite*, Pontificium Athenaeum S. Anselmi de Urbe (PIL exceptum ex diss. dott. 327), Rome 2006.

[29] A. DAWTRY, "Walter Frere", *They Shaped our Worship*, ed. Irvine, 49-56.

[30] DUDLEY, "J. Wickham Legg", 23.

[31] P. BRADSHAW, "Gregory Dix", *They Shaped our Worship*, ed. Irvine, 111-117.

Source criticism was used for the first time by Dom Bernard Capelle of Mont César in, "L'œuvre liturgique de S. Gélase" in 1951 and Mgr Antoine Chavasse used it in his comprehensive and influential *Le Sacramentaire Gélasien* in 1957. Dom Henry Ashworth of Quarr Abbey followed in his first article, "The Liturgical Prayers of St Gregory the Great" in 1959.

The study of Christian Latin was pioneered by Sr Mary Gonzaga Haessly, OSU, whose *Rhetoric in the Sunday Collects of the Roman Missal* already in 1938 developed the analysis of the structure of collects, identifying the protasis or prelude, (containing address and petition) and apodosis (result or purpose clause). Christine Mohrmann's publications on liturgical Latin appeared first in *Vigiliae Christianae* in 1949, and later in English in *Liturgical Latin: its Origin and Character*, in London in 1959 and in four volumes in *Raccolta di studi e testi* 65, 87, 103, 143 (1961-1977) in Rome.

Research tools were already being developed by E. Gaar with his first edition of *Clavis Patrum Latinorum* in Turnhout in 1951, and by P. Bruylants' *Les oraisons du Missel Romain* at Louvain in 1952.

Dom Augustin Meyer, rector of Sant'Anselmo, established an *Institutum Liturgicum* in 1950 for advancing liturgical research through the editing of historically important liturgical sources. The first volume, *Sacramentarium Veronense* (RED. Fontes 1), emerged from the *Institutum liturgicum* at Sant'Anselmo, Rome in 1956.

5. **1960-1979**

With the establishment of the PIL at Sant'Anselmo by Pope John XXIII in 1961 the faculty there began to develop its own scientific-liturgical method. Also in Rome, A. Pflieger continued the development of research tools with his *Liturgicae orationis concordantia verbalia* for the *Missale Romanum* of 1961, published in 1964.

Critical editions of important liturgical texts continued to be produced before, during and after the Second Vatican Council. The first edition of *La Tradition Apostolique de Saint Hippolyte* by Dom Bernard Botte, was published in Münster in 1963, and further editions continued to be produced until the fifth one in 1989. The *Institutum Liturgicum* at Sant'Anselmo came to its full flowering with the production of important editions. The *Sacramentarium Veronense* had been published first in 1956, with further editions following in 1966 and 1978. The *Sacramentarium Gelasianum*, was published in editions of 1961, 1968 and 1981. The *Missale Francorum* was published in 1957, the *Missale Gallicanum vetus* in 1958, and the *Missale Gothicum* in 1961.

Geoffrey Willis' article,[32] "The Collect", in *Further Essays in Early Roman Liturgy*, 1968, continued the valuable work of Church of England scholars on

---

[32] G. JEANES, "G. G. Willis", *They Shaped our Worship*, ed. Irvine, 132-137.

the collect, but few new major contributions would come from Britain for some time.

Dom Henry Ashworth continued his source critical work with his articles, "Further Parallels to the 'Hadrianum' from St Gregory the Great's Commentary on the First Book of Kings" in 1960, "The Psalter Collects of Pseudo-Jerome and Cassiodorus" in 1963, "The Relationship between Liturgical Formularies and Patristic Texts" in 1963 and 1966, "The Collect, Sixth Sunday after the Epiphany", in 1967, "The Prayers for the Dead in the Missal of Paul VI" in 1971 and "Les sources patristiques du nouveau Missel Romain" in the same year.

Renato De Zan wrote in 1997 of the development of the methodology of the PIL.[33] Because of his contribution elsewhere in this volume, here we shall refer only briefly to his invaluable contribution. A new path was opened up by F. Nakagaki in 1971,[34] and three years later in 1974 Matias Augé published his own principles for interpreting liturgical texts in the PIL's handbook *Anàmnesis*.[35] Augé extended Nakagaki's proposals considerably, focussing on the euchological texts themselves, carefully separating texts drawn from Scripture and those composed by the Church. Augé begins with a clear description of the biblical roots of euchology, observes the peculiarities of liturgical Latin and moves to the three steps of his method: the text's objective content, its structural elements and its stylistic or rhythmic elements. Thus he came to identify, as had Sr. Maria Gonzaga Haessly in 1938, three principal elements of a prayer; besides the invocation or address, there is the petition, the motive (expressive of anamnesis) and the purpose. The publication by A.-M. Triacca and R. Farina in 1977 of "Studio e lettura dell'eucologia: note metodologiche" developed the scientific method. In 1978 R.F. Taft added "The structural analysis of the Liturgical Units: An Essay in methodology".

---

[33] R. DE ZAN, "Criticism and Interpretation of Liturgical Texts", in *Introduction to the Liturgy*, ed. A.J. Chupungco (Handbook for Liturgical Studies 1), Liturgical Press (Pueblo Book), Collegeville MN 1997, 331-365 (En. tr. of R. DE ZAN, "Introduzione alla Liturgia, Ermeneutica", ed. A. J. Chupungco [*Scientia Liturgica: Manuale di Liturgia* 1] Piemme, Casale Monferrato 1998, 356-389).

[34] F. NAKAGAKI, "Metodo integrale: discorso sulla metodologia nell'interpretazione dei testi eucologici", in *Fons vivus: Miscellanea liturgica in memoria di don E.M. Vismara*, ed. A. Cuva (Bibliotheca Theologica Salesiana 1, 6), PAS Verlag, Zürich 1971, 269-286.

[35] M. AUGÉ, "Principi di interpretazione dei testi liturgici", in *Anàmnesis 1. La Liturgia momento nella storia della salvezza*, ed. S. Marsili et alii, Marietti, Casale Monferato, 1974, 159-179.

6. **1980-1999**: Developing hermeneutical studies.

In this period editors continued to produce further diplomatic and critical editions. Irmgard Pahl's first volume of Eucharistic texts of Reformation Churches, *Die Abendmahlsliturgie der Reformationskirchen im 16. und 17. Jhdt* appeared in 1983. Jean Deshusses published *Le sacramentaire grégorien* in three volumes in 1992, establishing a stemma for the evolution of the manuscripts and thus abandoning any hope of re-establishing a text originally composed by St Gregory the Great.

Anthony Ward and Cuthbert Johnson's very useful *Missale Romanum anno 1975 promulgatum: orationes et benedictiones*, was published in 1994 and is a useful addition to the list of research tools available.

Matias Augé developed his important work on textual analysis with a lengthy article, "Orazione colletta" in the *Nuovo Dizionario di Liturgia* in 1984.

Studies by Anglicans on the collect and on methodology also continued. Martin Dudley compiled a useful compendium of Anglican Collects in *The Collect in Anglican Liturgy: Texts and sources 1549-1989* published in 1994. Ronald Jasper[36] also mentions the collect in his historical work, *The Development of the Anglican Liturgy 1662-1980*, published in 1989. Bridget Nichols published her doctoral thesis from Durham University, "Liturgical Hermeneutics: Interpreting Liturgical Rites in Performance", as *Liturgical Hermeneutics* in 1996. The thesis compared eucharistic, baptismal and funeral rites of the First & Second *Prayer Books* of Edward VI (1549 & 1552), the *Book of Common Prayer* of 1662, and *The Alternative Service Book* of 1980, using Paul Ricoeur's model to develop a model for the world (the Kingdom of God) proposed to worshippers by the liturgical rite.

De Zan, continuing his account of the history of hermeneutical studies after 1980 in his chapter in the *Handbook of Liturgical Studies*, describes the contributions of J. Shermann's *Die Sprache im Gottesdienst* of 1987, M. Merz' *Liturgisches Gebet als Geschehen* of 1988, J.A. Zimmermann's *Liturgy as Language of Faith* also 1988 and Silvano Maggiani's contribution, "Interpretare il libro liturgico" of 1989.[37] The remainder of De Zan's article is divided into seven other sections of unequal length and importance. These topics have all been examined by De Zan himself in chapter three of this volume, which draws from the book of E. Lodi *Liturgia della Chiesa* published in 1981. Central to De Zan's argument is his "Methodological proposal"[38] with nine subsections. Among these, we find a summary statement, not to be omitted here:

---

[36] D. GRAY, "R.C.D. Jasper", *They Shaped our Worship*, ed. Irvine, 155-160.

[37] DE ZAN, "Criticism and Interpretation of Liturgical Texts", section 2, 335-337.

[38] DE ZAN, "Criticism and Interpretation of Liturgical Texts", section 4, 341-344.

All the data that have emerged from the process thus far must be organised and understood according to established rules. Since a celebration has intrinsic dimensions and foundations, the material must be organised according to its four dimensions (anamnesis, epiclesis, doxology, and koinonia) and its four foundations (theandric, Christological-pneumatological, ecclesial and symbolic.[39]

These are the theological interpretative keys to be used in any textual analysis of prayers and now form part of the methodology of the PIL, learned and inherited by the present generation of students and graduates. De Zan's article continues with five further sections: "The Meaning of the Text", "Historical Identity of the Text", "Event and Communication", "History of the Tradition of the Text" and "Literary Identity of the Text".[40]

Two further interesting contributions, one in Italian by Alceste Catella, "Analisi filologica e critico-letteraria in ordine alla dinamica storica della liturgia" in 1993, and one in Spanish by C. Urtasun- Irisarri, *Las oraciones del misal: Escuela de espiritualidad de la Iglesia: Domingos y solemnidades* 1995, should not go unnoticed.

A. Meneghetti's article, "'*Oblatio spiritalis*' Un cammino di maturità cristiana nella partecipazione all'Eucaristia", published in 1986, would have important consequences for the study of the collect in the following decade. This hermeneutic of human development, to be observed and developed by later authors as we shall see, was based securely upon the clausal structure of the collects.

Especially valuable for his study of the vocabulary of the collects of the *Missale Romanum* of 1975 is the fundamental volume by Gerard Moore, *Vatican II and the Collects for Ordinary Time*, published in 1998, though the work is out of print and certainly deserving of republication.[41] His study continues with a contribution on the biblical vocabulary and ways of addressing God in the collects, included in the present volume.

7. **2000 onwards**: Recent developments: The two pillars of a new methodology.

Three new editions of valuable sources appeared in 2005. The *Liber sacramentorum paduensis* edited by A. Catella and others was published in Rome, the *Missale gothicum* edited by Els Rose in Turnhout and *Die*

---

[39] DE ZAN, "Criticism and Interpretation of Liturgical Texts", section 4, 444, citing E. LODI, "La liturgia: teologia mistagogica. Introduzione generale allo studio della liturgia", *Liturgia della Chiesa*, EDB, Bologna 1981, 21-226.

[40] DE ZAN, "Criticism and Interpretation of Liturgical Texts", 345-355.

[41] G. MOORE, *Vatican II and the Collects for Ordinary Time. A Study in the Roman Missal (1975)*, International Scholars Publications, San Francisco – London – Bethesda 1998.

Abendmahlsliturgie der Reformationskirchen vom 18. bis zum frühen 20. Jhdt edited by Irmgard Pahl in Fribourg.

New on-line research tools have grown in popularity and give free access to texts via sites such as *Liturgia*[42] and the Vatican website.[43] Others give access to societies, libraries and collections such as to Alcuin Club Publications,[44] the Deutsches Liturgisches Institut,[45] the Henry Bradshaw Society,[46] the Institut Supérieur de Liturgie, Paris,[47] The Parker Society Archives,[48] the Publications of the Surtees Society.[49] Subscriptions to commercial search engines are also available, such as, *The Library of Latin Texts Online* (CLCLT) from Brepols, Turnhout,[50] and the *American Theological Libraries Association*.[51]

On-line commentaries also exist for the minor euchologies of both the 1962 and the 2002 *Missalia Romana*.[52] These are not always accurate or scientific and are sometimes biased, but can be useful as an introduction. Such commentaries do highlight the need not only for a detailed knowledge of the Latin language, which we call the first pillar of liturgical research, but also for a highly detailed and consistent hermeneutical method, the second pillar.

To the first pillar Els Rose adds a great contribution in the chapter on Medieval Latin in her new edition of the *Missale gothicum*, already mentioned. Rose says that by the time of the middle ages, Latin had become a working language and was subject to developments and deteriorations, as does any other language. Thus, it can no longer be considered as a hieratic and fixed language as Christine Mohrmann had previously considered.

At the beginning of the new millennium in 2001 A.M. Savage produced a rather eccentric doctoral study of both Anglican Collects for Advent and Roman Rite Collects for Lent using a phenomenological approach.

Lauren Pristas, one of the few others writing on the collects today, has produced five articles which certainly deserve attention: "Theological principles that guided the redaction of the Roman Missal (1970)" and "The Orations of the Vatican II Missal: Policies for Revision" both published in 2003, "The Pre- and Post-Vatican II Collects of the Dominican Doctors of the Church" and "The Collects at Sunday Mass: An Examination of the Revisions

---

[42] www.liturgia.it

[43] www.vatican.va

[44] http://www.alcuinclub.org.uk/alcuin_club_publications.htm.

[45] http://www.liturgie.de/liturgie/index

[46] http://www.henrybradshawsociety.org/booklist.html

[47] http://www.icp.fr/isl/

[48] http://library.truman.edu/microforms/parker_society_publications.htm

[49] http://www.boydell.co.uk/pubocity.htm

[50] http://www.brepolis.net/info/info_clt_en.html

[51] http://search.ebscohost.com/

[52] http://wdtprs.com/blog/wdtprs-series/

of Vatican II" both in 2005 and "The Post-Vatican II Revision of the Lenten Collects" in 2007. Her detailed analysis of the collects is always her starting point. Her comparison between the collects of the 1962 and 1970 *Missalia Romana* concludes that the prayers in the 1970 *Missale*, which have been altered or newly composed, show a different emphasis than do those in the 1962 *Missale*.

Pristas alerts the reader to the contrast in emphasis between the prayers of the 1962 *Missale* on the "internal" or private dimension with that in the 1970 *Missale* on the "external" or "active". In the 2005 *Nova et Vetera* essay on the Advent collects, for example, Pristas calls attention to how the 1962 prayers ask God (or Christ) to work within us, while the 1970 collects use the language of external assistance.

Pristas is reluctant to concede that the results of the liturgical renewal that we now have were, in fact, mandated by the Council, and obliquely calls this matter into question (see, for example, the comments on "the needs of modern man" in the conclusion of her 2003 essay in *The Thomist*). In the 2007 article she carefully observes how the language of fasting has been excised from the Lenten collects.

Pristas is prudent in that she makes no generalizations, for an essay can examine only a few prayers out of the thousand or two in the Missal and it would be very rash to draw conclusions based on such small samples. We look forward to her forthcoming volume on the collects.

Dom Patrick Hala of the Abbey of Solesmes has produced three commentaries on the Latin and French collects of Ordinary time, Advent and the Christmas season in 2002, 2004 and 2006 respectively. They are a very useful addition to our resources.

Peter Scagnelli's 2003 doctoral study for Boston University of the proposed ICEL Scriptural Collects, *Creativity within Continuity: The ICEL Scriptural Collects*, published in 1997, concludes that the new compositions retain the form and content of ancient orations, are suitable for use with the Revised Lectionary and favour ecumenical cooperation.

Guibert Michiels' 2004 article "Les oraisons du Missel Romain au temps de l'Avent" is a useful presentation of Latin texts of the prayers of that season with the official French translation and a spiritual commentary.

Thomas Whelan's as yet unpublished thesis "Deus auctor pacis et amator": *The Liturgical-Theological Response of the Church in Time of War*, from the PIL in 2006 is very dependent upon Greimas' semiology and is a useful entry into that methodology.

Dom Daniel McCarthy of St Benedict's Abbey, Atchison has published a weekly column, "Listen to the Word", in *The Tablet* of London, where he has analysed the collect and then the prayer over the gifts in two series, from Lent 2006 to Easter 2007, and from Advent 2007 to November 2008. These all use the analysis of literary forms as practiced in the methodology of the PIL as outlined by Renato De Zan below on p 57.

McCarthy together with James Leachman of Ealing Abbey, London worked together on two articles due for publication in 2008, using the same elements of the methodology. The first, "The Formation of the Ecclesial Person Through Baptismal Preparation and the Celebrations in the *OICA*: The Collects for the Scrutinies", brings out the key force of the divine-human exchange in the structure of these collects. The second article, "Preparation for the Piazza: The Preface of the Second Scrutiny (the Fourth Sunday in Lent)", was given as a paper at the *Societas Liturgica* Conference in Palermo, August 11th 2007, and, although it refers to the preface, uses the same methodology and emphasis on the twin pillars of Latin Language and the hermeneutical methodology of the PIL.

For his series on the collects, Daniel McCarthy developed the following chart from his notes from a class taught by Renato De Zan on liturgical hermeneutics. McCarthy, as does De Zan, distinguishes the two basic languages, two basic vocabularies: one is literary-critical, the other is grammatical. The basic form of the collect is thus, but there are many elaborations.

Literary critical vocabulary	Vocabulary of Latin Language
Invocation	1. Simple = vocative noun 2. Complex = vocative noun and adjectives
Amplification	1. Nouns in apposition 2. Relative clause
Petition	1. Imperative 2. Exhortative subjunctive
Purpose	1. *ut* + subjunctive (classical form) 2. *ad* + gerund (or infinitive) (less classical form) 3. *ad* + gerundive (or passive necessity participle) 4. relative pronoun + subjunctive (relative clause of purpose)
Cause or motive	1. *quia* + subjunctive nestled in the purpose clause (classical form) 2. relative clause nestled in the purpose clause: e.g.: *domine fac ut qui te amant perducantur.*
Premise	Ablative absolute (especially in the post communion)

The benefit of writing a weekly article employing a consistent methodology was the opportunity to see the great variety of combinations and the insistent confrontation with several difficulties to be clarified. In addition to this column, the more profound writing projects shared with James Leachman led the two to clarify several perennial difficulties in understanding the texts, including:

1. To the above chart, they have added the participial phrase as an expression of motive.
2. To the above chart, they have added the independent indicative sentence as expressive of the premise, which is particularly applicable to the prayers over the gifts. This has been confirmed by A. Meneghetti in the article mentioned above.
3. Learning from Reginaldus Foster, they confronted the one Latin verbal form that is expressive of both the historical perfect and the present perfect time. Distinguishing between these times is essential to understanding the verbal times of the prayers.
4. With Foster's help too, they clarified the difference between a result and a purpose clause, both of which may have the same grammatical form in Latin but are to be translated differently into English, a purpose clause is translated into the subjunctive and a result clause into the indicative.
5. From Foster again they clarified their understanding of purpose clauses: relative to the verb on which it depends, the first subjunctive (present subjunctive) is contemporaneous, ongoing, incomplete, unending, future and eternal. One of their proper contributions arises from the consequences this has for the understanding of eschatology in its contemporaneous self-realisation.
6. One of their proper contributions is to understand in the Latin prayer the function of object clauses formed by the accusative followed by the infinitive. Often these clauses are latent expressions of purpose.
7. A second proper contribution is to understand a purpose clause as indicating that the way in which God gives is part of the gift.
8. Corresponding to realizing eschatology, they have come to understand that the anamnetic elements of the prayers are often presented as instruments through which God works today.
9. From the interpretative keys of De Zan and Lodi, they have taken the divine-human exchange.
10. A third proper contribution is to realize that we are drawn into the divine human exchange through steps.
11. When we identify the times of the verbal forms in the prayers their succession often reveals what we have come to see as developmental steps of Christian maturation. This interpretative key is added to those of De Zan and Lodi.[53]
12. Drawing on the writings of Crispino Valenziano,[54] in addition, they used the nuptial union between God and humanity as an interpretative key for understanding the collect genre.

---

[53] n. 37, above.
[54] C. VALENZIANO, *L'anello della Sposa: mistagoga eucaristica*, Centro Liturgico Vincenziano edizioni liturgiche, Rome 2005.

In which direction collect studies will now move, we cannot divine; but this short history of collect studies is offered as an orientation and reference for those who will continue the patient study of the texts.

Conclusion

This necessarily brief and rather general sweep across the history of liturgical studies shows how gradually the attention of liturgists has come first to focus on the collect form, then by degrees of patient study upon its structure, content, context and meaning.

Bibliography

A. Holy Scripture

Biblia Sacra Vulgata, ed. R. Weber, Deutsche Bibelgesellschaft, Stuttgart [4]1994
    (Vulgate).
New Revised Standard Version, Oxford UP, Oxford – New York 1989 (NRS).

B. Research tools

BRUYLANTS, P., *Concordance verbale du Sacramentaire Léonien*, Mont César, Louvain
    1945.
_____, *Les oraisons du Missel Romain*, 2 vol.; vol. 1. *Tabulae synopticae fontium
    Missalis Romani, Indices*; vol. 2. *Orationum textus et usus iuxta fontes* (Études
    liturgiques 2 vol.), Mont César, Louvain 1952.
*Clavis Patrum Latinorum qua in Corpus christianorum edendum optimas quasqe scriptorum
    recensiones a Tertulliano ad Bedam*, ed. E. Dekkers – E. Gaar (Corpus
    christianorum series latina), Brepols, Turnhout [1]1951, [2]1961, [3]1995.
Concordantia et Indices Missalis Romani, editio typica tertia, ed. M. Sodi – A. Toniolo
    (Monumenta studia instrumenta liturgica 29) Libreria editrice Vaticana, Città
    del Vaticano 2002.
Concordantia verbalia missalis romani: Partes euchologicae, ed. T.A. Schnitker – W.A.
    Slaby, Aschendorff, Münster 1983.
O'CONNOR, G., *The sources of the Orations of the* Missale Parisiense *of 1738: A study of the
    Concordances*, Pontificium Athenaeum S. Anselmi de Urbe (PIL exceptum ex
    diss. dott. 316), Rome 2004.
Corpus orationum, 14 vol., ed. E. Moeller – J.-M. Clément – B.C. 't Wallant (Corpus
    christianorum series latina 160-160 M), Brepols, Turnhout 1992-2004.
Corpus praefationum, 5 vol. ed. E. Moeller – J.-M. Clément – B.C. 't Wallant (Corpus
    christianorum series latina 161-161 D), Brepols, Turnhout 1980-1981.
GILDERSLEEVE, B.L, – G. LODGE, *Gildersleeve's Latin Grammar*, Bolchazy-Carducci,
    Wauconda IL 2003, reprint of [3]1985.
LEWIS, C.T.,- C. SHORT, *A Latin Dictionary*, Oxford UP, Oxford – New York 1879,
    reprinted 1995.
*The Parker Society for the Publication of the Works of the Fathers and Early Writers of the
    Reformed English Church*, Cambridge UP, Cambridge 1841-55.
PFLEIGER, A., *Liturgicae orationis concordantia verbalia. Prima pars. Missale Romanum*,
    Herder, Rome 1964.
WHEALE, W.H.J., – H. BOHATTA, *Catalogus Missalium ritus latini ab anno 1474
    impressorum*, Quaritch, London 1928.

C. Historical studies

BRADSHAW, P., "Gregory Dix", *They Shaped our Worship: Essays on Anglican Liturgists*,
    ed. C. Irvine (Alcuin Club Collections 75), SPCK, London 1998, 111-117.

CHUPUNGCO, A.J., "The Pontifical Liturgical Institute", *Sant'Anselmo: saggi storici e di attualità*, ed. G.J. Békés (Studia Anselmiana 97), Pontificium Athenaeum S. Anselmi de Urbe, Rome 1998, 193-226.

CRICHTON, J.D., "The First Liturgical Saint, Giuseppe Tommasi (1649-1713)", *Lights in the Darkness: Forerunners of the Liturgical Movement*, Columba, Blackrock 1996, 11-13.

_____, "Lodovico Antonio Muratori (1627-1750)", *Lights in the Darkness: Forerunners of the Liturgical Movement*, Columba, Blackrock 1996, 14-24.

DAWTRY, A., "Walter Frere", *They Shaped our Worship: Essays on Anglican Liturgists*, ed. C. Irvine (Alcuin Club Collections 75), SPCK, London 1998, 49-56.

DUDLEY, M., "J. Wickham Legg", *They Shaped our Worship: Essays on Anglican Liturgists*, ed. C. Irvine (Alcuin Club Collections 75), SPCK, London 1998, 22-28.

ENGELBERT, P., *Geschichte des Benediktinerkollegs St. Anselm in Rom von den Anfängen (1888) bis zur Gegenwart* (Studia Anselmiana 98), Pontificium Athenaeum S. Anselmi de Urbe, Rome 1998.

GRAY, D., "R.C.D. Jasper", *They Shaped our Worship: Essays on Anglican Liturgists*, ed. C. Irvine (Alcuin Club Collections 75), SPCK, London 1998, 155-160.

GUNTER, P.C.F., *Edmund Bishop and the Genius of the Roman Rite*, Pontificium Athenaeum S. Anselmi de Urbe (PIL exceptum ex diss. dott. 327), Rome 2006.

JAGGER, P., *The Alcuin Club and its Publications 1897-1987*, Alcuin Club, Norwich 1986.

JEANES, G., "G.G. Willis", *They Shaped our Worship: Essays on Anglican Liturgists*, ed. C. Irvine (Alcuin Club Collections 75), SPCK, London 1998, 132-137

SCICOLONE, I., *Il Cardinale Giuseppe Tomasi di Lampedusa e gli inizi della scienza liturgica* (Studia Anselmiana 82, Analecta Liturgica 5), Pontificium Athenaeum S. Anselmi de Urbe, Rome 1981.

They Shaped our Worship: Essays on Anglican Liturgists, ed. C. Irvine (Alcuin Club Collections 75), SPCK, London 1998.

TOVEY, P., "Francis Procter", *They Shaped our Worship: Essays on Anglican Liturgists*, ed. C. Irvine (Alcuin Club Collections 75), SPCK, London 1998, 7-13.

VOGEL, C., *Medieval Liturgy: An Introduction to the Sources*, tr., rev. W.G. Storey – N.K. Rasmussen (National Association of Pastoral Musicians Studies in Church Music and Liturgy), Pastoral Press, Washington DC 1986 (of *Introduction aux sources de l'histoire du culte chrétien au moyen âge*, Centro italiano di studi sull'alto medioevo, Spoleto 1981).

WARD, A., *The Publications of the Henry Bradshaw Society* (Bibliotheca Ephemerides Liturgicae, Subsidia 131. Instrumenta Liturgica Quarreriensia 1), Centro Liturgico Vincenziano edizioni liturgiche, Rome 1992

D. **Study of Christian Latin**

ELLEBRACHT, M.P., *Remarks on the Vocabulary of the Ancient Orations in the Missale Romanum*, (Latinitas christianorum primaeva 22), Dekker, Nijmegen – Utrecht 1963; Dekker and Van De Vegt, Nijmegen – Utrecht ²1966.

HAESSLY, M.G., *Rhetoric in the Sunday Collects of the Roman Missal*, St Louis Univ. PhD thesis, The Manufacturers Printery, St Louis 1938.

Il latino e i cristiani: Un bilancio all'inizio del terzo millennio, ed. E. Dal Covolo – M. Sodi, (Monumenta Studia Instrumenta Liturgica 17) Libreria Editrice Vaticana, Città del Vaticano 2002.

MOHRMANN, C., "Les origines de la latinité chrétienne à Rome", *Vigiliae Christianae* 3 (1949) 67-106, 163-183.

_____, "Les emprunts grecs dans la latinité chrétienne", *Vigiliae Christianae* 4 (1950) 206 ff.

_____, "Sacramentum dans les plus anciens textes chrétiennes", *Harvard Theological Review* 47 (1954) 141-152.

_____, "Problèmes stylistiques dans la littérature latine chrétienne", *Vigiliae Christianae* 9 (1955) 222-246.

_____,"Linguistic Problems in the Early Christian Church", *Vigiliae Christianae* 11 (1957) 11-36.

_____, *Liturgical Latin. its Origin and Character*, Burns & Oates, London 1959.

_____, *Études sur le latin des chrétiens* (Raccolta di studi e testi 65, Études sur le latin des chrétiens 1), Edizioni di storia e letteratura, Rome ²1961.

_____, *Latin chrétien et médiéval* (Raccolta di studi e testi 87, Études sur le latin des chrétiens 2), Edizioni di storia e letteratura, Rome 1961.

_____, *Latin chrétien et liturgique* (Raccolta di studi e testi 103, Études sur le latin des chrétiens 3), Edizioni di storia e letteratura, Rome 1979.

_____, *Études sur le latin des chrétiens* (Raccolta di studi e tesi 143, Études sur le latin des chrétiens 4), Edizioni di storia e letteratura, Rome 1977.

_____, "Sakralsprache und Umgangssprache", *Archiv für Liturgiewissenschaft* 10 (1968) 344-354.

ROSE, E., "Medieval Latin", *Missale gothicum e codice vaticano reginensi latino 317 editum*, ed. E. Rose (Corpus christianorum series latina 159 D), Brepols, Turnhout 2005, 94-187.

E. Studies by period

1. Pre 1600: Collecting and publishing liturgical sources.
These sources are helpfully listed in VOGEL, *Medieval Liturgy*, 10-17.
Vogel writes, "By the XVI century, the process of liturgical codification was over, … [and] the documents liturgical scholars collected were to prove helpful for the study of medieval liturgy" (VOGEL, *Medieval Liturgy*, 17).

PAMELIUS, J. (Jacques de Joigny de Pamèle), *Liturgicon ecclesiae latinae*, 2 vol., Cologne 1571, reprint Farnborough 1970. Contains *Sacramentorum libri tres*, (Gregorian Sacramentary, pp 177-387) and others.
ROCCA, A., *Opera S. Gregorii Magni*, 8 vol., Rome 1593.

2. 1600- 1799: Collections and commentaries.
Vogel writes, "many scholarly works appeared during this period, remarkable both for the documents they assembled and for the learned commentaries which accompanied them". (VOGEL, *Medieval Liturgy*, 17-18). Some of the more important, still used in the study of collects, are listed (VOGEL, *Medieval Liturgy*, 18-20).

BIANCHINI, F., (Veronense), Rome 1735, see Vogel, *Medieval Liturgy*, 38-39.

MABILLON, J., *De liturgia gallicana libri tres*, Paris 1685, reprint PL 72, 99-448.

MABILLON, J., – M. GERMAIN, *Museum italicum seu collectio veterum scriptorum ex bibliothecis italicis*, Paris 1687-1689.

LE BRUN, P., *Explication littérale, historique et dogmatique des prières et des cérémonies de la messe*, 4 vol., Paris 1716-1726, reprinted Farnborough 1970.

MARTÈNE, E., *De antiques Ecclesiae ritibus libri tres*, 3 vol. Rouen [1]1700-1702; 4 vol. Antwerp [2]1736-1738, reprinted Hildesheim 1967-69.

MÉNARD, H., *Divi Gregori papae Liber Sacramentorum nunc demum correctior et locupletior editus ex missali Mss. S. Eligii bibliothecae Corbeiensis*, Paris 1642 (a mixed Gelasiano-Gregorian).

MURATORI, L.A., *Liturgia romana vetus*, 2 vol., Venice 1748.

TOMASI, J.M., *Codices Sacramentorum nongentis annis vetustiores*, Rome 1680, includes the Gelasian Sacramentary = vat. Reg. 316, the *Missale Gallicanum, Missale Francorum, Missale Gallicanum Vetus*.

3. 1800-1899: Beginning scientific studies. Anglican pre-eminence.

Liturgical Sources:
Missale ad usum insignis et praeclarae ecclesiae Sarum, ed. F.H. Dickinson, J. Parker, Oxford – London 1861, [2]1883, repr. Gregg International Publishers, Farnborough 1969.

The Westminster Missal: Missale ad usum Ecclesiae Westmonasteriensis, ed. J. Wickham Legg (Henry Bradshaw Society 1, 5, 12), Oxford 1891, 1893, 1897; repr. in 1 vol. Boydell & Brewer, Woodbridge 2000.

Sacramentarium Leonianum, ed. C.L. Feltoe, Cambridge 1896.

Studies:
DOWDEN, J., *The Workmanship of the Prayer Book*, Methuen, London 1899.

GUÉRANGER, P., *Institutions liturgiques*, 2 vol., Le Mans – Paris 1840, 1842.

PROCTOR, F., *A History of the Book of Common Prayer*, Macmillan, London – New York 1855.

DUCHESNE, L., *Origines du Culte Chrétienne*, Ernest Thorin, Paris 1889, tr. M.L. McClure, *Christian Worship*, SPCK, London [5]1923.

GOULBURN, E.M., *The Collects of the Day*. vol. 1. *Preliminary Essays and Collects from Advent to Whitsunday*, Longmans, Green & Co., London 1891.

NEALE, J.M., "The Collects of the Church", *Essays on Liturgiology and Church History*, Saunders, London 1863, 47-88.

PALMER, W., *Origines Liturgicae or Antiquities of the English ritual: and a dissertation on primitive liturgies*, 2 vol., Oxford vol. 1. 1836, 1845; vol. 2 1839.

4. 1900-1964: Source criticism, critical editions, diplomatic editions.

Liturgical sources:
The Stowe Missal (MS. D.II.3 in the Library of the Royal Irish Academy, Dublin), ed. G. F. Warner (Henry Bradshaw Society 31), vol. 1. facsimile 1906; vol. 2. (Henry Bradshaw Society 32) text 1915 (issued for 1906).

The Sarum Missal, edited from Three Early Manuscripts, ed. J. Wickham Legg, Oxford
    1916; reproduced Clarendon, Oxford 1969.

Missale Gothicum: A Gallican Sacramentary (MS. Vatican. Reg. Lat. 317), vol. 1. *Text and
    Introduction*, ed. H.M. Bannister (Henry Bradshaw Society 52), 1917.

The Bobbio Missal: A Gallican Mass-Book, (MS. Paris. Lat. 13246), ed. E.A. Lowe (Henry
    Bradshaw Society 53), Facsimile, 1917.

Missale Gothicum: A Gallican Sacramentary (MS. Vatican. Reg. Lat. 317), vol. 2. *Notes and
    Indices*, ed. H.M. Bannister (Henry Bradshaw Society 54), 1919 (issued for
    1917).

The Bobbio Missal: A Gallican Mass-Book (MS. Paris. Lat. 13246) Text, ed. E.A. Lowe
    (Henry Bradshaw Society 58), 1920.

The Bobbio Missal (MS. Paris. Lat. 13246) Notes and Studies, ed. A. Wilmart – E.A. Lowe
    – H.A. Wilson (Henry Bradshaw Society 59), 1924.

Les Ordines Romani du haut moyen âge. Tome 2. Les textes (Ordines I-XIII), ed. M.
    Andrieu, (Spicilegium Sacrum Lovaniense 23), Louvain 1948.

Sacramentarium Veronense, ed. L.C. Mohlberg – L. Eizenhöfer – P. Siffrin (Rerum
    ecclesiasticarum documenta. Series maior, Fontes 1), Rome 1956.

Studies:

ASHWORTH, H., "The Liturgical Prayers of St Gregory the Great", *Traditio* 15 (1959)
    107-161.

BISHOP, E., "The Genius of the Roman Rite", *Liturgica Historica*, Clarendon Press,
    Oxford 1918, 1-19.

CAPELLE, B., "L'œuvre liturgique de S. Gélase", *The Journal of Theological Studies* 2
    (1951) 139-143.

CHAVASSE, A., *Le Sacramentaire Gélasien (Vaticanus Reginensis 316): Sacramentaire
    presbytéral en usage dans le titres Romains au VIIe siècle* (Bibliothèque de
    théologie. Série 4: Histoire de la Théologie 1), Desclée, Tournai 1958.

DIX, G., *Shape of the Liturgy*, Dacre, London 1945.

DUCHESNE, L., *Christian Worship*, tr. M.L. McClure SPCK, London ³1910 (of *Origines du
    culte chrétien*, Thorin, Paris ⁴1908).

PROCTOR, F. – W.H. FRERE, *A New History of the Book of Common Prayer with a Rationale
    of its Offices*, Macmillan & Co., London 1901.

5. <u>1960-1980</u>: The Scientific-Liturgical Methodology at the PIL. Dictionaries and
    research tools.

Liturgical sources:

Missale gothicum (Cod. Vat. Reg. Lat. 317), ed., L.C. Mohlberg (Rerum ecclesiasticarum
    documenta. Series maior, Fontes 5), Herder, Rome 1961.

Sacramentarium Veronense, ed., L.C. Mohlberg – L. Eizenhöfer – P. Siffrin (Rerum
    ecclesiasticarum documenta. Series maior, Fontes 1), Herder, Rome ³1978.

*Liber sacramentorum romanae aeclesiae ordinis anni circuli (Cod. Vat. Reg. Lat. 316/Paris
    Bibl. Nat. 7193, 41/56) (Sacramentarium Gelasianum)*, ed. L.C. Mohlberg – L.
    Eizenhöfer – P. Siffrin (Rerum ecclesiasticarum documenta. Series maior,
    Fontes 4), Herder, Rome ³1981.

La Tradition Apostolique de Saint Hippolyte: *Essai de reconstruction*, ed. B. Botte
   (Liturgiewissenschaftliche Quellen und Forschungen 39), Aschendorff,
   Münster [5]1989.

Studies:
ASHWORTH, H., "Further Parallels to the 'Hadrianum' from St Gregory the Great's
   Commentary on the First Book of Kings", *Traditio* 16 (1960) 364-373.
_____, "The Psalter Collects of Pseudo-Jerome and Cassiodorus", *The Bulletin of the
   John Rylands Library Manchester* 45 (1963) 287-304.
_____, "The Relationship between Liturgical Formularies and Patristic Texts", ed.
   F.L. Cross (Studia Patristica 8, 2), Papers presented to the Fourth
   International Conference on Patristic Studies held at Christ Church, Oxford
   1963, Akademie Verlag, Berlin 1966 (= Texte und Untersuchungen zur
   Geschichte der altchristlichen Literatur, Band 93), 149-155.
_____, "Practical Commentaries on Some Prayers of the Missal", *Studies in Pastoral
   Liturgy*, vol. 3, ed. Placid Murray, The Furrow Trust – Gill, Dublin 1967, 74-
   115.
_____, "The Collect, Sixth Sunday after the Epiphany", *Liturgy* (Quarterly of the
   Society of St Gregory) 36 (1967) 89-91.
_____, "Le nuove messe per i defunti nel Messale Romano di Paolo VI", *Rivista
   Liturgica* 58 (1971) 354-381.
_____, "The Prayers for the Dead in the Missal of Pope Paul VI," *Ephemerides
   Liturgicae* 85 (1971) 3-15.
_____, "Les sources patristiques du nouveau Missel Romain", *Questions liturgiques*
   4 (1971) 295-304.
AUGÉ, M., "Le collette del proprio del tempo nel nuovo Messale", *Ephemerides
   Liturgicae* 84 (1970) 275-298.
_____, "Principi di interpretazione dei testi liturgici", *Anàmnesis 1. La Liturgia
   momento nella storia della salvezza*, ed. S. Marsili et alii, Marietti, Casale
   Monferato, 1974, 159-179.
BRAGA, C., "Il nuovo messale romano," *Ephemerides Liturgicae* 84 (1970) 249-74.
_____, "Il 'proprium de sanctis,'" *Ephemerides Liturgicae* 84 (1970) 401-403.
CAPELLE, B., "L'oraison 'veneranda' à la messe de l'Assomption", *Histoire* (Travaux
   liturgiques 3 vol.), Centre Liturgique, Mont César, Louvain 1967, 3, 387-397.
DUMAS, A., "Les oraisons du nouveau Missel Romain," *Questions liturgiques* 25 (1971)
   263-270.
FERRETTI, W., "Le orazioni 'post communionem' de tempore nel nuovo messale
   romano," *Ephemerides Liturgicae* 84 (1970) 323-341.
HOPE, D.M., *The Leonine Sacramentary: A reassessment of its nature and purpose*, Oxford
   1971.
MIAZEK, J., *La* "Collecta" *del* "Proprium de Tempore" *nel* "Missale Romanum" *di Paolo
   VI. Avviamento ad uno studio critico-teologico*, Pontificium Athenaeum S.
   Anselmi de Urbe (PIL exceptum ex diss. dott. 44), Rome 1977.
NAKAGAKI, F., "Metodo integrale: discorso sulla metodologia nell'interpretazione dei
   testi eucologici", in *Fons vivus: Miscellanea liturgica in memoria di don E.M.
   Vismara*, ed. A. Cuva (Bibliotheca Theologica Salesiana 1, 6), PAS – Verlag,
   Zürich 1971, 269-286.
RAFFA, V., "Le orazioni sulle offerte del proprio del tempo nel nuovo messale,"
   Ephemerides Liturgicae 84 (1970) 299-322.

TAFT, R.F., "The structural analysis of the Liturgical Units: An Essay in methodology", *Worship* 52 (1978) 314-329.

TRIACCA, A.-M., - R. FARINA, "Studio e lettura dell'eucologia: note metodologiche", *Teologia, liturgia e storia: Miscellanea in onore di C. Manziana*, Brescia 1977.

WILLIS, G.G., "The Collect", in *Further Essays in Early Roman Liturgy* (Alcuin Club Series 50), SPCK, London 1968, 103-121.

VISENTIN, P., "Linee di spiritualità cristiana nell'eucologia del Messale Romano", *Rivista Liturgica* 61 (1974) 381-401.

WEISS, L., *Die Orationen im* Missale Romanum *von 1970*, Heidelberg 1978.

6. 1981-1999: Developing hermeneutical studies.

Liturgical sources:

Die Abendmahlsliturgie der Reformationskirchen im 16. und 17. Jhdt, ed. I. Pahl, (Spicilegium Friburgense 29. Coena Domini 1) Universitätsverlag Freiburg Schweiz, Fribourg 1983.

Le Sacramentaire grégorien, 3 vol., ed. J. Deshusses, Éditions Universitaires, Fribourg ³1992.

Studies:

AUGÉ, M., "Orazione colletta", *Nuovo Dizionario di Liturgia*, ed. D. Sartore – A.-M. Triacca, Paoline, Cinisello Balsamo 1984, 517.

AUGÉ, M., "Libri liturgici", *Nuovo Dizionario di Liturgia*, ed. D. Sartore – A.-M. Triacca, Paoline, Cinisello Balsamo 1984, 701-704.

CATELLA, A., "Analisi filologica e critico-letteraria in ordine alla dinamica storica della liturgia", *Celebrare il mistero di Cristo: La celebrazione: introduzione alla liturgia cristiana* vol. 1, Rome 1993, 121-130.

DE ZAN, R., "Criticism and Interpretation of Liturgical Texts", in *Introduction to the Liturgy*, ed. A.J. Chupungco (Handbook for Liturgical Studies 1), Liturgical Press (Pueblo Book), Collegeville MN 1997, 331-365 (En. tr. of R. DE ZAN, "Introduzione alla Liturgia, Ermeneutica", ed. A. J. Chupungco [*Scientia Liturgica: Manuale di Liturgia* 1] Piemme, Casale Monferrato 1998, 356-389).

DONGHI, A., "Il Messale, sorgente di spiritualità", *Rivista Liturgica* 71 (1984) 361-380.

DUDLEY, M., *The Collect in Anglican Liturgy: Texts and sources 1549-1989* (Alcuin Club Collection 72), Liturgical Press, Collegeville MN 1994.

JASPER, R.C.D., *The Development of the Anglican Liturgy 1662-1980*, SPCK, London 1989.

JOHNSON, C., - A. WARD, *Missale Romanum anno 1975 promulgatum: orationes et benedictiones* (Bibliotheca Ephemerides Liturgicae, Subsidia 71, Instrumenta Liturgica Quarreriensia 3), Centro Liturgico Vincenziano edizioni liturgiche, Rome 1994.

KRASÓN, *Per un profilo del 'cristiano' dall'eucologia del Sacramentario Veronese. Contributo per l'approfondimento della liturgia come vita del fedele*, Pontificium Athenaeum S. Anselmi de Urbe (PIL exceptum ex diss. dott. 120), Rome 1987.

LODI, E., *Liturgia della Chiesa*, Edizioni Dehoniane, Bologna 1981.

_____, "L'ideal éthique dans les sources des Sacramentaires du Missel Romain", in *Liturgie, éthique et people de Dieu. Conferences Saint-Serge, XXXVIIe Semaine d'études liturgiques*, ed. A.M. Triacca – A. Pistoia, Centro Liturgico Vincenziano edizioni liturgiche, Rome 1991, 191-218.

MAGGIANI, S., "Interpretare il libro liturgico", *Il mistero celebrato: Per una metodologia dello studio della liturgia*, Rome 1989, 157-192.

MENEGHETTI, A., "*Oblatio spiritalis*": Un cammino di maturità cristiana nella partecipazione all'Eucaristia. Studio metodologico di teologia liturgica sull'eucologia minore del Messale Romano di Paolo VI", *Ephemerides Liturgicae* 100 (1986) 28-72, 224-269.

MERZ, M., *Liturgisches Gebet als Geschehen*, Münster 1988.

MOORE, G., *Vatican II and the Collects for Ordinary Time: A Study in the Roman Missal (1975)*, International Scholars Publications, San Francisco – London – Bethesda 1998.

NICHOLS, B., *Liturgical Hermeneutics*, Peter Lang, London 1996.

SCHERMANN, J., *Die Sprache im Gottesdienst*, Innsbruck-Vienna 1987.

URTASUN-IRISARRI, C., *Las oraciones del misal: Escuela de espiritualidad de la Iglesia. Domingos y solemnidades* (Biblioteca liturgica 5), Centre de Pastoral Litúrgica, Barcelona 1995.

ZIMMERMANN, J.A., *Liturgy as Language of Faith: A Liturgical Methodology in the Mode of Paul Ricoeur's Textual Hermeneutics*, New York- London 1988.

7. 2000 onwards: Recent developments. The two pillars of a new methodology.

Liturgical sources:

Liber sacramentorum paduensis (Padova, Biblioteca Capitolare, cod. D 47), ed. A. Catella – F. dell'Oro – A. Martini (Bibliotheca Ephemerides Liturgicae, Subsidia 131. Monumenta italiae liturgica 3), Centro Liturgico Vincenziano edizioni liturgiche, Rome 2005.

Missale gothicum e codice vaticano reginensi latino 317 editum, ed., E. Rose (Corpus christianorum series latina 159 D), Brepols, Turnhout 2005.

Die Abendmahlsliturgie der Reformationskirchen vom 18. bis zum frühen 20. Jhdt, ed. I. Pahl, (Spicilegium Friburgense 43. Coena Domini 2) Academic Press, Fribourg 2005.

Studies:

GUIBERT, M., "Les oraisons du nouvel Missel Romain: les fêtes des apôtres", *Questions Liturgiques* 64 (1993) 120-133.

_____, "Les oraisons du Missel au temps de l'Avent", *Questions Liturgiques* 85 (2004) 216-243.

HALA, P., *Habeamus gratiam: commentaire des collectes du temps ordinaire*, Solesmes, 2002.

_____, *La spiritualité de l'Avent à travers les collectes*, Solesmes, 2004.

_____, *Méditations sur les oraisons du temps de Noël*, Solesmes, 2006.

LEACHMAN, J.G., – D.P. McCARTHY, "The Formation of the Ecclesial Person through Baptismal Preparation and the Celebrations in the *OICA*: The Collects for the Scrutinies," *The Liturgical Subject: Subject, Subjectivity, and the Human Person in Contemporary Liturgical Discussion and Critique*, ed. J. Leachman, SCM – Notre Dame, London – South Bend IN 2008, 172-200.

LEACHMAN, J.G., – D.P. McCARTHY, "Preparation for the Piazza: The Preface of the Second Scrutiny (the Fourth Sunday in Lent): The Mystagogical Formation of the Neophytes and the Assembly", Societas Liturgica Conference, 11 August 2007, *Studia Liturgica* 38 (2008) 114-133.

McCarthy, D.P., *Listen to the Word: Commentaries in Selected Opening Prayers of Sundays and Feasts*, weekly series in *The Tablet*, 2006-2007, and published privately, Rome 2007.

_____, *Listen to the Word: Commentaries in Selected Prayers over the Gifts of Sundays and Feasts*, weekly series in *The Tablet* 2007-2008.

O'Connor, G., *The sources of the Orations of the* Missale Parisiense *of 1738: A study of the Concordances*, Pontificium Athenaeum S. Anselmi de Urbe (PIL exceptum ex diss. dott. 316), Rome 2004.

Pascher, J., *Die Orationen des Missale Romanum Papst Paulus VI*, 4 vol. Eos, St. Ottilien 1989.

Pristas, L., "Theological principles that guided the redaction of the Roman Missal (1970)", *The Thomist* 67 (2003) 157-195.

_____, "The Orations of the Vatican II Missal: Policies for Revision", *Communio* 30 (2003) 621–653.

_____, "The Pre- and Post-Vatican II Collects of the Dominican Doctors of the Church", *New Blackfriars* (2005) 604–621.

_____, "The Collects at Sunday Mass: An Examination of the Revisions of Vatican II", *Nova et Vetera* 3 (2005) 5–38.

_____, "The Post-Vatican II Revision of the Lenten Collects", *Ever directed to the Lord: The Love of God in the Liturgy of the Eucharist Past, Present, and Hoped For*, ed. M.U. Lang, T & T Clark, Aldershot 2007, 62-89.

Savage, A.M., *A Phenomenological Understanding of Certain Liturgical texts: The Anglican Collects for Advent and the Roman Catholic Collects for Lent*. University Press of America, Lanham MA 2001.

Scagnelli, P.J., *Creativity within Continuity: The ICEL Scriptural Collects*, Boston University ThD Diss. 2003.

Valenziano C., *L'anello della Sposa: mistagoga eucaristica*, Centro Liturgico Vincenziano edizioni liturgiche, Rome 2005.

Whelan, T.R., *Deus auctor pacis et amator: The Liturgical-Theological Response of the Church in Time of War*, Pontificium Athenaeum S. Anselmi de Urbe (PIL tesi dott. unpubl.), Rome 2006.

F. **Internet resources**

Alcuin Club Publications, retrieved 14 May 2008.
    http://www.alcuinclub.org.uk/alcuin_club_publications.htm
American Theological Libraries Association, retrieved 14 May 2008.
    http://search.epnet.com
Centre Nationale de Recherches (France) , retrieved 19 June 2008.
    http://www.cnrs.fr/
Consiglio Nazionale delle Ricerche (Italy), retrieved 15 May 2008.
    http://www.cnr.it/sitocnr/home.html.
COPAC: online access to major British and Irish university libraries, retrieved 15 May 2008. http://copac.ac.uk/
CURSUS: an Online Resource of Medieval Liturgical Texts, retrieved 15 May 2008.
    http://www.cursus.uea.ac.uk/
Deutsches Liturgisches Institut, with library search, retrieved 14 May 2008.
    http://www.liturgie.de/liturgie/index

Henry Bradshaw Society, retrieved 14 May 2008.
     http://www.henrybradshawsociety.org/booklist.html
Institut Supérieur de Liturgie (Paris), retrieved 15 May 2008.
     http://www.icp.fr/isl/
JUSTUS: Online Anglican resources, retrieved 15 May 2008.
     http://justus.anglican.org/resources/
Missale Parisiense, retrieved 19 May 2008. www.clerus.org (/library/liturgy). OR:
     http://www.clerus.org/pls/clerus/cn_clerus.h_start_consult_ext?ric_key_g
     lobale=Missalis+Parisiensis&dicastero=2&tema=&argomento=&sottoargome
     nto=&lingua=2&classe=&operazione=ges_ric&rif=&rif1=&vers=2
The Parker Society Archives, Pickler memorial Library, Truman State University, MI,
     retrieved 14 May 2008.
     http://library.truman.edu/microforms/parker_society_publications.htm.
Publications of the Surtees Society, retrieved 14 May 2008.
     http://www.boydell.co.uk/pubocity.htm
URBE: Pontifical Roman University Library catalogues online, retrieved 17 May 2008.
     http://librivision.urbe.it/lvansbin/librivision

CHAPTER 2

Collectarum latinitas

Reginaldus Thomas Foster
with
Daniel P. McCarthy

Introduction

These items from my[1] method of presenting the Latin language were selected to help the student develop a clear understanding of Latin and the collects. The selection here is not a full presentation of the language.

1. The times of verbs

- In Latin, there are 6 verb times in the Indicative.
- The word 'indicative' means that the verb indicates a fact.
- I number the times to prevent the confusion that other systems cause and perpetuate.

---

[1] This paper presents the Latin Language as understood and taught by Reginaldus Thomas Foster, using a pedagogy that he has developed over many years of experience. Examples from the collects are provided to help the student of the Liturgy to apply this presentation of the Latin language to the study of the liturgy.

- Take for example the dictionary entry, *volo, velle volui, irregular verb,* "to wish, to want":

Time	Example: *tu*	English Meaning	Others' categories
T1	*vis*	you want, you are wanting (*progressive*) you do want (*intensive or emphatic*)	Present
T2	*volebas*	you were wanting you used to want you would want (*whenever it happened*) you always did want	Imperfect
T3	*voles*	you will want you will be wanting	Future
T4a	*voluisti*	you have wanted (*up to present*) you have been wanting	Present perfect or Pure perfect
T4b	*voluisti*	you wanted you did want	Historical perfect
T5	*volueras*	you had wanted you had been wanting	Pluperfect
T6	*volueris*	you will have wanted you will have been wanting	Future perfect

1.1 *Times 4 A and 4 B*

There is a problem between T4a (Time 4a) and T4b (Time 4b):[2]

- In Latin their form is the same, but their meanings are different.
- In English their forms are different and so we must choose between them.
- T4a refers to an event in the past that touches on the present situation. Often the event is in the recent past, but not always. In Italian this is the *passato prossimo,* in Greek the perfect.

---

[2] What I call T4a is called the pure or present perfect in B.L. GILDERSLEEVE – G. LODGE, *Gildersleeve's Latin Grammar,* Bolchazy-Carducci, Wauconda IL 2003, reprint of [3]1985 (hereafter GL) n° 235-38. What I call T4b is called the historical perfect or the aorist in GL n° 239-240. Their difference is explained:
"1. The Pure Perfect differs from the Historical Perfect, in that the Pure Perfect gives from the point of view of the Present an instantaneous view of the development of an action from its origin in the Past to its completion in the Present, that is, it looks at both ends of an action, and the time between is regarded as a Present [what I liken to a video]. The Historical Perfect obliterates the intervening time and contracts beginning and end into one point in the Past [what I liken to a photo].
"2. An intermediate usage is that in which the Perfect denotes an action in the Past (Historical), whose effect is still in force (Pure)" (GL n° 235).

- T4b refers to an event in the past that is unrelated to the present. Usually it is in the distant past, but not always. In Italian this is the *passato remoto*, in Greek the aorist. Italian is losing the distinction between the *passato prossimo* (T4a) and the *passato remoto* (T4b).

Another way to compare them is to say that:
- T4a presents a past event as if it were a video touching on the present, whereas
- T4b presents a past event as if it were a photo.

The reader has to judge the intent of the author in order to translate texts into English. The range of difficulties in understanding the difference between T4a and T4b are present in the following collect for the feast of the Triumph of the Cross celebrated on 14 September in the Roman Calendar. For example, the following prayer from the *Missale Romanum* of 2002.

> *Deus, qui Unigenitum tuum crucem subire voluisti,*
> *ut salvum faceret genus humanum,*
> *praesta, quaesumus,*
> *ut, cuius mysterium in terra cognovimus,*
> *eius redemptionis praemia in caelo consequi mereamur.* [3]

The author's translation for study purposes only:

> God, you who willed your Only-begotten to endure the cross
> that he would save the human race,
> grant, we ask,
> that, whose mystery we have come to know on earth,
> of his redemption we may deserve to attain the rewards in heaven.

In the Latin text, the two verbs *voluisti* and *cognovimus* are Time 4. In order to understand them, however, and then to express them accurately in English, we must decide for each one whether it is T4a or T4b. In this case, the difference is clear.

- *Voluisti* is T4b because it presents a photo image of the will of God in human history and is considered in its historical context. Thus *voluisti* is an historical perfect similar to the Greek aorist. This is made clear by the purpose clause *ut ... faceret*. The only way to get that second subjunctive *faceret*, is if *voluisti* is understood as T4b,

---

[3] *Missale Romanum ex decreto Sacrosancti Oecumenici Concilii Vaticani II instauratum auctoritate Pauli PP. VI promulgatum Ioannis Pauli PP. II cura recognitum, editio typica tertia*, Typis Vaticanis, Città del Vaticano ³2002 (hereafter *MR* ³2002), 827.

thereby establishing Track 2, as I explain in the sequence of tenses. Had *voluisti* been T4a, *faceret* would have been *faciat*.

• *Cognovimus* is T4a because it presents our knowing from some point in the past all the way up to and touching on the present. *Cognovimus* literally means "we have come to know" (T4a) and, thus, in the present means "we know".

1.2 *The passive historical times*

The passive forms of Times 4-6 do not follow the same system as the passive forms of times 1-3. This creates a problem not found in other languages because the passive forms of T4-6 look like and come to be confused with Times 1-3. This confusion is common. The passive form of T5 and T6 do not appear in the collects of the *Missale Romanum* of 2002. For T4a and T4b the passive forms are the following:

T4a and T4b passive

• Both T4a and T4b of the passive have the same form.
• This leads to no end of confusion.
• T4a and T4b are formed by taking fourth principal part of the verb and joining it to T1 of the verb *esse*, "to be".
• Take for example, the dictionary entry[4] *mangifico, avi, atum* 1, "to praise, worship":

Example: *tu*	Time	Meaning in English
magnificatus es[5]	**T4a**	you have been praised
	T4b	you were praised

T4a and T4b of deponent verbs

Several deponent verbs show up in the collects.
• Their form is passive but their meaning is active.
• Thus, to form T4a and T4b of these verbs, we must use the passive forms as indicated above, then assign an active meaning.
• This leads to no end of confusion, because T4a and T4b have the same form.

---

[4] All dictionary entries are based on those given in: C.T. LEWIS – C. SHORT, *A Latin Dictionary*, Oxford UP, Oxford – New York 1879, reprinted 1995.

[5] "Deus, qui in beato Martino episcopo sive per vitam sive per mortem magnificatus es, innova gratiae tuae mirabilia in cordibus nostris, ut neque mors neque vita separare nos possit a caritate tua" (*MR* [3]2002, 866).

- Take for example the dictionary entry *dignor, atus*, 1 v. dep. ... "to deem worthy, deserving":

Example: *tu*	Time	Meaning in English
dignatus es[6]	T4a	you have deemed worthy (*up to present*) you have been deeming worthy (*progressive*)
	T4b	you deemed worthy you did deem worthy (*intensive* or *emphatic*)

- Take for example the dictionary entry *patior, passus*, 3, v. dep. "to bear, endure":

Example: *tu*	Time	Meaning in English
passus es[7]	T4a	you have endured (*up to present*) you have been enduring (*progressive*)
	T4b	you endured you did endure (*intensive* or *emphatic*)

Difficulties with passive verbs

In various eras, however, the use of the passive forms of T4a and T4b weakened by steps.
- The form of the verb *esse*, "to be", was considered to be the verb,
- and the fourth principal part of the verb was taken to be an adjective,
- thus, rendering a passive verb in T4a or T4b as a present indicative verb joined with an adjective.
- To compensate for this change in understanding, the verbal forms of *esse*, "to be", tended to be changed to an earlier time, for example:

> T4a T4b   *magnificatus est* became *magnificatus erat*.
> T5   *magnificatus erat* became *magnificatus fuerat*.
> T6   *magnificatus erit* became *magnificatus fuerit*.

Discerning the correct verbal form used is, consequently, important.

2. Principles of the subjunctive

The subjunctive is called the *conjunctive* in Latin, German, Italian.

---

[6] "Deus, qui splendorem gloriae tuae per sacrae Virginis partum mundo dignatus es revelare, tribue, quaesumus, ut tantae incarnationis mysterium et fidei integritate colamus, et devoto semper obsequio frequentemus" (*MR* [3]2002, 144).

[7] "Da nobis, quaesumus, omnipotens Deus, adversa mundi invicta mentis constantia tolerare, qui beatum Martinum papam et martyrem nec minis terreri nec poenis passus es superari" (*MR* [3]2002, 744).

The basic principles of the Subjunctive are:

1. The forms are super-simple,
    > but the use of the subjunctive is super-human.
2. Most of the time the sub-junctive is sub-joined to the main sentence:
    > Sub-junctive : con-junctive : joining with.
3. There are two big uses:
    > A. independent (subject all alone),
    > B. dependent (dependant on another clause, verb, sentence).
4. The Latin subjunctive is expressed in English by either:
    > A. subjunctive: may, might, should, would, may have, should have,
    > B. or simply indicative (v.g. did, came, was).
5. Rendering a Latin subjunctive into English depends on the type of subjunctive it is in Latin.
6. Of all the subjunctives used over the past 2500 years:
    > A. 80% of all Latin subjunctives are expressed by the English indicative. These include:
    > > all: **causal** clauses,
    > > **temporal** clauses,
    > > **result** clauses,
    > > **indirect** questions,
    > > half of all **conditional** clauses
    > B. 20% of all Latin subjunctives are expressed by the English subjunctive (may, might, could, would, should). These include:
    > > all: purpose/final clauses,
    > > independent subjunctives,
    > > half of all conditional clauses.
7. Remember, fully 80% of all Latin subjunctives will sound indicative when expressed in English. Most uneducated Latinists will translate all Latin subjunctives into English subjunctives. You will not make that mistake.
8. Only three uses of the subjunctive in Latin are expressed in English by the subjunctive. If it is not one of these three cases, the English must sound indicative.
9. Some of the most certain things can be expressed in the subjunctive;
    > some of the most uncertain things can be expressed in the indicative.
    > We must cut out the prejudice that the subjunctive is for uncertain things, as the potential subjunctive appears only 4 times in a year of reading Latin.
10. The Latin subjunctive may be used for many reasons.
    > In Latin literature, you may never know the exact reason for the appearance of many subjunctives as their uses overlap.

11. In our class, as beginners, we do not attach any definite meaning to any subjunctive time. Because of the overlapping, we leave the thing afloat.

12. Four subjunctive times must express every human concept; this is the problem.
Greek has 12 subjunctive forms but Latin only four. Thus their meanings overlap.

13. We have no future or future perfect forms in the subjunctive,
but we have the future and future perfect ideas and concepts;
this creates its own problem.

14. When determining what subjunctive time to use in a Latin sentence:
English is no guide, nor is dreaming or sentimentality.
A definite system is used called the sequence of tenses.

3. *Consecutio temporum* : The following of the times or sequence of tenses

1. The subjunctive can be independent or dependent.
2. *Consecutio* occurs only with a dependent subjunctive.
3. Dependent subjunctives can depend on:
an indicative verb,
a subjunctive verb,
an infinitive,
a participle,
the supine.
4. The choice of the time of the subjunctive is not arbitrary, a feeling or a guess.
5. The *Consecutio* is a definite system of times.
6. To use Latin one must know the *consecutio*;
to understand literature, one needs the sequence of tenses.
7. The system depends on the times of Latin verbs, ideas and concepts, not upon English.
8. *Consecutio* covers 97% of the language. The remaining 3% is a strange phenomenon.
9. I organize the *Consecutio* according to a two track method.
10. What decides which track to use?
The verbal form upon which the subjunctive depends determines whether the sentence is on track 1 or 2, even if it is the last word in the sentence.
11. Track 1 is used if the verbal form upon which the subjunctive depends is present or future.[8] These are:

---

[8] Track 1 is also called the primary sequence. It refers to the principal tenses as described in GL n° 509-511.

Time	Otherwise called
T1	present
T3	future
T4a	present perfect: what I liken to a video, e.g.: "I have done"
T6	future perfect

12. Track 2 is used if the main verbal form upon which the subjunctive depends is
Past or Historical.[9] These are:

Time	Otherwise called
T2	imperfect
T4b	perfect, photo: what I liken to a photo, e.g.: "I did"
T5	past perfect

13. Once the track is established by the verbal form on which the subjunctive depends, the choice of the subjunctive time depends on the kind of action in the subjunctive verb. With regard to the main verbal form, either the subjunctive verb is:
A. contemporaneous or future,
B. antecedent or previous.

14. On track 1:
A. If, relative to the verbal form on which the subjunctive depends, the action of the subjunctive is incomplete, unfinished, ongoing, eternal, future or contemporaneous, then the subjunctive is Time 1 subjunctive (T1s).[10]
B. If, relative to the verbal form on which the subjunctive depends, the action of the subjunctive is completed, finished, past or future perfect, then the subjunctive is Time 3 subjunctive (T3s).[11]

15. On track 2:
A. If, relative to the verbal form on which the subjunctive depends, the action of the subjunctive is incomplete, unfinished,

---

[9] Track 2 is also called the secondary sequence. It refers to the historical tenses as described in GL n° 509-511.

[10] Also called the present subjunctive. We do not use this term because T1s also refers to the future.

[11] Also called the perfect subjunctive. We do not use this term because T3s also refers to the future anterior.

ongoing, eternal, future or contemporaneous, then the
subjunctive is Time 2 subjunctive (T2s).

B. If, relative to the verbal form on which the subjunctive depends,
the action of the subjunctive is completed, finished, past or
future perfect, then the subjunctive is Time 4 subjunctive
(T4s).

We may summarize the choice of subjunctive in the following chart.[12]

Track 1[13]

If time of verbal form is:	Time of the subjunctive verb must be:

T1 present
T3 future
 	
T4a present perfect
       (video, "I have done")
T6 future perfect
	T1s if action of subjunctive with regard to indicative
	       is: incomplete, unfinished, ongoing, eternal,
	       future, contemporaneous.
	
	T3s if action of subjunctive with regard to indicative
	       is: completed, finished, past, future perfect.

Track 2[14]

If time of verbal form is:	Time of the subjunctive verb must be:

T2 imperfect
T4b perfect
       (photo, "I did")
T5 past perfect
	T2s if action of subjunctive with regard to indicative
	       is: incomplete, unfinished, ongoing, eternal,
	       future, contemporaneous.
	
	T4s if action of subjunctive with regard to indicative
	       is: completed, finished, past, future perfect.

16. T1s in other systems is called the present subjunctive. We do not use this
term because relative to the verbal form on which it depends T1s is
incomplete, unfinished, ongoing, eternal, future or
contemporaneous.

17. T3s in other systems is called the perfect subjunctive. We do not use this
term because relative to the verbal form on which it depends T3s is
incomplete, unfinished, ongoing, eternal, future or
contemporaneous.

---

[12] Cf.: GL n° 510-11.

[13] Also called the primary sequence for the principal tenses. See: GL n° 510-11.

[14] Also called the secondary or historical sequence. See: GL n° 510-11.

18. T2s in other systems is called the imperfect subjunctive. We do not use this term because relative to the verbal form on which it depends T2s refers to any action that is completed, finished, past or future perfect.

19. T4s in other systems is called the pluperfect subjunctive. We do not use this term because relative to the verbal form on which it depends T4s refers to any action that is completed, finished, past or future perfect.

4. **Purpose and result clauses**[15]

1. Both purpose and result clauses contemplate the end of an action.
    The purpose clause considers the end as an aim.[16]
    A result clause considers the end as a result.[17]

2. Purpose and result clauses may have the same Latin construction;
    therefore they are difficult to discern and are often confused.

3. Purpose and result clauses are translated into English in different ways:
    Purpose clauses are translated into the subjunctive in English.
    Result clauses are translated into the indicative in English.

4. "It is to be remarked that the difference between Final [purpose] and Consecutive [result] often consists only in the point of view. What is final [purpose] from the point of view of the doer is consecutive [result] from the point of view of the spectator".[18]

5. For example: *Loquitur magister voce alta ut discipuli audire omnes possint.*

- If taken as a purpose clause, it describes the intent of the teacher. In English the subjunctive is then employed: "The teacher speaks with a loud voice in order that all the students may be able to hear".

- If taken as a result clause, it describes the result of the teacher's speech, without regard to the intent of the teacher. In English the indicative is employed: "The teacher speaks with a loud voice with the result that all the students are able to hear".

- While the difference between the result and purpose clause in the Latin sentence may consist only in one's point of view, in English one must choose between the subjunctive, which expresses purpose, and the indicative, which expresses result.

6. In this chapter we shall present purpose clauses. In a subsequent contribution we shall take up result clauses.

---

[15] This material is drawn largely from GL n° 543-553.

[16] What I call a purpose clause is called a sentence of design or a final sentence in GL n° 543-550.

[17] What I call a result clause is called a sentence of tendency or a consecutive sentence in GL n° 543, 551-558.

[18] GL n° 543, note 2.

4.1 *Purpose Clauses*[19]

1. Purpose clauses give the final objective of an action.

2. Purpose clauses express the wish or intention of the actor.

3. The subjunctive expresses a hope and thus is called the optative subjunctive.[20]

4. Purposes clauses are constructed by:

      A. *ut* or *uti* to make a positive statement,

      B. *ne*   to make a negative statement[21]

                   translated as "that ... not ..." and "least ..."

                   N.B.: *ut ne* ... means "so that ... not ..."

      C. *ut non* to negate one word.[22]

      D. Relative sentences of purpose where the relative stands in for:[23]

               qui + subjunctive stands in for "*ut is* + subjunctive",

               quae + subjunctive stands in for "*ut ea* + subjunctive",

               quod + subjunctive stands in for "*ut id* + subjunctive" etc.

5. Examples of relative sentences of purpose in the collects of the *MR* [3]2002 include:

> *Gratia tua ne nos, quaesumus, Domine, derelinquat,*
> quae et *sacrae nos deditos* faciat *servituti,*
> et *tuam nobis opem semper* acquirat.[24]

Here   *quae et ... faciat ... et ... acquirat* substitutes for
          ut ea ... et ... faciat ... et ... acquirat.

> *Corda nostra, quaesumus, Domine,*
> *tuae maiestatis splendor illustret,*
> quo *mundi huius tenebras transire* valeamus,
> et perveniamus *ad patriam claritatis aeternae.*[25]

Here   *quo valeamus, et perveniamus* substitutes for
          ut eo valeamus, et perveniamus.

---

[19] This material is drawn largely from GL n° 543-553.

[20] GL n° 262.

[21] One example is found among the collects in the *MR* [3]2002, 231: "Gratia tua ne nos, quaesumus, Domine, derelinquat, quae et sacrae nos deditos faciat servituti, et tuam nobis opem semper acquirat".

[22] One example is found among the collects in the *MR* [3]2002, 412: "Deus, qui ad aeternam vitam in Christi resurrectione nos reparas, da populo tuo fidei speique constantiam, ut non dubitemus implenda, quae te novimus auctore promissa".

[23] See: GL n° 630.

[24] *MR* [3]2002, 231.

[25] *MR* [3]2002, 173.

Domine, sancte Pater,
servorum tuorum N. et N.
propositum confirma benignus,
et fac ut baptismatis gratia,
quam novis cupiunt nexibus roborari,
plenum in eis sumat effectum,
quo *tuae maiestati debitum cultum* retribuant,
et *Christi regnum apostolico* dilatent *ardore.*[26]

Here   *quo retribuant, et ... dilatent* substitutes for
        ut eo retribuant, et ... dilatent.

Deus, qui humano labore immensum creationis opus
iugiter perficis atque gubernas,
exaudi preces populi supplicantis,
et praesta, ut omnes homines digno potiantur labore,
quo, *suam condicionem honestantes,*
arctius coniuncti fratribus suis valeant *inservire.*[27]

Here   *quo ... arctius ... valeant* substitutes for
        ut eo ... arctius *... valeant.*

Adveniat nobis, quaesumus, Domine,
virtus Spiritus Sancti,
qua *voluntatem tuam fideli mente retinere,*
et pia conversatione depromere valeamus.[28]

Here   *qua ... valeamus* substitutes for
        ut ea ... valeamus.

Deus, cui potestates humanae deserviunt,
da famulo tuo (regi nostro) N.
prosperum suae dignitatis effectum,
in qua, *te semper timens tibique placere contendens,*
populo sibi credito liberam ordinis
tranquillitatem iugiter procuret et servet.[29]

Here   *in qua ... procuret et servet* substitutes for
        ut in ea ... procuret et servet.

---

[26] *MR* ³2002, 1055.
[27] *MR* ³2002, 1125.
[28] *MR* ³2002, 435.
[29] *MR* ³2002, 1124.

> *Benedictionem tuam, Domine Deus,*
> *super populum tuum propitiatus infunde,*
> *quatenus, dante te benignitatem,*
> *terra nostra proferat fructus suos,*
> quibus *ad honorem sancti tui nominis*
> *grata semper mente* fruamur.[30]

Here   *quibus ... fruamur* substitutes for
       ut iis ... fruamur.

> *Fraterna nos, Domine,*
> *martyrum tuorum corona laetificet,*
> quae *et fidei nostrae* praebeat *incrementa virtutum,*
> *et multiplici nos suffragio* consoletur.[31]

Here   *quae ... praebeat ... et consoletur* substitutes for
       ut ea ... praebeat ... et consoletur.

> *Deus, qui pacificos revelasti filios tuos esse vocandos,*
> *praesta, quaesumus,*
> *ut illam instauremus sine intermissione iustitiam,*
> quae *sola firmam pacem* spondeat *et veracem.*[32]

Here   *quae ... spondeat* substitutes for
       ut ea ... spondeat.

4.2 *Purpose clause after verbs of will and desire*

Certain groups of verbs give rise to a special group of purpose clauses called complementary final sentences. These groups of verbs are listed below with some verbs of each class that appear in the collects of the *MR* [3]2002:

- Willing and wishing: *volo, do, oro, rogo, precor, deprecor,*[33]
- Urging and demanding: *impero, praecipio.*[34]

In regard to these verbs, note the following:

- The object of these verbs is expressed by the entire phrase composed of *ut* + subjunctive.
- Thus, these clauses are called complementary because they complete the verb.
- They are purpose clauses, because they express what is willed, wished, urged or demanded.

---

[30] *MR* [3]2002, 1128.
[31] *MR* [3]2002, 912.
[32] *MR* [3]2002, 1131.
[33] GL n° 546, n. 1.
[34] GL n° 546, n. 1.

Examples in the collects are:

- Verbs of willing and wishing: *volo*

   Deus, qui caritatis tuae praecepto voluisti, ut *nos affligentibus amorem* impendamus *sincerum, da nobis ita novae legis sequi mandata, ut bona pro malis reddere et alii aliorum onera portare studeamus.*[35]

   Deus, qui Unigenitum tuum crucem subire voluisti, ut *salvum* faceret *genus humanum, praesta, quaesumus, ut, cuius mysterium in terra cognovimus, eius redemptionis praemia in caelo consequi mereamur.*[36]

   Deus, qui pro nobis Filium tuum crucis patibulum subire voluisti, ut *inimici a nobis* expelleres *potestatem, concede nobis famulis tuis, ut resurrectionis gratiam consequamur.*[37]

   Da Ecclesiae tuae, quaesumus, Domine, spiritum fortitudinis zelumque iustitiae, quibus beatum Gregorium papam clarescere voluisti, ut, *iniquitatem reprobans, quaecumque recta sunt libera exerceat caritate.*[38]

   Deus, qui Ecclesiam tuam sacramentum salutis cunctis gentibus esse voluisti, ut *Christi salutiferum opus usque in fines saeculorum* perseveret, *excita tuorum corda fidelium, et praesta, ut ad omnem creaturam salvandam urgentius vocari se sentiant, quatenus ex omnibus populis una familia unusque tibi populus exsurgat et crescat.*[39]

- Verbs of warning and beseeching: *do*

   Deus, qui diversitatem gentium in confessione tui nominis adunasti, da, ut *renatis fonte baptismatis una sit fides mentium et pietas actionum.*[40]

   Deus, qui beato Hieronymo presbytero suavem et vivum Scripturae Sacrae affectum tribuisti, da, ut *populus tuus verbo tuo uberius* alatur, et *in eo fontem vitae* inveniat.[41]

---

[35] *MR* ³2002, 1142.
[36] *MR* ³2002, 1161 = *MR* ³2002, 827. In this prayer, *ut … faceret* could depend either on *subire* or *voluisti*. I have presented the latter. In either case it is an expression of purpose.
[37] *MR* ³2002, 289. In this prayer, *ut … expelleres* could depend either on *subire* or *voluisti*. I have presented the latter. In either case it is an expression of purpose.
[38] *MR* ³2002, 758.
[39] *MR* ³2002, 1117. In this prayer, *ut … perseveret* could depend either on *esse* or *voluisti*. I have presented the latter. In either case it is an expression of purpose.
[40] *MR* ³2002, 383.
[41] *MR* ³2002, 839.

Deus, qui populum tuum Ecclesiam vocare dignatus es, da, ut *plebs in nomine tuo congregata te* timeat, *te* diligat, *te* sequatur *et ad caelestia promissa, te ducente,* perveniat.[42]

Deus, qui beatam Margaritam eximia in pauperes caritate mirabilem effecisti, da, ut, *eius intercessione et exemplo, imaginem bonitatis tuae inter homines* referamus.[43]

Deus, qui beati Francisci praedicatione multos tibi populos acquisisti, da, ut *fidelium animi eodem fidei zelo* ferveant, et *uberrima ubique prole Ecclesia sancta* laetetur.[44]

Deus, qui Ecclesiam tuam sponsam vocare dignatus es, da, ut *plebs nomini tuo inserviens te* timeat, *te* diligat, *te* sequatur *et ad caelestia promissa, te ducente,* perveniat. *Per Dominum.*[45]

Deus, qui nos regeneras verbo vitae, da, ut, *corde sincero illud accipientes, veritatem alacres* faciamus, et *fraternae* afferamus *fructus plurimos caritatis.*[46]

Rerum conditor Deus, qui hominem iussisti laboris officia sustinere, da, ut *opus quod incipimus huius vitae* prosit *incrementis,* et *regno Christi dilatando tua benignitate* proficiat.[47]

- Verbs of warning and beseeching: *oro, imploro, exoro*

  Maiestatem tuam, Domine, suppliciter imploramus, ut, *quanto magis dies salutiferae festivitatis accedit, tanto devotius ad eius celebrandum* proficiamus *paschale mysterium.*[48]

  Annua recolentes mysteria, quibus per renovatam originis dignitatem humana substantia spem resurrectionis accepit, clementiam tuam, Domine, suppliciter exoramus, ut, *quod fide recolimus, perpetua dilectione* capiamus.[49]

  Deus, cuius providentia in sui dispositione non fallitur, te supplices exoramus, ut *noxia cuncta* submoveas, et *omnia nobis profutura* concedas.[50]

---

[42] *MR* ³2002, 864.
[43] *MR* ³2002, 869.
[44] *MR* ³2002, 875.
[45] *MR* ³2002, 895.
[46] *MR* ³2002, 980.
[47] *MR* ³2002, 1125.
[48] *MR* ³2002, 234.
[49] *MR* ³2002, 390.
[50] *MR* ³2002, 459.

Omnipotens sempiterne Deus, maiestatem tuam supplices exoramus, ut, *sicut Unigenitus Filius tuus hodierna die cum nostrae carnis substantia in templo est praesentatus, ita nos* facias *purificatis tibi mentibus praesentari.*[51]

Magnificantes, Domine, potentiam tuam, supplices exoramus, ut, *sicut beatus Georgius dominicae fuit passionis imitator, ita* sit *fragilitatis nostrae promptus adiutor.*[52]

Maiestatem tuam, Domine, suppliciter exoramus, ut, *sicut Ecclesiae tuae beatus Andreas apostolus exstitit praedicator et rector, ita apud* te sit *pro nobis perpetuus intercessor.*[53]

Deus, cuius nutu universa oboediunt elementa, te supplices exoramus, ut, *sedatis terrentibus procellis, in materiam* transeat *laudis comminatio potestatis.*[54]

Omnipotens sempiterne Deus, salus aeterna credentium, exaudi nos pro famulis tuis infirmis, pro quibus misericordiae tuae imploramus *auxilium,* ut, *reddita sibi sanitate, gratiarum tibi in Ecclesia tua* referant *actiones.*[55]

Deus, cui proprium est misereri semper et parcere, te supplices exoramus *pro famulo tuo N., quem (hodie)ad te migrare iussisti, ut, quia in te speravit et credidit,* concedas *eum ad veram patriam perduci, et gaudiis perfrui sempiternis.*[56]

Omnipotens sempiterne Deus, vita mortalium et exsultatio Sanctorum, te supplices exoramus *pro famulis tuis (N. et N.), ut, mortalitatis nexibus expediti, regnum tuum in gloria* possideant *sempiterna.*[57]

Omnipotens sempiterne Deus, qui vivorum dominaris simul et mortuorum, omniumque misereris, te suppliciter exoramus, ut, *pro quibus effundimus preces, pietatis tuae clementia delictorum suorum veniam* consequantur, et *de te beati* congaudeant ac *te sine fine* collaudent.[58]

---

[51] *MR* ³2002, 722.
[52] *MR* ³2002, 745.
[53] *MR* ³2002, 874.
[54] *MR* ³2002, 1138.
[55] *MR* ³2002, 1146.
[56] *MR* ³2002, 1191.
[57] *MR* ³2002, 1209.
[58] *MR* ³2002, 1212.

- Verbs of warning and beseeching: *rogo*

    Supplices te rogamus, *omnipotens Deus,* ut, *intercedente beato N. (episcopo), et tua in nobis dona multiplices, et tempora nostra in pace* disponas.[59]

- Warning and beseeching: *precor, deprecor*

    Deus, qui famulos tuos in tribulatione positos semper miseratus exaudis, pro benignitate tua gratias agentes, te supplices deprecamur, ut, *liberi a malis omnibus, in gaudio tibi iugiter* serviamus.[60]

    Maiestatis tuae clementiam suppliciter deprecamur, *omnipotens et misericors Deus,* ut, *sicut Unigeniti tui agnitionem per beatorum martyrum N. et N. praedicationem populorum cordibus infudisti, ita, eorum intercessione, fidei stabilitate* firmentur.[61]

    Deus, qui posuisti praesentis vitae terminum, ut aeternitatis reseres introitum, te supplices deprecamur, ut *nomen famuli tui N. in libro vitae miserationis tuae gratia* iubeas *conscribi.*[62]

    Inclina, Domine, aurem tuam ad preces nostras, quibus misericordiam tuam supplices deprecamur, ut *famulus tuus N., quem in hoc saeculo tuo populo misericorditer aggregasti, in pacis ac lucis regione* constituas, et *Sanctorum tuorum* concedas *esse consortem.*[63]

    Misericordiam tuam, Domine, pro famulo tuo N. supplices deprecamur, ut, *qui pro Evangelio dilatando allaboravit assiduus, ad praemia regni* mereatur *intrare securus.*[64]

- Verbs of warning and beseeching: *deposco*

    Clementiam tuam, Domine, supplici voto deposcimus, ut *nos famulos tuos, paenitentia emendatos et bonis operibus eruditos, in mandatis tuis* facias *perseverare sinceros, et ad paschalia festa pervenire illaesos.*[65]

---

[59] *MR* [3]2002, 933.
[60] *MR* [3]2002, 1153.
[61] *MR* [3]2002, 922.
[62] *MR* [3]2002, 1192.
[63] *MR* [3]2002, 1204.
[64] *MR* [3]2002, 1223.
[65] *MR* [3]2002, 249.

- Urging and demanding: *impero*

  > *Famulis tuis, quaesumus, Domine, caelestis gratiae munus* impertire, ut, *quibus beatae Virginis partus exstitit salutis exordium, Nativitatis eius festivitas pacis* tribuat *incrementum.*[66]

4.3 *Thirteen ways to express purpose in Latin*

The thirteen ways to express purpose in Latin are demonstrated using two sentences:

a. Deponent: They invited us to hunt boars.

                using the deponent verb: *venor, venari, venatus sum* 1

b. Active: They invited us to eat boars.

                using the verb: *comedo comedere, comedi, comesum* 3

Nos invitaverunt (T4b):

1. *ut* + subjunctive:
   a. dep.: *ut venaremur apros.*
   b. act.: *ut comederemus apros.*

2. *qui, quae, quod* + subjunctive = *ut is, ea, id* + subjunctive; a relative purpose sentence:
   a. dep.: *qui venaremur apros.*
   b. act.: *qui comederemus apros.*

3. *ut* + passive subjunctive:
   a. dep.: -----
   b. act.: *ut apri a nobis comederentur.*

4. *qui, quae, quod* + passive subjunctive = *ut is, ea, id* + subjunctive; a relative purpose sentence:
   a. dep.: -----
   b. act.: *a quibus apri comederentur.*

5. future active participle (as done by Livius):
   a. dep.: *Nos invitaverunt venaturos apros.*
   c. act.: *Nos invitaverunt comessuros apros.*

6. Supine (accusative):
   a. dep.: *venatum apros.*
   b. act.: *comessum apros.*

---

[66] *MR* ³2002, 823.

7. *Ad* + gerund:
>   a. dep.: *ad venandum apros.*
>   b. act.: *ad comedendum apros.*
8. *Ad* + gerundive:
>   a. dep.: *ad venandos apros.*
>   b. act.: *ad comedendos apros.*

9. Genitive gerund + gratia, causa, ergo:
>   a. dep.: *venandi apros gratia, causa, ergo.*
>   b. act.: *comedendi apros gratia, causa, ergo.*

10. Genitive gerundive + *gratia, causa, ergo*:
>   a. dep.: *venandorum aprorum gratia, causa, ergo.*
>   b. act.: *comedendorum aprorum gratia, causa, ergo.*

11. Dative case of the gerund
>   (because of the verb of motion, *idoneos* «suitable ones» is added):
>   a. dep.: *idoneos venando apros.*
>   b. act.: *idoneos comedendo apros.*

12. Dative case of the gerundive
>   (because of the verb of motion, *idoneos* «suitable ones» is added):
>   a. dep.: *idoneos venandis apris.*
>   b. act.: *idoneos comedendis apris.*

13. *quo* + comparative + subjunctive = *ut eo* + comparative + subjunctive
>   a. dep.: *quo facilius venaremur apros.*
>   (*quo facilius* = *ut eo facilius* = "so that by that much more easily",
>   which is rendered "so that all the more easily ...")
>   b. act.: *quibus promptiores comederemus apros.*
>   (*quibus promptiores* = *ut eis promptiores* = "so that we that much more enthusiastic people",
>   which is rendered "so that all the more easily ...")

The above thirteen constructions all express purpose. There is one final construction, which we do not use because it is poor Latin prose. Virgil and the poets use this for meter. Then, this construction is used from the Augustan period and following. Modern languages use this construction as well.

14. (The infinitive. We do not do this!)
>   a. (dep.: *venari apros.*)
>   b. (act.: *comedere apros.*)

5. Gerund

To understand the use of gerunds and gerundives, let us first look at how they are formed.
- A Gerund is a singular neuter noun.
- Thus,
  - o   it is not plural,
  - o   words that agree with it are in the neuter, and
  - o   as a noun a gerund has cases.

The forms of a gerund are:

Subject:	*Cantare hymnos est iucundum*: Singing hymns is pleasant. (*Iucundum* is neuter because *cantare* as a subject gerund is neuter.)
Object:	Either: *volo cantare*: I want singing. Or: *paratus sum ad cantandum*: I'm ready for singing.
of, possession:	*Habet facultatem cantandi*: she has the ability of singing.
to, for: by, with, from, in:	*Operam dedit cantando*: she gave effort to singing. *Vivit cantando*: she lives by singing. (The forms of the dative and ablative are the same.)

- Most of the time an infinitive can be translated by the "-ing" form of the verb.
- For example: *paratus sum ad cantandum hymnos*: I'm ready for singing hymns.
  - o   Thomas and scholastics like this as it flows easily.
  - o   Romans don't like it.
  - o   Romans use the gerund 5% of the time and the gerundive 95% of the time.
  - o   The gerundive is preferred, stylistically better and usual.

6. Gerundive

- A gerundive is a verbal adjective.
- There is no difference in meaning between gerunds and gerundives, only their forms are different.
- Gerund**ive** is the adject**ive** of the gerund.
- The gerundive has the same meaning as the gerund but uses the form of an adjective.
- Romans prefer the gerundive by 95%; and use the gerund only 5% of the time.
- The gerundive is preferred, stylistically better and usual.

- The form of the gerundive is, for example, *Cantandus, -a, -um.*
- The rule for forming the gerundive is:
    - o Put the object of the gerund in the case of the gerund
    - o and make the gerundive agree with it,

- For example:
    - o *Paratus sum **ad cantandum** hymnos*: I'm ready for singing hymns.
    - o First put the object of the gerund in the case of the gerund.
    - o In this case *hymnos* is already accusative.
    - o Then, make the gerundive agree with it.
    - o So, *cantandum* becomes plural masculine: *cantandos.*
    - o Thus: *Paratus sum **ad cantandos hymnos**.*
    - o Both phrases with the gerund and gerundive mean:
        "I'm ready for singing hymns".
    - o The object of *ad* is *cantandos.*
    - o *The object of cantandos is hymnos.*
    - o *Hymnos* is in the gender and number of its own object.

- Another example:
    - o *Habet facultatem **cantandi** hymnos*: She has the power of singing hymns.
    - o First, put the object of the gerund in the case of the gerund.
    - o In this case *hymnos* takes the genitive case here: *hymnorum.*
    - o Then, and make the gerundive agree with it.
    - o So, *cantandi* becomes plural masculine: *cantandorum.*
    - o Thus: *Habet facultatem **cantandorum hymnorum**.*
    - o Both phrases with the gerund and gerundive mean:
        "She has the power of singing".
    - o The object of *ad* is *cantandorum.*
    - o The object of *cantandorum* is *hymnorum.*
    - o *Cantandorum* is in the gender and number of its own object.

- The gerund contributes the case; its object contributes the gender and number.

Now let us see both the gerund and the gerundive in each of its function in the Latin sentence:

- *Subject*   *nominative, as others call it.*
- *Object*   *accusative, as others call it.*
- *Of, possession*   *genitive, as others call it.*
- *By, with, from, in (the form is the same as* to, for)   *ablative, as others call it.*
- *To, for (same form as* by, with, from, in)   *dative, as others call it.*

6.1 *Subject*

Gerund	Gerundive
Cantare hymnos est iucundum: Singing hymns is pleasant. *Iucundum* is neuter because *Cantare* is neuter.	

6.2 *Object*

Gerund	Gerundive
*Paratus sum **ad cantandum** hymnos.* * **in cantandum** hymnos.* * **inter cantandum** hymnos.*	*Paratus sum **ad cantandos hymnos.*** * **in cantandos hymnos.*** * **inter cantandos hymnos.***
both mean: I'm ready	for singing hymns. unto singing hymns. in the midst singing hymns.
the object of ad is *cantandum* as a gerund. The object of *cantandum* is *hymnos.*	The object of *ad* is *cantandos,* an adjective. The object of *cantandos* is *hymnos.* *Cantandos* is in the gender and number of its own object *hymnos.*

6.3 *Of, possession*

Gerund	Gerundive
*Habet facultatem **cantandi** hymnos:*	*Habet facultatem **cantandorum hymnorum.***
both mean: She has the power of singing hymns.	
The object of *cantandi* is *hymnos*	One can not see that *hymnorum* is the object of *cantandorum.* *Cantandorum* is in the gender and number of its own object *hymnorum.*

6.4 *By, with, from, in* (*the form is the same as to, for*)

Gerund	Gerundive
*Lucratur **cantando** hymnos.*	*Lucratur **cantandis hymnis.***
both mean: She makes money by singing songs	
The object of *cantando* is *hymnos.*	One can not see that *hymnis* is the object of *cantandis.* *Cantandis* is in the gender and number of its own object *hymnis.*

6.5 *To, for* (*same form as by, with, from, in*)

Gerund	Gerundive
*Operam dedit **cantando** hymnos.*	*Operam dedit **cantandis hymnis**.*

both mean: (She) gave effort to singing songs.

The object of cantando is hymnos.	One can not see that *hymnis* is the object of *cantandis*. *Cantandis* is in the gender and number of its own object *hymnis*.

7. Passive necessity formula

We will study the participles in our next article. I hesitate to even mention here the participle of passive necessity, because it looks like a gerundive and at times like a gerund, but its meaning is wholly different. The distinction between the participle of passive necessity and the other two (gerund and gerundive) is so difficult for students to understand that I separate them when I am teaching by one full year. So here I will only mention the difference and we will examine the participle of passive necessity next year when considering the four participles.

The problem is that one and the same form may be either:
- gerund,
- gerundive,
- participle of passive necessity.

Note the use of *ad liberandum humanum genus* in the following prayer:
> *Deus, qui, ad liberandum humanum genus a vetustatis condicione,*
> *Unigenitum tuum in hunc mundum misisti,*
> *largire devote exspectantibus supernae tuae gratiam pietatis,*
> *ut ad verae perveniamus praemium libertatis.*[67]

The phrase *ad liberandum humanum genus* may be either:
- a **gerund**:   the object of *ad* is the gerund *liberandum*, and the object of the gerund is *humanum genus*: "for freeing the human race".
- a **gerundive**:   the object of *ad* is the gerundive *liberandum humanum genus*: "for freeing the human race". Because *genus* is neuter, *liberandum* already agrees with it.

---

[67] *MR* ³2002, 127.

- a **participle of passive necessity**: the object of *ad* could be, although I do not believe it is here, *humanum genus*, which is in turn described by the participle of passive necessity *liberandum*, meaning "needing to be freed":

"for the human race needing to be freed".

The difference between these three is important, because:

- the participle of passive necessity describes the *humanum genus*;
- taken as either gerund or a gerundive the object of *ad* is *liberandum* and the object of *liberandum* is *genus humanum*.

This grammatical distinction is important because of its consequences for the hermeneutics of the prayer, because:

- only the gerund and gerundive are counted among the thirteen ways to express purpose;
- the participle of passive necessity is not listed among the thirteen ways to express purpose.
- Both the gerund and gerundive are active verbal forms;
- the participle of passive necessity is, as its title says, passive.

Here are several examples from the collects of the MR ³2002.

I have divided the following examples up into those which are clearly gerunds followed by an object, those which are clearly gerundives, and then those which could be taken as either of these two because the object of the gerund is a masculine or neuter singular accusative noun.

- Expressions of purpose: gerunds followed by an object

Omnipotens sempiterne Deus, infirmitatem nostram propitius respice, atque ad protegendum nos *dexteram tuae maiestatis extende.*[68]

Quaesumus, omnipotens Deus, ut nos, virtute Spiritus Sancti, et ad credendum dociles et ad confitendum fortes *efficias, qui beato Xysto eiusque sociis propter verbum tuum et testimonium Iesu animas suas ponere tribuisti.*[69]

Deus, qui beatum Ioannem presbyterum ad annuntiandum *investigabiles Christi* divitias *mirabiliter elegisti, da nobis, eius exemplis et monitis, ut, in tua scientia crescentes, secundum Evangelii lumen fideliter conversemur.*[70]

Quaesumus, omnipotens Deus, ut nos, virtute Spiritus Sancti, et ad credendum dociles et ad confitendum fortes *efficias, qui beatis martyribus N. et N. propter verbum tuum et testimonium Iesu animas ponere tribuisti.*[71]

---

[68] MR ³2002, 204.
[69] MR ³2002, 803.
[70] MR ³2002, 813.
[71] MR ³2002, 918.

- Expressions of purpose: gerundives

> *Excita, Domine, corda nostra* ad praeparandas *Unigeniti tui* vias, *ut, per eius adventum, purificatis tibi mentibus servire mereamur.*[72]

> *Deus, qui hodierna die Unigenitum tuum gentibus stella duce revelasti, concede propitius, ut, qui iam te ex fide cognovimus,* usque ad contemplandam speciem *tuae celsitudinis perducamur.*[73]

> *Deus, qui* ad *multas* illuminandas gentes *beatum Ansgarium episcopum mittere voluisti, eius nobis intercessione concede, ut in tuae veritatis luce iugiter ambulemus.*[74]

> *Deus, qui Ecclesiam tuam per beatum Cyrillum episcopum ad mysteria salutis profundius* attingenda *mirabiliter adduxisti, da nobis, eius intercessione, Filium tuum ita agnoscere, ut vitam abundantius habeamus.*[75]

> *Deus, qui* ad *christianam* iuventutem educandam *beatum Ioannem Baptistam elegisti, excita in Ecclesia tua institutores, qui humanae et christianae iuvenum disciplinae toto corde sese devoveant.*[76]

> *Deus, qui* ad dilatandam Ecclesiam *tuam beatum Petrum martyrio coronasti, da nobis, in his paschalibus gaudiis, ita Christi mortui et resurgentis mysteria frequentare, ut novitatis vitae testes esse mereamur.*[77]

> *Deus, qui in Ecclesia tua beatum Pium papam ad fidem* tuendam ac te *dignius* colendum *providus excitasti, da nobis, ipso intercedente, vivida fide ac fructuosa caritate mysteriorum tuorum esse participes.*[78]

> *Omnipotens sempiterne Deus, qui beatam Virginem Mariam, Filium tuum gestantem,* ad visitandam Elisabeth *inspirasti, praesta, quaesumus, ut, afflanti Spiritui obsequentes, cum ipsa te semper magnificare possimus.*[79]

> *Deus, qui* ad *maiorem tui nominis* gloriam propagandam *beatum Ignatium in Ecclesia tua suscitasti, concede, ut, eius auxilio et imitatione certantes in terris, coronari cum ipso mereamur in caelis.*[80]

---

[72] *MR* ³2002, 132.
[73] *MR* ³2002, 175.
[74] *MR* ³2002, 724.
[75] *MR* ³2002, 733.
[76] *MR* ³2002, 744.
[77] *MR* ³2002, 747.
[78] *MR* ³2002, 749.
[79] *MR* ³2002, 760.
[80] *MR* ³2002, 795.

Deus, qui, ad tuendam *catholicam* fidem et universa *in Christo* instauranda, *beatum Pium papam caelesti sapientia et apostolica fortitudine replevisti, concede propitius, ut, eius instituta et exempla sectantes, praemia consequamur aeterna.*[81]

Deus, qui ad *tuae* fidem *Ecclesiae* vindicandam *beatum Robertum episcopum mira eruditione et virtute decorasti, eius intercessione concede, ut populus tuus eiusdem fidei semper integritate laetetur.*[82]

Deus, qui beatum Dionysium eiusque socios ad praedicandam *gentibus* gloriam *tuam misisti, eosque virtute constantiae in passione roborasti, tribue nobis, quaesumus, ex eorum imitatione prospera mundi despicere, et nulla eius adversa formidare.*[83]

Deus, qui ad tuendam *catholicam* fidem *virtute et doctrina beatum Petrum presbyterum roborasti, eius intercessione concede, ut, qui veritatem quaerunt, te Deum gaudenter inveniant, et in tua confessione populus credentium perseveret.*[84]

Deus, qui ad illustrandam Ecclesiam *tuam beatum N. martyrii victoria decorare dignatus es, concede propitius, ut, sicut ipse dominicae passionis imitator fuit, ita nos, per eius vestigia gradientes, ad gaudia sempiterna pervenire mereamur.*[85]

Deus, qui infirmitati nostrae, ad terendam *salutis* viam, *in Sanctis tuis exemplum et praesidium collocasti, concede propitius, ut, qui beati N. natalicia colimus, per eius ad te exempla gradiamur.*[86]

Pater sancte, qui, licet fideles omnes ad perfectionem caritatis invitas, multos tamen excitare non desinis, ad Filii tui vestigia pressius sequenda, *concede, ut, quos tibi in sortem peculiarem elegeris, conversatione sua valeant regni tui signum ostendere Ecclesiae mundoque perspicuum.*[87]

Deus, qui Ecclesiam tuam sacramentum salutis cunctis gentibus esse voluisti, ut Christi salutiferum opus usque in fines saeculorum perseveret, excita tuorum corda fidelium, et praesta, ut ad omnem creaturam salvandam *urgentius vocari se sentiant, quatenus ex omnibus populis una familia unusque tibi populus exsurgat et crescat.*[88]

---

[81] *MR* ³2002, 814.
[82] *MR* ³2002, 832.
[83] *MR* ³2002, 845.
[84] *MR* ³2002, 883.
[85] *MR* ³2002, 921.
[86] *MR* ³2002, 956.
[87] *MR* ³2002, 1105.
[88] *MR* ³2002, 1117.

- The following could be taken as either gerunds or gerundives because the object of the gerund is a neuter or masculine accusative singular noun.

> *Deus, qui, ad liberandum humanum genus a vetustatis condicione, Unigenitum tuum in hunc mundum misisti, largire devote exspectantibus supernae tuae gratiam pietatis, ut ad verae perveniamus praemium libertatis.*[89]

> *Concede nobis, omnipotens Deus, ut, per annua quadragesimalis exercitia sacramenti, et ad intellegendum Christi proficiamus arcanum, et effectus eius digna conversatione sectemur.*[90]

> *Maiestatem tuam, Domine, suppliciter imploramus, ut, quanto magis dies salutiferae festivitatis accedit, tanto devotius ad eius celebrandum proficiamus paschale mysterium.*[91]

> *Omnipotens sempiterne Deus, qui humano generi, ad imitandum humilitatis exemplum, Salvatorem nostrum carnem sumere, et crucem subire fecisti, concede propitius, ut et patientiae ipsius habere documenta et resurrectionis consortia mereamur.*[92]

> *Deus, qui, ad populum fidelem in angustiis confortandum, beatum Ioannem suscitasti, praesta, quaesumus, ut nos in tuae protectionis securitate constituas, et Ecclesiam tuam perpetua pace custodias.*[93]

> *Deus, qui beatos (episcopos) N. et N. ad pascendum populum tuum spiritu veritatis et dilectionis implevisti, praesta, ut, quorum festivitatem venerando agimus, eorum imitatione proficiamus, et intercessione sublevemur.*[94]

> *Omnipotens aeterne Deus, qui per glorificationem Sanctorum novissima dilectionis tuae nobis argumenta largiris, concede propitius, ut, ad Unigenitum tuum fideliter imitandum, et ipsorum intercessione commendemur, et incitemur exemplo.*[95]

> *Deus, qui ancillam tuam beatam N. ad quaerendum te ante omnia vocasti, eius exemplo et intercessione concede, ut, puro et humili corde tibi servientes, ad gloriam tuam perveniamus aeternam.*[96]

---

[89] *MR* ³2002, 127.
[90] *MR* ³2002, 206.
[91] *MR* ³2002, 234.
[92] *MR* ³2002, 272.
[93] *MR* ³2002, 851.
[94] *MR* ³2002, 932.
[95] *MR* ³2002, 952.
[96] *MR* ³2002, 960.

Deus, qui beatum N. ad *tuum* regnum *in hoc saeculo* perquirendum, *per caritatis perfectae prosecutionem vocasti, concede, ut, eius intercessione roborati, in dilectionis via spiritu gaudentes progrediamur.*[97]

Deus clementiae et reconciliationis, qui praecipuos dies salutis hominibus praebes ad te *omnium creatorem et patrem* agnoscendum, (*per hoc acceptabile tempus*) *propitius nos adiuva, ut, libenter verbum pacis a te accipientes, omnia in Christo instaurandi tuae deserviamus voluntati.*[98]

Deus, cuius Filius, ad redimendum genus *humanum a captivitate peccati, formam servi accipere dignatus est, da famulis tuis in vinculis constitutis, ut illa libertate potiantur, qua omnes homines, filios tuos, voluisti donari.*[99]

Domine Deus, qui beatum Paulum apostolum ad praedicandum Evangelium *mirabiliter designasti, da fide mundum universum imbui, quam ipse coram regibus gentibusque portavit, ut iugiter Ecclesia tua capiat augmentum.*[100]

- In one case, the object of the preposition *ad* is the gerund *serviendum* which takes a dative complement, *tibi*

  Deus, qui sanctum Brunonem ad serviendum tibi *in solitudine vocasti, eius nobis intercessione concede, ut, per huius mundi varietates, tibi iugiter vacemus.*[101]

- Dative gerundive

  Deus, qui naturalium rerum virtutes hominum labori subdere voluisti, concede propitius, ut, operibus nostris christiano spiritu intenti, sinceram caritatem cum fratribus exercere, et creationi divinae perficiendae *sociam operam praestare mereamur.*[102]

  Praesta, quaesumus, omnipotens et misericors Deus, ut Spiritus Sanctus adveniens templum nos gloriae suae dignanter inhabitando *perficiat.*[103]

  Concede nobis, omnipotens Deus, ut salutare tuum, quod ad redemptionem mundi luce nova caelorum processit, nostris semper innovandis cordibus *oriatur.*[104]

---

[97] *MR* [3]2002, 963.
[98] *MR* [3]2002, 1109.
[99] *MR* [3]2002, 1144
[100] *MR* [3]2002, 1185.
[101] *MR* [3]2002, 843.
[102] *MR* [3]2002, 1126.
[103] *MR* [3]2002, 436.

Deus, qui beatum Iosephum presbyterum tanta caritate et patientia decorasti, ut pueris erudiendis omnique virtute exornandis constanter incumberet, concede, quaesumus, ut, quem sapientiae praeceptorem colimus, veritatis cooperatorem iugiter imitemur.[105]

Conclusion

In this chapter we have

- given the times in their numerical order,
- distinguished between T4a and T4b and shown the importance of this distinction in a collect,
- shown how the understanding of the passive T4a, T4b, T5, T6 evolved,
- established the principles of the subjunctive,
- explained simply the sequence of tenses using the two track system,
- begun to distinguish between purpose and result clauses,
- examined the result clause in detail, presenting numerous examples from the collects of its various forms of construction,
- presented thirteen ways to express purpose, with numerous examples from the collects,
- distinguished between a gerund and a gerundive, both of which can be expressions of purpose,
- and begun to distinguish the passive necessity formula from the gerund and gerundive.

In a subsequent article, I intend to:

- present the four participles
- including the passive necessity formula,
- examine result clauses in detail,
- present the object sentence composed of the accusative and infinitive,
- with numerous examples from the collects.

You may now:

- teach Latin through the collects,
- begin your patient and detailed analysis of the minor euchology,
- better appreciate the liturgy.

---

[104] *MR* ³2002, 182.
[105] *MR* ³2002, 817.

Bibliography

A. **Research tools**

GILDERSLEEVE B.L., – G. LODGE, *Gildersleeve's Latin Grammar*, Bolchazy-Carducci, Wauconda IL 2003, reprint of [3]1985.

LEWIS, C.T.,– C. SHORT, *A Latin Dictionary*, Oxford UP, Oxford – New York 1879, reprinted 1995.

B. **Liturgical source**

Missale Romanum ex decreto Sacrosancti Oecumenici Concilii Vaticani II instauratum auctoritate Pauli PP. VI promulgatum Ioannis Pauli PP. II cura recognitum, editio typica tertia, Typis Vaticanis, Città del Vaticano [3]2002.

CHAPTER 3

How to Interpret a Collect[1]

Renato De Zan

Introduction

Until the Second Vatican Council the *consuetudo Ecclesiae* gave no exact name to the prayer which today is called the collect (*Collecta*).[2] Before the liturgical reform born of the Second Vatican Council, this prayer was normally given the generic name of *Oratio*[3] in the writings of earlier authors. One already finds the term *Collecta* with a certain frequency in the *Ordo Romanus* 10 (of the

---

[1] Translated from the Italian by: J.G. Leachman and E. Carr.

[2] For a brief bibliography on the collect refer to V. RAFFA, *Liturgia eucaristica: Mistagogia della Messa, dalla storia e dalla teologia alla pastorale pratica*, Rome, Edizioni Liturgiche [2]2003, 294-295, 300; B. CAPELLE, "Collecta", *Revue Bénédictine* 42 (1930) 197-204; J. COCHEZ, *La structure rythmique de oraisons*, Louvain 1928, 139-150; L. BROU, "Étude historique sur les oraisons des dimanches après la Pentecôte dans la tradition romain", *Sacris Erudiri* 2 (1941) 123-224; P. BRUYLANTS, *Les oraisons du missel romain. Texte et histoire* (Études liturgiques 2 vol.), Mont César, Louvain 1952; M. RIGHETTI, *Storia Liturgica*, vol 3, Ancora, Milano [3]1966, 177-182; A. MARTIMORT, *La Chiesa in preghiera*, vol. 1, Brescia, Queriniana 1987, 178-179; vol. 2, 72-73; S. MARSILI - A. NOCENT - M. AUGÉ - A.J. CHUPUNGCO, *Anàmnesis. La Liturgia Eucaristica*, vol 3/2, Casale Monferrato, Marietti 1983, 205-208.

[3] *Oratio* is the name given to the *Collecta* already by the Gregorian Sacramentary (*Gregor* 193,194,195,196) and by the *Ordines Romani* (*OR* 1, 53; 2,23; 4, 24; etc.) until the Missal of Pius V in its final edition promulgated by John XXIII in 1962. In *OR* 2, 214 we find however: "Sequitur oratio prima, quam collectam dicunt [the first prayer, which they call the Collect, follows]".

tenth century and composed in the Rhineland) and in the Franco-germanic liturgical authors of the tenth to twelfth centuries (cf. Remigius of Auxerre, Bernoldus of Constance, Rupert of Deutz, and others).[4] In his *Micrologus de ecclesiasticis observationibus*, published around 1085, Bernoldus[5] writes: "*Sequitur oratio quam Collectam dicunt, eo quod sacerdos, qui legatione fungitur pro populo ad Dominum, omnium petitiones et orationes colligat atque concludat*"[6] (PL 151, 979).

The current *Instructio Generalis Missali Romani* states that the collect is the Latin name commonly given to the prayer "per quam indoles celebrationis exprimitur"[7] (*IGMR*-2000, 54), and that the prayer gathers and summarizes the prayers of the assembly. In fact the *IGMR*-2000, 54, states: "Deinde sacerdos populum ad orandum invitat; et omnes una cum sacerdote parumper silent, ut conscii fiant se in conspectu Dei stare, et vota sua in animo possint nuncupare".[8]

In 1983 the Italian episcopate underlined a new aspect of the proper Sunday collect. The introduction to the Italian edition states: "Based on the mature experience of the local churches in these past years, the 1983

---

[4] It should not be forgotten that John Cassian already writes of the one "*qui orationem collecturus est*" or "*qui precem colligit*" (*De institutis coenobitorum* 2, 7, ed. M. Petschenig, [Corpus scriptorum ecclesiasticorum latinorum 17], Vienna 1888, 23-24).
Cassian was born around 360, perhaps in Scythia (modern Romania). He stayed in Palestine (Bethlehem) and Egypt, where he was ordained presbyter by St John Chrysostom. He moved to Rome and straightaway to Marseille. In 415 he founded a men's monastery (Saint Victor) and a women's one. He wrote the *De institutis coenobitorum* and the *Collationes*, important for monastic formation. He died 23 July 435 and was buried at St Victor, a monastery which would be destroyed in the French Revolution.
[5] Bernoldus of Constance, born in Sciaffusa (Switzerland) about 1054, was educated in Constance with Bernard of Hildesheim. In 1079 he took part in the synod called by Gregory VII (when Berengarius of Tours was condemned). After having been present at the Council of Piacenza, he returned to Germany, was briefly counsellor to Herman of Luxemburg and in 1086 became a Benedictine monk. In 1091 he returned to Sciaffusa (the abbey of All Saints) where he died 16 September 1100. A supporter of Papal supremacy over the Emperor, upon which he wrote at least seventeen tracts, he edited the *Chronicon* and, in the study of Liturgy, the *Micrologus de ecclesiasticis observationibus* (ca. 1085) which is a commentary on the Papal Liturgy.
[6] "The prayer named the Collect follows, because the presbyter, who carries out his ministry on behalf of the faithful before God, gathers and concludes the requests and the prayers of all", translator.
[7] "By means of which is expressed the character of the celebration".
[8] "Il sacerdote invita il popolo a pregare e tutti insieme con lui stanno per qualche momento in silenzio, per prendere coscienza di essere alla presenza di Dio e poter formulare nel cuore le proprie intenzioni di preghiera" (official translation of the CEI).

edition ... establishes a connection between the collects and the Word of God distributed throughout the three-year cycle of the Sunday lectionary".[9]

All that has been said above helps us to appreciate that the collect is a rich and complex text, a richness that former students of the liturgy have ever been careful not to lose.

1. In search of a methodology

The science of interpreting the Liturgy is as old as the history of the Church. It should be emphasised, however, that a systematic treatment using a historical-critical method for the study of liturgical texts is quite recent.[10] The beginning of such a methodology can traced to the brief study by P. Alfonso on the stylistic and historical features of the ancient Roman euchology, published in 1931.[11] His observation, no longer totally tenable, is that: "The study of the Liturgy ... is principally a euchological study".[12] After the Council, in the ferment of methodological studies on the Liturgy,[13] a good deal of attention was given to the study of the euchology in the conviction that any methodology has to go beyond the historical-critical, since the

---

9 "Presentazione", *Messale Romano: Riformato a norma dei decreti del Concilio Ecumenico Vaticano II e promulgato da Papa Paolo VI*, Conferenza Episcopale Italiana, Libreria Editrice Vaticana, Città del Vaticano 1983, no. 3, translator.

10 Simply to give a few titles as examples, L. BEAUDUIN, *La piété de l'Eglise: Principes et faits*, Louvain 1914; P. DE PUNIET, "La méthode en matière de liturgie", *Cour et Conférences des semaines liturgiques. Tome II. Cinquième semaine. Louvain du 10 au 14 août 1913*, Louvain 1914, 41-77; A. BAUMSTARK, *Liturgie comparée: Principes et méthodes pour l'étude historique des liturgies chrétiennes*, Chevetogne – Paris 1920; ed. and supplemented B. Botte ³1953; R. GUARDINI, "Über die systematische Methode in der Liturgiewissenschaft", *Jahrbuch für Liturgiewissenschaft* 1 (2/1921), 97-108; C. CALLEWAERT, "La méthode dans l'étude de la liturgie", *Sacris erudiri*, Steenbrugge 1940, 41-52.

11 P. ALFONSO, *L'eucologia romana antica. Lineamenti stilistici e storici*, Subiaco 1931.

12 "Lo studio della liturgia ... è principalmente uno studio eucologico", ALFONSO, 7.

13 Among the various studies should be noted: P. LUCIER, "Le statut epistémologique de la situation liturgique", *Liturgie et vie chrétienne* 82 (1972) 256-278; F. BROVELLI, "Per uno studio della liturgia", *La scuola cattolica* 104 (1976) 567-635; A. CAPRIOLI, "Linee di ricerca per uno statuto teologico della liturgia", *Communio* 41 (1978) 35-44; *La liturgie: son sens, son esprit, sa methode. Liturgie et théologie*, Rome 1982; R. VOLP, *Zeichen: Semiotik in Theologie und Gottesdienst*, München – Mainz 1982; R. LE GALL, "Pour une conception intégrale de la liturgie", *Questions liturgiques* 65 (1984) 181-202; J. HERMANS, "L'étude de la liturgie comme discipline théologique: Problèmes et méthodes", *Revue théologique de Louvain* 18 (1987), J.A. ZIMMERMANN, *Liturgy as Language of Faith. A Liturgical Methodology in the Mode of Paul Ricoeur's Textual Hermeneutics*, Lanham – New York – London 1988; D.W. FAGERBERG, *What Is Liturgical Theology? A Study in Methodology*, Liturgical Press, Collegeville MN 1992; K.W. IRWIN, *Context and Text: Method on Liturgical Theology*, Liturgical Press, Collegeville MN 1994.

euchology is inserted into a ritual programme often conditioned by anthropology.[14]

a) A first methodological proposal was formulated in 1971 by F. Nakagaki.[15] His "integral method" includes five moments (liturgical, historical, literary, contextual and unitary). The liturgical moment examines the text within its context of the liturgical year. The historical moment endeavours to identify the author of the formula and its date and place of composition and use, as well as any other elements useful in determining its cultural context.

b) In 1974 M. Augé took up the methodology of Nakagaki and expanded it.[16] He asserts that the liturgical texts should be examined both in their historical context (date, author, geographical location, function, witness of authors and citations, etc.) and in their doctrinal identity (content, expressive force, specific liturgical sense, links with the thought of ancient Christian authors and with the theological environment of the time). In particular the biblical roots and particular philology (liturgical Latin) of the euchological texts must be studied further by looking for the theologies within, and the structural, stylistic and rhythmical characteristics.

c) Just a few years later, in 1977, A.-M. Triacca and R. Farina published a substantial article on the method of reading and studying euchology.[17] The argument is rather complex (and sometimes repetitive), but the meaning of the authors is clear. They intend to examine the euchology itself (philological analysis of each word and of the particular formula, analysis of the overall structure, grammatical and stylistic analysis), the collect's historical relationships (the euchology and its context, the specific euchology and the different euchological traditions, etc.), the collect's literary system (literary or formal criticism) and its relationship with its object or the receiver, called by the authors "the reader" (the believer, the *orans* or the student of literary-criticism).

---

[14] We refer here to the organisation of the studies of the Institute of Pastoral Liturgy of Sta. Giustina in Padua, incorporated in the Faculty of Theology of the Pontifical Atheneum of St. Anselmo in Rome, which gives a privileged position to the anthropological approach to the Liturgy.

[15] F. NAKAGAKI, "Metodo integrale: Discorso sulla metodologia nell'interpretazione dei testi eucologici", in *Fons vivus: Miscellanea liturgica in memoria di don E. M. Vismara*, ed. A. CUVA, [Bibliotheca Theologia Salesiana 1, 6], PAS Verlag, Zürich 1971, 269-286.

[16] M. AUGÉ, "Principi di interpretazione dei testi liturgici", in *Anàmnesis 1. La Liturgia momento nella storia della salvezza*, ed. S. Marsili et alii, Marietti, Casale Monferato, 1974, 159-179.

[17] A.M. TRIACCA – R. FARINA, "Studio e lettura dell'eucologia: Note metodologiche", in *Teologia, Liturgia, Storia: Miscellanea in onore di C. Manziana*, ed. C. Ghidelli, Morcelliana, Brescia 1977, 197-224.

d) In 1978 R.F. Taft opened up the dialogue between studies of euchology and of the human sciences,[18] proposing a method of structural analysis of the celebration in which the texts are situated. This stimulus produced some worthwhile results. In 1987 J. Schermann published his doctoral thesis[19] in which he presented a linguistic-semiotic approach to the Liturgy. In 1988 there appeared two further publications, one from Europe and one from the USA. From Europe, M.B. Merz,[20] studying the phenomenon of what occurs between the written and spoken text, examined the text in light of pragmatics, textual linguistics and communication. From the USA, J.A. Zimmermann[21] sought to understand the celebration through the form of the texts and to understand the Christian life through a study of the texts. Following the line of thought of P. Ricoeur, Zimmerman tackles the understanding of texts by studying single words (the synchronic linguistic criteria of the syntagmas and of the paradigms), by studying the way expressions or phrases are used in the text (in relation to the celebration, in relation to the performative, illocutory and perlocutory dimensions and in relation to the non-linguistic), by studying the text (its structure, literary form and style) and by studying the written text as an ever-renewed written and read communication. The purpose of Zimmerman's method is to go beyond the text first to a necessary pre-comprehension (by means of a participation in the liturgical event), then to an explanation (through a distancing from the event) and finally to an understanding (through the appropriation of the liturgical event).

e) Finally, the position of E. Mazza, a specialist in ancient liturgical texts, may seem curious.[22] He states that many "oremus" carry an excellent theology, but have no effect at all upon the celebration: "What is celebrated in the celebration is simply the rite as such in its complexity. In other words, the text is relevant, not in itself as text, but for its place within the rite, either for the connections it has with what goes before and what follows, or for the totality of the rite as such. This does not invalidate the text, but situates it

---

[18] R.F. TAFT, "The Structural Analysis of the Liturgical Units: An Essay in Methodology", *Worship* 52 (1978) 314-329.

[19] J. SCHERMANN, *Die Sprache im Gottesdienst*, Tyrolia Verlag, Innsbruck – Wien 1987.

[20] M. MERZ, *Liturgisches Gebet als Geschehen*, Aschendorff, Münster 1988.

[21] J.A. ZIMMERMAN, *Liturgy as Language of Faith: A Liturgical Methodology in the Mode of Paul Ricoeur's Textual Hermeneutics*, University Press of America, New York – Lanham – London 1988.

[22] E. MAZZA, "Teologia liturgica centrata sul vissuto celebrativo", *Qualità pastorale delle discipline teologiche e del loro insegnamento*, ed. M. MIDALI – R. TONELLI, Libreria Ateneo Salesiano, Rome 1993, 143-144. "Nella celebrazione, ciò che viene celebrato è il rito in quanto tale, nella sua globalità, come fatto sintetico. In altri termini: il testo ha rilievo non per se stesso, in quanto testo, ma per il suo rilievo all'interno del rito. Ossia per i legami che ha con ciò che precede e con ciò che segue, nonché con la totalità del rito in quanto fatto globale. Ciò non significa negare validità al testo, ma situarlo nel contesto rituale nel quale viene celebrato".

within its ritual context where it is celebrated". The author highlights the ritual context of the prayer in order to avoid its being understood only from a literary-theological point of view.

f) We published in English, in 1997, and in Italian, in 1998, a short chapter on the interpretation of liturgical texts.[23] The method we offered there takes account of the delicate problem which provoked a good deal of interest in the second half of the last century. H.G. Gadamer[24] had proposed a rather intransigent position in his account of the relationship between text and author: that one may not know the intention of the author. The response, sometimes polemical, of different authors and particularly of E.D. Hirsch[25] redefined the problem: it is possible to search and to discover, even if not in an exhaustive way, the intention of the author ("the meaning" of the text); it is possible to search and find the meaning of the text within the text by synchronic methods which reveal the imaginative capacity of the reader upon the text, yet omitting what the author intended to say about the text ("the significance" of the text). The method proposed here takes account of two hermeneutical aspects: the *intentio auctoris in textu* (the intention of the author within the text) and the *intentio textus in lectore* (the intention of the text according to the reader). The method presented, furthermore, confirmed by the work of my own teachers (in particular that of prof. Matias Augé) and by the progress of liturgical, linguistic, philologico-critical and literary sciences, offers a method that responds to the questions left to us by previous studies even as it formulates new ones.

After all that has been said above, we can now present a methodological process which maintains the riches of the past (historical-critical studies) and combines them with new methods suggested by the synchronic methodologies reported above. Given the necessary brevity of these pages, we can merely outline the analytical process enumerated below, with examples, in the following points: textual criticism, philological analysis, semantic analysis, the analysis of the text's authenticity and history, literary criticism (sources, context, structure, literary type and style) and the celebrative analysis.

Two other treatments should be part of the method: the theology of the collect and its translation. These we shall omit, and they will need to be treated elsewhere.

---

[23] R. DE ZAN, "Criticism and Interpretation of Liturgical Texts", in *Introduction to the Liturgy*, ed. A.J. Chupungco (Handbook for Liturgical Studies 1), Liturgical Press (Pueblo Book), Collegeville MN 1997, 331-365 (En. tr. of R. DE ZAN, "Introduzione alla Liturgia, Ermeneutica", ed. A. J. Chupungco [*Scientia Liturgica: Manuale di Liturgia* 1] Piemme, Casale Monferrato 1998, 356-389).

[24] H.G. GADAMER, *Wahrheit und Methode*, J.C.B. Mohr, Tubingen [3]1972. The first edition is of 1960.

[25] E.D. HIRSCH, *Validity in Interpretation*, Yale UP, New Haven – London 1967.

2. Textual criticism: Which text for the collect?

The collect may belong to the rich tradition comprising the patrimony of the liturgical texts of the Church or it may be of recent composition. The ancient texts of the *Collectae* or *Orationes* have been handed down for centuries through copying by hand. Such is one way of handing down the text of a formula, even if the formula might have been handed down more accurately in printed liturgical works. Not infrequently manual transmission has produced variants, which in their turn may be real errors or simple corrections that either improve or detract from the language and theology.

Nor are misunderstandings rare events, whether through copying by hand or through the printing process. For both manuscripts and printed books, therefore, it is necessary to use the steps of the critical-textual method. The study of the collect requires that the text be checked. For brevity's sake, we give an example of a collect in a printed work containing critical-textual errors.

When Holy Week was reformed in 1955, this was the new opening *Oratio*[26] for Good Friday:

> Deus, qui peccati veteris hereditariam mortem, in qua posteritatis genus omne successerat, Christi tui, Domini nostri, passione solvisti: da, ut, conformes eidem facti; sicut imaginem terren*ae* naturae necessitate portavimus, ita imaginem caelestis gratiae sanctificatione portemus.

Whoever reads the Latin text with a certain attention notes that there are two inconsistencies. The children of Adam bear not only the "image of earthly nature" – as the prayer says – but also the "reality". Furthermore, sanctification – says the text – is presented as if it were brought about only by personal ascesis. We know, rather, that sanctification is, first of all, brought about by grace. The original formula of the collect, no. 398 of *Sacr. Gelasianum Vetus*, says:[27]

---

[26] H.A.P. SCHMIDT, *Hebdomada Sancta. Vol 1. Contemporanei textus Liturgici, documenta paina et bibliographia*, Herder, Rome 1956, 93.
The translation is deliberately literal: "O God who has paid with the Passion of your Christ, our Lord, for the hereditary death of the ancient sin, in which every generation of posterity had followed, grant, that having being made like to the one, as by necessity we have carried the likeness of earthly nature, so may we carry by sanctification the likeness of heavenly grace", translator.
[27] *Liber Sacramentorum Romanae Aeclesiae ordinis anni circuli (Cod. Vat. Reg. Lat. 316/Paris Bibl. Nat. 7193, 41/56) (Sacramentarium Gelasianum)*, ed. L. C. Mohlberg – L. Eizenhöfer – P. Siffrin (Rerum ecclesiasticarum documenta. Series maior, Fontes 4] Herder, Rome ³1981, 65.
Literal translation: "O God who has paid with the Passion of your Christ, our Lord, for the hereditary death of the ancient sin, in which every generation of posterity had followed, grant, that having being made like to Him, as by necessity we have carried

Deus, qui peccati veteris hereditaria(m) mortem, in qua posteritatis genus omne successerat, Christi tui, Domini nostri, passione solvisti: da, ut, conformes eidem facti; sicut imaginem terreni naturae necessitate portavimus, ita imaginem caelestis gratiae sanctificatione portemus.

The opposing parallelism between *terreni* and *caelestis* is evident in the prayer. The words here refer to Adam and to Christ.[28] In the case of *terreni* the human race bears the image of Adam, by the necessity of nature, and it will bear, the image of Christ, *caelestis*, by a sanctification given by grace. The text of the collect, already corrected for the 1962 edition of the Missal, has also been used in the three editions of the Missal of Paul VI.

3. What meaning is found in the words and in the Latin constructions? (Philological analysis)

Christianity has reformed the Latin language,[29] shaping it to her own confession of faith. To the accusation that the pagans made of Christians that they had altered the purity of the Latin language, St Augustine replied: "Nec quaerant grammatici quam sit latinum, sed christiani quam verum. 'Salus' enim latinum nomen est. 'Salvare' et 'salvator' non fuerunt haec latine

---

the likeness of the nature of the earthly one, so may we carry by the sanctification (fruit – De Zan) of grace the likeness of the Heavenly one", translator.

[28] Cfr 1Cor 15,49; S. Leo the Great, *Tractatus* 63, 6. "Dum enim renuntiatur diabolo, et creditur Deo, dum in nouitatem a uetustate transitur, dum terreni hominis imago deponitur, et caelestis forma suscipitur, quaedam species mortis et quaedam similitudo resurrectionis interuenit, ut susceptus a Christo Christumque suscipiens non idem sit post lauacrum qui ante baptismum fuit, sed corpus regenerati fiat caro Crucifixi" (*Tractatus* 63, 6 in *Sancti Leonis Magni Romani pontificis tractatus septem et nonaginta*, ed. A. Chavasse [Corpus christianorum series latina 138 A] Brepols, Turnhout 1973, 387; PL 54, 357).
S. Leo the Great, *Tractatus* 71, 2. "Accordingly, since the Apostle says, 'the first man is of the earth earthly, the second man is from heaven heavenly. As is the earthy, such also are they that are earthy; and as is the heavenly, such also are they that are heavenly. As we have borne the image of the earthy, so let us also bear the image of Him Who is from heaven'" : "Dicente ergo Apostolo: *Primus homo de terra terrenus, secundus homo de caelo caelestis. Qualis terrenus, tales et terreni, et qualis caelestis, tales et caelestes. Sicut portauimus imaginem terreni, portemus et imaginem eius qui de caelo est*" (*Tractatus* 71, 2 in *Sancti Leonis Magni Romani pontificis tractatus septem et nonaginta*, ed. A. Chavasse (Corpus christianorum series latina 138 A) Brepols, Turnhout 1973, 435; cf.:1 Cor 15, 47–49).
[29] Cfr J. SCHRIJNEN, *Charakteristik des Altchristlichen Latein*, Nijmegen 1932 (tr. it.: *I caratteri del latino cristiano antico*, Bologna 1986); A. Dumas, *Manuel du latin chrétien*, Strasbourg 1955; C. MOHRMANN, *Etudes sur le latin des Chrétiens*, 4 vol., Rome 1958-1977.

antequam veniret salvator: quando ad Latinos venit, et haec Latina fecit".[30]
Nor has Liturgical Latin[31] always remained constant, for it has undergone
definite changes across the centuries, both in its vocabulary (cultural
variations and new forms coming from deeper theological reflection) and in
its syntactic-stylistic construction.[32] In Gaul, in Spain, in Germany and in
Ireland it was influenced by the "genius" of the various cultures where Latin
was spoken and used as a non-native tongue. If one knows the history of the
liturgical books, one may also understand how certain cultural and
theological influences passed into liturgical Latin from the local Latin usages.
Liturgical formularies from several areas (Italy, Gaul, Spain, Germany and
others) and from several epochs (liturgical Latin from the sixth to the ninth
centuries and of the rather different styles of later centuries) have been
introduced into the church's deposit of liturgical texts. All these facts require
that the text be read with great attention, taking account at least of such
influences as the language and the historical-geographical context. The play
between the following elements constitutes a fundamental element in the
philological understanding of each word of the text of the collect.

§1. If the text of the collect is found in its original formulary, present in
the Sacramentary (say: the *Sacr. Veronese*), one reads the formulary within its
original linguistic and theological context for which the formula had been
thought out and redacted. The linguistic context is similar: the Roman
liturgical Latin of the fifth and sixth centuries. The theological context is
similar too. The philological and theological analyses done from within the
closed field of the Sacramentary has a uniform language and is not difficult.
Today we have tools for knowing the particular use of words and
expressions of a particular liturgical book.[33]

---

[30] AUGUSTINUS HIPPONENSIS, *Serm.* 299. 6, "And let grammarians not ask whether the
word is Latin, nor Christians whether it is true. *Salus* is a Latin word, *salvare* and
*salvato*r never existed before the coming of the *salvator*: when he came to the Latins he
made this Latin", tr. from Italian; PL 38 1371; Cf. *De Trin.* 13. 10: "Quod verbum
[salvator] latina lingua antea non habebat, sed habere poterat; sicut potuit quando
voluit" (Ed. J. Mountain – F. Gloire [CCL 50 A, 401], Brepols, Turnhout 1973).

[31] Cfr C. MOHRMANN, *Études sur le latin des Chrétiens, vol. 3. Latin chrétien et liturgique*,
Rome 1965.

[32] For an example one may see: D. NORBERG, *Manuel pratique de latin médiéval*, Paris
1968 (tr. it., *Manuale di Latino medioevale*, Firenze 1974); V. PALADINI – M. DE MARCO,
Lingua e letteratura mediolatina, Bologna ²1980; V. VÄÄNÄNEN, *Introduzione al latino
volgare*, Bologna 1982.

[33] For the use of particular words within ancient texts, other than P. BRUYLANTS,
Concordance verbale du Sacramentaire léonien, Louvain 1945, there is J. DESHUSSES – B.
DARRAGON, *Concordances et Tableaux pour l'étude des grands Sacramentaires*, 6 vol.,
Fribourg, Editions Universitaires 1982-83 ; see also: A. BLAISE, *Dictionnaire latin-
français des auteurs chrétiens*, rev. H. Chirat, Brepols, Turnhout 1962; A. BLAISE, *Le
vocabulaire latin des principaux thèmes liturgiques*, rev. A. Dumas, Turnhout 1966; cfr
M.P. ELLEBRACHT, *Remarks on the Vocabulary of the Ancient Orations in the* Missale

If one wishes to express the word *epulae* (in many texts, *aepulae*) well in another language one needs to remember that in the *Sacr. Veronese* the word is never used in a deprecative sense (cfr n. 70: "puris mentibus ad aepulas aeternae salutis accedant"), whereas one may encounter the negative meaning in the Gelasian and Gregorian Sacramentaries (cfr *Sacr. Gelasianum Vetus*, 106: *cum aepularum restrictione carnalium*). A rare word may also occur on occasion. At n. 93 of the *Sacr. Veronese* one reads this formula: "Da nobis haec, quaesumus, Domine, frequentata mysteria: quia quotiens hostiae tibi placatae commemoratio celebrantur, opus nostrae redemptionis exeritur: per". A textual critic would correct *celebrantur* to *celebratur*, whereas *exeritur* presents difficulties to a philological critic. The analysis of the text's tradition tells us that the word does not make sense. The *Sacr. Gelasianum Vetus* presents *exercitum*, the Gregorian tradition reports *exercetur*, the Gelasian of Angoulême has *exere* and the Sacramentary of Prague, in two places, has *exercitus* and *exercitur*. The verb *ex(s)ero*, present only once in the *Sacr. Veronese* (n. 93), means not only "to appear, to show oneself", but also "to show oneself decisively". The expression *opus nostrae redemptionis exeritur* means "the work of our redemption (when it happens in the celebration of the sacrifice of Christ) *show itself in a decisive way* in our life".[34]

§2. When, however, the formulary or the individual formula, in this case the collect, is taken out of its original context and placed in a new context (Missal of Pius V or Missal of Paul VI), one can easily understand how the new general context would modify the original meaning of the text. The general context of the Missal will affect the understanding of the whole formulary. For the individual formula (cf. the collect) the simple context of the new formulary (as well as the general context of the Missal) will affect the understanding of the formula.

Let us give particular attention now to how the Missal of Paul VI came to be composed. First of all, it is important to note that we are dealing with a

Romanum (Latinitas Christianorum Primaeva 18), Dekker & Van De Vegt, Nijmegen — Utrecht ²1966. There are numerous monographs which treat individual words or expressions, for example, M. STEINHEIMER, *Die "DOXA TOY THEOY" in der römischen Liturgie* (Münchener theologische Studien, 2. Systematische Abteilung 4), Zink, München 1951; W. DIEZINGER, *'Effectus' in der römischen Liturgie*, Bonn 1961; B. DROSTE, *"Celebrare" in der römischen Liturgiesprache*, München 1963; etc.
There are some excellent dictionaries, C. DU CANGE, *Glossarium mediae et infimae latinitatis*, 10 vol., Graz 1954 (anastatic copy of original ed., Didot, Paris 1840-1850); A. ERNOUT – A. MEILLET, *Dictionnaire étymologique de la langue latine: Histoire des mots*, Paris ⁴1959; A. FORCELLINI, *Totius latinitatis lexicon*, 6 vol., Padova 1965 (anastatic copy); *Thesaurus Linguae Latinae, editus auctoritate et consilio Academicarum quinque Germanicarum, Berolinensis, Gottingensis, Lipsiensis, Monacensis, Vindobonensis*, Leipzig 1903.
[34] cfr J. PINELL, "I testi liturgici, voci di autorità, nella costituzione *Sacrosanctum Concilium*", *Costituzione liturgica* 'Sacrosanctum Concilium'. *Studi*, ed. Congregazione per il Culto Divino, Rome 186, 331-341

missal in which texts have been brought together from diverse periods and places.[35] We are dealing with a "closed field" that has a variety of language styles. The best method currently available for analyzing a "closed field" (a missal) with a variety of language styles (*multistylistic*) is semasiological or semantic analysis.[36] This contextual theory involves the analysis of the meaning of a word in its context, for a word being analyzed is classified according to its use within its particular context. The procedure is simple. Once the word in a collect is chosen for examination, other formulae in which the same word occurs are selected.[37] The 'syntagmas' (expressions, phrases) where the word is found are isolated and classified according to their semantic area, highlighting their model or 'paradigm'. The classification of the word's associations (verb, noun, determinative) proceeds by taking account of the semantic fields. Finally the equivalent or similar 'commutations' are examined while taking account of the model or paradigm. At this point one estimate value of meaning with which the examined word is used.

If we wish to know the meaning of the word *gloria* in the collect for Saturday of the second week of Advent as found in the Missal of Paul VI, *editio typica altera*,[38] which for convenience is labelled 140-C2[39] we begin with the text of the collect:

> Oriatur, quaesumus, omnipotens Deus, in cordibus nostris splendor gloriae tuae ut, omni noctis obscuritate sublata, filios nos esse lucis Unigeniti tui manifestet adventus.

---

[35] To accomplish an initial and basic research into the sources of the euchology of the Missal of Paul VI, consult: A. DUMAS, "Les sources du Missel Romain" *Notitiae* 7 (1971) 37-42, 74-77, 94-95, 134-136, 276-280, 409-410.

[36] G. Mounin in the second half of the last century gave a definition that is still clear and valid today:
"Before Bréal the term 'semasiology' used to indicate what today we call 'semantics'. 'Semasiology' has a more restricted meaning now indicating the study of the significations or meanings, or concepts which derive from the words which name them: making a list of all the meanings that are attributed to the word 'semantics', is itself a problem of semasiology. Diversely, 'onomasiology' is now understood as making a list of all the different denominations – the meanings – that can be attributed to the same concept or meaning" (MOUNIN, *Guida alla semantica*, Milano 1975, 8-9).

[37] Such formulae should preferably (but not necessarily) belong to the same literary type (collect) and to the same time (Advent, Christmas, etc.) or liturgical section (Sanctoral, *Ad diversa*, etc.).

[38] Because there are some errors in the *editio typica tertia* of the Missal it is better for the moment not to take examples from this edition and to wait for a revised publication of the volume.

[39] The sigla 140-C2 shows in the first number (140) the page of the second edition, in the sigla (C) that the formula is a collect and in the final number (2) that it is the second collect formula on page 140.

Given the brevity of the example, let us take one further collect (132-C)[40] and identify the syntagmas with the following result:

> - perducamur ad *gloriam* resurrectionis   : 132-C
> - splendor *gloriae* tuae oriatur in cordibus nostris   : 140-C2

Now we shall classify them according to their semantic fields:

> * semantic field of eschatological movement
>   - perducamur ad *gloriam* resurrectionis   : 132-C
>
> * semantic field of revelation
>   - splendor *gloriae* tuae oriatur in cordibus nostris   : 140-C2

Let us examine the type or paradigm of each syntagma:

> - 132-C: - we or equivalents + passive verb of direction + *ad* + accus. of X[41]
>   - God + verb of direction + we or equivalent + *ad* + accus. of X
> - 140-C2:   - X + verb of comparison + *in* + personal "state of place"

Having prepared the material, one may proceed in the classification of the associations (verbal, nominal and determinative), showing the association of function (VERBS, NOUNS, DETERMINANTS):

a) Verbal associations

> * field of eschatological movement
>   - PERDUCAMUR ad *gloriam* resurrectionis   : 132-C
> * field of revelation
>   - splendor *gloriae* tuae ORIATUR in cordibus nostris   : 140-C2

b) Nominal associations

> * field of revelation
>   - SPLENDOR *gloriae* tuae   : 140-C2

c) Determinative associations

> * field of eschatological movement
>   - *gloriam* RESURRECTIONIS   : 132-C
> * field of revelation
>   - *gloriae* TUAE   : 140-C2

---

[40] In Advent five texts contain the word *gloria*: 132-C; 135-C1; 140-C2; 144-C; 149-So.
[41] One may have a passive type of syntagma, but one may also have an active type. The X indicates any eschatological reality or goal.

Once the material has been classified, the commutations are established, and here attention to the paradigm of the syntagmas becomes important. If we search the concordances for the entry indicated by the associations (the word in CAPITALS), the syntagmas present in the Missal of Paul VI, which respond either to the semantic field or to the paradigm of the syntagma in question, are brought to light:

a) Verbal commutations

* field of eschatological movement
    paradigm   - we or equivalent + passive verb of direction + *ad* + accus. of X
                      - God + verb of direction + we or equivalent + *ad* + accus of X

- PERDUCAMUR	ad *gloriam* resurrectionis	: 132-C
- perducas familiam tuam	ad dona superna	: 196-C
- perducas nos	ad illam lucem in qua ipse es	: 199-C
- perduxisti beatum Martinum	ad caelestem *gloriam*	: 638-C1
- concedas perduci	ad veram patriam	: 881-C2

*field of revelation
    paradigm: - X + verb of comparison + *in* + personal "state of place"

| - splendor *gloriae* tuae | ORIATUR | in cordibus nostris | : 140-C2 |
| - salutare tuum | oriatur | cordibus nostris | : 173-C1 |

The verbal commutations indicate that the expression *gloria resurrectionis* (132-C) may be considered as almost interchangeable (with a similar meaning) with *dona superna* (196-C), *illa lux in qua ipse es* (199-C) and *vera patria* (881-C2). The expression *caelestis gloria* (638-C) is a tautology of 132-C and adds nothing.

Splendor GLORIAE tuae and *salutare tuum* are two biblico-liturgical, christological titles. Their interchangeability (commutation) is possible because the text concerns the same person. Their equivalence, though not complete, is very close for they express two different properties or functions exhibited by Christ: one in relation to God (in 140-C2 Jesus is the experiential manifestation in regard to humanity: cfr 374-C), the other in relation to humanity (in 173-C1 Jesus works the salvific will of the Father on behalf of humanity).

b) Nominal commutations

* field of revelation

- SPLENDOR	gloriae tuae	: 140-C2*
- splendor	animarum fidelium	: 164-C
- splendor	gratiae tuae	: 209-Pc*
- splendor	claritatis tuae	: 311-C2*
- splendor	veritatis	: 352-C
- splendor	doctrinae et virtutis	: 693-C1

In this series of words we must immediately exclude the expression *doctrina et virtus* (693-C1) because it clearly indicates realities predicated of a creature and not of God or Christ, as is represented by the word *gloria*. One may well have a good dose of uncertainty whether one should accept or reject the word *veritas*. The context does not indicate whether it is a "group of truths" or God's self (352-C). Furthermore, in 164-C the syntagma *splendor animarum fidelium* is a case apart because it is equivalent to God's self. The other cases (marked *) allow a good equivalence with *gloria*, even though not completely so. One may assert, furthermore, that the believer may see the *gloria* of God (140-C2) as grace *gratia* and as brightness *claritas* (one should note the presence of the possessive adjective *tuus* in all three sub-syntagmas).

c) Determinative associations (connections)

* field of eschatological movement

- *gloriam*	RESURRECTIONIS	: 132-C
- gaudia sempiterna	resurrectionis	: 883-Pc2

Certainly in the Missal of Paul VI only the syntagma *gaudia sempiterna resurrectionis* (883-Pc2) is inserted in a paradigm equal to the one in which our syntagma (132-C) is found. The similarity of the two allows us to say that *gloria* is interchangeable, in this case, with *gaudia sempiterna*.

At the end of this rapid and simplified treatment we may at least understand how the term *gloria*, as a word very rich in meaning, cannot easily be substituted by any other single word. In the field of eschatological movement it has the meaning of "supreme gift", of "grace", of "light (in which God dwells)" and of "definitive state", whilst in the field of revelation it points both to "Jesus as revelation of the Father" and to "eternal joy".

4. What fabric of meaning exists in the text of the collect? (Semantic analysis)

Just as there exists a semantic problem of the word (and of the respective grammatical and syntactical constructions), there also exists a semantic problem of the text. Since the *textus* consists of a real and proper "fabric" of relationships, these new diachronic methodologies have been able to tease out these semantic relationships, which make up the *textus*. The process of decodifying a text, through reading or listening, traces the production of the text in reverse. Among the various possibilities, only the two methodologies emerging from the studies of C. Bremond[42] and of A. Greimas[43] will be examined here. Since the texts of the collect formulae are very short, it is clearly not possible to apply the methodologies in their full complexity, rather an adaptation of each will be provided for our purpose.

a) The methodology, which springs from the studies of Bremond, is set out in three steps. First of all, the inventory of the lexemes (elements of communication) is assembled and the lexemes are subdivided into semantic areas. This first step provides the outline meaning of a text and its network of meanings. We shall apply this methodology to the same text as before, that is 140-C2. The semantic inventory is simple:

area of movement	area of stasis	area of divine realities
orior	*corda nostra*	*omnipotens Deus*
subfero	*omnis obscuritas noctis*	*splendor gloriae tuae*
adventus	*Nos*	*Unigenitus tuus*
Unigenitus	*esse filii lucis*	
manifesto		

The fabric of meaning is composed of God's action in favour of the deixis[44] "*nos*" with the purpose of making "*nos*" children of God and revealing "*nos*" to be such. The divine action is set out in the following manner. The divine action begins with the generation of the Son (*Uni-genitus*) by God (*Deus*), continues with the arrival (*adventus*) of the Son at the deixis "*nos*" and comprises three subsequent actions. The first of these is rising in the hearts of the ones praying, the second is scattering the darkness of the night and the third is revealing the effect of the splendour of glory in the hearts of those who represent the "*nos*": who are the children of light.

The second step consists in picking out the semantic oppositions of each *lexeme*, whether explicit or implicit (in parenthesis in the scheme below):

area of divine action	area of stasis (opposition)
omnipotens Deus	(that which is not omnipotent:) *corda nostra*
splendor gloriae tuae	(that which is in the shadows:) *corda nostra*
Unigenitus tuus	*Nos*
orior	(place of action:) *in cordibus nostris*
subfero	(that which has dominated:) *omnis obscuritas noctis*
adventus	(that which is alone and waits:) *nos*
manifesto	(that which is found hidden:) *nos, filii lucis*
filii lucis	(that which was child of all darkness of the night)

---

[42] C. BREMOND, *Logique du récit*, Seuil, Paris 1973.

[43] A.J. GREIMAS, *Sémantique structurale*: *Recherche de méthode*, Larousse, Paris 1966 (latest edition, Presses universitaires de France, 1986).

[44] *Deissi* (Italian), deixis (English) – an indeterminate and imprecise object, e.g. *nos* – who the 'we' are is not defined.

The basic opposition is between the area of movement and the area of stasis. The divine realities have come together in the area of movement, thereby revealing the power and the breadth of the saving power of God (described as *omni-potens*).

The third and final step consists of bringing to dialogue the first and the second steps in order to discover the transformations that the linguistic text brings to light. In our example, the opposition darkness – light is clear. This opposition is considered as the foundational text (genotext) of the prayer text. The condition of the ones represented by the deixis "*nos*" (the ones who pray) is that of living in the "shadows". God intervenes as light (*splendor*) and affects the ones who are in the shadows, transforming them into children of light (*filii lucis*) and revealing them to themselves and to others as such. This type of "reading" demonstrates how the "genotext" shadows-light is not anthropological, but definitely theological, and more precisely Johannine. The transformation, however, is expressed with the vocabulary of the letter to the Hebrews (*splendor gloriae*: Heb 1:3).

b) The methodology proceeding from the studies of Greimas (actantial analysis) consists of three activities: the analysis of the initial situation, identifying the three tests (qualifier, principal, glorifier) and the analysis of the final situation.

If we examine 140-C in its initial situation we have to say that the action of God is drawn towards a missing Object at the Receiver ("*nos*"). The missing Object might be "*filii lucis*" or the "*manifestatio filiorum lucis*". The Subject or Hero is the "*splendor gloriae tuae*" which is also "*Unigenitus*". The Opposer is represented by all that is symbolically in the "*obscuritas noctis*". In table form, this appears as:

Deus	*esse filios lucis*	*nos*
(sender)	(object)	(receiver)

	Unigenitus tuus	
Omnipotens	Splendor gloria tuae	*Omnis obscuritas noctis*
(helper)	(subject)	(opposer)

Identifying the three tests is not difficult.[45] In the qualifying test, the Subject or Hero is qualified to accomplish its mission because it is both the *Uni-genitus* (as the Son of Almighty God) and the *splendor gloriae* of Almighty

---

[45] There are two essential questions for identifying the qualifying proof: What is the proof (present in the text or presupposed) which qualifies the Hero-Subject as such? Who is the Helper? There are three essential questions for the principal proof: Where is the place of the principal proof expressed or understood in the text? What is the proof? How does is overcome the Opposer? There are two essential questions for the glorifying proof: When and how does the Hero-Subject make him or herself recognised as Hero-Subject? How is the Object changed or moved or how is the situation changed in favour of the Receiver.

God. In the principal test, the Hero, who is *splendor*, scatters the darkness and, giving himself in history, is able to give to the Receiver (*nos*) both adoption-sonship and light. In the glorifier test, at his arrival (*adventus*) the Hero reveals himself by illuminating hearts and revealing himself in them, carrying therefore the Object (*esse filios lucis*) to the Receiver (*nos*).

The final situation (condition) consists in the fact that the darkness is taken away and the Receivers (*nos*) are manifested for the Object they are in reality: children of the light.

5. To what historical period is the text connected? (Analysis of authenticity and historical analysis)

The text of a collect, ancient or modern, contains within itself slivers of history. These splinters offer different clues: facts about a particular period, the situation of a community, doctrinal problems, theological forms of thought of the author, etc. This physiognomy is certainly not easily identifiable in the texts of the collects. It is not always easy, therefore, to put this type of analysis (historical analysis and ascertaining the authenticity [author, period, place, cause, objective, etc.]) into practice, because not all the texts lend themselves to it. When possible, however, this analysis is very useful for lifting the veil that covers the past and for enabling us better to understand a particular collect. B. Capelle[46] shows how formula n° 193 of the *Sacr. Gregorianum Hadrianum* might be the fruit of the genius of Gregory the Great himself:[47]

> *Deus, qui nos in tantis periculis constitutos, pro humana scis fragilitate non posse subsistere, da nobis salutem mentis et corporis, ut ea, quae pro peccatis nostris patimur, te adiuvante, vincamus. Per.*

This formula becomes even more interesting when we know that the Lombards (Arian Christians) had besieged Rome in the years 593-594, during Gregory's pontificate, and the tension of these circumstances is almost tangible in the prayer.

The adventure, which we call the handing down of a text through history, must be considered when addressing the problem of a text's historical authenticity. The successive literary and theological retouchings of a text give rise to a new text, better adapted to the situation in which it will

---

[46] B. CAPELLE, "La main de S. Grégoire dans le Sacramentaire Grégorien", *Revue Bénédictine* 49 (1937) 13-28.

[47] "O God, you know that we, being set in such great difficulties, are not able to bear them because of human fragility, grant us salvation of spirit and of body in order that we may be able, with you helping, to conquer those things which we are suffering because of our sins. Through".

be re-used. Sometimes these changes are minimal, sometime considerable. One of the most disruptive elements that a text can undergo is a change of function (contextual changes). Such is the case of the embolism of the preface of the QUINTA DOMINICA POST CLAUSUM PASCHAE in the *Gelasianum Vetus*,[48] which has become a collect in the Missal of Paul VI (323-C3). Although the strong eschatological character of the original text accorded with the literary-theological content of the formulary, this is less easy to explain in its new literary clothing as a collect.

6. What is the literary identity of the text? (Literary criticism)

The collect is situated within a context, contains sources from which vocabulary and concepts have been drawn, shows a structure and expresses itself in a literary style.

§1. The context of a collect is quite complex, being both literary-theological and celebrative-theological.

* The literary-theological context reflects the cultural and theological situation of the collect. The collect is found within a formulary (its immediate context), within a series of formularies of a liturgical cycle (its remote context) and within a specific Missal or Sacramentary (its general context). The context allows us to distinguish the more important themes from the secondary ones.

* The celebrative-theological context, on the other hand, is the given celebrative context and is treated below in the 'pragmatic' analysis.

When we examine the text 140-C2, the context certainly can help us to understand how the collect functions within its larger context. The celebration is fundamentally understood (experienced) as a preparation for feasts which are already near (141-Pc: *Ut haec divina subsidia, a vitiis expiatos, ad festa ventura nos praeparent*). The "shadows" of the collect are named "vices" in the *Post communionem*, and the uprooting of the shadows is called "divine salvation" in the *Super oblata* and "divine clemency" in the *Post communionem*.

§2. A collect is not born by accident. Although very often anonymous, the author possesses his own, particular, biblico-theological heritage. The texts witness to this very fact. Within a collect, therefore, the attentive reader may find both citations and allusions to pre-existing texts, which are called 'sources'. Such sources may be defined according to two types: the primary source is Holy Scripture, and the 'material' source may be either a text from one of the ancient Christian authors, a previous liturgical text, documents of the Magisterium, hagiographical records, or some other source. Identifying the sources (citations or allusions) of a collect provides a better

---

[48] *Sacramentarium Gelasianum* n° 564, ed. Mohlberg (RED. Fontes 4), 87.

understanding of the formula itself. In the text 140-C2 the expression *splendor gloriae tuae* is not a baroque form that the Liturgy has taken over, but an exact citation of Hebrews 1:3 (*qui [= Filius] cum sit splendor gloriae et figura substantiae eius*). Thus this citation from the Letter to the Hebrews is certainly one of the sources of 140-C2. One of the material sources of formula n° 398 of the *Sacr. Gelasianum Vetus* (*imago terreni / imago Celestis*), however, is without doubt Homily 63, 6 of St Leo the Great (*dum terreni hominis imago deponitur et Caelestis forma suscipitur*).

§3. The structure of a collect contains various elements: the invocation (simple as in *Deus*; composite as in *Deus Omnipotens*), the amplification of the invocation (simple as an apposition such as *Deus, pater pauperum*; relative as in a relative phrase such as *Deus, qui splendorem gloriae tuae per sacrae Virginis partum mundo dignatus es rivelare*), petition (imperative as in *tribue, quaesumus*; exhortative subjunctive as in *Oriatur in cordibus nostris splendor gloriae tuae*), purpose or goal (*ut* + subjunctive as in *ut digne tuis servire semper altaribus mereamur*; *ad* + gerund as in *ad tuam misericordiam illis conferendam*), motive (*quia* + indicative as in *quia in hac vita tibi manserunt fideles*; a relative clause which follows immediately on the *ut* purpose clause as in *ut, qui per abstinentiam temperantur in corpore, per fructum boni operis reficiamur in mente*).

§4. The literary style of an oration has three elements: the form, the content and the function. In regard to the form, the most obvious structural element which distinguishes the collect from other formulae is the extended conclusion.[49] The content of the collect is always linked to very broad theological themes, often corresponding to the liturgical season and at times in dialogue with biblical themes of the Liturgy of the Word. One can clearly distinguish the collect from the other formulae of the formulary (*Super oblata, Post communionem*) in that these latter, using precise words and literary expressions, are closely linked to their particular situation in the celebration, one at the presentation of the gifts, and the other at communion.

§5. The style of a collect is also very rich. Here we need to limit ourselves to certain aspects of the rhetorical dimension, of the properties of the language and of the metre.

With reference to the rhetorical dimension it is worth pointing out certain phenomena such as parallelisms, inclusions, hendiadys and iteration.

Parallelism is the repetition of two words, two expressions, two lines etc. In one type of parallelism a concept is repeated (synonymous parallelism: *Fac nos, omnipotens Deus, sanctis exsultare gaudiis, et pia gratiarum actione laetari ...*: 307-C). In another type two concepts are opposed (antithetic parallelism: *da, quaesumus, nobis eius divinitatis esse consortes, qui humanitatis nostrae fieri dignatus est particeps*: 157-C). In a third type the second element completes what has been summarised within the first (synthetic or summary parallelism: *et ad intellegendum Christi proficiamus arcanum, et effectus eius digna*

---

49 *IGMR*-2000, 54.

conversatione sectemur: 184-C). Parallelism may contain progression (... *quo lavacro abluti, quo spiritu regenerati, quo sanguine sunt redempti*: 299-C) or a chiasm (a - b : b' - a'). A particular form of parallelism is inclusion, whereby two words or phrases begin and end the formula. A hendiadys is the stylistic phenomenon by which a single concept or idea is expressed with two words (*gratia et veritas* = *gratia veritatis*; "law and order" = "the order of law"). Iteration, on the other hand, consists of the repetition of an element (*da fidelibus tuis cor unum et animam unam*: 849-C).

Among the properties of language, both *concinnitas* and the divine passive deserve particular emphasis. *Concinnitas* consists in the equilibrium and harmony of content and form, whereby the maximum meaning of a concept finds expression in a minimum of words (*Omnipotens sempiterne Deus, deduc nos ad societatem caelestium gaudiorum, ut eo perveniat humilitas gregis, quo processit fortitudo pastoris*: 302-C). The divine passive, rather, is the use of a passive verb without the explicit expression of its complement of agent, which is understood to be God (*ad gloriam perducamur [ab te, Domine]*).

In regard to metrification, the *cursus* deserves consideration. The *cursus* is a succession of words and syllables at the end of a phrase or semiphrase or of a sense line which create rhythmical cadences pleasing to the ear.[50] There are four types of *cursus* found in liturgical texts: the *cursus planus*, the *tardus*, the *velox*, the *trispondaicus*.[51] Ancient formulae (cfr *Sacr. Veronese*) are characterized by the use of the *cursus*, but its use has gradually diminished through the centuries. In the Missal of Paul VI several formulae have been composed by placing different sources together, thereby altering the *cursus*. As a result, not all the sense lines of the contemporary Collects possess this characteristic.

7. What does the text of the collect do? (Pragmatic analysis)

During the celebration, the collect is offered at the end of the introductory rites, before the Liturgy of the Word, and expresses the character of the celebration of which the collect is a part. The collect, therefore, plays a multifunctional role, and any understanding of it is conditioned by its

---

[50] A. MOCQUEREAU, *Le cursus et la psalmodie, Paléographie musicale*, vol. 1 of 4, Berne 1974, 27, (anastatic publication of the Solesmes edition, 1894); L.P. Wilkinson, *Golden Latin Artistry*, Cambridge UP, Cambridge 1963.

[51] One always begins at the final part of the phrase or line to work out the syllables and emphases, which must be worked out not by the length of the syllable (which exists and which however is not to be counted), but from the accent. The *cursus planus* is extended over five syllables ($\leq$ _ _ $\leq$ _): *libe-ràn-te sal-và-ri*. The *tardus* has six syllables ($\leq$ _ _ _ $\leq$ _ _): *sèm-per ob-tì-ne-at*. The *cursus velox* seven syllables ($\leq$ _ _ $\leq$ _ $\leq$ _): *mè-ri-tis a-diu-vè-mur, praè-m-i-a praest-i-tì-sti*. Finally, the *trispondaicus* has six syllables ($\leq$ _ _ _ $\leq$ _): *adversi-tà-te li-be-rén-tur*.

position within the ritual programme. Just as the silence preceding the collect provides the assembly with a moment of prayer to be concluded by the collect itself, so the collect in turn provides the theological character of the particular celebration and at the same time may function as an introduction to the Liturgy of the Word. Each of these characteristics is the present in the text of the collect and should be emphasised according to the interest of whoever is studying the text.

Conclusion

The methodological journey we have traced has been presented in as linear a fashion as possible, gathering all the major riches found by the historico-critical methodologies and from linguistic-anthropological approaches.

Certainly the proposed methodology is as yet unfinished, for it shows only one stage of that never-ending journey of understanding the riches of the faith present in the Church's euchological heritage. This wealth is not static, but remains a foundation and a treasure to guard, to understand and to hand on. From this foundation, through the true dynamism which animates every tradition and practice in the journey of the Church through history, there will be born new formulae which will express the ability of the Church to celebrate the Lord Jesus, always the same, yesterday, today and forever (cfr Heb 13:8).

Glossary of Linguistic and Hermeneutical Terminology

a. *Linguistic or literary-critical terminology*:

> deixis (English), *deissi* (Italian) – an indeterminate and imprecise object.
> hendiadys (English), *endiadi* (Italian) – the stylistic phenomenon which
> expresses one idea with two words, e.g. "law and order".
> hyperbaton – a "transposition of words or clauses". Words that are out of
> order "overstep" their correct place in a sentence, e.g. All, in my
> opinion, people …
> iteration – the repetition of an element, e.g. *da fidelibus tuis cor unum et*
> *animam unam.*
> lexeme (English), *lesseme* (Italian) – an item of vocabulary, a word
> occurrence, a word in the most abstract sense.
> stanza – a group of lines of verse of poetry composed of several stichoi.
> stichos (English), *stico* (Italian) – a line of text; not necessarily a sense line,
> literally meaning a series, [as in a … of trolleys, *hamaxostichos* = a
> train (Latin)], e.g. "to give praise and thanksgiving to God".
> syntagma – a sense line, a regular or orderly collection of statements, a
> sequence of linguistic units in a syntagmatic relationship to one
> another, e.g. "I will arise in the morning, to give praise and
> thanksgiving to God".

b. *Literary-critical analysis*:

Literary-critical vocabulary	Vocabulary of the Latin language
invocation –	The address or title of the addressee of the prayer, vocative. simple or complex.
amplification –	Typically expands upon the invocation, 1) relative clause, 2) words in apposition to the invocation
petition –	Imperative or exhortative subjunctive
purpose clause –	There are thirteen ways of expressing purpose in the Latin language, most frequently expressed by ut + subj., translated with the subj. Gives intention or goal, not to be confused with a result clause.
result clause –	Expressed by ut + subj., translated in the indicative in English. Gives a concrete result.
motive or motor –	1) *quia* + subjunctive (classical); 2) relative clause, typically in a purpose clause; 3) participial clause.
premise –	Ablative absolute

For a reference work on literary-critical analysis of liturgical prayers we recommend this volume and Renato De Zan's previous writings:

DE ZAN, R., "Criticism and Interpretation of Liturgical Texts", in *Introduction to the Liturgy*, ed. A.J. Chupungco (Handbook for Liturgical Studies 1), Liturgical Press (Pueblo Book), Collegeville MN 1997, 331-365 (En. tr. of R. DE ZAN, "Introduzione alla Liturgia, Ermeneutica", ed. A. J. Chupungco [*Scientia Liturgica: Manuale di Liturgia* 1] Piemme, Casale Monferrato 1998, 356-389).

For an English key to Latin language we recommend:

B.L. GILDERSLEEVE - G. LODGE, *Gildersleeve's Latin Grammar*, Bolchazy-Carducci, Wauconda IL 2003, reprint of [3]1985.

c. *Semantic analysis – semiological hermeneutic*:

hermeneutical vocabulary	
object –	goal or final state
receiver –	addressee
sender –	source of communication, speaker, singer, *orans*
helper –	an assisting force to an action
opposer –	an opposing force to an action
subject –	hero, principal actor or protagonist

A useful reference work for semiological analysis is:
B. MARTIN – F. RINGHAM, *Key Terms in Semiotics*, Continuum, London 2006.

Bibliography

A. Research tools

BLAISE, A., *Dictionnaire latin-français des auteurs chrétiens*, rev. H. Chirat, Brepols, Turnhout 1962.
_____, *Le vocabulaire latin des principaux thèmes liturgiques*, rev. A. Dumas, Turnhout 1966.
BRUYLANTS, P., *Concordance verbale du Sacramentaire Léonien*, Mont César, Louvain 1945.
_____, *Les oraisons du Missel Romain, texte et histoire* (Études liturgiques 2 vol.), Mont César, Louvain 1952.
Deshusses, J., – B. Darragon, *Concordances et Tableaux pour l'étude des grands Sacramentaires*, 6 vol., Editions Universitaires, Fribourg 1982-83.
DU CANGE, C., *Glossarium mediae et infimae latinitatis*, 10 vol., Akademische Druck- und Verlagsanstalt, Graz 1954 (anastatic copy of original ed., Didot, Paris 1840-1850).

ERNOUT, A., - A. MEILLET, *Dictionnaire étymologique de la langue latine: Histoire des mots*, Paris ⁴1959.

FORCELLINI, A., *Totius latinitatis lexicon*, 6 vol., Padova 1965 (anastatic copy).

SCHRIJNEN, J., *Charakteristik des Altchristlichen Latein*, Nijmegen 1932 (tr. it.: *I caratteri del latino cristiano antico*, Bologna 1986).

Thesaurus Linguae Latinae, 10 vol. to date, Teubner, Leipzig - Stuttgart 1900-1999, K.G. Saur-Verlag, Munich 2000-2006; Walter de Gruyter, Berlin – New York 2006-present.

B. Patristic sources

AUGUSTINUS HIPPONENSIS, *Sermon* 299, in ed. J.P. Migne (*Patrologia cursus completa, Series latina* 38), Garnier, Paris 1865, 1371.

_____, *De Trinitate libri XV*, ed. J. Mountain – F. Gloire (Corpus christianorum series latina 50, 50 A) Brepols, Turnhout 1968.

JOHANNES CASSIANUS *De institutis coenobiorum*, ed. M. Petschenig (Corpus scriptorum ecclesiasticorum latinorum 17), Tempsky – Freytag, Vienna - Leipzig 1888; suppl. G. Kreuz ²2004.

LEO MAGNUS, *Tractatus* 63, ed. A. Chavasse (Corpus christianorum series latina 138 A) Brepols, Turnhout 1973 (PL 54, 357).

LEO MAGNUS, *Tractatus* 71, ed. A. Chavasse (Corpus christianorum series latina 138 A) Brepols, Turnhout 1973.

C. Liturgical sources

Liber sacramentorum romanae aeclesiae ordinis anni circuli (*Cod. Vat. Reg. Lat. 316/Paris Bibl. Nat. 7193, 41/56*) (*Sacramentarium Gelasianum*), ed. L. C. Mohlberg – L. Eizenhöfer – P. Siffrin (Rerum ecclesiasticarum documenta. Series maior, Fontes 4), Herder, Rome ³1981.

D. Magisterial documents

"Presentazione", *Messale Romano: Riformato a norma dei decreti del Concilio Ecumenico Vaticano II e promulgato da Papa Paolo VI*, Conferenza Episcopale Italiana, Libreria Editrice Vaticana, Città del Vaticano 1983, vii-x.

E. Studies

ALFONSO, P., *L'eucologia romana antica: Lineamenti stilistici e storici*, Subiaco 1931.

AUGÉ, M., "Principi di interpretazione dei testi liturgici", in *Anàmnesis 1. La Liturgia momento nella storia della salvezza*, ed. S. Marsili et alii, Marietti, Casale Monferato 1974, 159-179.

BAUMSTARK, A., *Liturgie comparée: Principes et méthodes pour l'étude historique des liturgies chrétiennes*, Chevetogne – Paris 1920; ed., suppl. B. Botte ³1953.

BEAUDUIN, L., *La piété de l'Eglise: Principes et faits*, Mont César, Louvain 1914.

BLAISE, A., *Manuel du latin chrétien*, Le Latin Chrétien, Strasbourg 1955.

BREMOND, C., *Logique du récit* (Collection Poétique) Seuil, Paris 1973.

BROU, L., "Étude historique sur les oraisons des dimanches après la Pentecôte dans la tradition romain", *Sacris Erudiri* 2 (1949) l23-224.

BROVELLI, F., "Per uno studio della liturgia", *La scuola cattolica* 104 (1976) 567-635.

CALLEWAERT, C., "La méthode dans l'étude de la liturgie", *Sacris erudiri*, Steenbrugge 1940, 41-52.

CAPELLE, B., "Collecta", *Revue Bénédictine* 42 (1930) 197-204.

_____, "La main de S. Grégoire dans le Sacramentaire Grégorien", *Revue Bénédictine* 49 (1937) 13-28.

CAPRIOLI, A., "Linee di ricerca per uno statuto teologico della liturgia", *Communio* 41 (1978) 35-44.

La Chiesa in preghiera: Introduzione alla liturgia, 4 vol., ed. A.-G. Martimort, tr. A. Biazzi, Brescia, Queriniana 1984-1987 (of *L'Église en prière: introduction à la Liturgie*, Desclée, Paris – Tournai c. 1961 ff.).

COCHEZ, J., *La structure rythmique de oraisons*, Louvain 1928.

DE PUNIET, P., "La méthode en matière de liturgie", *Cours et Conférences des semaines liturgiques. Tome II Cinquième semaine, Louvain du 10 au 14 août 1913*, Louvain 1914, 41-77.

DE ZAN, R., "Criticism and Interpretation of Liturgical Texts", in *Introduction to the Liturgy*, ed. A.J. Chupungco (Handbook for Liturgical Studies 1), Liturgical Press (Pueblo Book), Collegeville MN 1997, 331-365 (En. tr. of R. DE ZAN, "Introduzione alla Liturgia, Ermeneutica", ed. A. J. Chupungco [*Scientia Liturgica: Manuale di Liturgia* 1] Piemme, Casale Monferrato 1998, 356-389).

DIEZINGER, W., '*Effectus' in der römischen Liturgie: Eine kultsprachliche Untersuchung Theophaneia* (Beiträge zur Religions- und Kirchengeschichte des Altertums 15), Peter Hanstein, Bonn 1961.

DROSTE, B., '*Celebrare' in der römischen Liturgiesprache: Eine liturgie-theologische Untersuchung* (Münchener theologische Studien 2. Systematische Abteilung 26), Max Hueber, München 1963.

DUMAS, A., "Les sources du Missel Romain" *Notitiae* 7 (1971) 37-42, 74-77, 94-95, 134-136, 276-280, 409-410.

ELLEBRACHT, M.P., *Remarks on the Vocabulary of the Ancient Orations in the* Missale Romanum (Latinitas Christianorum Primaeva 18), Dekker & Van De Vegt, Nijmegen – Utrecht ²1966.

FAGERBERG, D.W., *What Is Liturgical Theology? A Study in Methodology*, Liturgical Press, (Pueblo Book), Collegeville MN 1992.

GADAMER, H.G., *Wahrheit und Methode*: Grundzüge einer philosophischen Hermeneutik, J.C.B. Mohr, Tubingen ³1972 (¹1960).

LE GALL, R., "Pour une conception intégrale de la liturgie", *Questions liturgiques* 65 (1984) 181-202.

GREIMAS, A.J., *Sémantique structurale: Recherche de méthode*, Larousse, Paris 1966 (latest edition, Presses universitaires de France, 1986).

GUARDINI, R., "Über die systematische Methode in der Liturgiewissenschaft", *Jahrbuch für Liturgiewissenschaft* 1 (2/1921), 97-108.

HERMANS, J., "L'étude de la liturgie comme discipline théologique: Problèmes et méthodes", *Revue théologique de Louvain*, 18 (1987) 337-360.

HIRSCH, E.D., *Validity in Interpretation*, Yale UP, New Haven – London 1967.

IRWIN, K.W., *Context and Text: Method in Liturgical Theology*, Liturgical Press (Pueblo Book), Collegeville MN 1994.

La Liturgia Eucaristica, ed. S. Marsili, – A. Nocent – M. Augé – A.J. Chupungco, (Anàmnesis 3/2), Marietti, Casale Monferrato, 1983.

La liturgie: son sens, son esprit, sa méthode: Conférence saint-Serge XXVIIIe semaine d'études liturgique, Paris, 30 Juin – 3 Juillet 1981, ed. A.M. Triacca – A. Pistoia, (Liturgie et théologie. Bibliotheca Ephemerides Liturgicae, Subsidia 27), Rome 1982.

LUCIER, P., "Le statut epistémologique de la situation liturgique", *Liturgie et vie chrétienne*, 82 (1972) 256-278.

MAZZA, E., "Teologia liturgica centrata sul vissuto celebrativo", *Qualità pastorale delle discipline teologiche e del loro insegnamento*, ed. M. MIDALI – R. TONELLI, Libreria Ateneo Salesiano, Rome 1993, 143-144.

MERZ, M., *Liturgisches Gebet als Geschehen*, Aschendorff, Münster 1988.

MOCQUEREAU, A., *Le cursus et la psalmodie, Paléographie musicale*, vol. 1 of 4., Berne 1974, (anastatic publication of the Solesmes edition, 1894).

MOHRMANN, C., *Etudes sur le latin des Chrétiens*, 4 vol., Rome 1958-1977.

_____, *Études sur le latin des Chrétiens, vol. 3. Latin chrétien et liturgique*, Rome 1965.

MOUNIN, G., *Guida alla semantica*, Milano 1975.

NAKAGAKI, F., "Metodo integrale: Discorso sulla metodologia nell'interpretazione dei testi eucologici", in *Fons vivus: Miscellanea liturgica in memoria di don E. M. Vismara*, ed. A. Cuva, (Bibliotheca Theologia Salesiana 1, 6) PAS Verlag, Zürich 1971, 269-286.

NORBERG, D., *Manuel pratique de latin médiéval*, Paris 1968 (tr. it., *Manuale di Latino medioevale*, Firenze 1974).

PALADINI, V. – M. DE MARCO, *Lingua e letteratura mediolatina*, Bologna ^{2}1980;

PINELL, J., "I testi liturgici, voci di autorità, nella costituzione *Sacrosanctum Concilium*", *Costituzione liturgica* 'Sacrosanctum Concilium': *Studi*, ed. Congregazione per il Culto Divino, Rome 186, 331-341

RAFFA, V., *Liturgia eucaristica: Mistagogia della Messa, dalla storia e dalla teologia alla pastorale pratica*, Rome, Edizioni Liturgiche ^{2}2003.

RIGHETTI, M., *Storia Liturgica*, vol. 3, Ancora, Milano ^{3}1966.

SCHERMANN, J., *Die Sprache im Gottesdienst*, Tyrolia Verlag, Innsbruck – Wien 1987.

SCHMIDT, H.A.P., *Hebdomada Sancta. Vol. 1. Contemporanei textus Liturgici, documenta paina et bibliographia*, Herder, Rome 1956.

STEINHEIMER, M., *Die "DOXA TOY THEOY" in der römischen Liturgie* (Münchener theologische Studien, 2. Systematische Abteilung 4), Zink, München 1951.

TRIACCA, A.M., – R. FARINA, "Studio e lettura dell'eucologia: Note metodologiche", in *Teologia, Liturgia, Storia: Miscellanea in onore di C. Manziana*, ed. C. Ghidelli, Morcelliana, Brescia 1977, 197-224.

TAFT, R.F., "The Structural Analysis of the Liturgical Units: An Essay in Methodology", *Worship* 52 (1978) 314-329.

VÄÄNÄNEN, V., *Introduzione al latino volgare*, Bologna 1982.

VOLP, R., *Zeichen: Semiotik in Theologie und Gottesdienst*, München – Mainz 1982.

ZIMMERMAN, J.A., *Liturgy as Language of Faith: A Liturgical Methodology in the Mode of Paul Ricoeur's Textual Hermeneutics*, University Press of America, Lanham MA 1988.

WILKINSON, L.P., *Golden Latin Artistry*, Cambridge UP, Cambridge 1963.

CHAPTER 4

The Collect in Context

Patrick Regan

Introduction

In 1970 the Roman Missal of Paul VI adopted the term 'collect' to designate the prayer which the priest recites in the name of the assembly at the end of the introductory rites of the Mass. Consequently, above every such prayer in the Latin missal is printed the word *Collecta*. This, however, is not a Roman term and its appearance in the newly reformed Roman Missal could be considered somewhat incongruous. The *General Instruction*, which was included in the 1970 edition of the missal, seems aware of this and explains, "Tunc sacerdos profert orationem, quae solet 'collecta' nominari".[1] Unchanged in the 2002 version of the document, the sentence is translated, "Then the priest says the prayer which is customarily known as the Collect".[2]

Previous English translations of the *General Instruction* as well as of the missal avoid the term "collect" and replace it with "opening prayer",[3] as does the French translation which has "prière d'ouverture". The German missal renders it "Tagesgebet", which means "prayer of the day". So whose custom

---

[1] *Institutio generalis Missalis Romani* n° 32 (hereafter *IGMR*), in *Missale Romanum ex decreto Sacrosancti Oecumenici Concilii Vaticani II instauratum auctoritate Pauli PP. VI promulgatum, editio typica*, Typis polyglottis Vaticanis, Città del Vaticano ¹1970, (hereafter *MR* ¹1970).

[2] *General Instruction of the Roman Missal*, tr. the International Commission on English in the Liturgy (Liturgy Documentary Series 2), United States Conference of Catholic Bishops, Washington DC ³2002, n° 54.

[3] The term 'collect' was introduced into the English text of the *Ordo Missae* before the word 'collecta' appeared in the Latin version of the *Ordo missae* in the *Missale Romanum*: "Afterwards he says: Let us pray, and the collects, in accordance with the rubrics" : "Postea dicit: Oremus, et orationes, iuxta rubricas" (*The English-Latin Sacramentary for the United States of America: The Prayers of the Celebrant of Mass together with the Ordinary of the Mass: English Translations Approved by the National Conference of Bishops of the United States of America and Confirmed by the Apostolic See*, Benziger Brothers, New York 1966, 203, n° 11).

is it to call this prayer the collect, when did it originate and what does it mean? The following paragraphs aim to answer those questions and then to explore the function of this formula in the larger context of the introductory rites.

1. From an unnamed prayer to the oration

In the Verona collection of Roman *libelli missarum*, compiled in the second half of the sixth century,[4] some of the contents of which stretch back to the previous century, none of the prayers have names, though prefaces are recognizable by their characteristic opening phrase, *Vere dignum*. Six groups of formulas bear titles which include the words *orationes*,[5] *praeces*[6] or *orationes et praeces*,[7] indicating that all the items listed beneath them are understood to be orations and prayers without any sharp distinction between the two.

The *Old Gelasian Sacramentary*, used in the titular churches of Rome during the seventh century,[8] retains many lists of *orationes et praeces* and some of *orationes* but proper prefaces are fewer than in the Verona manuscript and the Mass formularies are more stable. They usually consist of five components. The last three have acquired a specific finality and are titled *Secreta*, *Post communionem* and *Ad populum* respectively, the *Ad populum* being a blessing of the people imparted before the dismissal. The first two, however, lack titles and are generic orations and prayers. Why they are two in number and at what points before the Secret they were recited is not entirely clear.[9] The *Sacramentary of Gellone* and other Gelasians of the eighth century[10] ordinarily follow the same scheme as the *Old Gelasian* and employ

[4] *Sacramentarium veronense*, ed. L.C. Mohlberg – L. Eizenhöfer – P. Siffrin (Rerum ecclesiasticarum documenta. Series maior, Fontes 1), Herder, Rome [3]1978 (hereafter *Leon*); see, C. VOGEL, *Medieval Liturgy: An Introduction to the Sources*, tr., rev. W.G. Storey – N.K. Rasmussen (National Association of Pastoral Musicians Studies in Church Music and Liturgy), Pastoral Press, Washington DC 1986, (of *Introduction aux sources de l'histoire du culte chrétien au moyen âge*, Centro italiano di studi sull'alto medioevo, Spoleto 1981), 38-42.
[5] *Leon* n° 187-199.
[6] *Leon* n° 169-186.
[7] *Leon* n° 413-586.
[8] *Liber sacramentorum romanae aeclesiae ordinis anni circuli (Cod. Vat. Reg. Lat. 316/Paris Bibl. Nat. 7193, 41/56) (Sacramentarium Gelasianum)*, ed. L.C. Mohlberg – L. Eizenhöfer – P. Siffrin (Rerum ecclesiasticarum documenta. Series maior, Fontes 4), Herder, Rome 1960. VOGEL, *Medieval Liturgy*, 64-70.
[9] See: A. CHAVASSE, *Le Sacramentaire Gélasien (Vaticanus Reginensis 316): Sacramentaire presbytéral en usage dans le titres Romains au VIIe siècle* (Bibliothèque de théologie. Série 4: Histoire de la Théologie 1), Desclée, Tournai 1958, 190-195.
[10] See: C. VOGEL, *Medieval Liturgy*, 70-78.

the same nomenclature except in rare cases when a copyist incorporates non-Roman material.[11]

In all forms of the Gregorian sacramentary, which reflect various stages of the papal liturgy at Rome in the seventh and eighth centuries,[12] the typical Mass formulary consists of only three prayers. The first has no title but the second and third are marked *Super oblata* and *Ad complendum* respectively and correspond to the *Secreta* and *Post communionem* of the *Old Gelasian*. The *Ad populum* appears only on weekdays of Lent. In these sacramentaries, unlike earlier ones, *praeces* is never used in headings. The word *oratio* has clearly established itself as the generic term to designate all prayers at Mass. Those pronounced over the offerings or after communion have proper names indicating their purpose: *Super oblata* and *Ad complendum*. The first does not; making no mention of offering or receiving the eucharistic gifts, it is simply an *oratio* with no further specification.

Six sets of Masses in the *Hadrianum*[13] and nine in the *Paduense*[14] feature two orations before the *Super oblata*. The second is always marked *Ad missas*, indicating that it is meant to be said at the beginning of the Mass at the stational church named in the title above the formulary. In the *Paduensis* the first prayer is almost always preceded by *Oratio ad collectam*, sometimes only *Ad collectam*[15] or *ad colleta*,[16] meaning that it is intended for use at the *collecta*, that is, the church at which clergy and faithful gather before moving in procession to the stational church where the Eucharist is celebrated.

In three of the six formularies of the *Hadrianum* the name of the *collecta* is disclosed in the rubric above the prayer destined to be said there: *Oratio collecta ad sanctum Hadrianum*,[17] *Collecta ad sanctam anastasiam*[18] and *Collectam*

---

[11] The Sacramentary of Angoulême, for example, inserts a Gallican prayer after the *Exultet* which it entitles *Collecta post hymnum caerei* and contains two Gallican prayers for blessing church bells each of which it calls *Collecta*; see: *Liber sacramentorum engolismensis (Cod. B. N. Lat. 816)*, ed. P. Saint-Roch (Corpus christianorum series latina 159 C), Brepols, Turnhout 1987, n° 739, 2045, 2049.

[12] Editions of all versions of the Gregorian Sacramentary are found in *Le Sacramentaire Grégorien: Ses principales formes d'après les plus anciens manuscrits*, 3 vol., ed. J. Deshusses (Spicilegium Friburgense 16), Éditions universitaires, Fribourg, 1, ³1992, 2 ²1988, 3 ²1992; see: C. VOGEL, *Medieval Liturgy*, 79-102.

[13] "Hadrianum ex authentico", *Le Sacramentaire Grégorien: Ses principales formes d'après les plus anciens manuscrits*, 3 vol., ed. J. Deshusses (Spicilegium Friburgense 16), Éditions universitaires, Fribourg ³1992, 1, 83-348 (hereafter *Gregor*).

[14] "Gregorianum paduense ad fidem codicis Paduensis D 47, Fragmentis collatis Salisburgensibus", *Le Sacramentaire Grégorien*, 3 vol., ed. J. Deshusses (Spicilegium Friburgense 16), Éditions universitaires, Fribourg ³1992, 1, 607-684 (hereafter *Pad* 1992)

[15] *Pad* 1992, n° 726.

[16] *Pad* 1992, n° 480.

[17] *Gregor* n° 123.

[18] *Gregor* n° 153.

ad sanctos cosmam et damianum.[19] The Sacramentary of Padua does so only once: *Ad collectam ad sanctos Cosmam et Damianum.*[20] Some claim that 'collect' as the name of a prayer derives from its being recited at the *collecta* before the procession to the *statio*. This is without foundation. As is clear from both papal sacramentaries, especially the *Paduensis*, the word *collecta* always refers to the place of assembly, never to a prayer. The prayer is the *oratio ad collectam.*[21]

Masses in the Carolingian supplement to the *Hadrianum*,[22] like those in the sacramentary itself, always consist of three orations. With rare exceptions the second is entitled *Super oblata* and the third, *Ad complendum*. The first, as usual, is never identified.

An important piece of information is forthcoming in *Ordo Romanus Primus*.[23] Composed at Rome between 700 and 750,[24] it is "the first surviving *ordo* of the solemn papal Mass" and "the first full description of eucharistic worship in Rome".[25] This document discloses the exact point at which this first prayer listed in the sacramentaries is to be recited. After describing the elaborate entrance procession and noting that the pontiff intones the *Gloria in excelsis Deo*, the earlier version of the *ordo* states that "he does not sit down before they say 'Amen' to the first oration", "non sedit antequam dicant, post orationem primam, Amen".[26] A Gallican interpolation adds that after the Gloria the pontiff says *Pax vobiscum*, then *Oremus*. It continues, "The oration follows. After it is finished he sits". *Sequitur oratio. Post finitam sedit.*[27] Both versions agree that the pontiff pronounces the first oration at the end of the ceremonial entrance, then sits.

This is confirmed by the short explanation of how the Roman Mass is to be celebrated copied at the beginning of the *Hadrianum*. Having mentioned the Introit, Kyrie and Gloria, it states, *Postmodum dicitur oratio, deinde sequitur apostolum.*[28] "Afterwards, the oration is said, then follows the apostle". The

---

[19] *Gregor* n° 735.

[20] *Pad* 1992, n° 726 = *Gregor* n° 735.

[21] See: B. CAPELLE, "Collecta", *Revue Bénédictine* 42 (1930) 197-204; reprinted in *Histoire: La Messe* (Travaux Liturgiques 3 vol.), Centre Liturgique, Mont César, Louvain 1962, 2, 192-199.

[22] "Hadrianum revisum anianense cum supplemento ad fidem codicis augustodunensis 19", *Le Sacramentaire Grégorien: Ses principales formes d'après les plus anciens manuscrits*, 3 vol., ed. J. Deshusses (Spicilegium Friburgense 16), Éditions universitaires, Fribourg ³1992, 1, 349-605.

[23] "Ordo Romanus Primus", *Les Ordines Romani du haut moyen age*, ed. M. Andrieu (Spicilegium Sacrum Lovaniense. Études et documents 23), Spicilegium Sacrum Lovaniense, Leuven 1971, 2, 1-108 (hereafter *OR* 1).

[24] VOGEL, *Medieval Liturgy*, 159-160.

[25] VOGEL, *Medieval Liturgy*, 155.

[26] *OR* 1 n° 53. Unless otherwise indicated all translations are by author.

[27] *OR* 1 n° 53 MSS GA.

[28] *Gregor* n° 2.

first of the three orations in the typical Gregorian formulary, then, is said at the conclusion of the entrance chants and before the reading from the Apostle, that is, before the beginning of the service of the word.

In Mass formularies contained in the *Romano-Germanic Pontifical*, assembled at Mainz in the mid-tenth century,[29] the first prayer usually is without a title. Occasionally *Oratio* or *Sequitur oratio* is printed in front of the prayer. This becomes more frequent in the pontificals compiled in Rome in the twelfth and thirteenth centuries, although by this time the content of these books is more and more restricted to ceremonies reserved to a bishop – ordinations and confirmation, consecrations and blessings.

Only in the Roman Missal of Pius V,[30] published in 1570 after the Council of Trent, is the first prayer at Mass consistently assigned a name. The name assigned it, of course, is *Oratio*. This name is printed above every such prayer in the Missal. Here, then, Oration becomes a proper noun on a par with the names of the two other sacerdotal prayers, the Secret and Post-communion. This terminology remains unaltered in every revision and reprinting of the Tridentine missal, including the most recent one, made under Pope John XXIII in 1962[31] and now recognized as the extraordinary form of the Roman Mass.

The *Ritus servandus in celebratione Missarum* printed at the beginning of the Missal of Pius V, however, stipulates that the priest "says the Post-communion prayers [*orationes Postcommuniones*] in the same manner, number and sequence as the above mentioned Collects [*Collectae*]".[32] Since the word *oratio* is generic and applies to any prayer, in order to distinguish the *orationes* recited after communion from the ones recited at the conclusion of the entrance rites, the document refers to the latter as *Collectae*. This is the only place in the 1570 Missal in which this term appears. It becomes a bit more frequent, though still narrowly confined, in the *Additiones et Variationes*, which appear in a 1920 reprinting of the Tridentine Missal and reflect disciplinary changes introduced by Pope Pius X and subsequent pontiffs.[33] Section VI of these additions, entitled *De Orationibus*, deals with the complicated matter of the number, kinds and content of the orations at Mass.

---

[29] *Le pontifical Romano-germanique du dixième siècle*, 3 vol. ed. C. Vogel – R. Elze (Studi e testi 226, 227, 269) Biblioteca Apostolica Vaticana, Città del Vaticano 1963-1972; see: VOGEL, *Medieval Liturgy*, 230-237.

[30] *Missale Romanum, editio princeps (1570)*, ed. M. Sodi – A.M. Triacca (Monumenta liturgica Concilii Tridentini 2), Libreria editrice Vaticana, Città del Vaticano 1998 (hereafter *MR* 1570).

[31] *Missale Romanum ex decreto SS. Concilii Tridentini restitutum summorum pontificum cura recognitum, editio typica*, Typis polyglottis Vaticanis, Città del Vaticano 1962.

[32] *MR* 1570 n° 30*.

[33] "Additiones et variationes in rubricis missalis ad normam bullae 'Divino afflatu' et subsequentium S.R.C. decretorum: VI. De orationibus", *Missale Romanum ex decreto SS. Concilii Tridentini restitutum summorum pontificum cura recognitum, editio XXXI post typicam*, Pustet, Regensburg [31]1920, (30-31).

These vary according the season of the year, rank of feasts and decision of the ordinary. Although the first prayer is usually designated as the *Oratio*, in order to distinguish it from the other two *orationes* - the one over the gifts and the one after communion - this section of the document, but nowhere else, frequently refers to the first oration as the collect.

As the foregoing survey shows, apart from the aforementioned exceptions, no Roman liturgical book prior to the Missal of Pope Paul VI ever called the first prayer at Mass anything but the oration. On what grounds, then, can n. 52 of the General Instruction of 2002 assert that this prayer "is customarily known as the collect?"[34]

2. A prayer known as the collect

For information about the collect as the name of a prayer we must make another survey, this time of non-Roman liturgical documents. One of the earliest occurrences of "collect" as a prayer formula is in Canon 30 of the Council of Agde, held in 506, which enjoins, "after the antiphons let collects be said in order by the bishops or priests", "post antiphonas collectiones per ordinem ab episcopis uel presbyteris dicantur".[35] The context here is morning and evening prayer, not the Eucharist. But the same word abounds in Gallican sacramentaries some two hundred years later.

In the *Missale Gothicum*, a collection of Gallican rite Masses made at Autun in Burgundy between 690 and 710,[36] practically all the prayers are called *collectiones*. Sometimes the word stands alone, sometimes it is followed by a prepositional phrase expressing its purpose. *Collectio post nomina* and *Collectio ad pacem* are very frequent; *Collectio post Sanctus* less so. Also found are *Collectio post prophetia, collectio post praecem, collectio ante orationem Dominicam, collectio post orationem Dominicam, collectio ad panis fraccionis, collectio post communionem, collectio post eucharistiam*. Despite the overwhelming use of *collectio*, *oracio* occurs occasionally.

---

[34] *IGMR* n° 32, in *Missale Romanum ex decreto Sacrosancti Oecumenici Concilii Vaticani II instauratum auctoritate Pauli PP. VI promulgatum, editio typica altera*, Typis Vaticanis, Città del Vaticano ²1975.

[35] *Concilia Galliae A. 314-A. 506*, ed. C. Munier (Corpus christianorum, Series latina 148), Brepols, Turnhout 1963, 206. The canon ends by saying, "plebem collecta oratione ad vesperam ab episcopo cum benedictione dimitti". Here "collecta oratione" does not mean "by a collect prayer" but "after the prayer is finished". The same phrase is found in the description which Uranius, a fifth century presbyter, gives of the death of John, bishop of Naples: "collecta oratione spiritum exhalavit", "after the prayer was finished, he breathed forth his spirit". See: URANIUS PRESBYTER, *Epistola de obitu Paulini ad Pacatum* 11, ed. J.P. Migne (*Patrologia cursus completa, Series latina* [hereafter PL] 53), Garnier, Paris, 1865, 866 A.

[36] *Missale Gothicum* (*Cod. Vat. Reg. Lat. 317*), ed. L.C. Mohlberg (Rerum ecclesiasticarum documenta. Series maior, Fontes 5) Herder, Rome 1961, xxiii.

Collectio is likewise the usual term for a prayer in the eighth century *Missale Gallicanum Vetus* as well as in the so-called Mone Masses and fragments of other Gallican sacramentaries printed by Mohlberg in his edition of the *Missale Gallicanum Vetus*.[37] The term is also common in the Bobbio Missal, though *oratio* is sometimes found. In Gallican liturgical books, therefore, *collectio* is the standard word to designate a prayer, whether used at Mass or elsewhere. It begins to be applied to the first oration of the Roman Eucharist by Frankish and Germanic scribes in the ninth century in their accounts of how the Eucharist is celebrated at Rome.

Vigorously promoted by Pepin the Short in the middle of the eighth century and completed by his son, Charlemagne, in the early part of the following century, the Roman liturgy supplanted the indigenous Gallican rites north of the Alps.[38] Signs of this process of Romanization are visible to varying extents in the Gallican sacramentaries just reviewed. One of the main purposes of the *Ordines Romani*, however, is to describe how services were conducted in Rome so that they could be imitated by bishops, clerics and monks throughout the Frankish kingdom.

As was already stated, the principal source of information about the eucharistic celebration at Rome is *Ordo Romanus Primus*. Some Frankish scribes copy it faithfully. The ninth century *Ordo* 4, written somewhere in Gaul, maintains the Roman term for the first prayer at Mass. It declares that "having finished the oration, the Pontiff sits in his chair", *oracione expleta, sedet pontifex in sede sua*.[39] *Ordo* 6, perhaps copied at Metz but later than Amalarius,[40] does the same. It insists that the Pontiff not sit down before the 'Amen' *post primam orationem*.[41] Before the end of the ninth century, probably in the Germanic section of the Frankish kingdom,[42] *Ordo* 9 likewise retains the Roman term, remarking that once the Gloria is over, "let the oration be said by the pontiff, as is the custom", "*dicatur a pontifice, ut mos est, oratio*".[43]

On the other hand *Ordo* 5, composed in the Rhineland between 850 and 900,[44] adds the Gallican term *collecta* to the Roman one, *oratio*. It declares, "*Deinde dicit: Oremus. Sequitur oratio prima, quam collectam dicunt*",[45] "then he says *Oremus*. There follows the first oration, which they call the

---

[37] *Missale Gallicanum Vetus* (*Cod. Vat. Palat. lat. 493*), ed. L.C. Mohlberg (Rerum ecclesiasticarum documenta. Series maior, Fontes 3) Herder, Rome 1958.
[38] See: VOGEL, *Medieval Liturgy*,147-150.
[39] "Ordo Romanus 4", n° 24, *Les Ordines Romani*, ed. Andrieu (SSL 23), 2, 135-170.
[40] M. ANDRIEU, OR 2, n° 238, Vogel, *Medieval Liturgy*,162.
[41] "Ordo Romanus 6, n° 25, *Les Ordines Romani*, ed. Andrieu (SSL 23), 2, 239-250.
[42] C. VOGEL, *Medieval Liturgy*,164
[43] "Ordo Romanus 9", n° 13, *Les Ordines Romani*, ed. Andrieu (SSL 23), 2, 327-336.
[44] "Ordo Romanus 5", *Les Ordines Romani*, ed. Andrieu (SSL 23), 2, 207-227, (hereafter OR 5); see commentary of Andrieu, p. 205-206; C. VOGEL, *Medieval Liturgy*, 161.
[45] *OR* 5 n° 25.

collect". It is not clear whom the scribe means by "they". It is certainly not the Romans. We should probably take it as an indefinite subject. In any case the first prayer has now acquired two designations, *oratio* and *collecta*. This is confirmed by the *Eclogae de officio missae* attributed to Amalarius of Metz upon which this *ordo* depends. It observes that, "the first oration is sometimes called *oratio*, sometimes called *collecta*".[46]

Ordo 10, used by the compilers of the *Romano-Germanic Pontifical* and written between 900 and 950, perhaps at Mainz,[47] substitutes the Gallican term for the Roman one: "Cumque collecta finierit, lectio legatur",[48] "when the collect will have finished, let the lesson be read". At the beginning of the tenth century Remigius of Auxerre not only designates the first oration as the *collecta*, but refers to the prayer over the gifts as *collecta super oblata*.[49] The practice of identifying the first prayer of the Roman Mass and even others by the Gallican term "collect", therefore, begins north of the Alps during the Carolingian and Ottonian epochs. This is the origin of the custom to which the *General Instruction of the Roman Missal* is referring when it states, "Then the priest says the prayer which is customarily known as the collect".[50]

In the English speaking world diffusion of the word 'collect' as the name of the first prayer at Mass may be due in great measure to the *Book of Common Prayer* which adopted the term in 1549 and retained it in all subsequent revisions. The Anglican scholar Gregory Dix, throughout his highly influential *The Shape of the Liturgy*, refers to the prayer in question as the collect and occasionally speaks of it as the prayer of the day and even opening prayer.[51] Louis Duchesne also uses the term in his classic *Christian Worship* and, like Remigius of Auxerre, even applies it to the other sacerdotal orations. He writes, "After saluting the congregation, the celebrant calls upon them to pray with him in the introductory prayer, which was called the *collecta*, because it was said as soon as the people had fully assembled. This is the first of the three 'collective prayers', or collects in the Roman Mass".[52] Adrian Fortescue employs no other term but collect to designate the first

---

[46] "*Prima oratio aliquando oratio dicitur, aliquando collecta*" (AMALARIUS METENSIS, *Eclogae de officio missae*, PL 105, 1327 D; cf.: citation in the critical apparatus to *OR* 5 n° 25).
[47] VOGEL, *Medieval Liturgy*, 164.
[48] "Ordo Romanus 10", n° 23, *Les Ordines Romani*, ed. Andrieu (SSL 23), 2, 349-362. This shows that while Gallican rites were being Romanized, Roman rites were being Gallicanized.
[49] ALCUINUS, *De divinis officiis liber*, ch. 11 of "De celebratione Missa et ejus significatione", in PL 101, 1249 C, 1252 D. The work is falsely attributed to Alcuin.
[50] IGMR n° 52, in *Missale Romanum ex decreto Sacrosancti Oecumenici Concilii Vaticani II instauratum auctoritate Pauli PP. VI promulgatum Ioannis Pauli PP. II cura recognitum, editio typica tertia*, Typis Vaticanis, Città del Vaticano [3]2002, (hereafter *MR* [3]2002).
[51] G. DIX, *The Shape of the Liturgy*, Dacre, London 1945, 488-492.
[52] L. DUCHESNE, *Christian Worship*, tr. M.L. McClure, SPCK, London 1912 (of *Origines du culte chrétien*, Thorin, Paris [3]1903), 166-167.

prayer at Mass.[53] The title of the chapter treating this prayer in Joseph Jungmann's *The Mass of the Roman Rite* is "The Collect".[54] Finally in the widely used *Saint Andrew Daily Missal* the word "collect" appears as a heading above each of these prayers.[55]

Innumerable other authors and titles could be brought forth but those listed above suffice to show that, although the Tridentine missal always identified the first prayer as *oratio* and never as *collecta*, in popular usage it was very common to refer to the oration as the collect. Hence when the Missal of Paul VI introduced the term *collecta* in 1970 the *General Instruction* was perfectly correct in saying that this *oratio* was customarily known as the collect. The translation of *collecta* as "opening prayer" in 1970, however, met with immediate and widespread acceptance. Paradoxically this led to the virtual disappearance of the word collect. As a result the statement that this prayer "is customarily known as the collect"[56] now sounds strange because in fact for more than thirty years it was known in English *not* as the collect but as the opening prayer!

3. The collect collects

One of the oldest explanations of the meaning of *collecta* as a type of prayer is that of Walafrid Strabo, abbot of Reichenau in the first half of the ninth century. He writes that we call prayers 'collects', because in them "we collect, that is, conclude their necessary petitions with compendious brevity".[57] In this short statement we see the main distinguishing characteristics of the collect. It is a prayer of petition, not praise, thanksgiving or lament. It is succinct – unlike Gallican and Mozarabic compositions, which are lengthy and verbose, frequently containing narrative material and biblical citations. It concludes a ritual unit and hence usually comes last, at the culminating point of the action. Finally, as the word itself suggests, it "collects", that is, gathers together and sums up in one compact, carefully crafted formula, the range of sentiments, needs, desires and aspirations of all present.

---

[53] A. FORTESCUE, *The Mass: A Study of the Roman Rite*, Longmans, Green & Co., London 1930 reprint of 1912, 244-253.

[54] The title of the same chapter in German begins "Die Kollekte": J.A. JUNGMANN, *The Mass of the Roman Rite: Its Origins and Development*, 2 vol., tr. F.A. Brunner, Benziger Brothers, Westminster MD 1986 (of *Missarum sollemnia: Eine genetische Erklärung der römischen Messe*, 2 vol. Herder, Wien – Freiburg – Basel ⁵1962, 462), 359.

[55] *The Saint Andrew Bible Missal*, ed. Center for Pastoral Liturgy, The Catholic University of America, William J. Hirten – Brepols, Brooklyn NY – Turnhout 1982.

[56] *IGMR* n° 54, in *MR* ³2002.

[57] "... quia necessarias earum petitiones compendiosa brevitate colligimus, id est, concludimus" (WALAFRIDUS STRABO, *Ecclesiasticarum rerum exordiis et incrementis. Liber unus, ad Reginbertum eipscopum*, in PL 114, 945 D).

Though not always called such, collects are found not only at the beginning of Mass, but also at the divine office and innumerable other ceremonies. One of the earliest and clearest portrayals of how the collect functions is that which John Cassian provides in the early fifth century in his description of the morning and evening offices of the monks of Egypt. Each service consists of twelve psalms read by soloists. At the end of each psalm the monks rise, pray silently with arms outstretched, then prostrate on the ground, and again stand with outstretched arms. After the silent prayer of each individual, the superior recites aloud a concluding prayer. Cassian does not call this prayer a collect, but twice refers to the one who recites it as, "qui orationem collecturus est", "he who is to collect the prayer", or, "qui precem colligit", "he who collects the prayer".[58] Obviously the purpose of the concluding prayer is to synthesize and articulate in the hearing of all the private prayers made by each individual in silence and perhaps without words.

The alternation of psalms and prayers is also seen in Egeria's account of the morning offices, both daily and on Sunday, in late fourth-century Jerusalem.[59] Her word for prayer, however, is always *oratio*, never *collecta*. In the Rule of the Master, composed in southern Italy in the early sixth century, each psalm of the divine office ends with the *Gloria Patri*, followed by silent prayer on bended knee concluded by prayer aloud.[60] The master's term for this prayer is *oratio*.

Three sets of orations intended to be recited after psalms have survived. Dom Louis Brou published them in 1949 under the title of *Psalter Collects*.[61] 'Collects', however, is his term. The word never appears in any of the manuscripts. Each of these compositions 'collects' the content of the foregoing psalm and transforms it into prayer. A series of such prayers were published with the post-conciliar *Liturgy of the Hours* in 1971.[62] The title of Dom Brou's book not withstanding, the accompanying General Instruction does not call them psalter collects but "psalm-prayers", *orationes super psalmos*. It explains that "when the psalm has been completed and a short silence observed, the psalm-prayer sums up the aspirations and emotions of

---

[58] IOHANNES CASSIANUS, *De Institutis coenobiorum* 2, 7, *Jean Cassien. Institutions cénobitiques*, ed. J.-C. Guy (Sources Chrétiennes 109), Le Cerf, Paris 1965, 72.

[59] EGERIA, *Itinerarium* 24, *Egeria's Travels*, ed. J. Wilkinson, Ariel, Jerusalem ²1981, 123-125.

[60] See: R.F. TAFT, *The Liturgy of the Hours in East and West: The Origins of the Divine Office and its Meaning for Today*, Liturgical Press , Collegeville MN ²1993, 122-124.

[61] *The Psalter Collects from V-VIth Century Sources*, ed. L. Brou (Henry Bradshaw Society 83), Harrison and Sons, London 1949.

[62] *Liturgia horarum iuxta ritum Romanum: Officium divinum ex decreto Sacrosancti Oecumenicum Concilium Vaticanum II instauratum atque auctoritate Pauli PP. VI promulgatum, editio typica*, 4 vol. Typis polyglottis Vaticanis, Città del Vaticano 1971-1972.

those saying them".[63] What is here translated as "sums up" in Latin is *colligat et concludat*, words which echo those of Cassian and Walafrid Strabo cited above.

Returning now to the eucharistic liturgy, the *General Instruction* of the 2002 Roman Missal designates the collect, prayer over the offerings and prayer after communion as *orationes praesidentiales*, "presidential prayers".[64] The explanation of the collect in the same *Instruction* is very similar to the way Cassian describes the prayer of the Egyptian monks, in that four elements can be distinguished. First "the priest invites the people to pray".[65] Then, "all, together with the priest, observe a brief silence so that they may be conscious of the fact that they are in God's presence and may formulate their petitions mentally".[66] After this short pause "the priest says the prayer itself".[67] Finally, "the people, uniting themselves to this entreaty, make the prayer their own with the acclamation, *Amen*".[68] Interestingly, this paragraph of the *General Instruction* points out that this prayer said by the priest "is customarily known as the collect",[69] it does not explain the meaning of the term or that the prayer gathers together and expresses aloud the silent prayers of the individual faithful. It simply states that in it "the character of the celebration is expressed".[70]

At the paschal vigil the orations following the seven readings from the Old Testament have the same function as psalm prayers. In each case a lector proclaims the reading and a cantor chants a responsorial psalm. Then, the 2002 Missal says, "with everyone standing, the priest says 'Let us pray' and, after all will have prayed for some time in silence, he says the oration corresponding to the reading".[71] Once again we find a period of silent prayer by individuals being concluded by an oration recited aloud. In the present case the oration sums up the content of the reading, not of the psalm, and transforms it into prayer. All these prayers are called *orationes*, not *collectae*.

---

[63] N. 112 cited from A.-M. ROGUET, O. P., *The Liturgy of the Hours: The General Instruction on the Liturgy of the Hours with a Commentary*, tr. P. Coughlan – P. Purdue, Liturgical Press, Collegeville MN 1971, 43.

[64] "Accedunt deinde orationes, idest collecta, oratio super oblata et oratio post Communionem... Merito igitur 'orationes praesidentiales' nominantur" (*IGMR* n° 30, in *MR* ³2002).

[65] "sacerdos populum ad orandum invitat" (*IGMR* n° 54, in *MR* ³2002).

[66] "omnes una cum sacerdote parumper silent, ut conscii fiant se in conspectu Dei stare et vota sua in animo possint nuncupare" (*IGMR* n° 54, in *MR* ³2002).

[67] "Tunc sacerdos profert orationem" (*IGMR* n° 54, in *MR* ³2002).

[68] "Populus, precationi se coniungens, acclamatione Amen orationem facit suam" (*IGMR* n° 54, in *MR* ³2002).

[69] "quae solet 'collecta' nominari" (*IGMR* n° 54, in *MR* ³2002).

[70] "per quam indoles celebrationis exprimitur" (*IGMR* n° 54, in *MR* ³2002).

[71] "Omnibus deinde surgentibus, sacerdos dicit 'Oremus', et, postquam omnes per aliquod tempus in silentio oraverint, dicit orationem lectioni respondentem" (VIGILIA PASCHALIS IN NOCTE SANCTA n° 23, in *MR* ³2002).

Only the prayer following the Gloria is so called. "When the hymn is finished", the Missal declares, "the priest says the collect in the usual manner".[72]

Another set of prayers, which are known as orations, not collects, are those which comprise the *Oratio universalis* on Good Friday, formerly known as *orationes sollemnes*.[73] Here too is found an invitation to prayer, a pause for silent prayer and then the concluding formula said aloud by the priest. On this day the invitation to prayer, "Oremus", is followed by a specification of the person or group on whose behalf the supplication is being offered, together with a declaration of what grace or favour is being sought. The faithful are then enjoined to kneel by the injunction "Flectamus genua". All remain kneeling for a short period of silent, personal prayer, then rise upon hearing "Levate". Although these prayers of the priest summarize the silent prayer previously enjoined upon the faithful, they are always called orations. Even the Gallican sacramentaries identify them as *oracciones*, probably as a result of Romanization.

Some claim that originally every oration was preceded by a call to prayer similar to those still used on Good Friday and that currently the priest's *Oremus* is but the relic of what was formerly a much longer exhortation. Jungmann asserts that "in the West this invitation to prayer was especially amplified in the Gallican liturgy. The formula, called a *praefatio*, precedes various prayers and series of prayers, both within the Mass and without; its form is sometimes reminiscent of a little homily".[74] The English translation of the 1970 *Roman* Missal provides longer formulas as optional additions to the "Let us pray" before the opening prayer.[75]

Besides Walafrid Strabo, already noted, other medieval authors explain the meaning of the word 'collect' as well as the significance of the invitation and response which precede it, and the 'Amen' which follows. In these comments the theological import of the prayer likewise comes to the fore. The late eleventh-century *Micrologus* of Bernold of Constance, for example, alluding to 2 Corinthians 5:20, states that the first prayer at Mass is called the collect "because the priest, who functions as an ambassador for the people before God, by that prayer collects and concludes [*colligat atque concludat*] the

---

[72] "Expleto hymno, sacerdos dicit collectam, more solito" (VIGILIA PASCHALIS IN NOCTE SANCTA n° 32, in *MR* ³2002).

[73] See: FERIA VI IN PASSIONE DOMINI n° 11, in *MR* ³2002.

[74] JUNGMANN, *The Mass of the Roman Rite*, 1, 366.

[75] *The Roman Missal Revised by Decree of the Second Vatican Council and Published by Authority of Pope Paul VI: The Sacramentary Approved for Use in the Dioceses of the United States of America by the National Conference of Catholic Bishops and Confirmed by the Apostolic See*, International Commission on English in the Liturgy, Catholic Book Publishing, New York 1985.

petitions of all".[76] The recurrence of the words *colligere* and *concludere* is noteworthy because they emphasize that the formula synthesizes the entreaties already made silently by the assembled faithful and gives them climactic expression. The collect, then, is corporate prayer. Though recited by the priest, it is not his own prayer but that of the entire community whose ambassador he is and whose petitions he presents to the Lord on their behalf. Latent here is a rich expression of the relation between priest and people, the ordained and the baptized.

In other passages too Bernold stresses the communal nature of liturgical action. Commenting on the priest's greeting, *Dominus vobiscum*, and the people's response, *Et cum spiritu tuo*, he points out that these words imply that those addressed and responding are several, not one. "Just as it would be improper", he asserts, "to answer *Et cum spiritu vestro* when a single individual issues the greeting, so it is incongruous to be greeted by *Dominus vobiscum* when only one person is present or even no one".[77] For this reason, he declares, Popes Anicetus and Soter (mid second century) insisted that when a priest celebrates Mass there should always be a third person present. This remark is very interesting, coming from a time when private Masses were widespread.

The author also emphasizes the importance of the people's 'Amen' at the end of the prayer and explains its significance: "According to the ancient tradition of the holy Fathers, everyone present should add *Amen* as a sign of confirmation in order to confirm the common prayer [*communem orationem*] which the priest offered for all".[78] Here Bernold refers to the collect as 'common prayer'. Though recited by the priest, it is the prayer of the entire assembly. By the response of 'Amen' the body of faithful 'confirm' what the priest asks on their behalf, that is, they give their approval to it, corroborate and ratify it, thereby making it authentic precisely as common prayer. Once again the ministerial character of the priest is underscored. He is a *legatio*, an ambassador, speaking and acting for the benefit of those whom he represents before God. The *General Instruction of the Roman Missal* adopts the opposite point of view and presents the priest as representing Christ before the people. Explaining the importance of the three presidential prayers the *General Instruction*, declares that they "are addressed to God in the name of

---

[76] "Sequitur oratio quam Collectam dicunt, eo quod sacerdos, qui legatione fungitur pro popolo ad Dominum (II Cor. V), omnium petitiones ea oratione colligat atque concludat" (PL 151, 979 D).

[77] "Sicut enim inepte responderetur, Et cum spiritu vestro, cum unus esset salutator, sic incongrue salutatur per, Dominus vobiscum, cum unus tantum adsit vel nullus" (PL 151, 979 C).

[78] "Omnes autem astantes, juxta antiquam sanctorum Patrum traditionem, in signum confirmationis Amen subjungere debent, ut communem orationem, quam sacerdos pro omnibus Domino libavit, confirment" (PL 151, 981 D).

the entire holy people and all present, by the priest who presides over the assembly in the person of Christ".[79]

In the thirteenth century Sicard, bishop of Cremona in central Italy, speaks of the communal nature of the collect in explicitly ecclesial terms. The priest, he declares, "praying and inviting others to pray, says: *Oremus*. He gathers [*colligit*] the whole church to himself as the representative of the whole speaking in the name of the many".[80] The priest is here understood as the point around which the assembly actualizes itself as church. By inviting the faithful to pray he "collects" them, joins them together and, having made them a single whole, addresses God in their name. Sicard concludes that the collect is so named "because by it people are collected and their petitions collected into one so as to be presented to God by the priest".[81] This union of priest and congregation begins even before the prayer, for Sicard remarks that the greeting and response, which precede the collect, make priest and people to be of one disposition and will.[82]

4. The collect in context

The collect concludes not only the silent prayer, but everything else which precedes it, even as the *Super oblata* concludes the presentation of the offerings and the *Post communionem* concludes the communion rite, each prayer coming at the end of a procession accompanied by the chanting of a psalm or at least of an antiphon taken from a psalm. The collect, then, is the culminating point of all that comes before the service of the word. This is nowhere more evident than in the oldest complete account of a papal Mass, the *Ordo Romanus Primus*, composed at Rome near the beginning of the eighth century.[83] The Pontiff emerges from the sacristy near the entrance to the basilica flanked by the archdeacon and another deacon and preceded by seven acolytes carrying burning candles and a subdeacon with the smoking thurible. The schola begins singing the Introit antiphon, followed by the psalm. Along the processional route the Pope pauses to reverence a container of consecrated bread remaining from a previous Mass. Upon reaching the

---

[79] "Hae preces a sacerdote, qui coetui personam Christi gerens praeest, ad Deum diriguntur nomine totius plebis sanctae et omnium circumstantium" (*IGMR* n° 30, in *MR* ³2002).

[80] "Orans autem, et alios invitans orare, dicit: Oremus. Universalem colligit ad se Ecclesiam, vel ut syndicus universitatis loquens sub persona multorum" (PL 213, 99 A).

[81] "Dicitur et collecta, quia sub ea populus colligitur, et petitiones populi in unum colliguntur, ut per sacerdotem ad Dominum referantur" (PL 213, 99 B).

[82] "Ex his mutuis salutationibus innuitur quod sacerdotis et populi debet esse unus affectus" (PL 213, 98 D).

[83] VOGEL, *Medieval Liturgy*, 159-60.

altar he gives the kiss of peace to one of the bishops, the archpriest and all the deacons. He then signals the schola to conclude the Introit psalm and to chant the *Gloria Patri* and then repeat the antiphon. After kissing the gospel book and altar he makes his way to the chair and stands there while the schola chants the *Kyrie eleison*. He intones the *Gloria in excelsis Deo*, at the end of which he recites the oration to which everyone responds 'Amen'. Then he sits down.[84]

This, of course, is the Roman entrance rite in its most magnificent form and on its grandest scale. During the stately movement of the procession featuring multiple ministers and numerous ceremonial intricacies, the chanting of the Introit psalm with its antiphon and doxology provides interpretation, focus and direction. Music and people move together through formal space. The movement stops when the Pontiff reaches his chair. With everyone still standing, the Kyrie is sung, then the Gloria. The climactic moment, that toward which everything has been building up, is the *oratio prima* – the spare but eloquent formulation of the entreaties of the assembled faithful, followed by their resounding 'Amen'. In this context the collect stands out in all its splendour as the pinnacle of a protracted and complex entrance ceremony.

At the opposite extreme is the practice which was common between the Council of Trent and the Second Vatican Council, that of a priest offering a Low Mass using the Missal of Pius V.[85] Mass began with the prayers at the foot of the altar, consisting of the sign of the cross, Psalm 42, the Confiteor and versicles with responses, all said in a barely audible voice by priest and servers on the floor before the first of at least three steps beneath the altar. As the priest ascended to the predella, he said a prayer quietly. As he kissed the altar stone in the middle of the altar, he said another prayer quietly. After reading the Introit from the Missal at the right side of the altar, he returned to the middle of the altar and exchanged with the servers the nine supplications of the Kyrie. Still standing at the middle of the altar he recited the Gloria on days when it was prescribed. He then kissed the altar again, turned toward the congregation, and said "Dominus vobiscum" in a low voice, to which the servers replied "Et cum spiritu tuo". Finally he returned to the epistle side, said "Oremus" and whispered the collect from the Missal . Upon hearing "per omnia secula seculorum", the servers answered 'Amen', immediately after which the priest began reading the epistle.

In contrast to the grandeur of the *Ordo Romanus Primus*, the scale of the Tridentine Low Mass could not be smaller – everything read by one person, from one book, in one tone of voice, at one place, in one posture, nothing lyrical, nothing poetic or dramatic, nothing to see or hear. In this context the collect is but one of a string of formulas read by the priest at the epistle side

---

[84] *OR* I, n° 44-53.

[85] As presented in the *Ritus servandus in celebratione Missarum*, in *MR* 1570, 20*-24*.

of the altar before moving to the other side of the altar to read the gospel. It is neither climatic nor conclusive and is heard by no one. Usually there were two or three collects. In medieval times there could be as many as five or seven. Legislation insisted that their number be uneven. And, of course, symbolic interpretations abounded.[86]

At a High Mass and especially a Solemn High Mass with deacon and subdeacon, things were noticeably different. But in a normal parish High Mass was sung only once on Sunday – rarely during the summer months before air conditioning – and Solemn High Mass perhaps only on Christmas and Easter. Worth recalling is that at these Masses, during the prayers at the foot of the altar, the choir was singing the Introit and Kyrie, and would take up the Gloria as soon as it had been intoned by the priest. After the Gloria the priest would chant "Oremus", followed by the collect, likewise chanted aloud.

In contrast to a Low Mass, here the collect has prominence. It is chanted and hence heard, and it calls forth a strong 'Amen' from the choir. Furthermore, aside from the intonation of the Gloria, it is the first time the priest is heard.[87] Prior to this the choir and organ occupied the foreground. Finally there is a change of posture. The congregation stands when the *Oremus* before the collect is sung and sits after the 'Amen'. So in this context the collect is both climactic and conclusive.

The opening rites of the eucharistic liturgy in the Roman Missal of Paul VI promulgated in 1970, 1975 and 2002, may be the weakest section of the post-conciliar Mass and have been widely criticized, sometimes severely.[88] Edward Foley reports that "the Consilium proposed a much sparer set of introductory rites in 1967 for its so-called '*Missa normativa*', consisting of a chant to accompany the procession of liturgical ministers, a greeting and an opening presidential prayer".[89] Unfortunately, this proposal was not accepted. The present format is considerably more than an entrance rite, because between the procession of ministers and the collect there is the sign of the cross, the greeting by the priest, the introduction to the Mass, the invitation to the penitential act followed by a brief pause for silence, the

---

[86] See: JUNGMANN, *The Mass of the Roman Rite*, 1, 385-388.

[87] Jungmann writes, "Keeping in mind the original plan of the Roman Mass, we perceive that the oration is the first place – and, until the so-called *secreta*, the only place – in which the celebrating priest himself steps before the assembly to speak. All the other things are singing and reading which – aside from the intonation of the *Gloria* – are carried out by others, or they are prayers inserted later on which the priest says quietly to himself" (JUNGMANN, *The Mass of the Roman Rite*, 1, 359).

[88] See especially: R.A. KEIFER, "Our Cluttered Vestibule: The Unreformed Entrance Rite", *Worship* 48 (1974) 270-277.

[89] E. FOLEY, "The Structure of the Mass: Its Elements and Its Parts", *A Commentary on the General Instruction of the Roman Missal*, ed. E. Foley – N.D. Mitchell – J.M. Pierce, Liturgical Press (Pueblo Book), Collegeville MN 2007, 135.

penitential act itself and at times the Kyrie and Gloria. Beginning with the sign of the cross these are all done after the priest has arrived at the chair, which is much more appropriate than the Tridentine practice of doing everything at the altar. Because of the insertion of so many new elements between the end of the procession and the collect this part of the Mass is no longer called the entrance rite but introductory rites, "Ritus initiales".[90]

The most common objection to the revised arrangement is that it is a juxtaposition of too many disparate components insufficiently developed or co-ordinated and requiring changes in thought and feeling which are considered to be too abrupt and jarring. Particularly disturbing is the shift from an invigorating opening song to an examination of conscience and confession of sin, then to a joyful Gloria. Moreover starting with the sign of the cross the person of the priest leaps into the foreground. Use of the optional intentions after "Let us pray" only increases the oppressiveness of the beginning of Mass.

When all the introductory rites, including the Introit, are spoken – as is usually the case on weekdays – the constituent parts tend to lose their distinctiveness and run together into an undifferentiated jumble of words ending only with the congregation's 'Amen' to the collect. In rare cases, when everything is sung including the sign of the cross and call to repentance, the length and solemnity of these rites can seem out of proportion to their stated purpose, which is "to ensure that the faithful who come together as one establish communion and dispose themselves to listen properly to God's word and to celebrate the Eucharist worthily".[91] People seem relieved when the priest finishes the collect, after which they can sit down and be quiet. When some parts are sung and others spoken, as is typical of most Sunday Masses, the incoherence of these various introductory rites is glaring. In all these cases the collect is conclusive. Whether it is also climactic is debatable. The only days on which this prayer stands out as being unmistakably conclusive and climactic are Ash Wednesday, Palm Sunday, Good Friday and the Presentation of the Lord. On these four occasions the sign of the cross, greeting, penitential act and even *Oremus* are omitted and the collect shines forth in all its pristine splendour as both the culmination and conclusion of the entrance procession.

---

[90] *IGMR* n° 46-54, in *MR* ³2002.

[91] "ut fideles in unum convenientes communionem constituant et recte ad verbum Dei audiendum digneque Eucharistiam celebrandam sese disponant" (*IGMR* n° 46, in *MR* ³2002).

Bibliography

A. Liturgical sources

The English-Latin Sacramentary for the United States of America: The Prayers of the Celebrant of Mass together with the Ordinary of the Mass: English Translations Approved by the National Conference of Bishops of the United States of America and Confirmed by the Apostolic See, Benziger Brothers, New York 1966.

"Gregorianum paduense ad fidem codicis Paduensis D 47, Fragmentis collatis Salisburgensibus", *Le Sacramentaire Grégorien*, 3 vol., ed. J. Deshusses (Spicilegium Friburgense 16), Éditions universitaires, Fribourg [3]1992, 1, 607-684 (*Pad* 1992).

"Hadrianum ex authentico", *Le Sacramentaire Grégorien: Ses principales formes d'après les plus anciens manuscrits*, 3 vol., ed. J. Deshusses (Spicilegium Friburgense 16), Éditions universitaires, Fribourg [3]1992, 1, 83-348 (*Gregor*).

"Hadrianum revisum anianense cum supplemento ad fidem codicis augustodunensis 19", *Le Sacramentaire Grégorien: Ses principales formes d'après les plus anciens manuscrits*, 3 vol., ed. J. Deshusses (Spicilegium Friburgense 16), Éditions universitaires, Fribourg [3]1992, 1, 349-605, n° 1019a-1805.

Liber sacramentorum engolismensis (Cod. B. N. Lat. 816), ed. P. Saint-Roch (Corpus christianorum series latina 159 C), Brepols, Turnhout 1987.

Liber sacramentorum romanae aeclesiae ordinis anni circuli (Cod. Vat. Reg. Lat. 316/Paris Bibl. Nat. 7193, 41/56) (Sacramentarium Gelasianum), ed. L.C. Mohlberg – L. Eizenhöfer – P. Siffrin (Rerum ecclesiasticarum documenta. Series maior, Fontes 4), Herder, Rome 1960.

Liturgia horarum iuxta ritum Romanum: Officium divinum ex decreto Sacrosancti Oecumenicum Concilium Vaticanum II instauratum atque auctoritate Pauli PP. VI promulgatum, editio typica, 4 vol. Typis polyglottis Vaticanis, Città del Vaticano 1971-1972.

Missale Gallicanum Vetus (Cod. Vat. Palat. lat. 493), ed. L.C. Mohlberg (Rerum ecclesiasticarum documenta. Series maior, Fontes 3) Herder, Rome 1958.

Missale Gothicum (Cod. Vat. Reg. Lat. 317), ed. L.C. Mohlberg (Rerum ecclesiasticarum documenta. Series maior, Fontes 5) Herder, Rome 1961.

Missale Romanum, editio princeps (1570), ed. M. Sodi – A.M. Triacca (Monumenta liturgica Concilii Tridentini 2), Libreria editrice Vaticana, Città del Vaticano 1998 (*MR* 1570).

Missale Romanum ex decreto SS. Concilii Tridentini restitutum summorum pontificum cura recognitum, editio XXXI post typicam, Pustet, Regensburg [31]1920.

Missale Romanum ex decreto SS. Concilii Tridentini restitutum summorum pontificum cura recognitum, editio typica, Typis polyglottis Vaticanis, Città del Vaticano 1962.

Missale Romanum ex decreto Sacrosancti Oecumenici Concilii Vaticani II instauratum auctoritate Pauli PP. VI promulgatum, editio typica, Typis polyglottis Vaticanis, Città del Vaticano [1]1970, (*MR* [1]1970).

Missale Romanum ex decreto Sacrosancti Oecumenici Concilii Vaticani II instauratum auctoritate Pauli PP. VI promulgatum, editio typica altera, Typis Vaticanis, Città del Vaticano [2]1975, (*MR* [2]1975).

Missale Romanum ex decreto Sacrosancti Oecumenici Concilii Vaticani II instauratum auctoritate Pauli PP. VI promulgatum Ioannis Pauli PP. II cura recognitum, editio typica tertia, Typis Vaticanis, Città del Vaticano [3]2002, (*MR* [3]2002).

"Ordo Romanus Primus", *Les Ordines Romani du haut moyen age*, ed. M. Andrieu
    (Spicilegium Sacrum Lovaniense. Études et documents 23), Spicilegium
    Sacrum Lovaniense, Leuven 1971, 2, 1-108 (*OR* 1).
"Ordo Romanus 4", *Les Ordines Romani du haut moyen age*, ed. M. Andrieu
    (Spicilegium Sacrum Lovaniense. Études et documents 23), Spicilegium
    Sacrum Lovaniense, Leuven, 2, 135-170.
"Ordo Romanus 5", *Les Ordines Romani du haut moyen age*, ed. M. Andrieu
    (Spicilegium Sacrum Lovaniense. Études et documents 23), Spicilegium
    Sacrum Lovaniense, Leuven, 2, 207-227, (*OR* 5)
"Ordo Romanus 6", *Les Ordines Romani du haut moyen age*, ed. M. Andrieu
    (Spicilegium Sacrum Lovaniense. Études et documents 23), Spicilegium
    Sacrum Lovaniense, Leuven, 2, 239-250.
"Ordo Romanus 9", *Les Ordines Romani du haut moyen age*, ed. M. Andrieu
    (Spicilegium Sacrum Lovaniense. Études et documents 23), Spicilegium
    Sacrum Lovaniense, Leuven, 2, 327-336.
"Ordo Romanus 10", *Les Ordines Romani du haut moyen age*, ed. M. Andrieu
    (Spicilegium Sacrum Lovaniense. Études et documents 23), Spicilegium
    Sacrum Lovaniense, Leuven, 2, 349-362.
Le pontifical Romano-germanique du dixième siècle, 3 vol. ed. C. Vogel – R. Elze (Studi e
    testi 226, 227, 269) Biblioteca Apostolica Vaticana, Città del Vaticano 1963-
    1972.
The Psalter Collects from V-VIth Century Sources, ed. L. Brou (Henry Bradshaw Society
    83), Harrison and Sons, London 1949.
Sacramentarium veronense, ed. L.C. Mohlberg – L. Eizenhöfer – P. Siffrin (Rerum
    ecclesiasticarum documenta. Series maior, Fontes 1), Herder, Rome ³1978
    (*Leon*).
Le Sacramentaire Grégorien: Ses principales formes d'après les plus anciens manuscrits, 3
    vol., ed. J. Deshusses (Spicilegium Friburgense 16), Éditions universitaires,
    Fribourg, 1, ³1992, 2 ²1988, 3 ²1992.

B. Translations of liturgical sources

*The Roman Missal Revised by Decree of the Second Vatican Council and Published by
    Authority of Pope Paul VI: The Sacramentary Approved for Use in the Dioceses of
    the United States of America by the National Conference of Catholic Bishops and
    Confirmed by the Apostolic See*, International Commission on English in the
    Liturgy, Catholic Book Publishing, New York 1985.
The Saint Andrew Bible Missal, ed. Center for Pastoral Liturgy, The Catholic University
    of America, William J. Hirten, Brooklyn NY – Brepols, Turnhout 1982.

C. Patristic sources

ALCUINUS, *De divinis officiis liber*, ch. 11 of "De celebratione Missa et ejus
    significatione", in ed. J.P. Migne (*Patrologia cursus completa, Series latina* 101),
    Garnier, Paris 1863, 1249 C, 1252 D
AMALARIUS METENSIS, *Eclogae de officio missae*, ed. J.P. Migne (*Patrologia cursus completa,
    Series latina* 105), Garnier, Paris, 1864, 1315-1332;

Concilia Galliae, ed. C. Munier (Corpus christianorum series latina 148), Brepols, Turnhout 1963.

EGERIA, *Itinerarium, Egeria's Travels*, ed. J. Wilkinson, Ariel, Jerusalem ²1981.

IOHANNES CASSIANUS, *De Institutis coenobiorum*, in *Jean Cassien: Institutions cénobitiques*, ed. J.-C. Guy (Sources Chrétiennes 109), Le Cerf, Paris 1965, corr. 2001.

URANIUS PRESBYTER, *Epistola de obitu Paulini ad Pacatum* 11, ed. J.P. Migne (*Patrologia cursus completa, Series latina* 53), Garnier, Paris, 1865, 866 A. (PL)

WALAFRIDUS STRABO, *Ecclesiasticarum rerum exordiis et incrementis: Liber unus, ad Reginbertum eipscopum*, in ed. J.P. Migne (*Patrologia cursus completa, Series latina* 114), Garnier, Paris, 1879, 919-966.

D. Magisterial sources

"Additiones et variationes in rubricis missalis ad normam bullae 'Divino afflatu' et subsequentium S.R.C. decretorum. VI. De orationibus", in *Missale Romanum ex decreto SS. Concilii Tridentini restitutum summorum pontificum cura recognitum, editio XXXI post typicam*, Pustet, Regensburg ³¹1920, (25-32).

General Instruction of the Roman Missal, tr. the International Commission on English in the Liturgy (Liturgy Documentary Series 2), United States Conference of Catholic Bishops, Washington DC ³2002.

Institutio generalis Missalis Romani (IGMR), in *Missale Romanum ex decreto Sacrosancti Oecumenici Concilii Vaticani II instauratum auctoritate Pauli PP. VI promulgatum*, Typis Vaticanis, Città del Vaticano ²1975, (MR ²1975).

E. Studies

CAPELLE, B., "Collecta", *Revue Bénédictine* 42 (1930) 197-204; reprinted in *Histoire: La Messe* (Travaux Liturgiques 3 vol.), Centre Liturgique, Mont César, Louvain 1962, 2, 192-199.

CHAVASSE, A., *Le Sacramentaire Gélasien (Vaticanus Reginensis 316). Sacramentaire presbytéral en usage dans le titres Romains au VIIᵉ siècle* (Bibliothèque de théologie. Série 4: Histoire de la Théologie 1), Desclée, Tournai 1958.

DIX, G., *The Shape of the Liturgy*, Dacre, London 1945.

DUCHESNE, L., *Christian Worship*, tr. M.L. McClure, SPCK, London 1912 (of *Origines du culte chrétien*, Thorin, Paris ³1903).

FOLEY, E., "The Structure of the Mass: Its Elements and Its Parts", *A Commentary on the General Instruction of the Roman Missal*, ed. E. Foley – N.D. Mitchell – J.M. Pierce, Liturgical Press (Pueblo Book), Collegeville MN 2007, 113-197.

FORTESCUE, A., *The Mass: A Study of the Roman Rite*, Longmans, Green & Co., London 1930 reprint of 1912.

JUNGMANN, J.A., *The Mass of the Roman Rite: Its Origins and Development*, 2 vol. tr. F.A. Brunner, Benziger Brothers, Westminster, MD 1986 (of *Missarum sollemnia: eine genetische Erklärung der römischen Messe*, 2 vol. Herder, Wien – Freiburg – Basel ⁵1962).

KEIFER, R.A., "Our Cluttered Vestibule: The Unreformed Entrance Rite", *Worship* 48 (1974) 270-277.

ROGUET A.-M., *The Liturgy of the Hours: The General Instruction on the Liturgy of the Hours with a Commentary*, tr. P. Coughlan – P. Purdue, Liturgical Press, Collegeville MN 1971.

TAFT, R.F., *The Liturgy of the Hours in East and West: The Origins of the Divine Office and its Meaning for Today*, Liturgical Press , Collegeville MN 1993.

VOGEL, C., *Medieval Liturgy: An Introduction to the Sources*, tr., rev. W.G. Storey – N.K. Rasmussen (National Association of Pastoral Musicians Studies in Church Music and Liturgy), Pastoral Press, Washington DC 1986 (of *Introduction aux sources de l'histoire du culte chrétien au moyen âge*, Centro italiano di studi sull'alto medioevo, Spoleto 1981).

CHAPTER 5

The Collect for the Easter Vigil

James G. Leachman

Introduction

We present here the collect of the Easter vigil as it appears in the current *Editio typica tertia* of the *Missale Romanum* of 2002 in synopsis with the same prayer as we find it in the official English translation of the Roman Missal of 1974. This prayer is offered when the catechumens are baptised during the Easter vigil.

Missale Romanum 2002	The Roman Missal
Deus, qui hanc sacratissimam noctem gloria dominicae resurrectionis illustras, excita in Ecclesia tua adoptionis spiritum, ut, corpore et mente renovati, puram tibi exhibeamus servitutem.[1]	Lord God, you have brightened this night with the radiance of the risen Christ. Quicken the spirit of sonship in your Church; renew us in mind and body to give you whole hearted service.[2]

---

[1] *Missale Romanum ex decreto Sacrosancti Oecumenici Concilii Vaticani II instauratum auctoritate Pauli PP. VI promulgatum Ioannis Pauli PP. II cura recognitum, editio typica tertia*, Typis Vaticanis, Città del Vaticano ³2002 (hereafter *MR* ³2002), 360. See: *Corpus orationum*, 14 vol., ed. E. Moeller – J.-M. Clément – B.C. 't Wallant (Corpus christianorum series latina 160 A), Brepols, Turnhout 1992-2004, 2, n° 1651; P. BRUYLANTS, *Les oraisons du Missel Romain, texte et histoire* (Études liturgiques 2 vol.), Mont César, Louvain 1952, 2, n° 346.

[2] *The Roman Missal, revised by decree of the Second Vatican Council and published by the authority of Paul VI, official English texts,* Collins, London 1974, 206. (*The Sunday Missal*, Collins, London 1974, 229).

Through this prayer we petition God, during the night which God illuminates with the glory of the dominical resurrection, to stir up the spirit of adoption in God's Church, that, having been renewed in body and mind, we may show pure service to God.

Like many of the orations also used in the re-established *Ordo initiationis christianae adultorum (Rite of Christian Initiation of Adults)*,[3] this prayer first appears in the *Sacramentarium gelasianum vetus*[4]. Unlike nearly all of the other recently restored prayers of the *OICA*, however, this collect has been retained throughout the Roman liturgy's history, appearing largely unchanged in forty-five western manuscripts and subsequent printed books, including the first printed *Missale Romanum* of 1474, the first edition of the *Missale* of Trent of 1570, the *Missale Parisiense* of 1747 and the last edition of the *Missale* of Trent of 1962.

The liturgical reform mandated by the Second Vatican Council altered or eliminated several of this collect's phrases so that it might reflect its new position before the baptismal rite in the Easter vigil. Thus, in its new position, it now refers to all members of the Church and not only to those baptised at that Easter vigil. We shall show below how the revisers of the *Missale* worked with those who produced the *OICA* to produce the revisions of the prayer. The present form of the prayer is found in all three editions of the *Missale Romanum* of 1970, 1975 and 2002. The only Latin edition of *OICA* was issued in 1972, and thereafter various English language translations and adaptations, called *RCIA*, were published in 1987 and 1988.[5]

The purpose of this short contribution is to show how the collect for the Easter vigil embodies in its very structure an expression of the divine-human exchange, our co-operation with the divine grace, and of our human maturation, all expressions of the prayer's dynamic power to change lives. This article follows two previous ones in which I examined the theology of the Holy Spirit in the catechumenal preparation for baptism[6] and in the

---

[3] *Rituale Romanum ex decreto Sacrosancti Oecumenici Concilii Vaticani II instauratum auctoritate Pauli PP. VI promulgatum, Ordo Initiationis Christianae Adultorum*, Typis polyglottis Vaticanis, Città del Vaticano 1972 (hereafter *OICA*).

[4] *Liber sacramentorum romanae aeclesiae ordinis anni circuli (Cod. Vat. Reg. Lat. 316/Paris Bibl. Nat. 7193, 41/56) (Sacramentarium Gelasianum)* n° 454, ed. L.C. Mohlberg – L. Eizenhöfer – P. Siffrin (Rerum ecclesiasticarum documenta. Series maior, Fontes 4), Herder, Rome ³1981 (hereafter *GelasV*).

[5] *The Roman Ritual: Rite of Christian Initiation of Adults, Approved for use in England and Wales, Scotland*, The International Commission on English in the Liturgy, Geoffrey Chapman, London 1987; *The Roman Ritual: Rite of Christian Initiation of Adults, Study Edition*, ICEL – US Bishops' Committee on the Liturgy, Liturgy Training Publications, Chicago IL 1988.

[6] J.G. LEACHMAN, "The Role of the Holy Spirit in the Catechumenal Preparation for Baptism in *OICA*", in *Spiritus spiritalia nobis dona potenter infundit*, ed. E. Carr (Studia Anselmiana 139. Analecta liturgica 25), Centro Studi S. Anselmo, Rome 2006, 277-292.

period of enlightenment and purification.[7] It also builds upon work done for a chapter in a forthcoming book in which Daniel McCarthy and I examine the structure and dynamic of the collects of the scrutinies.[8] We continued that discussion in a further paper, on the preface of the second scrutiny, given at the meeting of *Societas Liturgica* in Palermo on 11th August 2007, and now due for publication in *Studia Liturgica*.[9] In both of these later studies we show how the enquirer is formed by a step-by-step process, *per ritus et preces*, into a fully initiated member of the catholic community, that, as they are born into a new ecclesial identity, they may come to participate in the divine-human exchange. In this article we develop this research further and show how the baptised, through their participation in the divine-human exchange, mature in the faith and come to service of God and neighbour.

The collect examined in this short paper is proclaimed during the Easter vigil, even when there are no baptisms. At the Easter vigil in the *OICA* the ritual and catechetical formation of candidates for full membership of the Roman Rite of the Catholic Church finds its culmination in the celebration of the sacraments of initiation. The *Ordo* begins with the rite of reception into the catechumenate, which continues until the rite of election. Then follows the period of purification and enlightenment, typically corresponding with the season of Lent, during which the three scrutinies are celebrated. The *Ordo* culminates in the sacraments of initiation, generally celebrated during the Easter vigil. Thereafter, the period of mystagogy leads into the remainder of Christian life.

1. The *Status quaestionis*

From the articles already published or submitted we have arrived at several conclusions.

1.1 *The Holy Spirit in the Catechumenate*[10]
The blessings and anointings celebrated during the catechumenate rarely mention the work of the Spirit, the *Praenotanda* only somewhat more

---

[7] J.G. LEACHMAN, "The Transforming Power of the Holy Spirit in the Period of Enlightenment and Purification in *RCIA*", *Studia Liturgica* 34 (2007) 185-200.

[8] J.G. LEACHMAN, - D.P. MCCARTHY, "The Formation of the Ecclesial Person through Baptismal Preparation and the Celebrations in the *OICA*: The Collects for the Scrutinies," *The Liturgical Subject: Subject, Subjectivity, and the Human Person in Contemporary Liturgical Discussion and Critique*, ed. J. Leachman, SCM – Notre Dame, London – South Bend IN 2008, 172-200.

[9] J.G. LEACHMAN, - D.P. MCCARTHY, "Preparation for the Piazza: The Preface of the Second Scrutiny (the Fourth Sunday in Lent): The Mystagogical Formation of the Neophytes and the Assembly", Societas Liturgica Conference, 11 August 2007, *Studia Liturgica* 38 (2008) 114-133.

[10] LEACHMAN, "The Role of the Holy Spirit", 277-292.

frequently. Wherever the Holy Spirit is mentioned in the texts, the *Ordo* looks forward to future events. So, I asked, "Why does the *OICA* give such a minimal emphasis to the Holy Spirit during the catechumenate?" I deduced that the intention of the editors of the *OICA* was to focus the Spirit's activity on the sacraments of initiation and in the life of the Spirit flowing from baptism. The Roman liturgical tradition sacramentally crystallizes the gift of the Spirit in the complex of rites constituting the sacraments of initiation; in the water bath blessed by the invocation of the Spirit,[11] in the sacramental anointing with chrism, and in the full participation in the Eucharist. Accordingly, the *OICA* is faithful to its Roman tradition, as the anointings with holy Chrism for the gift of the Spirit occur only after the water bath, be it in the post-baptismal anointing[12] or chrismation, as also in ordination.

More proper to the catechumenate is the more diffuse activity of the Spirit who moves the Church to pray for the catechumens in their gradual conversion. The whole of the catechumenate, indeed, is intended to be an experience of transformation in the Spirit, of passing from one way of life to another.[13]

1.2 *The Holy Spirit in the Period of Enlightenment*[14]
Once again, the Holy Spirit is rarely mentioned in the ritual texts of the period of enlightenment, except in the *Praenotanda*. Again, I saw that when the Spirit is mentioned, the liturgical text anticipates the anointings with holy Chrism after the water bath and in confirmation.

1.3 *The Scrutinies*
In the forthcoming chapter on the three collects of the scrutinies[15] and in the forthcoming article on the preface of the second scrutiny,[16] we discovered that the prayers express and mediate the elect's entering ever more deeply into the divine-human exchange.[17] Through the transformation of the elect into new ecclesial persons by developmental stages, as they are enabled, the elect come to co-operate with the divine self-revelation and gift, they share in God's self-transcending love as they participate in the life of the Church in the world, and thereby come to share in and mediate to the world the nuptial union of God and humanity, which alone satisfies our deepest longings.

---

[11] *OICA* 215; see also: D.E. SERRA, *The Blessing of Baptismal Water at the Paschal Vigil (GeV 444-448): Its Origins, Evolution and Reform*, (Thesis ad Lauream 136), Pontificium Athenaeum S. Anselmi de Urbe, Pontificium Institutum Liturgicum, Rome 1989.

[12] *OICA* 263.

[13] LEACHMAN, "The Role of the Holy Spirit", 290.

[14] LEACHMAN, "The transforming power of the Holy Spirit in the period of Enlightenment", 185-200.

[15] LEACHMAN - MCCARTHY, "The Formation of the Ecclesial Person".

[16] LEACHMAN - MCCARTHY, "The Preface of the Second Scrutiny".

[17] LEACHMAN - MCCARTHY, "The Formation of the Ecclesial Person", 174.

1.4 *The Period of Mystagogy*
Because the neophytes are now full members of the Church, no proper prayer texts are provided in the *OICA* for them, rather the Sunday and weekday euchology becomes their own. From our research thus far we have deduced that, after the celebration of the sacraments of initiation at Easter, as the neophytes mature in their experience of mutual self-gift, they will discover that the divine-human exchange becomes a way of interpreting both their public worship and their behaviour and attitudes in the public domain.

1.5 *The Present Contribution*
In this examination of the collect for the Easter vigil, we continue to probe our hypothesis that the divine-human exchange is the liturgical-theological core of the sacraments of Christian initiation celebrated at the Easter vigil. The divine-human exchange is the hinge upon which our continual co-operation with grace and our on-going human maturation in the faith function. To examine our hypothesis more closely let us, after a brief historical summary, turn to the collect of the Easter vigil, and then to four linguistic elements of the prayer.

2. History

In the first three centuries of Christian history after the New Testament we find neither specific orations nor any collect tradition associated with baptisms at the Easter vigil. Prayers are indeed mentioned and described, as in the third-century *Apostolic Tradition*,[18] originally redacted in Greek, but most prayers in this text, with the exception of eucharistic prayers and prayers of ordination, are short, blunt and almost rudimentary. Some fine exceptions are the prayer after the first post-baptismal anointing,[19] the prayers for the blessing of light[20] and of fruit offered to the bishop, [21] all

---

[18] *La Tradition Apostolique de Saint Hippolyte: Essai de reconstruction*, ed. B. Botte (Liturgiewissenschaftliche Quellen und Forschungen 39), Aschendorff, Munster [5]1989.
[19] *La Tradition Apostolique*, ed. Botte (LQF 39), 52: "Domine Deus, qui dignos fecisti eos remissionem mereri peccatorum per lauacrum regenerationis spiritus sancti, inmitte in eos tuam gratiam, ut tibi seruiant secundum uoluntatem tuam; quoniam tibi est gloria, patri, filio cum spiritu sancto in ecclesia, et nunc et in saecula saeculorum".
[20] *La Tradition Apostolique*, ed. Botte (LQF 39), 64: "Gratias agimus tibi, Domine, per filium tuum Iesum Christum dominum nostrum, per quem illuminasti nos, revelans nobis lucem incorruptibilem. Cum perfecimus ergo longitudinem diei quam creasti ad satietatem nostram, et cum nunc non egemus luce vesperi per gratiam tuam, laudamus te et glorificamus te per filium tuum Iesum Christum dominum nostrum, per quem tibi Gloria et potentia et honor cum sancto spiritu, et nunc et in saecula saeculorum".
[21] *La Tradition Apostolique*, ed. Botte (LQF 39), 76: "Gratias tibi agimus, deus, et offerimus tibi primitiuas fructuum, quos dedisti nobis ad percipiendum, per uerbum

reclaimed in Latin translation from the fifth-century Latin Verona manuscript.[22] It was only in the fourth century and the passage of liturgical prayer at Rome into the Latin tongue that the collect form, unique to Western traditions, emerged, probably at the hand of Damasus.[23]

2.1 *Early History*

The earliest record of Latin collects is found in the *Verona sacramentary*[24] in the fifth century, but unfortunately the fascicles containing the orations of Lent and the Easter Season are missing. We thus find our earliest Latin prayers associated with these seasons in the *Gelasianum vetus*. This document comes from a manuscript of about 750, redacted 628-715, in part from earlier materials, but some of the prayers may have their own earlier histories.

It may be impossible ever to establish the authorship and date of this collect for the Easter vigil. It is perhaps worth noting the parallels of phrases with other prayers.

First, in the *Gelasianum*, both the collect for the vigil mass of Christmas[25] and our prayer for the vigil mass of Easter[26] have the first five words in common; both contain references to birth and salvation. These two prayers are also found in the *Paduense*,[27] a papal sacramentary originally adapted for use with pilgrims to St Peter's basilica on the Vatican hill around 670-680, well within the time frame during which the *Gelasianum* was redacted, although the earliest extant copy of the *Paduense* is much later (840-855) and shows signs of Gallican influence. It could be that this evidence points to a common ancestor once used for the Christian Passover feast when the liturgy was first proclaimed in the Latin tongue, presumably before the arrival of the Feast of the Nativity in the West, estimated by Thomas Talley as "earlier than 311, … and the place of the origin of the festival could well have been

---

tuum enutriens ea, iubens terrae omnes fructus adferre ad laetitiam et nutrimentum hominum et omnibus animalibus. Super his omnibus laudamus te, dues, et in omnibus quibus nos iubati, adornans nobis omnem creaturam uariis fructibus, per puerum Iesum Christum dominum nostrum, per quem tibi gloria in saecula saeculorum".

[22] See: *La Tradition Apostolique*, ed. Botte (LQF 39), xvii-xx.

[23] J. PINELL, "Liturgie locali antiche (origine e sviluppo)", *Nuovo Dizionario di Liturgia*, ed. D. Sartore – A.M. Triacca, Paoline, Cinisello Balsamo MI 1984, 776-783, esp. 779.

[24] *Sacramentarium Veronense*, ed., L.C. Mohlberg – L. Eizenhöfer – P. Siffrin (Rerum ecclesiasticarum documenta. Series maior, Fontes 1) Roma [3]1978 (hereafter *Leon*).

[25] *GelasV* n° 5

[26] *GelasV* n° 454.

[27] "Gregorianum Paduense", *Le Sacramentaire Grégorien* n° 4, ed. J. Deshusses (SpicFri 16), 1, 607-684 (hereafter *Pad* 1992); *Pad* 1992, n° 327; C. VOGEL, *Medieval Liturgy: An Introduction to the Sources*, tr., rev. W.G. Storey – N.K. Rasmussen, (National Association of Pastoral Musicians Studies in Church Music and Liturgy), Pastoral Press, Washington DC 1986 (of *Introduction aux sources de l'histoire du culte Chrétien au moyen âge*, Centro italiano di studi sull'alto medioevo, Spoleto 1981), 94.

North Africa".[28] One may surmise that such a common ancestor, or at least a common incipit used for various vigil celebrations, may have been proclaimed in Rome during the papacy of Damasus I (366-384) or of Innocent I (401-447).

Second, the phrase in the Gelasian source of our prayer (*GelasV* n° 454), *conserua in noua*[m] *familiae tuae progeniem sanctificationis spiritum/gratiam quem dedisti, ut, corpore et mente renouati* is found also in the collect for the Pentecost vigil, also in the *Gelasianum*, (*GelasV* n° 625), though the latter prayer does not share the initial five words of *GelasV* n° 454. This shared phrase may indicate that a common source for a baptismal vigil, originally used at Easter, was adapted to create the Pentecost vigil prayer. Pope Siricius (385-398) let it be known that baptism was to be administered only at the Easter and Pentecost vigils, the latter being seen as a repetition of the former.[29] Furthermore, the purpose phrase in the Gelasian source of our prayer (*GelasV* n° 454) is *ut ... puram tibi exhibeant seruitutem*, and in the collect for the Pentecost vigil in the *Gelasianum*, (*GelasV* n° 625), *ut ... in unitatem fidei seruentes tibi, domine, seruire mereantur*. The latter is more complicated theologically and therefore seems to be derived from the former.

These commonalities, parallels and developments hint at the development of a selection of prayers and of their distribution throughout the annual liturgical cycle. Both the prayers and the whole cycle of the liturgical year elicit, by making anamnesis, the different mysteries of the life of Christ.[30] Such an evolution of the annual cycle of prayers may have come about by new compositions, editing of existing prayers, or the selection and stitching together of phrases lifted from a common pool of expressions used in liturgical or domestic prayers. Our three prayers probably appeared in the *tituli*, perhaps during the pontificates of Gelasius (492-496), Vigilius (537-555) or Pelagius I (556-561), and then were later incorporated into the *Gelasianum* about a century later. Indeed, Chavasse prefers a date in the early 500's for the composition of the Gelasian baptismal ritual,[31] and our collect may have its origin in this period, though we cannot be sure that it was first proclaimed in one of the *tituli* of Rome, rather than St Peter's, St John Lateran. Thus the

---

[28] T.J. TALLEY, *The Origins of the Liturgical Year*, Liturgical Press (Pueblo Book), Collegeville MN ²1991, 87.

[29] S. DE BLAAUW, *Cultus et decor: Liturgia e architettura nella Roma tardoantica e medievale*, 2 vol., (Studi e Testi 355, 356), Biblioteca Apostolica Vaticana, Città del Vaticano 1994, 149; SIRICIUS, *Epist. 1 ad Himerium Episcopum*, 2, (*Patrologia cursus completa, Series latina* 13), 1134-35.

[30] See the forthcoming article on the Liturgical Year as Sacrament of Christ by M. Augé, *Ecclesia Orans* (2008).

[31] A. CHAVASSE, *Le Sacramentaire Gélasien (Vaticanus Reginensis 316): Sacramentaire presbytéral en usage dans le titres Romains au VIIᵉ siècle* (Bibliothèque de théologie. Série 4: Histoire de la Théologie 1), Desclée, Tournai 1958, 163.

prayer remained, virtually as it had stood from its first attestation, for nearly one thousand years.

2.2 *The Anglican Development*

The prayer we are studying appeared in many later medieval manuscripts, in the first printed *Missale Romanum* of 1474, and the Sarum,[32] Westminster[33] and many other Missals in England. It might have been treasured and passed in translation, via the *Book of Common Prayer*, into the English speaking world, yet it was not to be. The divines of the English Reformation, aware that the Church of England was in need of a general reform, undertook one of their most radical reorganisations of medieval practice and swept away the Holy Week services, and with them the traditional collect for the Easter vigil. Thus it was that the English-speaking world had to wait for 421 years, from 1549 to 1970, for the prayer to be offered in English.[34]

As there were, we may assume, no baptisms during the Easter vigil in the later Medieval era, it must have seemed reasonable to follow the Reformation logic, to abandon the Vigil altogether, together with the many other early medieval encumbrances to a Reformed liturgy. Yet, it seems to us a great loss that English-speaking Christians who inherited the Reformation have been deprived of a collect of such theological richness, depth and beauty.

The Church of England liturgist Goulburn writes in 1891, "Why they rejected the Sarum Collect, it is not easy to say; for it is entirely free from everything objectionable in point of doctrine, and contains, as our present Collect does, a pointed allusion to the Sacrament of Baptism, which in the early church it was customary to administer on Easter Even".[35] Thus matters stood; there was no Easter vigil liturgy and no collect for the day, and the unprecedented step of providing Epistle and Gospel, yet no collect, presumably for a hypothetical Communion Service, stood for eighty-eight

---

[32] *The Sarum Missal, edited from Three Early Manuscripts*, ed. J. Wickham Legg, Oxford 1916; reproduced Clarendon, Oxford 1969.

[33] *The Westminster Missal* (Missale ad usum Ecclesiae Westmonasteriensis), ed. J. Wickham Legg. (Henry Bradshaw Society vols. 1, 5, 12) Oxford 1891, 1893, 1897; reproduced in 1 vol. Boydell & Brewer, Woodbridge 2000.

[34] Notable exceptions include some not officially recognized Tractarian and Anglo-Catholic Prayer Books and Missals, such as *The Manual of Catholic Devotion*, published in London from the late 19th century, then by the Church Literature Association, London from 1950 to 1969, and most recently in Norwich 2001; *The Anglican Missal*, The Society of Saints Peter and Paul, London from the end of the nineteenth century; *The English Missal*, first published by W. Knott & Son, London 1912, and others. English translations for use by Catholics were made before 1970, but only for private reading and study, e.g. *The Office of Holy Week, in Latin and English according to the Roman Missal and Breviary*, Keating, Brown and Keating, London 12 1808, 355.

[35] E.M. GOULBURN, *The Collects of the Day*, 2 vol., Longmans, Green & Co., London – New York – Bombay 1891, 1, 341.

years from 1549. In 1633 King Charles I and Archbishop William Laud planned to introduce the English *Book of Common Prayer* into Scotland, and after certain revisions, including the provision of a brand new collect for Easter Eve composed by the Archbishop,[36] had been completed, they attempted to impose the new liturgy upon the unwilling Scots.

> The new liturgy was appointed ... to be read for the first time in the Scottish churches for the first time in July 1637. But the attempt ... was the signal for a burst of popular fury ....The Seventh Sunday after Trinity, on which the new form of Prayer was to be read, was known long after as 'the stony Sabbath', or 'the casting of the stools,' because stones and stools were hurled at the heads of such of the clergy as ventured to read it.[37]

The result was the overthrow of episcopacy in Scotland in the following year, 1638; a lasting warning to creators of new liturgical texts. It was only in 1661 that Bishop Cosin abbreviated the new prayer, rejected by the Scots, and it was rewritten and inserted in the third English *Book of Common Prayer* of 1662. Its text is as follows:

> Grant, O Lord, that as we are baptized into the death of thy blessed Son our Saviour Jesus Christ, so by the continual mortifying our corrupt affections we may be buried with him; and that through the grave, and gate of death, we may pass to our joyful resurrection; for his merits, who died, and was buried and rose again for us, thy Son Jesus Christ, our Lord. Amen.

This new Anglican prayer focuses on baptism as the image of death and resurrection of Christ, inherited from the late medieval tradition of theology. References to incarnation or to baptism as new birth are lacking. Yet there is, interestingly, reference to human co-operation with divine grace in "our continual mortifying our corrupt affections" whereby we come to enjoy the new life of the resurrection after death.

2.3 *A Period of Fixity*
Returning to consider the medieval prayer, probably first proclaimed in the early sixth-century in Rome, we see from the sources that it remained with few changes first in the Roman liturgical manuscripts and eventually in the *Missale Romanum*. The original context of the prayer is difficult to establish. In

---

[36] GOULBURN, *The Collects of the Day*, 1, 344, "O most gracious God, look upon us in mercy, and grant that as we are baptized into the death of thy Son our Saviour Jesus Christ; so by our true and hearty repentance all our sins may be buried with him, and we not fear the grave; that as Christ was raised up from the dead by the glory of thee, O Father, so we also may walk in newness of life, but our sins never be able to rise up in judgement against us; and that for the merit of Jesus Christ, that died, was buried, and rose again for us. Amen".

[37] GOULBURN, *The Collects of the Day*, 1, 342-343.

the written records certainly, the vigil celebration precedes the baptismal celebration, and the collect for the Eucharist follows. It could have been however that the vigil liturgy and the baptismal liturgy were celebrated in the basilica and its baptistery simultaneously; in these circumstances, the baptismal celebration having been completed, the neophytes would join the vigil and hear this Mass collect for the first time with the rest of the assembly. If this were in fact the case, when the prayers and rituals of Vigil, Baptism and Eucharist came to be written down in one manuscript, such as the *Gelasianum*, the scribe would have to choose an order in which to copy them out. The scribe for the *Gelasianum* chose to write down first the texts of the vigil, then baptism and then Eucharist. When the manuscript later came to be read and used as a liturgical source, it was interpreted as three sequential sections, thus all would go first to the vigil, then the baptisms and then finally to Eucharist, rather than begin in two assemblies in baptistery and nave and later join together.

Sible De Blaauw describes the development of the Roman baptismal liturgies at the Easter vigil in the Lateran from 312 to 1304. In his account of the period 312-600,[38] and of processions to and from the font, he suggests that in the fourth century the vigil was followed by the baptismal liturgy, rather than being celebrated at the same hour. In the period 600-1050 de Blaauw reports that the baptisms definitely followed the vigil,[39] as was the case from 1050 to 1304.[40]

Despite the almost complete stability of the prayer's text and its unaltered position in the liturgy up to, including and after the Council of Trent, during the twentieth-century pontificate of Pius XII momentous events came to hold sway. Up to this point in history the collect in the Easter vigil was proclaimed after the baptismal liturgy and after the *Gloria* at the beginning of the Mass. During the Pontificates of Pius XII and John XXIII, the Pian Commission of the Sacred Congregation of Rites (SCR), enjoyed the presence of Annibale Bugnini as its efficient secretary. As a result of the Pian Commission's work the Church restored the Easter vigil in 1951, and then in 1955 restored and renewed the whole of Holy Week. In the same year as they published the *Missale Romanum* 1962, permission was given by the SCR to

---

[38] DE BLAAUW, *Cultus et decor*, (StT 355), 149-155; (StT 356), fig 6.

[39] DE BLAAUW, *Cultus et decor*, (StT 355), 189-193; (StT 356), fig 6.

[40] DE BLAAUW, *Cultus et decor*, (StT 355), 300, 302-308; (StT 356), fig 6. This fits in with what we have discovered about Ordos XVII and XXIII if they are eighth-century French documents. In eighth and ninth century Gaul and Germany the number of litanies was increased to three and intercessions to the saints were included because of the longer processions. See: A. CHAVASSE, *La liturgie de la ville de Rome du Ve au VIIIe siècle: Une liturgie conditionnée par l'organisation de la vie in Urbe et extra muros* (Studia Anselmiana 112, Analecta Liturgica 18), Pontificium Athenaeum Anselmianum, Rome 1993, 56.

divide the Rite of Baptism into seven "steps"[41] for adults under the title, *Ordo baptismi adultorum per gradus catechumenatus dispositi*.

The Vatican Council mandated a further reform, both of the *Missale Romanum* and of the other liturgical books, whose results were published over a lengthy period of time from 1968 (*Ordo Confirmationis*) to 1977 (*Ordo dedicationis Ecclesiae et Altaris*)[42] and then finally to 2001 (*Martyrologium romanum*).[43] The work of the reform was steered by the *Consilium ad recte exsequendam Constitutionem de S. Liturgia*,[44] set up in January 1964 by Pope Paul VI and working directly under him. The *Consilium* set up various study groups (*coetus*)[45] to implement the mandated reform, and we can see from the results that there was collaboration between the Groups. Group 22, responsible for the *OICA*, and working in collaboration with Group 23,[46] had obtained approval for its text from the *Consilium* on November 13, 1969, and after two further years of inspection by the agencies of the Curia, the *OICA* text was published in 1972. It was only after the approval of the *OICA* text in 1969 that the Vigil liturgy could be restructured to accommodate the demands of *OICA*, since we find the prayer first in the *Missale Romanum* of 1970.

Presuming that there was collaboration between Group 22 and Group 23 working on *OICA*, and Group 17 responsible for preparing the texts of the missal for special celebrations throughout the year,[47] the collect for the Easter vigil in the *Missale Romanum* 1970 (and therefore of subsequent editions to 2002) was moved to before the baptismal liturgy. Because of its changed position in the Vigil, the prayer had to be rewritten in a collaborative effort of Group 18*bis*,[48] responsible for prayers and prefaces, and Group 13[49] responsible for the euchology for ritual masses, masses for various occasions and votive masses, to an appropriate form for its new position. The reasons for this we shall see in a later section after we have summarised the editorial changes and given an analysis of the literary forms found in the prayer.

---

[41] A. BUGNINI, *The Reform of the Liturgy 1948-1975*, tr. M.J. O'Connell, The Liturgical Press, Collegeville MN 1990, 585, note 5, referring to *Ordo baptismi adultorum per gradus catechumenatus dispositi*, in *Acta Apostolica Sedis* 54 (1962) 315-338.

[42] B. NEUNHEUSER, *Storia della Liturgia attraverso le epoche culturali* (Bibliotheca Ephemerides Liturgicae, Subsidia 11), Centro Liturgico Vincenziano edizioni liturgiche, Rome ²1983, 145.

[43] Already in second edition in 2004.

[44] PAUL PP. VI, Litterae apostolicae motu proprio datae, *Sacram liturgiam*, die 25 ianuarii 1964, *AAS* 56 (1964) 140.

[45] These are listed in BUGNINI, *The Reform of the Liturgy*, 63-65.

[46] BUGNINI, *The Reform of the Liturgy*, 584-597.

[47] BUGNINI, *The Reform of the Liturgy*, 402. The schemata were all approved by 16 October 1968.

[48] BUGNINI, *The Reform of the Liturgy*, 396, 399, n. 14.

[49] BUGNINI, *The Reform of the Liturgy*, 401, n. 18, 19, approved 8 October 1968.

2.4 *A Summary of the Editorial Changes*
Now let us look at the editorial changes made to the text of the source prayer in the *Gelasianum vetus*, and in subsequent ancient sacramentaries. First, only the *Gelasianum* has the word "*gloriosae*", whereas both the eighth-century Gellone and Phillips sacramentaries correct "*gloriosae*" to read "*gloria*", this rendering being also the same as in the *Hadrianum* and the *Sacramentary of Padua*. Second, only the *Gelasianum* has the curious phrase, "*in nova…progeniem*". This rendering was corrected in two ways. On the one hand, the Paduense has "*in nova…progenie*". On the other hand, both the Gellone and Phillips sacramentaries correct the *Gelasianum*, this time to read "*in novam…progeniem*" as does the *Hadrianum*. Third, we find the spelling, "*inlustras*" in the *Gelasianum*, which is repeated in the eighth century Gellone and Phillips, and the Gregorian sacramentaries, the Hadrianum and Paduense.

The 1474 *Missale* follows the *Paduense* in the phrase "*in nova…progenie*", rather than the *Hadrianum's* "*in novam…progeniem*". This is understandable, for the Gregorian sacramentary was not published until 1571 by Pamelius, and so the text of the *Hadrianum* was not available to the publishers of the 1474 *Missale*. In fact, the family tree of the various Gregorian sacramentaries was not clarified till the twentieth century. The 1474 *Missale* has three phonetic misspellings *dominice, familie tue*, but again we know that since the Gregorian sacramentary was published only in 1571, this is not a correction but a local usage following the *Paduense*. The Gregorian diverts from the tradition of the *Paduense* by changing "*inlustras*" to "*illustras*".

After the Council of Trent, the 1570 *Missale* redacts the text in several ways. The phrase "*in nova…progenie*" becomes the standard text following the 1474 *Missale* and the *Paduense*, rather than the *Hadrianum*. The three hidden diphthongs *dominice, familie* and *tue*, are restored to the text as, *dominicae, familiae* and *tuae*. The word "*illustras*" is maintained from the 1474 *Missale*.

In the *Missale* of 1970 the collect is transferred to before the baptismal liturgy. Thus, when the collect is proclaimed, the offspring have not yet been born, and so several changes had to be made. First, "*conserva*" was changed to "*excita*" and "*in nova familiae tuae progenie*" to "*in Ecclesia tua*". It was ingenious to substitute "*excita*" for "*conserva*", since the substitution elicits both the "*excita*" in two collects of Advent[50] and the birth of our salvation at Christmas, thus strengthening the idea of baptism as regeneration and new birth. The Spirit of adoption is "stirred-up" (*excita*) in this collect proclaimed before the baptismal liturgy, but the Spirit is not given (*emitte*) sacramentally until the blessing of water and in the anointings of the candidates. Second, "*in nova…progenie*" was dropped because there are not yet any newly-baptized; "*quem dedisti*" was dropped because the Spirit had not yet been

---

[50] The collects of the First and Second Sundays of Advent in *MR* 1962 were transferred to Thursday and Friday of Advent week 1 and Thursday of Advent week 2; see also the Thirty-fourth Sunday in Ordinary Time, collect, in *MR* ³2002.

given; *"familiae tuae"* became the church, *"Ecclesia tua"*; and finally *"exhibeant"* became *"exhibeamus"*, thus, "they" was changed to "us".

3. Analysis of literary forms

We now come to examine the language of the prayer, its words and phrases of the prayer and its deeper literary structures.

3.1 *Understanding Words and Phrases*
The following table presents the current prayer of the *Missale Romanum* of 2002 arranged according to its literary structure. The literary categories are presented in the left column in bold, the grammatical constructions in the centre column and their corresponding phrases in the prayer to the right.

Invocation:	simple:	*Deus*
Amplification:	relative:	*qui hanc sacratissimam noctem gloria dominicae resurrectionis illustras,*
Petition:	imperative:	*excita in Ecclesia tua adoptionis spiritum,*
Purpose:	ut + subj. (classical):	*ut, ... puram tibi exhibeamus servitutem*
Motive:	participial:	*corpore et mente renovati ...*

Invocation: The invocation is simple, *Deus*, "God", and rendered in the official English translation as "Lord God".

Amplification: The invocation is amplified in a relative clause, *qui hanc sacratissimam noctem gloria dominicae resurrectionis illustras*, literally, "you illumine this most holy night with the glory of the dominical resurrection", rendered in English as, "you have brightened this night with the radiance of the risen Christ".

Sacratissimam noctem (the most holy night) alludes to the *vigilias noctis*, the night of the incarnation when, "in that region there were shepherds living in the fields, keeping watch over their flocks by night", (Luke 2:8; *Vulgate*,[51] NRS[52] throughout). *Gloria* (Glory) relates to the song of the angels, "Glory to God in the highest", (Luke 2:14), and though *illustras* (illumination) finds no direct parallel in the Vulgate, we find a related word, *claritas* used to describe the lighting at the same event, "claritas Dei circumfulsit eos", "the

---

[51] *Vulgate = Biblia Sacra Vulgata*, ed. R. Weber, Deutsche Bibelgesellschaft, Stuttgart ⁴1994.

[52] NRS = *The Holy Bible Containing the Old and New Testaments with the Apocryphal / Deuterocanonical Books, New Revised Standard Version*, Oxford UP, New York – Oxford 1989.

glory of God shone around them" (Luke 2:9). Further, the word *inlustras* (you illumine) is used in the *Gelasianum* at Christmas, Lent, Easter and for the dedication of a church and of a font;[53] all associations with birth, rebirth and renewal.

The many verbal parallels we have already shown between the collects of the Easter and Christmas vigils in the *Gelasianum*, all reveal connections between this collect and the incarnation, therefore to both Christ's birth and by extension to our birth, the experience of which the Word of God shared with every member of the human race.

Petition: The imperative petition is, *excita in Ecclesia tua adoptionis spiritum*, literally, "stir up in your church the spirit of adoption", rendered in English as, "Quicken the spirit of sonship in your Church". The word, *excita*[54] means to stir up, excite or set in motion, and was used until 1962 as the first word, also in the imperative mood, of the collects for the first and second Sundays of Advent.[55] Here the word *excita* anticipates the rebirth of baptism as Advent anticipates Christmas.

Adoptionis, refers to *adoptionem* as in, "we ... groan inwardly while we wait for adoption" (Romans 8:23), and, "so that we might receive adoption as children" (Gal 4:5) and "he destined us for adoption as his children" (Eph 1:5). In classical Rome the act of adoption was the legal acceptance of paternity by a father after the birth of a child in which he formally lifted up (*suscipio suscipere suscepit susceptum*) and recognised the infant as his own. *Spiritum adoptionis* (the spirit of adoption) also appears in the passage: "you have received a spirit of adoption. When we cry 'Abba! Father!'" (Rom 8:15). As a further allusion to *adoptionem* we can refer to being *coheredes* and *comparticipes* with Christ, "fellow heirs, members of the same body and sharers in the promise in Christ Jesus" (Eph 3:6).

Purpose: God's intention in stirring up the Spirit of adoption is expressed classically by the purpose clause, *ut ... puram tibi exhibeamus servitutem*, literally, "in order that ... we may show forth to you pure service", and which is rendered in English as, "to give you whole hearted service".

The word *purus -a -um*, the complement of "*servitutem*", is an adjective we find associated with baptismal preparation back to the early third century. In the edition of the *Apostolic Tradition* edited by Dom Bernard Botte, traditionally ascribed to Hippolytus of Rome we find cognates of the word,

---

[53] The verb *inlustras* is found in *GelasV* n° 5 (Christmas), 156, 167, 279 (Lent), 453, 454 (Easter), 690, 707 (Dedication of a Church), 730 (Blessing a font).

[54] "*excitare*", in C.T. Lewis - C. Short, *A Latin Dictionary*, Oxford UP, Oxford - New York 1879, reprinted 1995, 330: *excitare* is derived from *excio*, call forth, wake, rouse up; *cio* or *cieo, cire, civi, citum*, from the Greek *kineo*, put in motion, move, stir, shake. Also *exhibeo*, from *habeo*, display or show.

[55] *Missale Romanum ex decreto SS. Concilii Tridentini restitutum summorum pontificum cura recognitum, editio typica*, Typis polyglottis Vaticanis, Rome 1962, 1,3.

"*purus*" three times.[56] The first two occasions refer to the required abstention by those who request baptism from professions that are not considered "pure", whereas the third refers to the state of the candidates immediately before baptism. Dom Bernard Capelle in his reconstruction uses a synonym "*mundus*".[57] Nor may catechumens give the kiss of peace, "*nondum enim osculum eorum sanctum est*"; their kiss is not holy, therefore not yet, presumably "pure".[58] However, it is interesting to see that the state of readiness of the catechumens for baptism is judged by their ethical behaviour, the touchstone of their purity, probity and readiness, in the following section:

Cum autem eliguntur qui accepturi sunt baptismum, examinatur vita eorum; an vixerint in honestate dum essent catechumeni, an honoraverint viduas, an visitaverint infirmos, an fecerint omnem rem bonam.[59]	And when they are chosen who are about to receive baptism, the life of them is examined: whether they have been living honestly while they were catechumens, whether they have been honouring the widows, whether they have been visiting the sick, whether they have been doing every good thing.[60]

From this text, I understand the qualification of purity in the preparation for baptism is ethical rather than ritual, and I explain it using the two-track system of the sequence of tenses. The independent main verb *examinatur* is a time 1 (present tense) verb and thus, establishes track 1 (the primary sequence). Then, the interrogative particle *an* gives rise to four indirect interrogatives, *vixerint*, *honoraverint*, *visitaverint* and *fecerint*, all third subjunctive (or perfect subjunctive) verbs. All four of these third subjunctive (perfect subjunctive) verbs are anterior to their main verb, *examinatur*, and, following track 1 (the primary sequence), are able to be translated by any anterior tense. Therefore, these four subjunctive verbs may validly be translated using the historical perfect (aorist) as "they lived", "they honoured", "they visited", "they did", or with these progressive perfect meanings, "they have been living", "they have been honouring", "they have been visiting" and "they have been doing".[61] It seems to me that the latter is

---

[56] *La Tradition Apostolique* n° 15, ed. Botte (LQF 39), 34: "donec purus sit"; 36, n° 16: "impuri enim sunt"; 42, n° 20: "ut sciat an purus sit".

[57] B. CAPELLE, "L'introduction du catéchuménat à Rome", *Histoire: varia, l'Assomption* (Travaux Liturgiques de doctrine et d'histoire 3 vol.), Centre Liturgique, Mont César, Louvain 1967, 3, 194: "ut mundus esse cognoscat".

[58] *La Tradition Apostolique* n° 18, ed. Botte (LQF 39), 40.

[59] *La Tradition Apostolique*, ch. 20, ed. Botte (LQF 39), 42.

[60] Translation by author.

[61] B.L. GILDERSLEEVE – G. LODGE, *Gildersleeve's Latin Grammar*, Bolchazy-Carducci, Wauconda IL 2003, reprint of ³1985 (hereafter GL) n° 235.

far more likely, as the candidates are still catechumens and, therefore, are still being examined for their practice of ethical purity.

Then, the reconstructed text shifts from track 1 (the primary sequence) to track 2 (the historical sequence), because the temporal phrase *dum essent*, using a second subjunctive (imperfect subjunctive) verb, is in turn dependent upon these third subjunctive (perfect subjunctive) verbs. Although the text shifts from track 1 to track 2 (from primary to historical sequence) the time frame of *essent* is contemporaneous with the third subjunctive (perfect subjunctive) verbs. Thus, the verb *essent* is contemporaneous with the full time frame of the four verbs that I have chosen to understand as progressive perfect verbs.

This understanding of the reconstructed Latin text is fully consistent with the context of the bishop's examining the ethical behaviour of the catechumens throughout their preparation for baptism including the present with hope for the future. The bishop would be obliged to inquire of the catechumens, whether "they have been living", "they have been honouring", "they have been visiting" and "they have been doing"[62] ethical actions "while being catechumens". This analysis is consistent with the note in the critical apparatus that Botte supplies with his reconstructed text. He indicates that three sources provide the basis for the reconstructed Latin text of the temporal phrase *dum essent catechumeni*, these are the Sahidic, the Arabic texts as well as the document *Testamentum Domini*, whereas the Ethiopic text is translated into Latin as *ante baptismum*, "before baptism".[63]

Returning to the Easter vigil collect, and its purpose clause *ut ... puram tibi exhibeamus servitutem*, we see that relative to the imperative verb, *excita* (stir up), the first subjunctive verb, *exhibeamus* (may we show) is grammatically contemporaneous, incomplete, unfinished, ongoing, future and eternal.[64] Thus, given the new context of the collect, offered now before baptism, the celebrating community, taking inspiration from the catechumens, who now at the point of baptism have been showing pure service throughout the catechumenate, now requests that the entire church, including the catechumens, may continue to show *puram servitutem* now and onwards into the future until the eschaton. Concretely this means that after baptism and confirmation, both the neophytes and all the previously baptised first proceed to the Eucharistic liturgy where they present at the altar their *puram servitutem*; then after the Easter vigil they go on presenting (*exhibeamus*) their *puram servitutem* as they go on being renewed through selfless living of their Christian lives. Finally, they hope at the end of an entire Christian life one day to enjoy the life of heaven, which is both praise and charity: *puram servitutem* of God and neighbour.

---

[62] GL n° 235.
[63] *La Tradition Apostolique* ch. 20, ed. Botte (LQF 39), 42.
[64] GL n° 510.

The *puram servitutem* of the neophytes, includes the full, conscious and active participation in the worship of the church, expressive of their active service of neighbour, as was illustrated above in the *Apostolic Tradition*. Jesus described this kind of ethical relationship with God and neighbour as a love with all of one's heart, soul, mind, and strength (Mark 12:29-33).

Yet further, in the letters to Timothy we find three references to pure worship. The first refers to *levantes puras manus* (lifting up pure hands) implying ethical living as a reflection of pure worship: "I desire then, that in every place, the men should pray, lifting up holy hands without anger or judgement" (1 Tim. 2:8). The second refers to a *conscientia pura* (with a pure conscience), establishing a similar link between an ethical life and worship: "they must hold fast to the mystery of faith with a clear conscience", (1 Tim. 3:9). The third also refers to a pure conscience, which it links with eucharistic thanksgiving, service and purity: *gratias ago Deo cui servio a progenitoribis in conscientia pura*, "I am grateful to God whom I worship with a clear conscience, as my ancestors did" (2 Tim. 1:3).

Finally, with the appearance of the word *exhibeamus* at the end of the purpose clause we find the first time the former elect have become part of "we", the Church.

Motive: Nestled at the beginning of the purpose clause and dependent upon it is the participial phrase expressing God's motive in stirring up the Spirit of adoption in the Church, *corpore et mente renovati*, literally, "ones having been renewed in body and mind", which is rendered in English as an imperative, "renew us in mind and body".

All alone, the participle *renovati* means "ones having been renewed". The implied subject of *renovati* is *nos*, the subject of *exhibeamus* in the purpose clause. As a passive participle, *renovati*, is a divine passive describing God's action and the co-operation of the faithful with the divine initiative. As an anterior participle, *renovati*, is antecedent to the first subjunctive (present subjunctive) verb, *exhibeamus*. Because *exhibeamus* refers to the on-going life of the faithful including the newly-baptised, *renovati* refers first to the entire period of formation of the elect leading up to the Easter vigil, including both the catechumenate and the period of purification and enlightenment, second and principally to their renewal in the sacraments of initiation, baptism, confirmation and Eucharist, and third to all subsequent renewal, for example in reconciliation, prayer, acts of charity and voluntary suffering.

In the *Missale gothicum* the formulary for Pentecost day includes the prayer *Ad pacem*, which contains a similar phrase, *ut corpore et mente renouati puram tibi animam cum securitatem pacis et purum pectus semper exhibeant,*[65] giving a link between Easter and Pentecost and the theme of purification.

---

65 *Missale gothicum e codice vaticano reginensi latino 317 editum* n° 361, ed. E. Rose (Corpus christianorum series latina 159 D), Brepols, Turnhout 2005.

Renovati also has explicit parallels with the collect of the third scrutiny in MR ³2002, which requests that the elect be renewed *renoventur*.[66] The subjunctive verb establishes a purpose clause: *ut ... renoventur fonte Baptismatis*, "that ... they may be renewed in the spring of Baptism". Although, in reference to that collect's main verb, *Concede*, the first subjunctive (present subjunctive) verb is contemporaneous, incomplete, unfinished, ongoing, future and eternal, there *renoventur* specifically looks forward to the imminent "renewal in ... Baptism" at the Easter vigil. So it seems that the primary focus of the renewal is in the sacraments of initiation. Here it is that God sends the *"spiritus adoptionis"* that the elect be sacramentally renewed.

Renovati alludes to *renovatur* (it is being renewed) in Colossians 3:10, "and have clothed yourselves with the new self, which is being renewed in knowledge according to the image of its creator", and to *Renovamini* (be renewed) in the passage, "be renewed in the spirit of your minds" (Eph 4:23). Now that we have examined the words and phrases of the prayer, let us turn to its deeper literary structure.

3.2. *Deeper Literary Structures*

For the moment, we shall leave aside the invocation and amplification of the prayer, which we shall consider later in the section on the theological-interpretative keys in section 5 of this paper.

If we lay out the remaining phrases of the prayer in five rows, let us begin our analysis by considering the three verbal forms presented in bold type in the chart below. We place the imperative *excita* in row 1, the anterior participle *renovati* in row 3 and the first subjunctive (present subjunctive) *exhibeamus* in row 5. These three verbal forms make a diagonal represented by the thin line (i-iv) in the following chart.

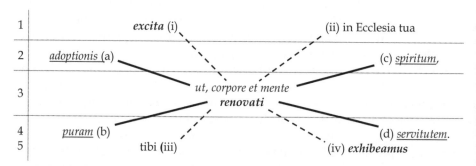

Verbal times. The imperative *excita* is present leading in to the future, as we ask God to stir up now, and to go on stirring up. The participle *renovati* is anterior the first subjunctive (present subjunctive) *exhibeamus*, which with

---

[66] MR ³2002, 976.

regard to *excita*, is contemporaneous, incomplete, unfinished, ongoing, future and eternal. Thus, diagonal i-iv moves from the present into the future.

Actors. God acts alone in the present imperative *excita*. God is the unnamed protagonist implied in the divine passive *renovati* and we passively undergo God's action upon us. Finally, we come to action in the subjunctive verb *exhibeamus*. Thus, in the diagonal i-iv the principal protagonist shifts from God to us, the Church.

Addressees. The addressee of God's action *excita* is *ecclesia tua*, "your church", while the addressee of our action *exhibeamus* is *tibi*, God. Thus, the two addressees form the axis ii-iii.

Objects. The object of God's stirring *excita* is *adoptionis spiritum* in row 2, and the object of our showing *exhibeamus* is *puram servitutem* in row 4.

Summary. This whole table shows how the verbal forms of the prayer express the stages of divine–human co-operation. First, the assembly invoking God, *Deus*, petitions for explicit divine action, *excita in Ecclesia tua adoptionis spiritum*. Second, the divine passive, *renovati*, expresses the hidden action of the divine protagonist and our passive co-operation with divine initiative. Third, the first subjunctive *exhibeamus* expresses our graced human initiative acting on God's part in the world.

The hinge-pin. In each of these elements we have examined initially, the times of the verbs, the actors, objects and addressees, the participle *renovati* acts as a hinge-pin for understanding the fabric of the whole prayer. Before continuing our examination of the various diagonal relationships that make up this prayer, we can prepare the way by offering the incarnation as an initial image of this prayer's hinge-pin.

Through God stirring the Spirit of adoption first over Mary, and now over the Church we, by the mystery of the incarnation, first share in the divine nature, and by baptism (*ut, corpore et mente renovati*), come to give pure service to God. This central mystery of the Christian faith, the divine-human exchange, is the cardinal point of the prayer, and thus central to each of the verbal pairs. Now that we have seen this basic structure, further patient study will reveal ten theological indicators in the prayer's deeper structure.

Let us first look at the two chiasms presented in the chart above, beginning with the chiasm indicated in bold lines formed by the letters a, b, c, d where we find our first two indicators.

1. **Diagonal a-d**. *Indicator of service*. The pair *adoptionis* (a) and *servitutem* (d) are related through the our sacramental adoption into the service of Jesus, who came not to be served but to serve and to lay down his life as a ransom for many (Mark 10:45a; Matt 20, 28).

2. **Diagonal b-c**. *Indicator of integral human nature*. The pair *puram* (b) and *spiritum* (c) are related in the psalm, "Give me a pure heart, O Lord, and renew a right spirit within me". The pair *puram – spiritum* is not exclusive of integral human nature for the hinge-pin of a pure spirit is a person renewed

(*renovati*) in body and mind (*corpore et mente*). This hints at the multi-dimentionality of human experience: physical, spiritual, psychological, emotional, social, familial, national and racial, without wishing to be exhaustive.

In the chiasm indicated in thin lines, formed by the numbers i, ii, iii, iv, we find two further indicators.

3. **Diagonal i-iv**. *Kenotic indicator.* We have already considered this indicator in the our analysis of the verbal times and actors. The activity of God is explicit in the verb *excita* (i), implied in the divine passive *renovati*, and hidden in the third verb *exhibeamus* (iv). Thus we see an increasing invisibility of God's activity, an image of God's self-emptying love.

4. **Diagonal i-iv**. *Indicator of divinization.* The obverse of the kenotic indicator is the increasing activity of the members of the church in response to God's self gift. God's initial action *excita* (i) does not imply any initiative on our part. Gradually, in response to the overtures of God, we begin to co-operate through passive means in our own renewal, *renovati*. As we begin to understand God's ways and are transformed, we learn to take more responsibility for acting autonomously and responsibly in God's name. Not only are we thus divinized, but our behaviour also becomes a bearer of Christ's action in the world.

Thus, the kenotic indicator and the indicator of divinization are in inverse proportion, for as God's action apparently decreases, so our activity empowered by God increases.

5. **Diagonal ii-iii**. *Teleological indicator.* We have already considered this diagonal formed by the two addressees, *Ecclesia* and *tibi*. God stirs up the Spirit *in Ecclesia tua* (ii), and through our participation in the divine-human exchange we come to show, *exhibeamus* our activity, *servitutem*, to God (*tibi*), who is the goal of our activity.

6. **Commutation of rows 2 and 4**. *Indicator of equivalence.* We have already seen that lines 2 and 4 give the objects of the verbs *excita* and *exhibeamus*. To understand the commutation between these two objects, let us consider them using the analogy of the *communicatio idiomatum* as applied to the incarnation, whereby Mary is called not only bearer of Jesus the man, but also bearer of God, *Theotokos*. The object of *excita* is the *adoptionis spiritum* (row 2), and the object of *exhibeamus* is *puram servitutem* (row 5). Thus, the faithful ask God to "stir up" the "spirit of adoption" in order that we the faithful, once *corpore et mente renovati*, may show "pure service". Through the commutation of properties brought about by the divine-human exchange, the two objects, *adoptionis spiritum* and *puram servitutem* the two elements are syntactically equivalent. Thus, we are able both to say "stir up ... pure service in your Church" and "in order that we may show you ... the Spirit of adoption".

7. **Left and right a-b, c-d**. *Indicator of transparency.* Not only are the objects in rows 2 and 4 commutable, but so are their verbal parts. Thus, as

our adoption (a) is pure (b) and our service (d) spiritual (c), so is everything accomplished in openness to ourselves, to neighbour and to God.

8. **Hinge pin**. *The divine-human exchange*. We have already considered how the participle *renovati* acts as the hinge pin for all the indicators of this prayer. By our baptism we share in the divine-human exchange in which God became human that we might share divine life.

9: **Inclusion and hyperbaton**. *Indicators of consummation*. The first and last words of this part of the prayer, *excita* (i) and *servitutem* (d), form an inclusion whereby the final goal of God's rousing is our service.

Rows 4 and 5 appear in the prayer as a single line: *puram tibi exhibeamus servitutem*. We have arranged these four words to indicate that *puram* describes *servitutem*, their separation forms a hyperbaton. This word order permits the Latin text to end with the word *servitutem*, thus, emphasizing the consummation of the prayer in service.

10. **Christological eschatocol**: *The doxological indicator*. The eschatocol or doxology following the prayer proper, *per Iesum Christum Dominum nostrum* juxtaposes the last word of the prayer, *servitutem*, in the context of Christ's own service. True glory is given to God in service.

3.3. *Conclusion*

Now that we have seen the hinge pin and the ten indicators which form the internal structure of the prayer, let us now proceed briefly to consider the prayer's context in the vigil and in the liturgical year, which will later help us to examine the five interpretative keys which provide us with a way of understanding how the prayer in context functions in the Church's liturgy, and how the dynamic of the divine-human exchange brings the prayer in context to its fruition in a life of service in the world.

4. **The context of the prayer**

We must first indicate the immediate context of the prayer in the Easter vigil and then its larger context in the liturgical year. We hope to treat the context of this prayer more fully in a later volume dedicated to the Easter vigil.

4.1 *The Immediate Context in the Easter Vigil*

Until 1970 the collect in the Easter vigil was proclaimed after the liturgy of Baptism. Now it is proclaimed after the liturgy of light, the Old Testament readings of the vigil and the "Glory to God in the highest", and thus precedes the Epistle, Gospel, homily, and the liturgies of baptism and Eucharist. The new position of the collect and its relationship with other elements of the vigil demanded changes in the text because, since the liturgical reform mandated by the Council, the elect are not yet baptised at the moment of the collect's proclamation.

4.2 *The Larger Context in the* OICA/RCIA *and the Liturgical Year*

The Easter vigil with its collect is situated at the heart of the liturgical year, and contains the rites of initiation for those who have been prepared by the prayers and rites of the *OICA*. The *"hanc sacratissimam noctem"* of the Easter vigil is closely connected with that of the Christmas vigil, thus emphasising the unity of the Paschal Mystery that begins at the Annunciation and concludes with Pentecost. The phrase *"gloria dominicae resurrectionis illustras"* also links the mystery of the resurrection with that of the incarnation by the words *gloria* and *illustras*.

The annual celebration of the liturgy first forms the people of God for service of others and of the world. The catechumens, for example are prepared for the sacraments of initiation, helped to take on a new vision and new values and, after initiation, are expected to give witness to their faith in the world of work.

Second, by enabling the people of God to respond together by giving a pure service of thanksgiving in unity (Didache and Malachi), the Church is bonded together. It is *puram servitutem* "pure service", because now washed, strengthened and consecrated by the Holy Spirit, the Holy Spirit leads Christians together to serve, accompanies our service and is our advocate before others.

Whereas baptism and confirmation are conferred only once, the Eucharist is the repeatable sacrament of initiation, and so this is what we do each Sunday; "In baptism the eucharist begins, and in the eucharist baptism is sustained. From this premier sacramental union flows all the Church's life".[67]

Nathan Mitchell states the mystery like this,

> "Because it is not just a rite but a way of life, because it celebrates not the past but the present coming-to-be of this assembly as church, because it announces not so much who we are as who we are to become...the eucharist is the climax of all those acts and processes by which human persons are called 'out of darkness into God's wonderful light' (1 Peter 2:9)".[68]

God continually pours out life and love for the world, offering the Word to us that our fears of rejection be assuaged by Jesus' humility, vulnerability and nearness to us, that we too may grow, change and be converted to serve.

---

[67] A. KAVANAGH, *The Shape of Baptism: The Rite of Christian Initiation*, Pueblo, New York 1978, 122.

[68] N. MITCHELL, *Eucharist as Sacrament of Initiation*, Liturgical Training Publications – North American Forum for the Catechumenate (Forum Essays 2), Liturgical Training Publications, Chicago IL 2003, 48.

5. Theological-interpretative keys

The goal of Christian initiation is to introduce people into a conscious participation in the divine-human exchange: full conscious and active participation in the divine liturgy and in God's action in the world. Following from our ten theological indicators, we now present five theological-interpretative keys. The first two help to further our analysis of our prayer, the second two further develop previous considerations, and the fifth is presented for the first time.

Enzo Lodi[69] and Renato De Zan[70] present eight interpretative keys, which we may use to further our analysis of the prayer. The keys are divided into two groups; four dimensions, (anamnesis, epiclesis, doxology, and koinonia) and four foundations of a Christian prayer, (theandric, christological-pneumatological, ecclesial and anthropological). Of these eight we have selected four and present them as theological-interpretative keys: first anamnesis, second epiclesis derived from the pneumatological foundation, third the divine-human exchange derived from the theandric foundation and fourth human cooperation derived from the anthropological foundation. Finally, we wish to introduce as a new interpretative key, heretofore either forgotten, unnoticed or overlooked, that of human maturation.

5.1 *Anamnesis as Interpretative Key*
The amplification of the prayer expresses its anamnetic dimension:
> *qui hanc sacratissimam noctem*
> *gloria dominicae resurrectionis illustras,*

God is ever acting now. God illumined the first Christmas night with glory, and the first Easter night with the glory of the Lord's resurrection. Not only does God illumine this particular paschal night, and each occasion when the prayer is proclaimed, God also illumines human life in every moment of our history.

God's first actions in the prayer is to illumine, *illustras*. The verb is time 1 (present indicative) indicating that God illumines now. God acts on "this most holy night", which refers to the annual cycle of remembrance in the liturgical year. That God illumines this night annually, provides an annual reminder that God illumines all of human history.

---

[69] E. Lodi, "La Liturgia: Teologia mistagogica: Introduzione generale allo studio della liturgia", *Liturgia della Chiesa*, Edizioni Dehoniane, Bologna 1999, 21-226.

[70] R. De Zan, "Criticism and Interpretation of Liturgical Texts", in *Introduction to the Liturgy*, ed. A.J. Chupungco (Handbook for Liturgical Studies 1), Liturgical Press (Pueblo Book), Collegeville MN 1997, 331-365 (En. tr. of R. De Zan, "Introduzione alla Liturgia, Ermeneutica", ed. A. J. Chupungco [*Scientia Liturgica: Manuale di Liturgia 1*] Piemme, Casale Monferrato 1998, 356-389), 344.

God illumines "with the glory of the dominical resurrection". This prayer does not refer to the resurrection of the Lord, God's saving work in Christ, in its quality as a historical event. The Lord's resurrection, while a saving deed of God in history, is also the goal of human history, for our eschatological glory is already revealed in the resurrected one. Not only is our eschatological hope already revealed in our history, but the resurrected Lord, who appeared to the disciples in history, is also the lamb that was slain, worthy to receive honour and glory and blessing (Rev. 5:12).

Because God ever illumines with glory, the assembly realises the transcendent nature of the present moment. Graced by the spirit, as the apostles after the resurrection, (John 20:19-23; Luke 24:13-49) the faithful see their divinized future in the glory of the Lord's resurrection and thereby reinterpret their past. Up to this point in the Easter vigil the assembly has proclaimed ritually the *mirabilia Dei* in salvation history. As this prayer is offered, the candidates, about to be incorporated into the community, come to reinterpret the whole of their lives in terms of the whole of Christ's life, and thereby come to a renewed view of their own personal past. As a document of the Canadian Bishops' Conference states, "Time is seen to extend to the whole length of … life. [The person's] … view of the past comes about through the eyes of the present person as he projects himself into the future and its challenges".[71]

5.2 *Epiclesis as Interpretative Key*

As anamnesis expresses God's action in the present, epiclesis expresses God's action "here", in this assembly. The epiclesis of our prayer is expressed by the petition: *excita in Ecclesia tua adoptionis spiritum*.

The classic fourth-century Greek and Latin model of epiclesis involves invoking the Spirit's descent upon people, gifts, water or oil. This spatial translocation of the Spirit is not apparent in our prayer, for the imperative *excita* petitions God to stir up the Spirit *in Ecclesia tua*, "within your Church". Rather than invoking a spatial translocation of the Spirit, here the epiclesis invokes an axiological change of state among the candidates. Thus, our prayer presents an immanent model of epiclesis that presupposes the presence of the Spirit already within the church.

This immanent model[72] of epiclesis is more frequent in oriental than western traditions. A list of such epicleses gives a wide selection of verbs, besides our *excita* to describe God's action. The *Euchologion of Serapion*, from the Nile Delta in the fourth century has two eucharistic epicleses, of which

---

[71] *The Integral Human Formation of Candidates for the Priesthood*, ed. Jeannine Guindon, tr. T. Prendergast, Éditions Paulines, Sherbrooke QC 1993, 47.

[72] I treated the different models of epiclesis in an earlier article: J. LEACHMAN, "Eucharistic Worship and Texts as Sources for Theological Reflection", *East Asian Pastoral Review* 42 (2005) 230-248.

the first requests that the Word come and 'fill'[73] the bread and wine. The *Dêr Balyzeh Fragment* asks the Spirit to 'fill us',[74] the *Manchester Fragment* also uses 'fill', [75] the Armenian *Anaphora of Isaac of Sahag* asks the Spirit to 'show' the bread and wine to be the body and blood of Christ,[76] the Syrian *Anaphora of the Twelve Apostles* also uses 'show',[77] and the Byzantine and Alexandrian anaphoras of Basil also have 'show'. The *Apostolic Constitutions* ask that bread and wine 'be revealed' as the body and blood of Christ,[78] and the Maronite *Anaphora of Xystus* asks the Holy Spirit to 'hover and rest upon' the gifts.[79]

Not only that, but a modern prayer, approved by the local conference of bishops and now included as part of the National Proper for the Philippines, and awaiting authorization, has an epiclesis that includes a word connoting the word "hover" of the Maronite *Anaphora of Xystus*. Anscar Chupungco writes that the 1976 version of this text of the Filipino Mass *Misa ng Bayang Filipino* has for both the consecratory and communion epicleses the verb *lukuban*, which calls to mind the action of a bird brooding its eggs,[80] as does the word *incubat* in the *Anaphora of Xystus*. The word *lukuban* is maintained in the slightly edited 1999 version of the Filipino text.[81] These words *lukuban*

---

[73] "πληρωσον" ("Anaphora in Euchologio Serapionis" 2, *Prex Eucharistica*, ed. A. Hänggi - I. Pahl (Spicilegium Friburgense 12), Éditions universitaires, Fribourg 1968, 130).

[74] "πληρωσον"("Fragmentum Dêr-Balyzeh" Epiclesis 1, *Prex Eucharistica*, ed. Hänggi – Pahl, 126).

[75] "πληρωσον"("Papyrus Manchester, John Rylands Library" Recto, *Prex Eucharistica*, ed. Hänggi – Pahl, 120).

[76] "*ostendat*"("Anaphora Isaac seu Sahag" Epiclesis, *Prex Eucharistica*, ed. Hänggi – Pahl, 335).

[77] "*ostendas*"("Anaphora duodecim Apostolorum" Epiclesis, *Prex Eucharistica*, ed. Hänggi – Pahl, 267).

[78] "ἀποφήνη"(*Les Constitutions Apostoliques*, 3 vol., ed. M. Metzger [Sources Chrétiennes 336], Le Cerf, Paris 1987, 3, 200).

[79] "*incubat … requiescat … requiescat*"("Anaphora Xysti" Epiclesis, *Prex Eucharistica*, ed. Hänggi - Pahl, 312).

[80] A.J. CHUPUNGCO, *Liturgies of the Future: Process and Methods of Inculturation*, Paulist, Mahwah NY 1989, 93; *Towards a Filipino Liturgy*, Benedictine Abbey, Manila 1976: Epiclesis 1 or Consecration epiclesis: "Ama naming Mapagmahal, ipagkaloob mo ang iyong Espiritu Santo upang kanyang *lukuban* at basbasan ang mga alay na ito, sapagkat tandang-tanda pa namin …" (106); "Our loving Father, grant us your Holy Spirit that he may *come upon* and bless these gifts, for how clearly we recall …" (128).
Epiclesis 2 or Communion epiclesis: "Ama, ipagkaloob mo ang iyong Espiritu Santo upang kaming nakikibahagi sa katawan at dugo ni Kristo ay kanyang tunghayan at *lukuban* nang kami'y magkaisa sa puso at diwa" (107); "Father, grant us your Holy Spirit. May he look upon us with favour and *take us under his wing*, so that we who share in the body and blood of Christ, may become one in heart and mind" (129-130).

[81] *Supplement to the Roman Missal for the Dioceses of the Philippines*, Paulines, Pasay City 1999. Epiclesis I or Consecration epiclesis: "Amang makapangyarihan, ipagkaloob mo sa iyong Simbahan ang Espiritu ng kabanalan: isinasamo namin na *lukuban* niya at italaga ang

and *incubat* also have overlapping connotations with the verb *rahhef*, "hover", in Genesis 1:2, when the Spirit "hovered" or "brooded" over the waters of chaos.

5.3 *The Theandric as Interpretative Key*

Just as anamnesis in our prayer expresses God's action now, and the epiclesis expresses God's action "here", the theandric dimension expresses the mutual incorporation of divine and human, and the growing interdependence of the protagonists of the prayer. Just as "the Word was made flesh", so is our humanity assumed into the divinity through the incarnation. The three verbs *excita, renovati*, and *exhibeamus* express the increasing divinisation of our humanity, as we are enabled by God's self-emptying grace (Phil 2:6-10).

God's gift, in this prayer, is not simply to impart a gift to humanity, rather, part of the gift of God's self is the way in which God gives. First, God's self gift is through self-emptying to assume our humanity. Then, God elicits from humanity a response so that, as we respond first by passive means of co-operation, we may come to full conscious and active participation in the gift of God's self.

5.4 *Human Co-operation as Interpretative Key*

As God is active (anamnesis) and present (epiclesis) drawing us into the divine-human exchange (theandric), our response to God's self-gift is to become protagonists for God in the world. Our human co-operation, expressed in our prayer as *corpore et mente renovati*, reveals how our divinization is effected through our graced co-operation with the divine initiative, which is understood as profoundly transformational not superficially theatrical.

Our ministerial participation occurs not only in the church building, for there are several altars at which we worship, where gifts are exchanged between God and humanity. The primary altar is the *christological* altar of Jesus' body, for the Word "assumed our humanity that we might share divine life" (Athanasius, *On the Incarnation* 54).[82] Second, we are Christ's

---

tinapay at alak na aming alay upang ang mga ito'y maging katawan at dugo ng aming Panginoong si Hesukristo ... " (155-156).

Epiclesis 2 or Communion epiclesis: "Ipagkaloob mo, Amang makapangyarihan, na kaming inaanyayahan mong sumalo sa hapag ng katawan at dugo ni Hesukristo ay *lukuban* ng Espiritu Santo, nang kami'y magkaisa sa puso, diwa at gawa" (160).

[82] ATHANASIUS ALEXANDRINUS, *De incarnatione*, tr. ed., F.L. Cross, Clapham Press, London 2007; confer: "tum, ut homines, in corruptionem reversos, iterum incorruptos redderet, atque a morte ad vitam revocaret, corpore quod sibi assumpserat et resurrectionis gratia mortem ab eis, non secus ac stipula ab igne consumitur, penitus amovens" (Augustinus Hipponensis, *Sermo Guelferbytanus* 3, in *Liturgia Horarum 2: Tempus Quadragesima et Tempus Pasquale*, Libreria Editrice Vaticana, Città del Vaticano 2000, "Die 2 maii. S. Athanasii, episcopi et ecclesiae doctoris", 1432).

body and so we exercise our baptismal priesthood primarily as the "altar of Christ's body". Third, during the Eucharist the church gathers at the *architectural* altar. Fourth, our lives of service in the world constitute the *cosmological* altar. Fifth, we gather at the *axiological* altar at which our status is changed and we are counted worthy to stand here (Eucharistic Prayer II), and finally, sixth, at the *maturational* altar, where we are changed from child to adult, to spouse of God.

5.5 *Human maturation as Interpretative key*

Our initial analysis of the minor euchology of the Roman liturgy has led us to propose a further interpretative key, in addition to those mentioned above by Lodi and De Zan. When we consider the three principal verbs of our prayer *excita, renovati* and *exhibeamus*, we can distinguish three steps of Christian maturation that correspond to increasing human activity in this prayer.

    i. *excita … adoptionis spiritum*. In this initial petition of the divine gift, God stirs up. We petition God to act, as a child asks a parent.

    ii. *renovati*. Here the verb is in the form of a divine passive. We co-operate with God, though our human activity is still passive or a co-operation by undergoing.

    iii. *exhibeamus*. The purpose clause of our prayer, expresses the goal of our Christian maturation, whereby, infused by divine gift, we come to adult action in the world.

As we are washed in baptism, transformed in body and mind, anointed in confirmation and nourished in the Eucharist we enter the sacred mysteries decisively, and we come to participate in them more and more throughout our lives, until we are definitively participating in the new way of life among the saints in heaven.

Summary

We see that the collect for the Easter vigil helps the candidates to perceive the divine-human exchange already at work in their lives, to name God's self-gift and to respond generously so that, as they may mature as Christians, they may come to that full stature of showing service in the world. The hinge-pin, (*corpore et mente renovati*) of our prayer, expressing the Divine-human exchange, links and coordinates the ten indicators which we have described, thus bringing the action of God and the response of believers to fruition in a "pure service" of the world.

    The *puram servitutem* of the Church in the world then informs the prayer of the community, which in turn responds in further service. As the cycle of the liturgical year continues on its way, each time the community meets for liturgy it offers further thanksgiving to God for what has been done in Jesus Christ, and further prayer for the gift of the Spirit to empower and change.

Thus do Christians mature in the faith year by year, responding to God's gift of self and showing service in the world.

Hugo Rahner sees how catechumens enter this experience of Christian maturation as they respond to the Risen Christ, and emerge as new Christians from the font. Citing an ancient homily, Rahner pictures their readiness for service in the world in terms of hope, fecundity and beauty. He writes,

> From these primal elements which are united on Easter Eve – the sunlight of Christ and the water which is man – there arises the new creature, the Christian.... And when the newly baptized Christian stepped forth into the daylight that had been made bright by the Easter Sun, he must have become newly alive.... For had he not himself taken part in this renewal, had he not himself become a new man in Christ? Had he not become even as one of those happy ones whom long ago a bishop had called the children of the new spring? "Ye sprigs of verdant holiness, who are my pious seed corn, my new-born swarm of bees, the wreath of blossoms that crowns my honour".[83]

The church petitions God to "stir up" the spirit of adoption within her and on those waiting to join her company, then she looks outside and beyond the celebration of the sacraments of initiation to the future service of the faithful in the world. Lactantius, in the Latin world of the fourth century, wrote about the need for a harmony of words offered inside and outside the place of worship. For him we serve God in our words not only in the church building, *sed et domi et in ipso etiam cubili suo*. Thus the Christian's life on Sunday is to be in harmony with that during the week.

> Uerbo enim sacrificari oportet deo, siquidem deus verbum est, ut ipse confessus est. summus igitur colendi dei ritus est ex ore iusti hominis ad deum directa laudatio, ... nec tantum hoc in templo putet sibi esse faciendum, sed et domi et in ipso etiam cubili suo. secum denique habeat deum semper in corde suo consecratum, quoniam ipse est dei templum:[84]

---

[83] H. RAHNER, *Greek Myths and Christian Mystery*, tr. B. Battershaw, Biblo and Tannen, New York 1971 (of *Griechische Mythen in christlicher Deutung*), 127-128. The internal quote is from the pseudo-Augustinian sermons, probably by Caesarius of Arles, *Sermo* 172 (PL 39, 2075).

[84] "For it is fitting that sacrifice be made to God in word; inasmuch as God is the Word, as He himself confessed. Therefore the chief ceremonial of worshipping God is praise from the mouth of a just one directed towards God .... And let him not suppose that this is to be done by him only in the temple, but at home, and even in his very bed. In short, let him always have God with himself, consecrated in his heart, inasmuch as he himself is a temple of God" (LUCIUS CAECILIUS FIRMIANUS LACTANTIUS, *Opera omnia Divinis institutis*, 6, ch. 25 [Corpus scriptorum ecclesiasticorum latinorum 19] ed. S. Brandt - G. Laubmann, Tempsky - Freitag, Prague - Vienna - Leipzig 1890, 579-580).

Ephrem the Syrian too, in fourth-century Syria, expressed these same ideas concerning God's initiative and our human co-operation and service in the divine-human exchange, which we have already identified in our Latin collect. They are all found in Ephrem's first and second Hymns on the Resurrection, of which I cite several strophes,

Hymn on the Resurrection 1

God's initiative: 3. He sprinkled dew and life-giving rain
on Mary, the thirsty earth.
Like a seed of wheat he fell again to Sheol
to spring up as a sheaf, as the new Bread.
Blessed is His offering.

    6. From on high He flowed like a river,
from Mary He [sprouted] as from a root,
from the Cross he descended as a fruit,
as the first fruit He ascended to heaven.
Blessed is His will!

Divine-human exchange:

    7. The Word came forth from the Father's womb,
He put on the body in another womb;
from one womb to another did he proceed,
and chaste wombs are filled with Him.
Blessed is He who has resided in us! [85]

---

[85] EPHREM THE SYRIAN, *Hymn on the Resurrection* 1, in *Select Poems*, tr., ed., S.P. Brock – G.A. Kiraz, Brigham Young UP, Provo UT 2006, 82-85.

Hymn on the Resurrection 2

Human co-operation and public service:

> 9. Let the chief pastor weave together
>   his homilies like flowers,
>
> Let the priests make a garland of their ministry,
>   the deacons of their reading,
>
> strong young men of their jubilant shout,
>   children of their psalms,
>
> chaste women of their songs,
>   chief citizens of their benefactions,
>
> ordinary folk of their manner of life.
>   Blessed is He who gave us so many
>   opportunities for good! [86]

In this last strophe each one of the faithful is called to serve the Lord according to their state of life and ministry in the Christian community. For Ephrem, first God communicates with humanity from the Silence of his ineffable Being by the divine Utterance, the Word, through the creation and incarnation; and we respond by moving towards God, participating in the divine life first by expressing gratitude vocally, then in the Christian way of life and finally in the silence of interior praise.[87]

In our Latin prayer too, we have seen many of the same characteristics; God's initiative, *excita in Ecclesia tua*; divine-human exchange, *corpore et mente renovati*; our human co-operation as response, *adoptionis spiritum*; and our Christian response throughout life, all leading to our showing God pure service, *ut ... puram tibi exhibeamus servitutem*.

The Christian experience of undergoing transformation, and the importance of our continual and definitive passing from one stage of maturation to the next through co-operating with divine grace, as we are enabled, is brought to light in the Latin prayer we have studied. It teaches that everyone belonging to God's Church (*Ecclesiae tua*), whether baptised this year at the vigil or not, is to make continual progress by co-operating actively and passively with the divine self-gift in an intimate union.

---

[86] EPHREM THE SYRIAN, *Hymn on the Resurrection* 2, in *Select Poems*, tr., ed., S.P. Brock, 176-177.

[87] S. BROCK, *The Luminous Eye: The Spiritual Vision of St Ephrem* (Cistercian Studies 124) Kalamazoo MI 1992, 79.

Bibliography

A. Holy Scripture

Biblia Sacra Vulgata, ed. R. Weber, Deutsche Bibelgesellschaft, Stuttgart [4]1994.
*The Holy Bible Containing the Old and New Testaments with the Apocryphal /
    Deuterocanonical Books, New Revised Standard Version*, Oxford UP, New York –
    Oxford 1989.

B. Research tools

BRUYLANTS, P., *Les oraisons du Missel Romain, texte et histoire* (Études liturgiques 2 vol.),
    Mont César, Louvain 1952.
Corpus orationum, 14 vol., ed. E. Moeller – J.-M. Clément – B.C. 't Wallant (Corpus
    christianorum series latina 160-160 M), Brepols, Turnhout 1992-2004.
GILDERSLEEVE, B.L, - G. LODGE, *Gildersleeve's Latin Grammar*, Bolchazy-Carducci,
    Wauconda IL 2003, reprint of [3]1985.
LEWIS, C.T.,- C. SHORT, *A Latin Dictionary*, Oxford UP, Oxford – New York 1879,
    reprinted 1995.
PAYNE-SMITH, R., *A Compendious Syriac Dictionary*, Clarendon, Oxford 1976.

C. Patristic sources

ATHANASIUS ALEXANDRINUS, *De incarnatione*, tr. ed., F.L. Cross, Clapham Press,
    London 2007.
AUGUSTINUS HIPPONENSIS, *Confessionum Libri XIII*, ed. L. Verheijen (Corpus
    christianorum series latina 27), Brepols, Turnhout 1981.
_____, *Sermo 375B. Sermo Aurelii Augustini in die primo sancti paschae 5* (= Sermo 375
    B in *Études critiques sur les sermons authentiques de Saint Augustin*, ed. P.P.
    Verbraken, [Instrumenta patristica 12] Abbatia S. Petri, Steenbrugge 1976), in
    Sancti Augustini sermones post Maurinos Reperti, ed. G. Morin (Miscellanea
    Agostiniana. Testi e studi 1), Typis polyglottis Vaticanis, Rome 1930.
_____, *Sermo Guelferbytanus 3*, ed. A. Hamman, (Patrologia Latina Supplementum
    2) Garnier, Paris 1960, 545-546; *Liturgia Horarum 2: Tempus Quadragesima et
    Tempus Pasquale*, Libreria Editrice Vaticana, Città del Vaticano 2000,
    "Hebdomada sancta, feria secunda", 347.
Les Constitutions Apostoliques, 3 vol., ed. M. Metzger (Sources Chrétiennes 320, 329,
    336), Le Cerf, Paris 1985, 1986, 1987.
CYRILLUS HIEROSOLYMITANIS, *Mystagogical Catechesis*, ed. F.L. Cross, SPCK, London
    1951.
EPHREM SYRUS, *Hymns on Paradise*, tr., ed. S.P. Brock, St Vladimir's Seminary Press,
    New York 1989.
_____, *Select Poems*, tr., ed., S.P. Brock – G.A. Kiraz, Brigham Young UP, Provo UT
    2006.
IRENAEUS LUGDUNENSIS, *Adversus Haereses*, in *Contre les heresies livre IV: Édition critique
    d'après les versions Arménienne et Latine, Texte et traduction*, ed. A. Rousseau –

B. Hemmerlinger – L. Doutreleau – Ch. Mercier (Sources Chrétiennes 100, 2), Le Cerf, Paris 1965.

LUCIUS CAECILIUS FIRMIANUS LACTANTIUS, *Opera omnia* (Corpus scriptorum ecclesiasticorum latinorum 19) ed. S. Brandt – G. Laubmann, Tempsky – Freitag, Prague – Vienna – Leipzig 1890.

SIRICIUS, *Epist. 1, ad Himerium Episcopum* 2 (*Patrologia cursus completa, Series latina* 13), 1131-1148.

La Tradition Apostolique de Saint Hippolyte: *Essai de reconstruction*, ed. B. Botte (Liturgiewissenschaftliche Quellen und Forschungen 39), Aschendorff, Münster ⁵1989.

D. Liturgical sources

The Anglican Missal, The Society of SS. Peter and Paul, London 1921.

"Gregorianum paduense ad fidem codicis Paduensis D 47, Fragmentis collatis Salisburgensibus", *Le Sacramentaire Grégorien*, 3 vol., ed. J. Deshusses (Spicilegium Friburgense 16), Éditions universitaires, Fribourg ³1992, 1, 607-684, (*Pad* 1992).

Les Ordines Romani du haut moyen âge. Tome II: Les textes (*Ordines I-XIII*), ed. M. Andrieu, (Spicilegium Sacrum Lovaniense. Études et documents 23), Spicilegium Sacrum Lovaniense, Louvain 1948.

Liber sacramentorum paduensis (*Padova, Biblioteca Capitolare, cod. D. 47*), ed. A. Catella – F. Dell'Oro – A. Martini (Bibliotheca Ephemerides Liturgicae, Subsidia 131. Monumenta italiae liturgica 3), Centro Liturgico Vincenziano edizioni liturgiche, Rome 2005 (*Pad* 2005).

Liber sacramentorum romanae aeclesiae ordinis anni circuli (*Cod. Vat. Reg. Lat. 316/Paris Bibl. Nat. 7193, 41/56*) (*Sacramentarium Gelasianum*), ed. L.C. Mohlberg – L. Eizenhöfer – P. Siffrin (Rerum ecclesiasticarum documenta. Series maior, Fontes 4), Herder, Rome ³1981 (*Gelas V*).

The Manual of Catholic Devotion, Church Literature Association, London 1950-1969, Canterbury Press, Norwich 2001.

Missale Anglicanum: *The English Missal*, W. Knott & Son, London 1912, Canterbury Press, Norwich 2001.

Missale gothicum (*Cod. Vat. Reg. Lat. 317*), ed., L.C. Mohlberg (Rerum ecclesiasticarum documenta. Series maior, Fontes 5) Herder, Rome 1961 (*Goth* 1961).

Missale gothicum e codice vaticano reginensi latino 317 editum, ed., E. Rose (Corpus christianorum series latina 159 D) Brepols, Turnhout 2005 (*Goth* 2005).

Missale Romanum ex decreto SS. Concilii Tridentini restitutum summorum pontificum cura recognitum, editio typica, Typis polyglottis Vaticanis, Città del Vaticano 1962.

Missale Romanum ex decreto Sacrosancti Oecumenici Concilii Vaticani II instauratum auctoritate Pauli PP. VI promulgatum Ioannis Pauli PP. II cura recognitum, editio typica tertia, Typis Vaticanis, Città del Vaticano ³2002 (*MR* ³2002).

Ordo baptismi adultorum per gradus catechumenatus dispositi, in *Acta Apostolica Sedis* 54 (1962) 315-338.

Prex Eucharistica, ed. A. Hänggi - I. Pahl, Éditions Universitaires, Fribourg 1968.

Rituale Romanum ex decreto Sacrosancti Oecumenici Concilii Vaticani II instauratum auctoritate Pauli PP. VI promulgatum, Ordo Initiationis Christianae Adultorum, Typis polyglottis Vaticanis, Città del Vaticano 1972 (*OICA*).

Sacramentarium Veronense, ed., L.C. Mohlberg – L. Eizenhöfer – P. Siffrin (Rerum ecclesiasticarum documenta. Series maior, Fontes 1) Herder, Rome [3]1978 (*Leon*).

The Sarum Missal. Edited from Three Early Manuscripts, ed. J. Wickham Legg, Oxford 1916; reproduced Clarendon, Oxford 1969.

Supplement to the Roman Missal for the Dioceses of the Philippines, Paulines, Pasay City 1999.

The Westminster Missal (Missale ad usum Ecclesiae Westmonasteriensis) ed. J. Wickham Legg. (Henry Bradshaw Society vol. 1, 5, 12) Oxford 1891, 1893, 1897; reproduced in 1 vol. Boydell & Brewer, Woodbridge 2000.

E. Translations of liturgical sources

The Office of Holy Week, in Latin and English according to the Roman Missal and Breviary, Keating, Brown and Keating, London [12]1808.

The Roman Missal, revised by decree of the Second Vatican Council and published by the authority of Paul VI, official English texts, Collins, London 1974.

The Roman Ritual: Rite of Christian Initiation of Adults, approved for use in England and Wales, Scotland, International Commission on English in the Liturgy, Geoffrey Chapman, London 1987.

The Roman Ritual: Rite of Christian Initiation of Adults, Study Edition. International Commission on English in the Liturgy and US Bishops' Committee on the Liturgy, Liturgy Training Publications, Chicago IL 1988.

The Sacramentary, Catholic Book Publishing Company, New York 1985.

The Sunday Missal, Collins, London 1974.

F. Magisterial sources

Coetus a studiis 22: De Sacramentis, Consilium ad exsequendam Constitutionem de Sacra Liturgia. Schemata. 1965-1969. Care of Hesburgh Library, University of Notre Dame IN (Archive material for the *Rite of Christian Initiation of Adults*).

Decrees of the Ecumenical Councils, 2 vol., ed. N. Tanner, Sheed & Ward – Georgetown UP, London-Washington 1990.

PAUL PP. VI, Litterae apostolicae motu proprio datae, *Sacram liturgiam*, die 25 ianuarii 1964, *AAS* 56 (1964) 139-144.

G. Studies

AUGÉ, M., "Le collette del Proprio del Tempo nel nuovo Messale", *Ephemerides Liturgica* 84 (1970) 275-298.

BÉRAUDY, R., "Le nouveau rituel du Baptême des adultes", *La Maison Dieu* 121 (1975) 122-142.

BROCK, S., *The Luminous Eye: The Spiritual World Vision of St Ephrem* (Cistercian Studies 124), Kalamazoo MI 1992.

BROVELLI, F., "Linee teologico-pastorali a proposito di iniziazione cristiana dall'analisi dei nuovi rituali", *Iniziazione cristiana e immagine di Chiesa*, ed. G. Angelini (Teologia pratica 2) Elle di Ci, Leumann (Turin) 1982, 185-219.

BUGNINI, A., *The Reform of the Liturgy 1948-1975*, tr. M.J. O'Connell, Liturgical Press, Collegeville MN 1990.

CAPELLE, B., "L'introduction du catéchuménat à Rome", *Histoire: varia, l'Assomption* (Travaux liturgiques de doctrine et d'histoire 3 vol.), Centre Liturgique, Mont César, Louvain 1967, 3, 186-210.

CHAVASSE, A., *La liturgie de la ville de Rome du Ve au VIIIe siècle: Une liturgie conditionnée par l'organisation de la vie in Urbe et extra muros* (Studia Anselmiana 112, Analecta Liturgica 18), Pontificium Athenaeum Anselmianum, Rome 1993.

_____, *Le Sacramentaire Gélasien (Vaticanus Reginensis 316): Sacramentaire presbytéral en usage dans le titres Romains au VIIe siècle* (Bibliothèque de théologie. Série 4: Histoire de la Théologie 1), Desclée, Tournai 1958.

CHUPUNGCO, A.J., *Liturgies of the Future: Process and Methods of Inculturation*, Paulist, Mahwah NY 1989.

_____, *Towards a Filipino Liturgy*, Benedictine Abbey, Manila 1976.

CLARK, N., "Spirit Christology in the Light of Eucharistic Theology", *Heythrop Journal* 23 (1982) 270-284.

DE BLAAUW, S., *Cultus et decor: Liturgia e architettura nella Roma tardoantica e medievale*, 2 vol. (Studi e Testi 355, 356), Biblioteca Apostolica Vaticana, Città del Vaticano 1994.

DE ZAN, R., "Criticism and Interpretation of Liturgical Texts", in *Introduction to the Liturgy*, ed. A.J. Chupungco (Handbook for Liturgical Studies 1), Liturgical Press (Pueblo Book), Collegeville MN 1997, 331-365 (En. tr. of R. DE ZAN, "Introduzione alla Liturgia, Ermeneutica", ed. A. J. Chupungco [*Scientia Liturgica: Manuale di Liturgia* 1] Piemme, Casale Monferrato 1998, 356-389).

DUMAS, A., "Le Missel Romain 1970", *Paroisse et Liturgie* 4 (1970) 291-296.

_____, "Les oraisons du nouveau Missel Romain", *Questions Liturgiques* 52 (1971) 263-270.

_____, "Le orazioni del Messale: Criteri di scelta e di composizione", *Rivista Liturgica* 58 (1971) 92-102.

_____, "Pour mieux comprendre les textes du Missel Romain", *Notitiae* 6 (1970) 194-213.

_____, "Les sources du nouveau Missel Romain", *Notitiae* 7 (1971) 37-42, 74-77, 94-95, 134-136, 276-280, 409-410.

GOULBURN, E.M., *The Collects of the Day*, 2 vol., Longmans, Green & Co., London – New York – Bombay 1891.

The Integral Human Formation of Candidates for the Priesthood, ed. Jeannine Guindon, tr. T. Prendergast, Éditions Paulines, Sherbrooke QC 1993.

KAVANAGH, A., "Christian Initiation in Post-Conciliar Roman Catholicism. A Brief Report", *Studia Liturgica* 12 (1977) 107-115.

_____, "The New Roman Rites of Adult Initiation", *Studia Liturgica* 10 (1974) 35-47.

_____, *The Shape of Baptism: The Rite of Christian Initiation*, Pueblo, New York 1978.

LEACHMAN, J.G., "Eucharistic Worship and Texts as Sources for Theological Reflection", *East Asian Pastoral Review* 42 (2005) 230-248.

_____, "The Role of the Holy Spirit in the Catechumenal Preparation for Baptism in *OICA*", in *Spiritus spiritalia nobis dona potenter infundit*, ed. E. Carr (Studia Anselmiana 139), Pontificium Institutum Liturgicum, Rome 2006, 277-292.

_____, "The Transforming Power of the Holy Spirit in the period of Enlightenment and Purification in *RCIA*", *Studia Liturgica* 34 (2007) 185-200.

_____, – D.P. McCARTHY, "The Formation of the Ecclesial Person through Baptismal Preparation and the Celebrations in the *OICA*: The Collects for the Scrutinies," *The Liturgical Subject: Subject, Subjectivity, and the Human Person in Contemporary Liturgical Discussion and Critique*, ed. J. Leachman, SCM – Notre Dame, London – South Bend IN 2008, 172-200.

_____, – D.P. McCARTHY, "Preparation for the Piazza: The Preface of the Second Scrutiny (the Fourth Sunday in Lent): The Mystagogical Formation of the Neophytes and the Assembly", Societas Liturgica Conference, 11 August 2007, *Studia Liturgica* 38 (2008) 114-133.

LODI, E., "La Liturgia: Teologia mistagogica: Introduzione generale allo studio della liturgia", *Liturgia della Chiesa*, Edizioni Dehoniane, Bologna 1999, 21-226.

McCARTHY, D.P., "Self-transcending Gift", *The Tablet* (10 February 2007) 18; "Giving as One and as Many", *The Tablet* (17 February 2007) 15.

MITCHELL, N., *Eucharist as Sacrament of Initiation*, Liturgical Training Publications – North American Forum for the Catechumenate (Forum Essays 2), Liturgical Training Publications, Chicago IL 2003.

MOORE, G., *Vatican II and the Collects of Ordinary Time: A Study in the Missal (1975)*, International Scholars Press, San Francisco – London – Bethesda 1998.

NEUNHEUSER, B., *Storia della Liturgia attraverso le epoche culturali* (Bibliotheca Ephemerides Liturgicae, Subsidia 11), Centro Liturgico Vincenziano edizioni liturgiche, Rome ²1983.

PINELL, J., "Liturgie locali antiche (origine e sviluppo)", *Nuovo Dizionario di Liturgia*, ed. D. Sartore – A.M. Triacca, Paoline, Cinisello Balsamo MI 1984, 776-783.

RAHNER, H., *Greek Myths and Christian Mystery*, tr. B. Battershaw, Biblo and Tannen, New York 1971 (of *Griechische Mythen in christlicher Deutung*).

REGAN, P., "Pneumatological and Eschatological Aspects of Liturgical Celebration", *Worship* 51 (1977) 332-350.

SERRA, D.E., *The Blessing of Baptismal Water at the Paschal Vigil (Ge 444-448): Its Origins, Evolution and Reform,* (Thesis ad Lauream 136) Pontificium Athenaeum S. Anselmi de Urbe, Pontificium Institutum Liturgicum, Rome 1989.

TALLEY, T.J., *The Origins of the Liturgical Year*, Liturgical Press (Pueblo Book), Collegeville MN ²1991.

VOGEL, C., *Medieval Liturgy: An Introduction to the Sources*, tr., rev. W.G. Storey – N.K. Rasmussen (National Association of Pastoral Musicians Studies in Church Music and Liturgy), Pastoral Press, Washington DC 1986 (of *Introduction aux sources de l'histoire du culte chrétien au moyen âge*, Centro italiano di studi sull'alto medioevo, Spoleto 1981).

CHAPTER 6

An Anglican Experiment in Appreciating the Liturgy: The Easter Day Collect (First Holy Communion) in The First Prayer Book of Edward VI

Bridget Nichols

Introduction

Anglicans have, historically, taken a keen interest in the style and diction of their prayers. More recently, and in line with a number of Churches, they have seen the need to develop a language of prayer capable of responding to contemporary culture. At its broadest, this realisation has entailed the search for an idiom, at once dignified and readily comprehensible to worshippers at all levels of sophistication. It has also drawn attention to particular constituencies, often those who have felt themselves excluded by the language of the Church's prayer. The grammatical structure of Anglican prayer has not, however, received much attention as a key to understanding and interpretation.[1] The invitation to join in an already well-established conversation about the method of analysing and interpreting liturgical texts has, therefore, been both a challenge and a revelation. It also brings with it a number of preliminary questions. Some of these are contained by the decision to use the collect as the subject matter. But within these limits, the choice of examples, and the clear articulation of the purpose for the exercise have had to be properly defined.

---

[1] Examples of close reading often depend more on the use of literary devices, e.g. G. CUMING, *The Godly Order*, SPCK/Alcuin Club, London 1983; D. GRAY, "Cranmer and the Collects" in *The Oxford Handbook of English Literature and Theology*, ed. A. HASS – D. Jasper, - E. Jay, Oxford UP, Oxford 2007, 561-574; B. NICHOLS, *Liturgical Hermeneutics*, Peter Lang, Frankfurt – New York 1996. A semiotic approach is well demonstrated in J.A. ZIMMERMAN, *Liturgy as Language of Faith: A Liturgical Methodology in the Mode of Paul Ricoeur's Textual Hermeneutics*, University Press of America, Lanham MA 1988.

This paper will concentrate on the collect for the first Holy Communion on Easter Day as it appeared in the *First Prayer Book of Edward VI* in 1549.[2] While there might have been strong arguments for choosing a prayer in contemporary language, perhaps much more recently composed, there are two major considerations in favour of a sixteenth-century example. The first of these concerns clarity. Here is an opportunity to observe a direct transmission process from Latin to English. Later on, the route becomes much more convoluted, as English prayers begin to evolve out of other English texts, and not – at any rate not directly – from Latin compositions. The second consideration is historical and doctrinal. The 1549 collect vividly expresses the Reformed mindset, whose formative influence on the Anglican tradition of prayer has been immense. Both of these factors have been important in establishing conditions for experimenting with an unfamiliar method of analysis. With some optimism, I hope that the process described in the paper may, at a further stage of development, be the foundation for readings of contemporary material.

1. Applying the methodology of the Pontifical Institute of Liturgy

By looking closely at the English text and its Latin models and predecessors, I want to offer some thoughts about what makes the distinctiveness of an Anglican collect, how it stands in a tradition and what its intentional and formational function might be, as an inherited tradition develops in a new direction. The method of reading that proceeds through grammatical and hermeneutical analysis towards a synthesis provides a shape and a discipline. What has become evident in the attempt to apply this analytical method to the English text, however, is a difference of objective.

A principal aim, in relation to the Latin text, is to work towards the best possible translation through a process of careful exposition of the grammatical and hermeneutical structures of the prayer itself. Only after the intricacies of the mechanism have been properly assimilated, and other features revealed (e.g. the pathway of a prayer's development, the transmission and sometimes rediscovery of texts, and the influence of particular doctrinal debates at the time of composition), will a translation emerge that represents not simply a faithful transfer of the words into another language, but also a rich set of insights into historical conditions, world view and doctrine at the time of the prayer's first appearance. As Renato De Zan explains, "[a] full-fledged translation will come only after we

---

[2] Collects for matins and for a second Holy Communion were also provided, the latter an original composition.

know and understand all the dynamics of the text – in other words, at the end of the methodological process".[3]

When we turn to the English prayer, the first aim, in applying a programme of clausal analysis, is not to produce a good translation, but to form an understanding of the way in which the vernacular text has come into being.[4] This might involve close reference to an original Latin text, and the 1549 Easter collect is a case in point, but the focus will be on the interpretative decisions made in arriving at an English formula. Where this has involved the substitution of material expressing a different doctrinal position from that of the original, or subtly nuancing the thought of the original, parallel examination of the two texts will often make things clearer. At every stage, though, we need to bear in mind that two different languages are involved, and that some things are possible in one which would be either impossible or unnatural in the other. Those considerations, as well as the guardianship of doctrine, have shaped our prayers.

2. General historical context

The *First Prayer Book of Edward VI*, issued in 1549 as the only legal rite of the English Church, was not a clean break from what had gone before. The Sarum Rite had *de facto* become the official order of worship across most of England through the later Middle Ages, although the preface to the *Prayer Book* mentions the Uses of Hereford, York, Bangor and Lincoln as well. In addition, primers, or collections containing English translations of the *Hours of the Virgin*, the *Office of the Dead*, and some psalms and familiar prayers, were popular aids to personal devotion.[5] The compilers of the *Prayer Book* preserved elements of the practice in which they had been nurtured, even as

---

[3] R. De ZAN, "Criticism and Interpretation of Liturgical Texts", in *Introduction to the Liturgy*, ed. A.J. Chupungco (Handbook for Liturgical Studies 1), Liturgical Press (Pueblo Book), Collegeville MN 1997, 331-365 (En. tr. of R. DE ZAN, "Introduzione alla Liturgia, Ermeneutica", ed. A. J. Chupungco [*Scientia Liturgica: Manuale di Liturgia I*, Piemme, Casale Monferrato 1998, 356-389]), 347.

[4] Daniel McCarthy's articles on the Collects and Prayers over the Gifts (*Tablet* 2007-2008) introduce discussion of published English translations, but their starting point and primary focus remain the Latin text. The English text is treated, amongst other things, in order to show where historical or pastoral considerations have led to significant departures from the original.

[5] A very useful and attractively produced survey of the use of the primers in England can be found in E. DUFFY, *Marking the Hours. English People and Their Prayers 1240-1570*, Yale UP, New Haven – London 2006. The standard work remains C. BUTTERWORTH, *The English Primers 1529-1545*, University of Pennsylvania Press, Philadelphia 1953; E. Hoskins, *Horae Beatae Mariae Virginis or Sarum and York Primers*, Longmans, Green & Co., London – New York 1901 has some textual variants which Butterworth omits.

they strove to introduce Reformed doctrine into the texture of the Church's prayer.

Eamon Duffy describes the 1549 *Prayer Book* as representing "radical discontinuity with traditional religion", but admits that it "preserved the basic pattern of parochial worship, matins, Mass, and evensong".[6] The most serious transformation, he believes, was in "lay experience of the Mass".[7] Geoffrey Cuming, on the other hand, suggests that the *Prayer Book's* components and the shape of its services had not in fact departed very far from its Sarum predecessor. The reasons for this were political – "it was wise to retain at any rate an outward appearance of continuity". At the same time, Cuming points out, "the sound of the English language in the new rite must have destroyed most of the traditional flavour that is apparent to the reader".[8] It is significant that the *Prayer Book* chooses the rite most obviously involving the liturgical formation of children – "The Order for Public Baptism of Infants" – as an occasion for acknowledging that important formulae were not yet written in English on the hearts of worshippers. The exhortation to parents and godparents at the end of the rite instructs them to "prouyde that [the newly baptised] maye learne the Crede, the Lordes prayer, and the ten commaundements in the english tong … ".[9]

Archbishop Thomas Cranmer, the principal architect of the first and second prayer books of Edward VI (published in 1552) had already gained some experience as a liturgical translator in 1544, when King Henry VIII commissioned him to produce an English text of the Litany, popularly known as 'processions' because it was sung as priest and people processed round the streets.[10]

By October 1545, a new litany for festival days had been added to the repertoire. In a much quoted letter to the King on 7th October of that year, Cranmer explained what he had done, and hinted strongly at the measures he had had to adopt in order to create something suited to the needs of the English Church at that time:

> I have translated into the English tongue, so well as I could in so short time, certain processions, to be used upon festival days, if after due correction and amendment of the same your highness shall think it so convenient. In which translation, forasmuch as many of the processions, the

---

[6] E. DUFFY, *The Stripping of the Altars. Traditional Religion in England 1400-1580*, Yale UP, New Haven – London 1992, 464.

[7] DUFFY, *The Stripping of the Altars*, 464.

[8] G. CUMING, "Thomas Cranmer. Translator and Writer" in *Language and the Worship of the Church*, ed. D. Jasper – R.C.D. Jasper, Macmillan, London 1990, 111.

[9] F.E. BRIGHTMAN, *The English Rite*, 2 vol. Rivingtons, London 1915, 2, 744.

[10] Jasper Ridley, in his biography of Cranmer, notes that this Litany "abolished the invocation of the Saints altogether by substituting a general appeal to Saints along with patriarchs and prophets" (J. RIDLEY, *Thomas Cranmer*, Clarendon Press, Oxford 1962, 247).

Latin, were but barren as meseemed, and little fruitful, I was constrained to use more than the liberty of a translator: for in some processions I have altered divers words; for by cause the matter appeared to me to be little to purpose, or by cause the days be not with us festival-days; and some processions I have added whole, because I thought I had better matter for the purpose, than was the procession in Latin: the judgment whereof I refer wholly unto your majesty ....[11]

When attention turned to the collects a little later, the limits of the "liberty of a translator" were tested further, for the saints' day provisions were not the only items to be keenly scrutinised and sometimes changed altogether to fit into the programme of reform. A new interpretation of the role of grace in salvation is, if not dominant, then certainly frequently articulated in a number of the *Prayer Book* collects.

3. Genesis of the *Prayer Book* collects

There was already a small but well-known collection of prayers in English, popularised by the primers. Cuming lists twelve collects which survived from the primers into the *Prayer Book*, four of them Sunday collects (notably Pentecost and Trinity) and three of them saints' day collects, including that for the Feast of the Annunciation, which was recited in a number of the hours during the day.[12]

He infers from the ratio of new collects to translations and adaptations that the 84 collects for Sundays and feast days were produced fairly fast: "It is ... noticeable that, whereas Cranmer begins the year at once with new collects for Advent 1 and 2, he is content to translate or adapt all the collects for the Sundays after Trinity. Either time or enthusiasm for new composition seems to have run out".[13]

In the end, it was only those collects expressing doctrine inconsistent with Reformed teaching, which were heavily revised or entirely rewritten. Most of these were for saints' days, where the Sarum source had asked for the saint's personal intercessions. Cuming notes, however, that Cranmer seemed to have a "psychological need ... to use someone else's work as a starting point" for producing a text, even though what he produced sometimes diverged quite widely from the original.[14]

What we can deduce about the process suggests an earnestness about the meaning of prayers, no doubt sharpened by the fact that prayers in the vernacular would be easily understood by churchgoers and should therefore

---

[11] "Letter 276 to King Henry VIII", *Miscellaneous Writings and Letters of Thomas Cranmer*, ed. J.E. Cox (Parker Society), Cambridge UP, Cambridge 1846, 412.

[12] G. CUMING, *The Godly Order*, Alcuin Club/ SPCK, London 1983, 51-55.

[13] CUMING, *The Godly Order*, 56.

[14] CUMING, "Thomas Cranmer", 112.

not encourage erroneous ideas. More was at stake, then, than producing good translations. Where new texts were composed (good examples are Advent I and Ash Wednesday), they were noticeably attentive to the day's readings. In the case of saints' days, where the scriptural record often said very little, the *Prayer Book* collects referred only to scripturally verifiable details of their lives and the importance of following their example. Thus there was already a new determination, not found in the rites on which the *Prayer Book* mainly modelled itself, to forge links between collect and lections.

4. The Easter Day collect

Although the new *Prayer Book* did not assume its status in law until Pentecost on 9th June 1549, the laborious nature of sixteenth-century printing required that it be with the printers much earlier in the year. Three printers were permitted to undertake the printing and the first copies were ready by 7th March.[15] A statute governing the Book's implementation required that it be put into use within three weeks of purchase, if copies had been acquired before the official inaugural date of 9th June. Contemporary evidence confirms that several London churches adopted the new provisions almost immediately.[16] The fact that the *Prayer Book* was introduced in some places several months before it became mandatory, suggests that, at least in London, there was little sense of compulsion and a significant measure of active enthusiasm. The exiled Strasbourg Reformer, Martin Bucer, wrote home soon after his arrival in England in the spring of 1549 to report his observations. He commented approvingly: "It much refreshed us...that everything in the churches is read and sung in the vernacular tongue, that the doctrine of justification is purely and soundly taught, and the eucharist is administered according to Christ's ordinance, private masses having been abolished".[17] We know that there was another side to the picture, and that riots broke out in Devon and Cornwall in response to the imposition of the *Prayer Book*. These were geographically contained, however, and a generally receptive climate seems to have prevailed.

---

[15] I. ROBINSON, *The Establishment of Modern English Prose in the Reformation and the Enlightenment*, Cambridge UP, Cambridge 1988, 87. Two London printers and a Worcester printer were engaged for this task.

[16] T. LATHBURY, *A History of the Book of Common Prayer and Other Books of Authority*, John Henry and James Parker, Oxford – London 1858, 27.

[17] D. McCulloch, *Thomas Cranmer. A Life*, Yale UP, New Haven – London 1996, 411-412 quotes from original printed in *Epistolae Tigurinae*, Parker Society, Cambridge 1848, 349-350; and in *Original Letters Relative to the English Reformation*, 2 vol., ed. H. Robinson, Parker Society, Cambridge 1846-1847, 535-536.

Easter fell on Sunday 21ˢᵗ April in 1549, and churches, which had taken advantage of the early arrival of copies, would have used the new *Order for Holy Communion*, including the new English collect. This marks a fascinating moment in liturgical history, since it is not often possible to say precisely when a prayer was first used. What the people heard was this:

> Almightie God, which through thy onely begotten sonne Iesus Christ, hast ouercome death, & opened vnto vs the gate of euerlasting life: we humbly beseeche thee, that as by thy speciall grace, preuentyng us, thou doest put in our mindes good desires: so by thy continuall helpe, we may bring thesame to good effect, thorough Iesus Christ our Lord: who liueth and reigneth.&c.[18]

The primary source is likely to have been the Sarum Missal:

> Deus qui hodierna die per Unigenitum tuum aeternitatis nobis aditum devicta morte reserasti: vota nostra quae praeveniendo aspiras etiam adjuvando prosequere.[19]

The Sarum version derives, in turn, from the *Hadrianum*:

> Deus qui hodierna die per unigenitum tuum eternitatis nobis aditum deuicta morte reserasti, uota nostra quae praeueniendo adspiras, etiam adiuuando prosequere. Per eundem dominum nostrum.[20]

5. Analysis and synthesis

5.1 *Analysis*
Invocation. The English prayer begins with the complex formula, "Almightie God", expanding its Latin source, which begins simply *Deus*, "God", or "O

---

[18] BRIGHTMAN, *The English Rite*, 1, 396.
[19] Sarum Missal n° 24, in M. DUDLEY, *The Collect in Anglican Liturgy: Texts and Sources 1549 –1989*, (Alcuin Club Collection 72), Liturgical Press, Collegeville MN 1994, 48. See also: F.H. DICKINSON, *The Sarum Missal*. J. Parker, Oxford – London 1861-1883, repr. Gregg International Publishers, Farnborough 1969, 359.
[20] "Hadrianum ex authentico" n° 383, *Le Sacramentaire Grégorien: Ses principales formes d'après les plus anciens manuscrits*, 3 vol., ed. J. Deshusses (Spicilegium Friburgense 16), Éditions universitaires, Fribourg ³1992, 1, 83-348, where it appears under the following heading: "88. ORTN IN DOMINICA SANCTA AD MISS". The only textual variant noted in the critical apparatus is the omission of *eundem* in the Sacramentary of Saint-Gall, Cologne 137. Daniel McCarthy draws attention to the *Veronense* text: *Deus, qui per unigenitum tuum aeternitatis nobis adytum deuicta morte reserasti, da nobis, quaesumus, ut qui resurrectionis sollempnia colimus, per innouatione tui spiritus a morte animae resurgamus.* (*Sacramentarium Gelasianum* n° 463 ed. L.C. Mohlberg – L. Eizenhöfer – P. Siffrin, [Rerum ecclesiasticarum documenta. Series maior, Fontes 4] Herder, Rome ³1981, 76).

God". This is typical of Prayer Book language, and probably reflects a style of formal invocation normally adopted when addressing social superiors or people in positions of authority. The conventions of letter-writing at the time may provide the best evidence of such forms of address, and a number of Cranmer's letters to Thomas Crumwell, the King's Vice-Gerent, survive. These never begin less formally than, "My Lord", and most often begin, "My most singular dear Lord".[21]

Prose rhythm is another factor to be taken into account. *Deus*, although it might invite translation by the single one-syllable word, God, has two syllables. An initial monosyllable in an English prayer has an odd and abrupt character, which distorts the recitation of what follows.[22] There are, admittedly, several modern examples of English collects which do not elaborate the address and simply begin, "God", but this does not fall attractively on the ear.[23]

The elaborate form is not merely rhetorical or prosodically convenient, however. John Dowden, a late nineteenth-century commentator, suggested that Cranmer and his colleagues sought to mitigate the "undue severity" and "deficiency of warmth" in translating certain Latin collects.[24] Dowden saw "their addition of adjectival epithets" not only as necessary for "rhythmical effect", but also as a means to add "emphasis", "colour", and "feeling", and singled out "Almighty" before the name of God as "a kind of homage of the heart that loves to dwell on divine attributes".[25]

This prayer's singling out of omnipotence as a divine attribute has to do with expectation as well as homage. In offering an initial description of God on which the rest of the prayer depends, the adjective functions proleptically. This is the God who can do all things, invoked by the people who can do nothing without him. Here, God is "Almightie" principally because he has "overcome death and opened unto us the gate of everlasting life". What follows will be based on this set of expectations.

Amplification. The address, "Almightie God", is amplified by the relative clause, "which through thy onely begotten sonne Iesus Christ, hast overcome death, & opened unto us the gate of everlasting life". While this is

---

[21] See examples in *Miscellaneous Writings*, ed. J.E. Cox (Parker Society).

[22] Oddly, this does not seem to affect other forms of statement or narrative, e.g. "James has left for Paris", presumably because there is not a caesura immediately following the monosyllable.

[23] See the following collects: Advent 3; Trinity 18; Trinity 20; 3rd Sunday before Advent, ARCHBISHOPS' COUNCIL OF THE CHURCH OF ENGLAND, *Common Worship Additional Collects*, Church House Publishing, London 2004. The 1549 *Prayer Book* collect for the Fifth Sunday after Easter begins 'Lord'. This seems exceptional, and in 1662 it was revised to 'O Lord'. The collect for the First Sunday after Trinity begins, 'God …'. The tendency of English prose to use iambic rhythms is not irrelevant here.

[24] J. DOWDEN, *The Workmanship of the Prayer Book*, Methuen, London 1899, 122.

[25] DOWDEN, *The Workmanship*, Methuen, 122.

closely dependent on its Latin source, "qui hodierna die per Unigenitum tuum aeternitatis nobis aditum deuicta morte reserasti",[26] it also departs from the Latin in significant ways. This amplification immediately makes the two claims of a resurrection faith – that God has overcome death and made available to us the way to eternal life. Whereas the Latin text partially isolates these two events from one another by according the conquest of death the independence of the ablative absolute, *deuicta morte*, they are given grammatical equivalence in the English text, which uses two finite verbs, both dependent on God, who acts through the Son. Thus, the grammatical link between God and the conquest of death becomes much more explicit. Literary devices offer strategic support, so that the statement of salvation, achieved through Jesus Christ, is internally tied together by assonance, as "*o*nely" leads to "*o*vercome" and then to "*o*pened". In a different way, the antithesis of "death" and "everlasting life" reinforces the same point.

The power of God which is conventionally declared in the invocation is now underpinned by a precise value. As the invocation works proleptically, here the direction is reversed: these two things, impossible for human beings, have been achieved because God is 'Almightie'. Since God acts through Christ, the relative clause and its embedded prepositional phrase (*per Unigenitum tuum*) also introduce the unique relationship between the Father and the Only-begotten, whose mutual generosity is extended to God's adopted children.

The phrase *hodierna die*, 'on this day', has been conspicuously omitted in the translation. This is consistent with a number of other collects, where *hodie* is not reflected in English, and exemplifies the Reformers' determination to avoid confusing repetition with re-enactment. This applies most obviously to the Prayer of Consecration, which makes the point emphatically by referring to Christ's 'one oblation once offered', and to his 'full, perfect and sufficient sacrifice, oblation and satisfaction'.[27] The doctrinal ambiguity, furthermore, is not ignored in shorter prayers such as collects, and in this case, any notion that the death and resurrection of Christ might recur annually in a realistic way is firmly discouraged.[28]

It would be easy to conclude from this that the prayer was inviting a purely commemorative interpretation, and that any hint of the continuing and lively effectiveness of the events of salvation, in other words their anamnetic content, was being suppressed. Yet two factors militate against a memorialist reading. The first is the use of the perfect tense, "hast overcome"

---

[26] Author's translation: "who on this day, through your Only-Begotten, have unsealed for us the entrance to eternity, death having been overcome".

[27] BRIGHTMAN, *The English Rite*, 2, 692.

[28] J.A. DEVEREUX, "Reformed Doctrine in the Collects of the *First Book of Common Prayer*", *Harvard Theological Review* 58 (1965), 58. Devereux notes that of eight Latin collects for feast days which use the word *hodie*, their English translations omit this in five cases.

and "[hast] opened", which, like the Latin perfect, is capable of expressing an event in the past whose consequences continue to be effective in the present. The second will be discussed in more detail when we come to the prayer's petition. Briefly, the "speciall grace" of God which goes before us is tacitly associated with his saving actions. We recall them in order to make eschatological sense of a providence which would otherwise be benevolent, but only effective within the finite limits of mortal life. Behind this lies the panoply of Reformation argument for justification by grace, through faith, and the refusal to allow good works any part in the process of salvation. I have delayed discussing this very important doctrinal background to the final part of this discussion.

Means. Encapsulated in the relative clause is a prepositional phrase signifying instrumentality. God acts 'through [his] onely sonne Iesus Christ', a form of words which adds significantly to the Latin source's *per Unigenitum tuum*, 'through your Only-begotten'. I am not aware of any English prayers in which 'only begotten' is not completed by Son, and often also by 'Jesus Christ', and would suggest that this has to do both with easier oral delivery, and with a preference in English for identifying persons by nouns rather than simply by adjectives.

Here, the prayer introduces the second part of a Trinitarian claim, begun in the address to God the Father, which will be completed in the petition. We have seen how the Latin divine passive, *deuicta morte*, gains direct association with God when it is translated in the active voice, as the necessary action that makes possible the offer of eternal life. Now that association acquires a further dimension, by being linked to Christ as means or instrument of divine action, participating in our mortal nature in order that we might participate in the life of eternity.

Petition. To an Anglican ear, "We humbly beseech thee" is a conventional introduction to a petition, expressing awareness of human insignificance in relation to the majesty of God. Yet, at this stage of its development, English was fast losing its capacity to mark status by the use of pronouns. By the early sixteenth century, the custom of addressing superiors as 'you', reserving 'thee' and 'thou' for members of the family, children and servants, had for the most part disappeared. As historians of language have pointed out, the 1549 Prayer Book reinvents a language of formality, but curiously, inverts the previous value of the pronouns in the ecclesiastical setting. Thus God comes to be addressed as 'thee' (with derivatives 'thou', 'thy' and 'thine'), while the congregation is addressed as 'you' or 'ye'.[29] Beyond the immediate situation of the Church, however, 'you' was rapidly

---

[29] A.C. PARTRIDGE, *Tudor to Augustan English*, Andre Deutsch, London 1969, 24-28. See also: D. CRYSTAL, *The Cambridge Encyclopedia of the English Language*, Cambridge UP, Cambridge 1995, 79. Crystal suggests some influence from Biblical translators, who learned their lessons from languages with different second person singular and plural pronouns.

taking over as the formal style of the second person pronoun. As a recent commentator has noted, biblical texts of the time might have had prophets addressing kings as 'thou', but "Cranmer would not have remained Archbishop long if he had done the same to Henry VIII".[30]

The petition does not reflect the grammatical indications of the Latin text, since the condition of humility in approaching God is certainly not implied in "uota nostra … prosequere", "encourage or foster our prayers", and the imperative petition (formed out of a deponent verb) would suggest a different English rendition.[31] "We humbly beseech thee" therefore introduces a new note into the prayer, and the decision to use a formula closer in meaning to *quaesumus supplices*, "we beseech you as supplicants", or *supplicamus*, "we entreat you", for example, should be seen in the context of the whole prayer's background and orientation. It is not the prayer of people who feel able to produce the visible results of God-given "good desires" by their own efforts. In a world where salvation is possible through the grace of God alone, and in which there is nothing we can do to help ourselves, or earn our hope of heaven, there is only one way for petitioners to place themselves before God – as beggars and supplicants.

Complementary final sentence. The petition gives rise to a complex sentence expressing the full weight of its content. This takes the form of "that", followed by the subjunctive, and would correspond to Latin models in which a verb of beseeching is followed by *ut* and the subjunctive. But that is not the form in the Latin prayer, where a single imperative petition, "uota nostra … etiam adiuuando prosequere", announces the request that God would support, nurture and encourage our prayers by giving us his help. One significant reason for the more convoluted English petition is a change of subject. God is named as the gracious author of "good desires"; but it is human beings who (with a good deal of divine assistance) must bring these desires to "good effect".

Instrument. How this is to be achieved depends on the second of two prepositional phrases, since it is only by God's "continuall helpe" – a forceful translation of the Latin *adiuuando*, "by helping" – that we can hope to match right action to a proper orientation of the will. Petitioners can only ever ask that God will assist them as they struggle against their fallible inclinations to live the life of the Kingdom. This is an ongoing struggle. Hence the need for the second condition, God's "continuall helpe". Echoing the Matthean promise, "I am with you always, even to the end of the world", and in that way, adding a pneumatological dimension, this part of the prayer completes the Trinitarian picture which begins in the amplification. The God who enters

---

[30] J. SCRIVENER, "Thee and Thou", *Faith and Worship* 62 (2008), 41. Scrivener quotes I. ROBINSON, *Who Killed the Bible?*, Brynmill Press, Hereford 2006.

[31] Nor is humility implied in the *Veronense* text, which adds an explicit petition, *da quaesumus*, to the earlier formula.

the world and through Jesus Christ redeems mortal nature continues to be present as Paraclete, inspiring, guiding, and directing.

Motive. So far, we have concentrated on the second of two correlatives – "that ... we may bring [good desires] to good effect". This answers an earlier indicative construction, "that as by thy speciall grace preventyng us thou doest put into our mindes good desires", which both explains the origin of the impulses which are to express themselves in practical outworking, and provides the motive for the good effects which will result. In this prayer, inspiration and motive, understood in its radical sense as a force directly impelling action or movement, are simultaneous. The temporal sequence of the Latin prayer, which also expresses the motive for further development in a relative clause embedded in the petition, "uota nostra quae praeueniendo adspiras prosequere", "encourage or nurture our prayers, which you assist by going before us", is thus sharply contracted in the English collect. In part, this is to be explained by the change of subject. There is no smooth continuity from one phase of a single agent's action to another here. Instead, the shift from God to humanity suggests a transfer of responsibility, admittedly carefully supervised "by [God's] continuall helpe".

Instrument. God plants "good desires" in us by "[his] speciall grace, preuentying us". Just as "continuall helpe" offers a strong reading of *adiuuando*, so this formulation offers a strong reading of *praeueniendo*. More than going before (the now obsolete sense in which "preuentyng" is used here), or even leading the way, God's prevenient grace in the English prayer has an added anticipatory force. Human need and weakness are identified and constantly confronted by grace. As careful students of the Pauline Epistles, the Reformers would surely have brought to bear on this subject such evidence as the assertion of God's righteousness acting independently of the law in Romans, so that "all are justified by God's free grace alone, through his act of liberation in the person of Christ Jesus",[32] or Paul's claim to be a minister of the gospel, "by God's gift, bestowed unmerited on me in the working of his power",[33] or his rejection of all worldly status "for the sake of gaining Christ and finding myself incorporate in him, with no righteousness of my own, no legal rectitude, but the righteousness which comes from faith in Christ, given by God in response to faith".[34] Co-operation with the divine will is central in bringing good desires to good effect. How the space between outright surrender of human will, and active, conscious response to divine initiative is negotiated, remains to be considered.

---

[32] Rom 3:21-24. All biblical quotations are from *The Revised English Bible* Oxford UP – Cambridge UP, Oxford – Cambridge 1989.
[33] Eph 3:7
[34] Phil 3:8-9

5.2 *Synthesis*

This prayer, which, as we have seen, is as much an adaptation as a translation, and marks a new doctrinal approach, has affinities with several others in the Prayer Book's sequence of Sunday collects. In different ways, all of these prayers express a desire for the convergence of the human and divine wills in a world where human beings are considered incapable of willing anything good in their own strength. Again and again, it is not the surrender of the independent will, but the positive discovery of the will that desires to work in harmonious obedience with the God who wills good things for his creation, that emerges in these collects.

Thus on the Second Sunday of Lent, the collect begins "Almighty God, which dost see that we have no power of ourselves to help ourselves".[35] On the Fourth Sunday after Easter the plea for convergent wills is more explicit: "Almighty God, which dost make the minds of all faithful men to be of one will; Grant unto thy people, that they may love the thing which thou commandest, and desire that which thou dost promise".[36] The Fifth Sunday after Easter, resembling Easter Day, returns to the question of grace and works: "Lord, from whom all good things do come: grant us thy humble servants, that by thy holy inspiration we may think those things that be good, and by thy merciful guiding may perform the same".[37] On the First Sunday after Trinity, the emphasis is firmly on grace as the sole origin of good works: "God, the strength of all them that put their trust in thee, mercifully accept our prayers; and because the weakness of our mortal nature can do no good thing without thee, grant us the help of thy grace, that in keeping of thy commandments we may please thee both in will and deed".[38] Finally, the collect for the Fourteenth Sunday after Trinity works around the difficulties of suggesting that salvation can be earned: "Almighty and everlasting God, give unto us the increase of faith, hope and charity; and that we may obtain that which thou dost promise, make us to love that which thou dost command".[39] All of these prayers, when compared with their Sarum predecessors, appear at first sight to be faithful translations. Yet closer inspection shows how subtle changes have altered the original emphasis, ruling out any possibility of an independent impulse to good, or of personal merit. Instead, they show a progressive movement from faith to the love of God that readily co-operates in a divinely directed course of action.

This evidence becomes more compelling when it is seen as the product of a climate of vigorous doctrinal argument. Ashley Null, in his

---

[35] *Gregor* n° 202.

[36] *Gelas V* n° 551; *Liber sacramentorum engolismensis* (*Cod. B. N. Lat. 816*) n° 922, ed. P. Saint-Roch (Corpus christianorum series latina 159 C), Brepols, Turnhout 1987, 137.

[37] *Gelas V* n° 556.

[38] *Gelas V* n° 566.

[39] *Gelas V* n° 1209; *Leon* n° 598. All of the examples cited are likely to have entered the Prayer Book directly from the Sarum Missal.

groundbreaking study of Cranmer's unpublished *Great Commonplaces*[40], presents a fascinating picture of the Archbishop's Evangelical interpretation of justification, grace and works, focusing on his doctrine of repentance. He shows how Cranmer referred to the same Augustinian evidence which his conservative opponents advanced, but used it to prove a very different position. This project became more urgent with the publication of the English Church's latest official manual of doctrine, *The King's Book*, in 1543. Cranmer subscribed to the book reluctantly, out of loyalty to the King, but disputed its teaching of "a doctrine of preparation for sanctifying grace through good works inspired by prevenient grace".[41] In this way, the book became an incentive to assemble a case in support of salvation by faith alone, and in particular to reinterpret the evidence from Augustine on which his conservative opponents relied. Null sums up his position as follows:

> Firstly, works done before justification had neither saving grace nor saving faith to make them pleasing in God's eyes. Secondly, in justification God pardoned sin by imputing Christ's alien righteousness to the ungodly, not by infusing in them an inherent personal merit. Concomitant with this externally based justification was an intrinsic renovation of the will and its affections by the indwelling of the Holy Spirit. Nevertheless, the Spirit's presence and the love he stirred in the believer's heart did not constitute a personal righteousness meritorious *de condigno*. When used in a broader sense to refer to both pardon and renewal, justification could be said to make the ungodly "right-willed" but never inherently righteous. Lastly, justification could never be contingent on either human preparation or personal merit because salvation was ultimately by unconditional predestination of God's elect.[42]

Cranmer's reading of Augustine was aimed at proving that Augustine "knew only one salvific grace, the justifying grace…[and] this grace renovated the will and its affections through the indwelling presence of the Holy Spirit".[43] Works of the law succeeded the event of justification, and did not take place before it. Grace was given, not as a reward for good works already accomplished, but in order that good works might be done.[44]

Unlike his conservative contemporaries, Cranmer understood the nature of saving grace not as something to which human beings assented, but something in which they trusted. The motion of the will, in other words,

---

[40] British Library. MS Royal 7B.

[41] A. NULL, *Thomas Cranmer's Doctrine of Repentance. Renewing the Power to Love*, Oxford UP, Oxford 2000, 157. *The King's Book* took a much more conservative stance than its predecessor, the so-called *Bishops' Book*, and was greeted with dismay by those who held Reformist views.

[42] NULL, *Thomas Cranmer's Doctrine of Repentance*, 158-159.

[43] NULL, *Thomas Cranmer's Doctrine of Repentance*, 161; cf. AUGUSTINUS HIPPONENSIS, *De spiritu et littera*, cap. 3. CRANMER, *Great Commonplaces*, 2, 82r.

[44] NULL, *Thomas Cranmer's Doctrine of Repentance*, 163. cf AUGUSTINUS HIPPONENSIS *De fide et operibus*, ca. 14. CGC II, 83r.

came first from God, and only subsequently from the believer. Null points to a telling section in the *Great Commonplaces* where Cranmer paraphrases Aquinas' teaching on the relationship between grace and free will (it also contains a remarkable summary of the function of 'motive' in prayer):

> "A man however is not able to turn to God, or prepare himself to receive the light of grace, unless through the gratuitous help of God he is moved inwardly"; "When the will first begins to wish the good, the will has only itself as the motion, but God alone is the mover"; "He works in us so that we will, but when we will, he co-operates with us so that we can bring our action to completion"; "a movement for free [choice] and consent to justification is the effect of grace, not the cause".[45]

The same ideas, now digested in popular form, find expression again in the *Book of Homilies*, published in 1547 as a resource for preachers, but also as a vehicle for imposing firm control on the teaching of doctrine from the pulpit.[46] A few extracts from the "Homily of Salvation", which is ascribed with some certainty to Cranmer, will illustrate the transfer from working notes to readily assimilated sermons. Total dependence on divine grace is stated on several occasions, as the following examples illustrate: "Righteousness cometh unto men by Christ's death and merits".[47] Summarising the writings of Hilary, Basil and Ambrose on salvation, the writer says: "What can be spoke more plainly than to say that freely without works, by faith only, we obtain remission of our sins?[48] He continues: "Justification by faith alone, freely and without works, takes away all merit of our works. [It therefore expresses] the weakness of man, and the goodness of God".[49]

At the same time, as commentators point out, the compilers of the *Book of Homilies* were not about to take the risk of declaring that, since the conduct of the faithful was irrelevant to their salvation, they need not practise good works. This would have been a recipe for disorder. The important message to convey, was that good works would not guarantee salvation, but that they were important as the visible fruit of God's saving grace working within his creation: "These great and merciful benefits of God, if they be well considered, do neither minister unto us occasion to be idle, and to live without doing any good works; neither yet stirreth up us by any means to do

---

[45] NULL, *Thomas Cranmer's Doctrine of Repentance*, 198. cf THOMAS AQUINAS *Summa Theologiae*, 1a2ae, q. 109, art. 6, CGC II, 113ᵛ; ibid. q. 111, art. 2, CGC II, 115ʳ.
[46] The right to preach through much of the 1540s was by licence only. In part, this was a measure against laziness and ignorance, but it was also a powerful means of inhibiting those unlikely to promote approved views.
[47] Attr. T. CRANMER, "Homily of Salvation", part II, in *Certain Sermons or Homilies to be Read in Churches*, ed. G.E. Corrie, John W. Parker, Cambridge 1850, 22.
[48] CRANMER, "Homily of Salvation", ed. G.E. Corrie, 24.
[49] CRANMER, "Homily of Salvation", ed. G.E. Corrie, 25.

evil things",[50] and "These be the fruits of true faith: to do good as much as lieth in us to every man; and above all things, and in all things, to advance the glory of God; of whom only we have our sanctification, justification, salvation and redemption".[51]

Cranmer's most recent biographer, Diarmaid McCulloch shrewdly observes that one subject is never mentioned in the Homilies – the matter of predestination. Here, he notes, "Cranmer's pastoral instinct muffled his presentation of the great soteriological themes of Augustine of Hippo". Although the Archbishop's notebooks and private writings clearly express his allegiance to the doctrine of predestination, he "never felt that this was a doctrine which would bring comfort to the motley congregations which crowded the churches of England". McCulloch points out that "the homilies of the Church of England were therefore composed as if all the hearers would be part of the elect".[52] Similar things might be said about the collects.

In the light of this material, the information embedded in the Easter Day collect makes a good deal more sense. The fact that human beings have good desires is wholly attributed to prevenient grace. God, for his part, anticipates the waywardness of human nature and suggests right action to receptive minds. None of this would be of any use, however, unless God remained present, continuing the gift of "good desires" with "continuall helpe". This significantly colours the interpretation of the petition. It is not a plea that we might *do* something, so much as a call for God to continue to work in us to develop the impulse towards right action which grace has planted in our minds. The subsequent assent of human wills, configured by the love of and for a gracious God, is the final part of the process. Here, the image of the motion and mover becomes especially significant. Our actions are evidence of God working in us.

In this way, the values of eternal life become part of the present life. But there is also a pragmatic side to that eirenic view. If human beings cannot earn eternal life, because it is given to them undeservedly by the grace of God, nevertheless, that does not absolve them from doing good works. The collect presents an elegant answer to some of the difficulties of faith and works. They will not guarantee a place in heaven, but they stand as important witnesses to God's grace at work in the people he has redeemed. The desire for conformity of the human will to the direction and purposes of the divine will can thus be seen in a positive light, as a process of growth and development towards the closest possible convergence with the divine will and purpose, underpinned, as the analysis has shown, by a well-integrated Trinitarian understanding of God.

---

[50] 'Homily of Salvation', part III. ed. G.E. Corrie, 30-31.

[51] CRANMER, "Homily of Salvation", ed. G.E. Corrie, 31.

[52] D. MCCULLOCH, *Thomas Cranmer*, 375.

Conclusion

The question that remains to be considered, is whether a method of interpretation based on clausal analysis offers a promising approach to the understanding of English language texts. As this has been an experimental exercise, the conclusions can only be preliminary, but several observations emerge. First of all, applying this method of reading raises self-consciousness in a useful way, and reminds us that the collect is a formal structure with its own conventions. Secondly, it provides a way of seeing that history, doctrine, grammar and poetics are inextricably interwoven in our prayers. Although it has been useful to demonstrate these functions separately, this is an artificial approach to elements which operate in a completely interdependent way to achieve their effects. Thirdly, it is a reminder that texts evolve, both for contextual reasons, and for reasons related to changes in colloquial language. This challenges the notion of the pure original, which is sometimes rather curiously invoked in relation to the Book of Common Prayer of 1662.

A fourth observation relates to the anthropology articulated in prayer. The method of analysis, as applied by Daniel McCarthy to Latin collects (and more recently in prayers over the gifts), places considerable weight on the way in which prayer can illustrate progress towards growth and maturity in faith. A much larger sample of English collects would have to be analysed before a similar argument could be confidently advanced. The view of the Tractarian writer who protested that in Cranmer's translations of Latin collects "there runs one prevailing tendency, to put into our mouths the language of servants rather than that of sons", has never been completely displaced.[53] A lurking sense that the Prayer Book collects never quite allow that people grow to adulthood in God is difficult to overcome.

What has not yet been tested in any way, is the applicability of the method to contemporary texts in current use. So far, we have studied a direct relationship between two texts, one in Latin, the other in English. Modern texts present a different situation. They tend to arise out of successive English revisions, in the case of Anglican collects, often occurring in different Provinces of the Anglican Communion. Many of them are newly composed, and have moved some way from Reformation views. The study of their grammar, and the attempt to discover a proper hermeneutical approach, must take account of such predecessors as can be found. It must also wrestle with the phenomenon of 'committee revision', with all the concomitant intermediary clumsiness which successive attempts to modify a prayer can bring. The often overt use of scriptural texts as the basis for composition, not

---

[53] Cuming, G. *The Godly Order*, 57 quotes I. WILLIAMS, *Tract 86: Indications of a superintending Providence in the preservation of the Prayer Book and in the changes which it has undergone*, 1841, 9. See: J.H. NEWMAN, et al., *Tracts for the Times by Members of the University of Oxford*, Rivingtons – J.H. Parker, London – Oxford 1834-1841. Also available at this URL http://anglicanhistory.org/tracts/tract86.html.

always resulting in a single developmental focus, is another factor to be considered.

Addressing these questions might be a useful way of developing a worshipping self-consciousness, necessary for growth in faith, but not obstructive in the communal practice of worship. It might also signal a welcome return of interest in the foundations of liturgical form and language, perhaps at long last laying down some principles which will inform revision and composition in the future.

Bibliography

A. Biblical source
The Revised English Bible Oxford UP – Cambridge UP, Oxford – Cambridge 1989.

B. Manuscript
British Library. MS Royal 7B.

C. Patristic sources
AUGUSTINUS HIPPONENSIS De fide et operibus, ed. J. Zycha (Corpus scriptorum ecclesiasticorum latinorum 41) Tempsky – Freytag, Wien – Prague 1900, 33-97.

AUGUSTINUS HIPPONENSIS, De spiritu et littera, ed. J. Zycha – C. Urba (Corpus scriptorum ecclesiasticorum latinorum 60), Tempsky – Freytag, Vienna – Leipzig 1913, 153-230.

D. Liturgical sources
ARCHBISHOPS' COUNCIL OF THE CHURCH OF ENGLAND, Common Worship Additional Collects, Church House Publishing, London 2004.

Liber sacramentorum engolismensis (Cod. B. N. Lat. 816), ed. P. Saint-Roch (Corpus christianorum series latina 159 C), Brepols, Turnhout 1987

Missale ad usum insignis et praeclarae ecclesiae Sarum, ed. F.H. Dickinson, J. Parker, Oxford – London 1861-1883, repr. Gregg International Publishers, Farnborough 1969.

Sacramentarium Gelasianum, ed. L.C. Mohlberg – L. Eizenhöfer – P. Siffrin (Rerum ecclesiasticarum documenta. Series maior, Fontes 4) Herder, Rome [3]1981, 76.

Le sacramentaire Grégorien: Ses principales formes d'après les plus anciens manuscripts, ed. J. Deshusses (Spicilegium Friburgense 16), Éditions universitaires, Fribourg, 1, [3]1992, 2 [2]1988, 3 [2]1992.

E. Tools
CRYSTAL, D., The Cambridge Encyclopedia of the English Language, Cambridge UP, Cambridge 1995.

F. Studies
BRIGHTMAN, F.E., The English Rite, 2 vol., Rivingtons, London 1915.

BUTTERWORTH, C., The English Primers 1529-1545, University of Pennsylvania Press, Philadelphia 1953;

CRANMER, T. attr., "Homily of Salvation", part II, in Certain Sermons or Homilies to be Read in Churches, ed. G.E. Corrie, John W. Parker, Cambridge 1850.

CUMING, G., The Godly Order, SPCK/ Alcuin Club, London 1983

―――, "Thomas Cranmer. Translator and Writer" in Language and the Worship of the Church, ed. D. Jasper – R.C.D. Jasper, Macmillan, London 1990, 110-119.

DE ZAN, R., "Criticism and Interpretation of Liturgical Texts", in Introduction to the Liturgy, ed. A.J. Chupungco (Handbook for Liturgical Studies 1), Liturgical Press (Pueblo Book), Collegeville MN 1997, 331-365 (En. tr. of R. DE ZAN, "Introduzione alla Liturgia, Ermeneutica", ed. A. J. Chupungco [Scientia Liturgica: Manuale di Liturgia 1] Piemme, Casale Monferrato 1998, 356-389).

DEVEREUX, J.A., "Reformed Doctrine in the Collects of the *First Book of Common Prayer*", *Harvard Theological Review* 58 (1965) 49-68.

DOWDEN, J., *The Workmanship of the Prayer Book*, Methuen, London 1899.

DUDLEY, M., *The Collect in Anglican Liturgy: Texts and Sources 1549 –1989*, (Alcuin Club Collection 72), Liturgical Press, Collegeville MN 1994.

DUFFY, E., *Marking the Hours. English People and Their Prayers 1240-1570*, Yale UP, New Haven – London 2006.

_____, *The Stripping of the Altars. Traditional Religion in England 1400-1580*, Yale UP, New Haven – London 1992.

GRAY, D., "Cranmer and the Collects" in *The Oxford Handbook of English Literature and Theology*, ed. A. Hass – D. Jasper, - E. Jay, Oxford UP, Oxford 2007, 561-574.

HOSKINS, E., *Horae Beatae Mariae Virginis or Sarum and York Primers*, Longmans, Green & Co., London – New York 1901.

LATHBURY, T., *A History of the Book of Common Prayer and Other Books of Authority*, John Henry and James Parker, Oxford – London 1858.

McCULLOCH, D., *Thomas Cranmer: A Life*, Yale UP, New Haven – London 1996, 411-412 quotes from original printed in *Epistolae Tigurinae*, Parker Society, Cambridge 1848, 349-350;

McCARTHY, D.P., *Listen to the Word: Commentaries in Selected Opening Prayers of Sundays and Feasts*, weekly series in *The Tablet*, 2006-2007, and published privately, Rome 2007.

_____, *Listen to the Word: Commentaries in Selected Prayers over the Gifts of Sundays and Feasts*, weekly series in *The Tablet*, 2007-2008.

Miscellaneous Writings and Letters of Thomas Cranmer, ed. J.E. Cox (Parker Society), Cambridge UP, Cambridge 1846, 412, Letter 276 to King Henry VIII.

Miscellaneous Writings and Letters of Thomas Cranmer, ed. J.E. Cox (Parker Society), Cambridge UP, Cambridge 1846.

NEWMAN, J.H., et al., *Tracts for the Times by Members of the University of Oxford*, Rivingtons – J.H. Parker, London – Oxford 1834-1841. Also available at this URL http://anglicanhistory.org/tracts/tract86.html.

NICHOLS, B., *Liturgical Hermeneutics*, Peter Lang, Frankfurt – New York 1996.

NULL, A., *Thomas Cranmer's Doctrine of Repentance. Renewing the Power to Love*, Oxford UP, Oxford 2000.

Original Letters Relative to the English Reformation, 2 vol., ed. H. Robinson, Parker Society, Cambridge 1846-1847.

PARTRIDGE, A.C., *Tudor to Augustan English*, Andre Deutsch, London 1969, 24-28.

RIDLEY, J., *Thomas Cranmer*, Clarendon Press, Oxford 1962.

ROBINSON, I., *The Establishment of Modern English Prose in the Reformation and the Enlightenment*, Cambridge UP, Cambridge 1988.

_____, *Who Killed the Bible?*, Brynmill Press, 2006.

SCRIVENER, J., "Thee and Thou", *Faith and Worship* 62 (2008) 38-50.

THOMAS AQUINAS, *Summa Theologiae*, 1a2ae, q. 109, art. 6, CGC II, 113^v; ibid. q. 111, art. 2, CGC II, 115^r.

WILLIAMS, I., *Tract 86: Indications of a superintending Providence in the preservation of the Prayer Book and in the changes which it has undergone*, 1841, in CUMING, G., *The Godly Order*, 57.

ZIMMERMAN, J.A., *Liturgy as Language of Faith. A Liturgical Methodology in the Mode of Paul Ricoeur's Textual Hermeneutics*, UP of America, Lanham MA – London 1988.

CHAPTER 7

The Opening Prayer for Epiphany:
A Linguistic and Literary Analysis

Anthony O. Igbekele

Introduction

The collect assigned to the feast of Epiphany, Mass during the day, in the *Missale Romanum* of 2002 and its official translation into English are presented in the following chart:

Missale Romanum 2002	The Roman Missal
Deus, qui hodierna die Unigenitum tuum, *gentibus stella duce revelasti,* *concede propitius, ut, qui iam te ex fide cognovimus,* *usque ad contemplandam speciem tuae celsitudinis* *perducamur.*[1]	Father, you revealed your Son to the nations by the guidance of a star. Lead us to your glory in heaven by the light of faith.[2]

The author's literal translation for study purposes is:

O God, you who on this day, with a star guiding,
have revealed your only Son to the nations,
favourably grant, we pray,

---

[1] *Missale Romanum ex decreto Sacrosancti Oecumenici Concilii Vaticani II instauratum auctoritate Pauli PP. VI promulgatum Ioannis Pauli PP. II cura recognitum, editio typica tertia*, Typis Vaticanis, Città del Vaticano ³2002 (hereafter MR ³2002), 175. Confer: *Corpus orationum*, 14 vol., ed. E. Moeller – J.-M. Clément – B.C. 't Wallant (Corpus christianorum series latina 160 A), Brepols, Turnhout 1993, 2, n° 1673; P. BRUYLANTS, *Les oraisons du Missel Romain, texte et histoire* (Études liturgiques 2 vol.), Mont César, Louvain 1952, 2, n° 351.

[2] *The Roman Missal, revised by decree of the Second Vatican Council and published by the authority of Paul VI, official English texts*, Collins, London 1974, 62.

that we who up to this moment have come to know you
as a result of the faith we have in you,
may be led to contemplating the vision of your greatness.

Epiphany celebrates the manifestation of Christ to the nations. The analysis of this collect requires a clear methodology. This study begins with its scriptural and historical sources, and the changing meaning of its text in subsequent use. Then an analysis of the prayer's clausal structure and a philological analysis of its individual words within the context of the *Hadrianum* prepares for an appreciation of the theological wealth of this prayer.[3] We will see that the theology of the collect which we are about to study marks a fitting close to the liturgical-theological *iter* begun at Advent.

1. *Status quaestionis*

We know that already some research has been carried out on this collect. Dom Henry Ashworth is of the opinion that Gregory the Great (540-604) could well be the author of some formularies which at some later date were "incorporated into an official, organized Roman Sacramentary for use at the Papal stational masses".[4]

In addition, Bernard Capelle's[5] research indicates that there exists affinity between some texts of Gregory and the Epiphany collect in the *Hadrianum*.[6] Capelle's research was limited in that he did not examine the words and expressions in this Epiphany collect vis-à-vis their appearance and usage in other sections of the *Hadrianum*. Nor did he use the results of his research to draw out a theology of the collect under our consideration. The present research hopes to contribute to the dialogue on the riches of the Epiphany collect by leading the way in these yet uncharted grounds.

---

[3] Cf. M. AUGÉ, "Principi di interpretazione dei testi liturgici", in *La Liturgia momento nella storia della salvezza*, ed. S. Marsili et alii (Anàmnesis 1), Marietti, Casale Monferato, 1974, 159-179.

[4] H. ASHWORTH, "The Liturgical Prayers of St Gregory the Great", *Traditio* 15 (1959) 111; A. CHAVASSE, *La liturgie de la ville de Rome du Ve au VIIIe siècle, une liturgie conditionnée par l'organisation de la vie in Urbe et extra muros* (Studia Anselmiana 112, Analecta Liturgica 18), Pontificium Athenaeum Anselmianum, Rome 1993, 283-295.

[5] B. CAPELLE, "La main de S. Grégoire dans le Sacramentaire Grégorien", *Revue Bénédictine* 49 (1937) 13-28.

[6] "Hadrianum ex authentico" n° 87, *Le Sacramentaire Grégorien: Ses principales formes d'après les plus anciens manuscrits*, 3 vol., ed. J. Deshusses (Spicilegium Friburgense 16), Éditions universitaires, Fribourg ³1992, 1 (hereafter *Gregor*).

In our analysis of the Epiphany collect we shall examine its historical identity and evolution, utilizing classical philological analysis,[7] to determine its meaning and theology.

2. Sources and redactional history

Liturgical source. Our collect is found in the *Hadrianum*[8] as the main collect for the celebration of Epiphany. Within the Gregorian tradition, the prayer appeared in the *Gregorianum Paduense*[9] as well as others.

Even though the prayer is not found in the *Sacramentarium gelasianum vetus*, which has a different collect for Epiphany,[10] it did appear in later sacramentaries of the Gelasian tradition, for instance, in the Frankish *Gelasianum of Saint-Gall 95*,[11] and the *Liber sacramentorum engolismensis*.[12] It is also found in the *Liber Sacramentorum Augustodunensis*[13] and the *Sacramentarium Bergomense*.[14]

---

[7] R. De Zan, "Criticism and Interpretation of Liturgical Texts", in *Introduction to the Liturgy*, ed. A.J. Chupungco (Handbook for Liturgical Studies 1), Liturgical Press (Pueblo Book), Collegeville MN 1997, 331-365 (En. tr. of R. De Zan, "Introduzione alla Liturgia, Ermeneutica", ed. A. J. Chupungco [*Scientia Liturgica: Manuale di Liturgia* 1] Piemme, Casale Monferrato 1998, 356-389), 343.

[8] *Gregor* n° 87.

[9] *Liber sacramentorum paduensis* (*Padova, Biblioteca Capitolare, cod. D 47*) n° 58, ed. A. Catella – F. dell'Oro – A. Martini (Bibliotheca Ephemerides Liturgicae, Subsidia 131. Monumenta italiae liturgica 3), Centro Liturgico Vincenziano edizioni liturgiche, Rome 2005; It appeared in the mixed Gelasian of the type "P" (Padua), composed about the 9th century in the imperial studio of Lothaire, for Verona Church. This Sacramentary was later taken to Padua, where it was completed. See: *Corpus Orationum*, ed. Moeller (CCL 160), 1, xxxv.

[10] *Liber sacramentorum romanae aeclesiae ordinis anni circuli* (*Cod. Vat. Reg. Lat. 316/Paris Bibl. Nat. 7193, 41/56*) (*Sacramentarium Gelasianum*) n° 61, ed. L.C. Mohlberg – L. Eizenhöfer – P. Siffrin (Rerum ecclesiasticarum documenta. Series maior, Fontes 4), Herder, Rome 1960.

[11] *Das fränkische* Sacramentarium Gelasianum *in alamannischer Überlieferung* (*Codex Sangall. 348*), ed. L.C. Mohlberg (Liturgiegeschichtliche Quellen und Forschungen 1-2), Aschendorff, Münster ²1939. This Sacramentary, whose origin is traced to Chur in Switzerland, from where it passed to the monastery of Saint Gall in the 9th Century. See: *Corpus Orationum*, ed. Moeller (CCL 160), 1, xliii.

[12] *Liber sacramentorum engolismensis* (*Cod. B. N. Lat. 816*) n° 101, ed. P. Saint-Roch (Corpus christianorum series latina 159 C), Brepols, Turnhout 1987.

[13] *Liber sacramentorum augustodunensis* n° 106, ed. O. Heiming (Corpus christianorum series latina 159 B), Brepols, Turnhout 1984.

[14] The formula also appears in the *Sacramentarium Bergomense* of the second half of the 9th Century, probably from Milan, on which the type "M" (Monza) of the mixed Gelasian depended. See: *Corpus Orationum*, ed. Moeller (CCL 160), 1, xi; *Sacramentarium Bergomense: Manoscritto del secolo IX della Biblioteca di S. Alessandro in*

Biblical sources. Our prayer contains two important allusions to scriptural sources. The first provides a link between the prayer and the liturgy of the word of the day, notably with the Matthean narration of the visit of the Magi.[15] Specifically, the ablative absolute *stella duce* refers to the account in the Gospel of Matthew in which a star guided the Magi to the newborn child at the manger in Bethlehem.[16] It is however instructive that the composer of this prayer did not simply use this story, he interpreted it. In his liturgical-theological interpretation, he substituted the original protagonists of Matthew's Gospel, the Magi, with the nations *gentibus*, without specifying the identity of these new protagonists. Does *gentibus* refer to all the nations or just to the community of Christians gathered from all nations?

The second scriptural allusion appears in the petition, where the combination of "*fides*" and "*speciem*" brings to mind Paul's statement in 2 Corinthians 5:7, which says: "per fidem ambulamus, et non per speciem".[17]

The redactional history of the text. The text as we have it in the *Missale Romanum* of 2002 reproduces the text as it appears in the *Hadrianum*. When we examine its editorial history, we immediately observe that the text is stable, apart from some minor redactional variants. Wherever we find the prayer, it is assigned as a collect for the Mass on the feast of Epiphany, with the exception of the *Sacramentarium Bergomense*. Here, it could be used as one of the prayers for the vigil or morning prayers of the divine office for Epiphany.[18] The sources also indicate that the papal stational mass was celebrated at Saint Peter's on the Solemnity of the Epiphany.[19]

3. Textual analysis

An analysis of the *cursus* shows that the verse lines of the prayer conform to the classical cursus in the following order: *planus, trispondaicus tardus,* and *velox.*

Colonna in Bergamo n° 193, ed. A. Paredi (Monumenta Bergomensia 6), Fondazione Amministrazione Provinciale, Bergamo 1962 (hereafter *Bergom*).

[15] Matt 2:1-12.

[16] "Ubi est, qui natus est, rex Iudaeorum? Vidimus enim stellam eius in oriente et venimus adorare eum" (Matt 2:2; Vulgate throughout); *Nova Vulgata Bibliorum Sacrorum editio: Sacrosancti Oecumenici Concilii Vaticani II ratione habita iussu Pauli PP. VI recognita auctoritate Pauli PP. II promulgata, editio typica altera,* Libreria editrice Vaticana, Città del Vaticano ²1998.

[17] "Audentes igitur simper et scientes quoniam, dum praesentes sumus in corpore, peregrinamur a Domino; per fidem enim ambulamus et non per speciem" (2 Cor 5:7).

[18] The prayer used in the *Sacramentarium Bergomense* is slightly different: "Deus qui hunc diem electionis gentium primitiis consecrasti. & per luminis tui stellam manifestum te nobis ostendisti. Tribue quaesumus ut nova caelorum mirabilis claritas in nostris semper cordibus oriatur" (*Bergom* n° 196).

[19] See: BRUYLANTS, *Les Oraisons* (ÉtL 1), 1, n° 29.

verse lines of the prayer	*cursus*
Deus, qui hodierna die Uni-gé-ni-tum tú-um,	5 syllables, *planus*
gentibus stella dú-ce re-ve-lá-sti,	6 syllables, *trispondaicus*
concede propitius, ut, qui iam te ex fí-de co-gnó-vi-mus,	6 syllables, *tardus*
usque ad contemplandam speciem	
tuae celsi-tú-di-nis pér-du-cá-mur.	7 syllables, *velox*

Our textual analysis continues with a careful grammatical analysis of the clausal structure of the Latin prayer. Each of these is then understood according to an interpretative process that reveals the meaning of the prayer itself. In the following chart, the clauses of the prayer are arranged in the column to the right. Its grammatical analysis is given in the centre column and the interpretative categories corresponding to each clause are placed in the column to the left.

Invocation:	simple:	*Deus*
Amplification:	relative clause:	*qui hodierna die Unigenitum tuum gentibus ... revelasti*
Premise:	ablative absolute:	*stella duce*
Petition:	imperative:	*concede propitius*
First purpose:	*ut* + subjunctive:	*ut ... perducamur*
Second purpose:	*usque ad* + gerundive:	*usque ad contemplandam speciem tuae celsitudinis*
Motive:	relative clause within purpose:	*qui iam te ex fide cognovimus*

Invocation. God is referred to simply as *Deus*, "O God", without any complementary apposition. The official translation in *The Roman Missal* of 1974 is, "Father".

Amplification. The Latin relative clause, *qui hodierna die Unigenitum tuum gentibus ... revelasti*, "who ... has revealed your only begotten Son to the nations", is translated in *The Roman Missal* as: "you revealed your Son to the nations". The verb *revelasti* is the syncopated form of *revelavisti*. This verb may be understood either as a present perfect meaning, "you have revealed" or "you have been revealing" or as an historical perfect, "you revealed" or "you did reveal".

The prayer's anamnetic force recounting the *mirabilia Dei*, the wondrous deeds of God, is expressed in the phrase *Deus qui ... revelasti*. Within our prayer, God is praised now (*hodierna die*) for that historical event in which he revealed his only begotten Son to the nations (*Unigenitum tuum gentibus revelasti*).

Premise. The premise *stella duce*, is an ablative absolute, meaning, "as the star leads", which is translated in *The Roman Missal* as, "by the guidance of a star". Thus, our interpretation of the whole relative clause is: "who, as the star leads, has revealed your only begotten Son to the nations".

The expression "*stella duce*" links our collect directly to the liturgy of the Word of this solemnity and presents the celebrative content of the *hodierna die*. Since the historical event being commemorated happened in the past, the expression *hodierna die* is intended to be understood not only in the spatio-temporal chronological sense but more so in the sacramental-mystery-celebrative sense. The celebration becomes a commemoration of the mystery of God's revelation of his only begotten Son to the nations, who become the recipients of the divine favour. God reveals his Son, as the star leads, to the nations. Thus, while the star points to the mystery, God is the ultimate protagonist.

Petition. The petition is expressed by the imperative *concede* followed by the adverb *propitius*, which mean, "favourably grant". This classic formula of introducing the petition is absent in the text of the prayer in *The Roman Missal*.

First purpose. The first purpose clause uses the classical construction composed of *ut* followed by the subjunctive, "*ut ... perducamur*", literally, "that we may be led", which is translated in *The Roman Missal* by the imperative, "lead us". The present subjunctive "*perducamur*" could be interpreted over a range of time including: contemporaneous, "that we may be led to"; unfinished, "that we may continue to be led to"; ongoing, "that we may go on being led to"; incomplete, "that we may further be led to"; future, "that [in the future] we may be led to"; eternal, "that we may [ever] be led to". If *perducamur* were interpreted as contemporaneous with "*concede*", then it would mean "grant [now] that we may be led [now]". While these shades might not be altogether ruled out of the interpretation of this subjunctive, further analysis of "*perducamur*" in the *Hadrianum* curiously reveals that the eschatological sense is closer to the intention of the composer, as we shall see below. Thus, we interpret the first purpose as: "that we may be led to".

Second purpose. The second purpose clause is composed of the expression *usque ad* followed by the gerundive *contemplandam speciem*, in the phrase, *usque ad contemplandam speciem tuae celsitudinis*. We translate this as, "all the way to contemplating the vision of your great glory". *The Roman Missal* renders this clause as, "to your glory in heaven". We shall see that noun *speciem* defines the hermeneutical boundaries of the contemplation and clarifies the context of the phrase *tuae celsitudinis* within this euchological formula.

Motive. The motive is expressed as a relative clause located within the purpose clause, *qui iam te ex fide cognovimus*. We could provisionally translate this motive clause as, "we who now have come to know you by means of faith". In *The Roman Missal*, this motive clause is translated as, "by the light of faith". The Latin original tells about how one arrives at this faith and its end. It says that we have known God through faith (*cognovimus*); that the object of our knowing through faith is God (*te*); and that this knowledge of God through faith is antecedent to the contemplation of God's glory, as expressed by the adverb *iam*.

4. Classical philological analysis

Following these preliminary observations, we may further unravel the theology of this collect by exploring the meaning of certain words and phrases, especially with regard to their stylistic elements. We shall examine three nouns, *fides*, *species* and *celsitudo*, then one verb, *cognoscere*, and finally two syntactical constructions, *cognovimus ex fide* and *perducamur ad contemplandam speciem celsitudinis tuae*. We shall limit this philological analysis to the *Hadrianum*, to help us better to determine the meaning and function of the selected words in the context of this ancient sacramentary.

fides – *species*. In our collect the nouns *fides* and *species* appear as a combination. We have already remarked that a similar combination is found in 2 Corinthians 5:7. In this text, according to Paul, we walk by faith, that is, by trust in God, and not by the ability to see God directly.[20] Central to this is the Pauline contrast between believing now, as we walk by faith, and seeing God face to face in the future.[21] This combination of *fides* – *species* is also found in a Sermon that Augustine of Hippo gave during the *traditio symbolorum*, when the creed was given to the catechumens about to be born in the womb of the faith (*utero fidei*), that they might in turn produce the fruit of faith (*fructum fidei*).[22] In this sermon, Augustine said, "*nunc enim ... in fide ... tunc autem in specie*".[23] Augustine stresses that the acceptance of the faith by the catechumens implies casting aside the old, "carnal" nature and having a "hatred" of the world so as obtain victory over the world.[24] While in their former lives the catechumens had lived in sin and in the shadow of

---

[20] According to Capelle, "il est clair que *species* ne désigne pas l'apparence, l'aspect, mais la réalité vue directement, par opposition à la foi qui ne la voit qu'à travers un voile" (CAPELLE, "La main de S. Grégoire", 15).

[21] J. LAMBRECHT, *Second Corinthians* (Sacra Pagina Series 8), Liturgical Press (Michael Glazier Book), Collegeville MN 1999, 85; A. BLAISE, *Le Vocabulaire Latin des principaux thèmes liturgiques*, Brepols, Turnhout 1966, 600.

[22] AUGUSTINUS HIPPONENSIS, *Sermo* 216, 1, in *Sant'Agostino, Discorsi 4,1 (184-229/v)*: *Su i tempi liturgici: testo Latino dell'edizione maurina e delle edizioni postmaurine*, tr. and notes P. Bellini – F. Cruciani – V. Tarulli (Opere di Sant'Agostino 32, 1), Città Nuova Editrice, Rome 1984, 248.

[23] "Nunc enim in Ecclesia in fide benedicitis Dominum; tunc autem in specie affluentissime rigabimini de fontibus Israel". AUGUSTINUS HIPPONENSIS, *Sermo* 216, 4, ed. Bellini (Opere di Sant'Agostino 32, 1), 252.

[24] AUGUSTINUS, *Sermo* 216, 2, ed. Bellini (Opere di Sant'Agostino 32, 1), 250-251.

death, they desired new life in God where faith and wisdom would be their food and drink. In his analysis of the Epiphany collect, B. Capelle points out that that the combination *fides – species* is not exact: "*fides* désignant un acte et *species* un objet".[25]

Let us now turn to the use of some of the important nouns and verbs in this collect and situate them within the *Hadrianum*.

fides. The noun *fides* appears in our collect in the absolute sense, without a determinant adjective or subjective complement. Faith is a grace (*fidei gratiam*).[26] It is the knowledge of God, the acknowledgement and acceptance of his purpose in human life and existence.[27] *Fides* also implies the confession of one's total adhesion and belonging to God, as it is demonstrated in the prayer for the vigil of the Solemnity of Saint Peter.[28] In this prayer, the amplification refers to God's consecrating the Church on the faith of the Apostle Peter,[29] an affirmation that alludes to Peter's confession of faith in Matthew 16:16-19. The Church needs this stable, true, integral, inviolable, sincere and constant faith in the proclamation of God's name.[30] Also, in an *oratio super oblata* used in the celebration of the Solemnity of the Annunciation, the Church asks God to confirm in her heart the sacred mysteries of the true faith, that is, the mysteries of the Incarnation, in which Christ became true God and true man.[31]

cognosco. The verb *cognosco* may refer to our awareness of our sinfulness.[32] According to the prayer used for the Christmas Vigil,[33] the worshipping community knows the mysteries of light on earth. In a prayer for the litany on the feast of Saint Lawrence, the phrase *qui pondus tuae animadversionis cognovimus* refers to the fact that though the Church is aware of and knows the burden of God's chastisement, she may still experience the

---

[25] Commenting on this, Capelle's concluded that: "Le parallélisme est absolu: même sens de *fides – species*; même influence de 2 Cor. non cité; même procédé qui transforme l'opposition en une gradation, la foi conduisant à la vision; même style". Capelle, "La main de S. Grégoire", 15.

[26] *Gregor* n° 428.

[27] BLAISE, *Le Vocabulaire Latin*, 598-599.

[28] *Gregor* n° 593.

[29] "Deus qui ecclesiam tuam apostolic tui petri fide et nomine consecrasti, quique beatum illi paulum ad praedicandum gentibus gloriam tuam sociare dignatus es, concede ut omnes qui ad apostolorum tuorum sollemnia convenerunt spiritali remuneratione ditentur. Per" (*Gregor* n° 593).

[30] *Gregor* n° 339.

[31] "In mentibus nostris domine vere fidei sacramenta confirma, ut qui conceptum de virgine deum verum et hominem confitemur, per eius salutifere resurrectionis potentiam ad aeternam mereamur pervenire laetitiam. Per dominum" (*Gregor* n° 142).

[32] *Gregor* n° 117.

[33] The prayer *Gregor* n° 36 indicates Christ as the true light that brightens that night with his presence.

favour of God's compassion (*gratiam pietatis*).[34] The brave and glorious martyrs are known by the witness they gave to Christ.[35] In a prayer assigned to the feast of the Annunciation, the Church petitions God to pour grace into her heart that, as the angel announces, we who have come to acknowledge the incarnation of Christ, may be led through his passion and cross to the glory of the resurrection.[36] In the Roman Canon, also present in the *Hadrianum*, God is asked to remember his children and all those whose faith is known to God (*quorum tibi fides cognita est*).[37] *Gregor* n° 921 gives us another interpretive nuance, where *cognoscere* is used in terms of an interior knowledge of God when it says, *ut et te tota mente cognoscat.*[38]

What is clear from this analysis is the fact that in the *Hadrianum*, *cognosco* refers to an earthly recognition, knowledge, acknowledgement, coming to an acceptance, experience, an earthly revelation of a divine mystery. This earthly knowledge however has the accomplishment of something else as its goal, for instance, the attainment of God's compassion,[39] God's grace that we may recognize the glory of Christ's resurrection,[40] which is a heavenly reality.[41] In our collect, *cognosco* therefore implies acknowledgement of and coming to terms with the mystery of the incarnation. Conversely, *cognosco* can also imply God's knowing our faith.

speciem.[42] In the Gospel of Luke, *species* is used in reference to the descent of the Holy Spirit on Jesus at his baptism (Luke 3:22). Here, *species* may be interpreted as exterior aspect or form. In the third anamnetical invocation of the divine name in the preface of the blessing of the baptismal font, the flood water (*effusione diluvii*, a reference to Gen 6-8), which God used to wash away the sins of the world (*mundi crimina*) represents a *speciem regenerationis*, a type or mystical image of baptismal regeneration.[43]

Species offers an antithesis to *veritas* in a ferial post communion prayer, where the opposition is expressed by the ablatives "*specie … veritate.*[44] The

[34] *Gregor* n° 467.
[35] *Gregor* n° 613; the idea here is that the Church knows them by the fruits of what they did, that is, their witness to Christ through their death.
[36] *Gregor* n° 143.
[37] *Gregor* n° 6.
[38] *Gregor* n° 921.
[39] *Gregor* n° 467.
[40] *Gregor* n° 143.
[41] *Gregor* n° 467.
[42] According to A. Blaise, *species* could mean "aspect extérieur, forme; aspect, aspect merveilleux; splendeur (de Dieu); vision direct; image mystique, symbolique; espèce, objet". "Species", in BLAISE, *Le Vocabulaire Latin*, 101.
[43] "Deus qui nocentis mundi crimina, per aquas abluens regenerationis speciem in ipsa diluuii effusione signasti, ut unius eiusdemque elementi mysterio, et finis esset uitiis et origo uirtutis" (*Gregor* n° 374a).
[44] "Perficiant in nobis domine quaesumus tua sacramenta quod continent, ut quae nunc specie gerimus rerum veritate capiamus" (*Gregor* n° 719).

praying Church petitions that the sacraments bring to perfection in us that which they contain, so that we may grasp the things, which we bear in outward appearance, by the truth of their realities. From this we know that the sacramental celebration has both an outward appearance (*species*) and a hidden reality (*veritas*).

Species thus refers to exterior aspect or form, appearance, beatific vision or beauty. Since it appears in our collect with the verb *contemplare* and refers to God, we interpret *species* as God's beauty, the beatific vision.

celsitudo. The noun *celsitudo*[45] is used in an optional prayer for the celebration of Vespers during the octave of Pentecost.[46]

perducamur. The verb *perducamur* is a divine passive where the complementary agent is implicit and not explicit. The verb *Perducere* is used in the *Hadrianum* with several fields of meaning:

i. It could mean a spiritual relocation, which implies a change of existence from something to another, with the new state always an improvement on the old. To hone this idea home, the composers of the euchological texts use the preposition *ad* with the simple accusative or the accusative of the gerund or gerundive. This new state is expressed in terms of joy, remedy, glory, salvation, premium, new life and the crown of glory. The composers expressed these ideas with terminologies such as *ad resurrectionis gloriam,*[47] *ad remedia ... aeterna,*[48] *ad sempiterna promissa,*[49] *ad salutaria cuncta;*[50] *ad caelestia dona.*[51] This new state is equally represented in terms of spatial boundaries, as in *ad caelestia regna.*[52] In one instance, however, this new state of reality could also be something terrestrial, as an increase of the church (*ad ecclesiae ... augmentum*).[53]

ii. It could also mean leading someone in the spiritual sense, for instance, to the mysteries of baptismal regeneration: *revela quem perducas ad gratiam baptismi tui.*[54]

iii. This change is however attained through a process, such as through the passion and cross of Christ.[55]

---

[45] *Celsitudo* is formed from the adjective *celsus. Celsus* can be interpreted in two ways: in a good sense, it means "raised high, extending upward, high, lofty ... elevated above that which is normal, great, elevated in rank or station, noble, eminent". In a bad sense, it means "haughty, proud, high-spirited" ("*celsus*", in C.T. LEWIS – C. SHORT, *A Latin Dictionary*, Oxford UP, Oxford – New York 1879, reprinted 1995, 348-349).

[46] *Gregor* n° 447.

[47] *Gregor* n° 143.

[48] *Gregor* n° 292.

[49] *Gregor* n° 710.

[50] *Gregor* n° 237.

[51] *Gregor* n° 210.

[52] *Gregor* n° 250, 266.

[53] *Gregor* n° 835.

[54] *Gregor* n° 980.

Perducamur therefore means a movement of spiritual relocation, leading or guiding, a change of state from terrestrial to heavenly reality, thus, it indicating "may we be led to".

5. The stages of salvation history

In our collect, we find a clear expression of the stages of salvation history.

Stage 1. In the first stage (*stella duce*), God makes his purpose known to the nations. We could refer to this as the time of the nations before their coming to Christ. The nations "read" the star, see in it an extraordinary expression of the divine purpose and follow it. The star that leads becomes the instrument of the divine purpose: divinity makes use of nature in the expression of the divine will. The ablative absolute thus expresses the premise that God reveals his initiative to the nations through nature. In this first stage, then, God uses what people can see in creation to express what they cannot see, his divine design. This first stage follows the biblical narrative[56] and the euchological tradition.[57]

Stage 2. The knowledge of the divine design through nature in stage 1 gives way to knowledge of the divine design through the incarnation in Stage 2. Revelation implies the presence of something hidden, a mystery that is now brought into the open or publicly manifested. This public manifestation is the mystery of this baby, God's only begotten Son. Thus revelation through nature gives way to theophany in God's revelation of his only begotten Son, and, indeed, theophany is the name given to Epiphany in some ancient Sacramentaries.

Stage 3. In the third stage the Church responds to God's revelation of his only begotten Son (*te cognovimus ex fide*). The church's response of faith involves her complete adhesion and assent to all that the only begotten represents, his life, mission and message: his whole person. The verb "*cognovimus*" expresses our on-going response, our active, not passive, assent as a people privileged with revelation. Thus, there are two responses in the prayer: the first though yet incomplete response of the nations, and the second now accomplished response of the Church.

Stage 4. The Church, having responded in faith, not just by sight or empirical knowledge, as do the nations, now moves on to the next stage in its encounter with God's revelation. This is the stage of the Church's accepting the need for God's ongoing gift expressed in the petition *concede propitius*.

Stage 5. The Church asks that we may be led (*perducamur*). As a divine passive, the verb implies that God is the mover, the guide, the director and

---

55 *Gregor* n° 143.
56 Mal 4:2; Luke 1:78.
57 See the following phrases in the prayers indicated: *veri luminis, lucis mysteria, (Gregor* n° 36); *nova ... luce, (Gregor* n° 42); *lux tuae claritatis infulsit (Gregor* n° 38).

that the church is the one moved and guided. Since the Church is on her earthly pilgrimage, this leading begins, is carried forward and continues throughout her earthly sojourn towards the eschaton.

Stage 6. The goal of this journey is the church's contemplation of the vision of God's great glory. The goal is, thus, eschatological.

Conclusion

In our collect, two important ideas stand out clearly: the necessity of faith and the eschatological vision of the glory of God. The star leads the nations to the earthly manifestation of the Only-begotten. God now leads the Church on to the eschatological manifestation of his divinity.

From this collect, we note a shift from a natural process of revelation to the nations, which leads to our knowing God by faith; a shift from a temporal to an eschatological manifestation; a movement from the primacy of divine action (*revelare*) to the human response of contemplation. Thus, revelation begins in God and ends in humanity's contemplation of God. God reveals to the nations his Only-begotten, the mystery now revealed: God the revealer, becomes God the revealed, first in nature, then in the incarnation, then in the Church by faith and finally at the eschaton.

The Epiphany collect draws towards the end of the liturgical-theological *iter* begun at Advent, that is, the expectant waiting for the coming of Christ, to the expectation of the eschaton, to which the celebrating community at Epiphany prays that she may be led.

Bibliography

A. Holy Scripture

Nova Vulgata Bibliorum Sacrorum editio: Sacrosancti Oecumenici Concilii Vaticani II ratione habita iussu Pauli PP. VI recognita auctoritate Pauli PP. II promulgata, editio typica altera, Libreria editrice Vaticana, Città del Vaticano ²1998.

B. Research tools

BLAISE, A., *Le Vocabulaire Latin des principaux thèmes liturgiques*, Brepols, Turnhout 1966.

BRUYLANTS, P., *Les oraisons du Missel Romain, texte et histoire* (Études liturgiques 2 vol.), Mont César, Louvain 1952.

Corpus orationum, 14 vol., ed. E. Moeller – J.-M. Clément – B.C. 't Wallant (Corpus christianorum series latina 160-160 M), Brepols, Turnhout 1992-2004.

LEWIS, C.T., – C. SHORT, *A Latin Dictionary*, Oxford UP, Oxford – New York 1879, reprinted 1995.

C. Patristic sources

AUGUSTINUS HIPPONENSIS, *Sermo* 216, in *Sant'Agostino, Discorsi 4,1 (184-229/v)*: *Su i tempi liturgici*: testo Latino dell'edizione maurina e delle edizioni postmaurine, tr. and notes P. Bellini – F. Cruciani – V. Tarulli (Opere di Sant'Agostino 32, 1), Città Nuova Editrice, Rome 1984.

D. Liturgical sources

Das fränkische Sacramentarium Gelasianum *in alamannischer Überlieferung*, ed. L.C. Mohlberg (Liturgiegeschichtliche Quellen und Forschungen 1-2), Münster ¹1918, ²1939, ³1971.

"Hadrianum ex authentico", *Le Sacramentaire Grégorien: Ses principales formes d'après les plus anciens manuscrits*, 3 vol., ed. J. Deshusses (Spicilegium Friburgense 16), Éditions universitaires, Fribourg ³1992, 1, 83-348 (*Gregor*).

Liber sacramentorum augustodunensis, ed. O. Heiming (Corpus christianorum series latina 159 B), Brepols, Turnhout 1984.

Liber sacramentorum engolismensis (*Cod. B. N. Lat. 816*), ed. P. Saint-Roch (Corpus christianorum series latina 159 C), Brepols, Turnhout 1987.

Liber sacramentorum paduensis (*Padova, Biblioteca Capitolare, cod. D 47*), ed. A. Catella – F. dell'Oro – A. Martini (Bibliotheca Ephemerides Liturgicae, Subsidia 131. Monumenta italiae liturgica 3), Centro Liturgico Vincenziano edizioni liturgiche, Rome 2005.

Liber sacramentorum romanae aeclesiae ordinis anni circuli (*Cod. Vat. Reg. Lat. 316/Paris Bibl. Nat. 7193, 41/56*) (*Sacramentarium Gelasianum*), ed. L.C. Mohlberg – L.

Eizenhöfer – P. Siffrin (Rerum ecclesiasticarum documenta. Series maior, Fontes 4), Herder, Rome 1960.

Missale Romanum ex decreto Sacrosancti Oecumenici Concilii Vaticani II instauratum auctoritate Pauli PP. VI promulgatum Ioannis Pauli PP. II cura recognitum, editio typica tertia, Typis Vaticanis, Città del Vaticano ³2002.

Sacramentarium Bergomense: Manoscritto del secolo IX della Biblioteca di S. Alessandro in Colonna in Bergamo, ed. A. Paredi (Monumenta Bergomensia 6), Fondazione Amministrazione Provinciale, Bergamo 1962 *(Bergom)*.

E. **Translations of liturgical sources**

The Roman Missal, revised by decree of the Second Vatican Council and published by the authority of Paul VI, official English texts, Collins, London 1974.

F. **Studies**

ASHWORTH, H., "The Liturgical Prayers of St Gregory the Great", *Traditio* 15 (1959) 107-161.

AUGÉ, M., "Principi di interpretazione dei testi liturgici", in *La Liturgia momento nella storia della salvezza,* ed. S. Marsili et alii (Anàmnesis 1), Marietti, Casale Monferato 1974, 159-179.

CAPELLE, B., "La main de S. Grégoire dans le Sacramentaire Grégorien", *Revue Bénédictine* 49 (1937) 13-28.

CHAVASSE, A., *La liturgie de la ville de Rome du Ve au VIIIe siècle, une liturgie conditionnée par l'organisation de la vie in Urbe et extra muros* (Studia Anselmiana 112, Analecta Liturgica 18), Pontificium Athenaeum Anselmianum , Rome 1993.

DE ZAN, R., "Criticism and Interpretation of Liturgical Texts", in *Introduction to the Liturgy,* ed. A.J. Chupungco (Handbook for Liturgical Studies 1), Liturgical Press (Pueblo Book), Collegeville MN 1997, 331-365 (En. tr. of R. DE ZAN, "Introduzione alla Liturgia, Ermeneutica", ed. A. J. Chupungco [*Scientia Liturgica: Manuale di Liturgia* 1] Piemme, Casale Monferrato 1998, 356-389).

LAMBRECHT, J., *Second Corinthians* (Sacra Pagina Series 8), Liturgical Press (Michael Glazier Book), Collegeville MN 1999.

CHAPTER 8

The Vocabulary of the Collects:
Retrieving a Biblical Heritage

Gerard Moore

Introduction

The original impetus driving this chapter was to explore the vocabulary of the collects in the Third Edition of the *Missale Romanum*. This broad focus has been narrowed to two general areas. One is the biblical nature of the vocabulary. The second is whether collects were composed in such a 'high' style in vocabulary and grammatical structure as to render them somewhat incomprehensible to the ordinary worshipper. Both questions, however, rely on finding a method for understanding the meaning of any word within the prayer itself, something much more than a dictionary exercise.

There are a number of excellent vocabulary studies of the collects. The dictionary by Albert Blaise is a classic text, complemented by the work of Mary Pierre Ellebracht and more recently the writings of Els Rose on the *Missale Gothicum*. In this paper I will also draw upon my own research into the collects.[1] These works remain relevant to any study of the vocabulary of the collects since the majority of collects for Ordinary Time, the seasons and

---

[1] These works are: A. BLAISE, *Dictionaire latin-français des auteurs chrétiens*, , rev. H. Chirat, Brepols, Turnhout 1954, reprint 1964; M.P. ELLEBRACHT, *Remarks on the Vocabulary of the Ancient Orations in the Missale Romanum* (Latinitas Christianorum Primaeva 18), Dekker & Van de Vegt, Nijmegen – Utrecht ²1966; *Missale gothicum e codice vaticano reginensi latino 317 editum*, ed. E. Rose (Corpus christianorum series latina 159 D), Brepols, Turnhout 2005 (hereafter *Goth*); G. MOORE, *Vatican II and the Collects for Ordinary Time: A Study in the Roman Missal (1975)*, Catholic Scholars Press, Bethesda 1998.

many feasts are ancient prayers still in use or retrieved from the past for reapplication in contemporary worship. Some research has been done on the grammatical structure of orations from the Missal of Pius V, prayers which have been carried into the present sacramentary.[2]

1. Reflections on the biblical nature of the collect vocabulary

The third edition of the General Instruction insists that the prayers of the Mass have a biblical foundation, however it does not develop what it means to draw upon the inspiration and spirit of the scripture.[3] In what manner, then, do the collects reflect a scriptural basis? Two influential positions have hindered the appreciation of the scriptural qualities of the prayers, despite the many biblical references and Hebraisms uncovered by Blaise, Ellebracht and Rose. One is the position of Theodore Klauser that the collects are non-biblical in nature. While not all have agreed with Klauser,[4] his assertion is the one that appears to be repeated almost habitually. The second is that of Christine Mohrmann on the highly stylized, 'sacral' nature of the prayers. We will open our essay in contention with Klauser, and close in dialogue with Mohrmann.

Klauser is quite emphatic that the collects are far from biblical. When discussing the biblical qualities of Roman liturgical texts he opines: "There is none of this in the Roman Collects ... I hope I shall not be misunderstood if I say that, fundamentally, the Roman liturgy is far removed from the Bible".[5] It

---

[2] In particular see: M.G. HAESSLY, *Rhetoric in the Sunday Collects of the Roman Missal*, St Louis Univ. PhD thesis, The Manufacturers Printery, St Louis 1938: F. GERDES, "The Language of the Roman Missal. Part III. Second Sunday after Epiphany to Quinquagesima Sunday", Saint Louis University thesis ad lauream, St Louis MO 1958. This dissertation is one of a series emanating from that university at the time.

[3] "... and it is drawing upon the inspiration and spirit of Sacred Scripture that prayers, orations, and liturgical songs are fashioned in such a way that from them [the scriptures] actions and signs derive their meaning". (*General Instruction of the Roman Missal*, tr. the International Commission on English in the Liturgy (Liturgy Documentary Series 2), United States Conference of Catholic Bishops, Washington DC [3]2002, n° 391).

[4] For example the comment from Blaise concerning the contents of the earliest extant Latin liturgical sources dating from seventh century Rome: "Compilers were concerned, firstly, to be understood by all when they expressed some religious feeling or thought pertaining to the feast being celebrated, and secondly, to avoid familiarity in creating a style especially fitting for prayer and sufficiently priestly and holy to be worthy of the mysteries expressed" (P. AUVRAY – P. POULIN – A. BLAISE, *The Sacred Languages*, tr. S.J. Tester (Faith and Fact Books 115), Burns & Oates, London 1961 (of *Les Langues sacrées*, Librairie Arthème Fayard, Paris, undated), 152.

[5] See: T. KLAUSER, *A Short History of the Western Liturgy: An Account and Some Reflections*, tr. J. Halliburton, Oxford UP, Oxford [2]1979 (of *Kleine abendländische*

is doubtful if this position, especially in regard to the collects, can be maintained.

1.1 *Establishing the biblical text in context*

The translation of the bible that was at the service of the creators of the ancient collects and of almost all prayers up until the present was the Vulgate.[6] It is rare to find a prayer in the ancient sacramentaries that reflects pre-Vulgate translations.[7] There is only a limited role for the Neo-Vulgate in understanding the vocabulary of collects written up until the present.

Yet it is not sufficient to identify that the vocabulary in a collect is also found in the bible. The vital questions are how that vocabulary is used within the prayer, whether this is true to the original scriptural usage, and what further meaning or even alternative meaning is established through a biblical allusion. A corollary is that the vocabulary cannot always be understood from the prayer alone. The context of the prayer is significant for appreciating the application of any biblical content. Context can include historical background to the collect itself, as well as the liturgical situations in which an oration is used.

1.2 *Collects derived directly from a scriptural passage*

Two collects in particular serve as prime examples of how a prayer can reflect and apply a passage from scripture. The collect for the Twenty-third Sunday in Ordinary Time is a distillation of Paul's Letter to the Galatians.[8] The text reads:

> *Missale Romanum* 1970
>
> *Deus, per quem nobis et redemptio venit et praestatur adoptio,*
> *filios dilectionis tuae benignus intende,*
> *ut in Christo credentibus*
> *et vera tribuatur libertas, et hereditas aeterna*[9]

Liturgiegeschichte. Bericht und Besinnung, Peter Hanstein, Bonn [5]1965), 41-42. To be fair to Klauser he goes on to recommend further close study of the vocabulary of the orations, the very type of research that somewhat undermines his position.

[6] There are variations in the editions of the Vulgate; throughout this paper I will use: *Bibliorum Sacrorum iuxta Vulgatam Clementinam, nova editio,* ed. A. Gramatica, Typis polyglottis Vaticanis, Città del Vaticano 1946.

[7] One possible example is the prayer AD POPULUM n° 591 in: *Liber sacramentorum romanae aeclesiae ordinis anni circuli (Cod. Vat. Reg. Lat. 316/Paris Bibl. Nat. 7193, 41/56) (Sacramentarium Gelasianum),* ed. L.C. Mohlberg – L. Eizenhöfer – P. Siffrin (Rerum ecclesiasticarum documenta. Series maior, Fontes 4), Herder, Rome 1960, (hereafter *GelasV*), 91.

[8] For a full study of the prayer see: Moore, *Vatican II,* 223-235.

[9] *Missale Romanum ex decreto Sacrosancti Oecumenici Concilii Vaticani II instauratum auctoritate Pauli PP. IV promulgatum, editio typica,* Typis polyglottis Vaticanis, Città del Vaticano [1]1970, (hereafter *MR* [1]1970), 362.

The author's translation for study purposes only is:

> God, through whom redemption comes for us and adoption is bestowed
> upon us,
> look favourably upon the children of your love,
> so that to those who believe in Christ,
> true freedom and eternal inheritance may be granted

The prayer is an adaptation of an oration first found in the *Gelasianum Vetus*[10] as a member of a set of orations for vespers during Paschaltide entitled, INCIPIUNT ORATIONES PASCHALES UESPERTINALES.[11] The adaptations to the prayer are themselves interesting, and are without precedent in the transmission of the prayer through the sources. The ancient text had a stronger baptismal reference. The current *in Christo credentibus* has replaced *in Christo renatis*, while *filios dilectionis tuae benignus intende* has replaced *respice in opera misericordiae tuae*. In the *Missale Romanum* 1970 the prayer is also found in Eastertide (on the fifth Sunday[12] and on Saturday of the second week[13]), adding weight to the baptismal sensibilities in the text. However in the *Missale Romanum* 2002 other collects have replaced these two Easter usages. The modified prayer now stands in Ordinary Time only, with its baptismal references and original paschal context deleted.

Nevertheless the biblical basis of the prayer remains potent. The outstanding feature of the prayer is its reflection of the Pauline matrix of redemption, adoption, baptism, inheritance and freedom. The structure, vocabulary and content of the prayer closely resemble certain passages in Paul's Letter to the Galatians. The following four features of the collect can be found in the Vulgate translation of Galatians 1) the conjunction of redemption (*redemptio*) and adoption (*adoptio*), 2) the association between baptism and inheritance, 3) the conjunction of inheritance (*hereditas*) and liberty (*libertas*), and 4) the relationship between the pair redemption/adoption and the pair inheritance/liberty.

Let us examine each of these in turn:

1) Redemptio/adoptio. Through redemption (*redimere*) by Christ from the law, comes adoption by God as children (*adoptio filiorum*) and as heirs (*heredes*): "ut eos qui sub lege erant redimeret, ut adoptionem filiorum reciperemus. Quoniam autem estis filii, misit Deus Spiritum Filii sui in corda vestra clamantem: Abba. Pater. Itaque iam non est servus, sed filius. Quod si filius, et heres per Deum" (Gal 4:5-7).

---

[10] *GelasV* n° 522.
[11] *GelasV* n° 516.
[12] *MR* ¹1970, 303.
[13] *MR* ¹1970, 322.

2) *Baptism*[14] *and inheritance.* Those who are baptized in Christ become heirs (*heredes*) to the promise first made to Abraham: "Quicumque enim in Christo baptizati estis Christum induistis ... Si autem vos Christi, ergo semen Abrahae estis, secundum promissionem heredes" (Gal 3:27-29).

3) Hereditas/libertas. Both the status of being an heir, and the gift of liberty from enslavement, come from being the free children (the children of the free woman) of God's promise (*filii liberae*). The free offspring share in the freedom by which Christ freed all who believe in him: "Sed quid dicit Scriptura? 'Ecce ancillam et filium eius'; non enim heres erit filius ancillae cum filio liberae. Itaque, fratres, non sumus ancillae filii, sed liberae, qua liberate Christus nos liberavit" (Gal 4:30-31).

4) Redemptio/adoptio *and* hereditas/libertas. It can be seen from the above that adoption and baptism provide the connection between redemption on the one hand, and the pairing of *hereditas* and *libertas* on the other.

It is important to note that various combinations of the themes of redemption, adoption, baptism, inheritance, and freedom are present in other Pauline writings. In Romans, adoption as God's children makes Christians heirs of God and coheirs with Christ (Rom 8:14-15, 17).[15] Believers live in the freedom of life in the Spirit, in which they are both free from sin and death, and freed for life and peace (Rom 8:2,6).[16] They receive this freedom through baptism (Rom 6:3-9). The blessing which opens the Letter to the Ephesians (Eph 1:3-14) combines adoption as children (*adoptio filiorum*) in Christ (v. 5),[17] redemption (*redemptio*) and the remission of sins (v. 7),[18] and the Spirit as the pledge of the eternal inheritance (*hereditas*) (v. 13-14),[19]

The collect, then, presents a concise version of key Pauline teachings, found throughout the Letter to the Galatians in particular, but not restricted

---

[14] For the connection between baptism and rebirth (*renasci*) see: BLAISE, *Vocabulaire*, n° 332, 333, 336.

[15] "Quicumque enim Spiritu Dei aguntur ii sunt filii Dei. Non enim accepistis spiritum servitutis iterum in timore, sed accepistis spiritum adoptionis filiorum in quo clamamus: Abba, Pater ... Si autem filii, et heredes: heredes quidem Dei, coheredes autem Chisti ..." (Rom 8:14-15,17).

[16] "Nihil ergo nunc damnationis est iis qui sunt in Christo Iesu, qui non secundum carnem ambulant; lex enim spiritus vitae in Christo Iesu liberabit me a lege peccati et mortis ... nam prudentia carnis mors est, prudentia autem spiritus vita et pax" (Rom 8:1-2, 6). See also: Rom 7:24.

[17] "qui praedestinavit nos in adoptionem filiorum per Iesusm Christum in ipsum, secundum propositum voluntatis suae" (Eph 1:5).

[18] "in quo habemus redemptionem per sanguinem eius, remissionem peccatorum secundum divitias gratiae eius" (Eph 1:7).

[19] "in quo et vos, cum audissetis verbum veritatis, evangelium salutis vestrae, in quo et credentes signati estis Spiritu promissionis sancto, qui est pignus hereditatis nostrae, in redemptionem adquisitionis, in laudem gloriae ipsius" (Eph 1:12-13).

to it. The original text, with its Paschaltide context, applied the vocabulary immediately to baptism. The *MR* 1970 has expunged this baptismal sensibility without altering the profound biblical nature of the oration.

The collect for the Third Sunday in Ordinary Time offers us an example of how a prayer encapsulates a particular biblical passage and applies it to a concrete situation. The collect reads:

> *Missale Romanum* 1970
>
> *Omnipotens sempiterne Deus,*
> *dirige actus nostros in beneplacito tuo,*
> *ut in nomine dilecti Filii tui*
> *mereamur bonis operibus abundare.*[20]

The author's translation for study purposes only is:

> Almighty eternal God,
> direct all our actions in what is pleasing to you,
> so that in the name of your beloved Son
> we may merit to abound in good works.

In structure, content and vocabulary, the collect corresponds with the Vulgate translation of the passage Ephesians 1:3-2:11. In terms of content and structure, the extended reference sets together the following elements: the divine favour (*beneplacitum*) (1:9), God's guidance of all things (1:11), the power of the name (*nomen*) of Christ (1:21), the abundance (*superabundare*) of grace (1:8, 2:7), and the good works (*bona opera*) designated by God for the faithful (2:10).

Yet historically the prayer contained an application of this scriptural passage to a particular situation. The original ancient liturgical context of the prayer either in the Masses for January or in a Mass for the octave of Christmas highlights certain features in the oration.[21] The preceding feast of the incarnation was one of the central acts of the mystery of God's saving will, the divine *beneplacitum* (Eph 1:9). Furthermore, the beginning of the

---

[20] *MR* ¹1970, 342.

[21] The original prayer is: "Hadrianum ex authentico" n° 85, *Le Sacramentaire Grégorien: Ses principales formes d'après les plus anciens manuscrits*, 3 vol., ed. J. Deshusses (Spicilegium Friburgense 16), Éditions universitaires, Fribourg ³1992, 1, 83-348 (hereafter *Gregor*). The following ancient sacramentaries contain the same Mass *prohibendum ab idolis* set alongside the Masses for the octave of the Nativity: *Gelas V* n° 54-56; *Liber sacramentorum gellonensis, textus* n° 82-87, ed. A. Dumas – J. Deshusses (Corpus christianorum series latina 159), Brepols, Turnhout 1981 (hereafter *Gellon*); *Liber sacramentorum engolismensis* (*Cod. B. N. Lat. 816*) n° 88-90, ed. P. Saint-Roch (Corpus christianorum series latina 159 C), Brepols, Turnhout 1987 (hereafter *Engol*). Our collect, *Gregor* n° 85, is the collect for an octave Mass in the sacramentaries of the *Gellon* n° 91; and *Engol* n° 91.

New Year (1 January) conjured up long standing pagan associations, focused around the festival of the god Janus.[22] These New Year festivities were markedly pagan and licentious, and as such were opposed by the church. Hence the petition to act according to what is pleasing to God, *in beneplacito tuo*. Further, imprecation of the 'name' of the beloved Son is a reminder to the faithful that God has set Christ above every power, dominion and name, now and in the future (Eph 1:20-21). In effect the time and influence of Janus, and all pagan belief and ceremony, had come to an end. This context serves to highlight the worship allusions of *bona opera* in that the related forms *agere*, *agenda* and *actio* carry a strong liturgical sense since they are often used to speak of the celebration of the Mass, and the Mass itself.[23]

The vocabulary of the collect, as used within a set structure, allows the prayer to unfold and reveal itself as a celebration of the passage Ephesians 1:1-2:10. Yet is it the liturgical context of the prayer within proximity to the celebration of the Nativity and its application to the cultural context of the continuing temptation of reverting to pagan worship and practice at the new year that gives the scriptural language a clear meaning and pastoral intent. While the current prayer, as the collect for the Third Sunday in Ordinary Time remains somewhat close to the celebration of Christmas, time and cultural change have erased much of the pastoral logic for the oration, and it resides in the Missal slightly diminished as a reflection of biblical language rather than an application of scripturally charged teaching to a contentious situation in the life of faith.

Collects that contain a 'play' on a scriptural text
Whereas not all collects are so explicitly scriptural, some exhibit an interplay between well known scriptural verses and tensions current at the time of writing. This is especially the case in the collect for the Fourth Sunday in Ordinary Time:

Missale Romanum 1970

Concede nobis, Domine Deus noster,
ut te tota mente veneremur,
et omnes homines rationabili diligamus affectu.[24]

---

[22] See: F. CABROL, "Circoncision (Fête de la)", in *Dictionnaire d'archéologie chrétienne et de liturgie*, ed. F. Cabrol – H. Leclercq, Letouzey et Ané, Paris 1948 (hereafter *DACL*), 3, 1717-1727.
[23] See: BLAISE, *Vocabulaire*, 242, n° 5.
[24] *MR* ¹1970, 343.

The author's translation for study purposes only is:

> Grant to us, Lord our God,
> to worship you with all our mind
> and to love all people with spiritual affection..

Until its inclusion in the Missal of Paul VI the prayer was found only in the *Veronense*.[25] Knowledge of the historical context of the oration is essential to understanding its vocabulary and the import of its use of scripture. G. Pomarès[26] in his study of a set of ancient Roman collects and prefaces identifies the prayer as from a series of Masses written by Pope Gelasius I (pope 492-496) to counter the celebration by Christians of the pagan Roman festival of Lupercalia, usually held in mid-February.[27] Our prayer was written for the Sunday liturgy of 29 January 495, just over two weeks before the festival was to take place.[28] The festival of Lupercalia was an ancient Roman tradition with a long, unclear and complicated history. At base are the metaphors of purification of the city from hostile forces and, from 276 B.C., the fructification of barren women. A central action of the celebration was the whipping of women by the *Lupercali*, a group of men. In ancient times the *Lupercali* were naked or dressed in a form of wolf costume, though after the time of Augustus (sometime after 44 B.C.) they dressed in goat skins. The festival persisted until the time of Gelasius, when it apparently had the following features. Prior to the festival the *Lupercali* would deliberately set about to seduce women. Then, as part of the festival, they would publicly denounce the women as having been seduced. These women, or perhaps others as well, once slandered publicly, would be either partially or fully stripped and subsequently whipped, to the delight of the crowd. The *Lupercali* also had affinities with the underworld and, as seducers, took on the aspect of *incubi*. As such their seducing of the women also carried a sense of the continuing fertility of Rome as based in the activities of the ancestors, the *parentalia*. The divulging of names and sins, and the whipping done by these representatives of the underworld, had a salutary significance not unrelated to the pagan notion of public confession and penance to secure salvation.

---

[25] *Sacramentarium veronense* n° 432, ed. L.C. Mohlberg – L. Eizenhöfer – P. Siffrin (Rerum ecclesiarticarum documenta. Series maior, Fontes 1), Herder, Rome [3]1978, 58 (hereafter *Leon*). See: *Corpus orationum*, 14 vol.,, ed. E. Moeller – J.-M. Clément – B.C. 't Wallant (Corpus christianorum series latina 160), 1, 59, n° 669.

[26] GELASIUS PP. I , *Lettre contre les Lupercales et dix-huit messes du Sacramentaire léonien*, ed., tr. G. Pomarès (Sources Chrétiennes 65), Le Cerf, Paris 1959.

[27] The main sources for this section are: GELASIUS, *Lettre*, ed. Pomarès (SCh 65) and A.W.J. HOLLEMAN, *Pope Gelasius I and the Lupercalia*, Adolf M. Hakkert, Amsterdam 1974, especially the summary of the book, 146-155.

[28] *Gélase*, ed. Pomarès, 142.

There was much for Gelasius to object to in the festival. It involved a general level of drunkenness and lascivious behaviour. Furthermore, there were the sexual sins of the *Lupercalia* and the slander and whipping of women. Because of its relationship to the forces of the underworld, it could not simply be seen as a piece of ancient Roman folklore, but remained a pagan ritual. Its metaphor of purification and fertility meant that there was a form of salvation and healing outside the Christian economy. It was clear to Gelasius that the participation of Christians in such an event was far from being harmless participation in a local folk custom. It compromised the worship of God, the love of God, the divine economy of grace and the love of neighbour.

The prayer is evocative of the Gospel episode in which Jesus is questioned concerning the greatest commandment of the Law. He answers by joining two Old Testament injunctions concerning the obligation to love God[29] and to love one's neighbour,[30] establishing that the entire law hangs on the combination of the pair: "'Diliges Dominum Deum tuum ex toto corde et in tota anima tua et in tota mente tua.' Hoc est maximum mandatum. Secundum autem simile est huic: 'Diliges proximum tuum sicut teipsum.' In his duobus mandatis universa lex pendet et prophetae" (Matt 22:37-40),[31] The Lucan parable of the Good Samaritan (Luke 10:29-37) shows that 'neighbour' refers to all humans. The biblical passage, then, provides the structure of the prayer and accounts for a good deal of its language: *Dominus Deus, in tota mente*, the use of the verb *diligere*, the directive to *omnes homines*. Further, the scriptural basis of the prayer means that *mens* does not signal the mind only, but is a 'short hand' for a love that includes the whole heart, soul and mind.

1.3 *Examples of 'play' on particular scriptural words*
In the collect for the Fourth Sunday in Ordinary Time the use of the words *veneremur* and *rationabilis* poses a different set of questions. We will deal with *veneremur* first. The term was introduced into Christian liturgical vocabulary from pagan Roman ritual language. In Roman cultic vocabulary *venerari* meant to honour the gods with reverence and ritual service so that they might be moved to grant the favours requested.[32] However, in Christian euchology the verb is not usually associated with direct acts of homage to God. Rather it is normally applied to the veneration of the saints, or to the veneration implied in carrying out mandates such as the Lenten fast. The use of *venerari* in our collect is highly unusual in that God is the direct object of

---

[29] "Audi, Israel: Dominus Deus noster Dominus unus est. Diliges Dominum Deum tuum ex toto corde tuo et ex tota anima tua et ex tota fortitudine tua. Eruntque verba haec, quae ego praecipio tibi hodie, in corde tuo ..." (Deut 6:4-6).
[30] "Diliges amicum tuum sicut teipsum, Ego Dominus" (Lev 19:18).
[31] The pericope is also found in Mark 12:29-31 and Luke 10:27-28.
[32] ELLEBRACHT, *Remarks*, 150-151.

the verb. This is found in only a few of the prayers in the earliest Roman sacramentaries examined in the Deshusses and Darragon concordance[33] and not at all in the Missal of Pius V.[34] This serves to emphasize the unusual nature of this prayer and further highlights that all actions of veneration must ultimately show honour to God and bring the faithful closer to the ways of God, in marked contrast to acts of pagan worship. By replacing the scriptural 'love of God' with the 'worship of God', the prayer highlights that worship belongs to God alone. As well, it points up that all acts of worship must be in line with the underlying commandment to love God totally. Furthermore, Gelasius is making it clear that those who engage in the festival of the Lupercalia are neither loving nor worshipping God as Christians ought. Yet in terms of vocabulary, Gelasius is retrieving for one off usage only the pagan sense of the word *venerari*, setting it within a biblical framework, tying it to the concept of divine love and then turning the word against its original sense to resolve a complex pastoral situation and a vexed theological dynamic. We require a comprehensive knowledge of the biblical basis, ancient liturgical usage and historical context to appreciate how the vocabulary is being used with such inventiveness and sophistication.

With the word *rationabili*[35] we encounter literary creativity of another sort. In early Christian writing, the Greek *logikos* was transposed into Latin as *rationabilis*. However it retained the Greek meaning of 'spiritual,' that is in keeping with the realm of the Spirit, rather than the Latin sense of 'rational', 'according to reason'.[36] This is established by examining the way the word is used in the Vulgate and also in liturgical sources from the same age.

In the Vulgate translation of the Letter to the Romans, Paul urges the community to live lives that are a spiritual service (*rationabile obsequium*) to God (Rom 12:1-2). Such lives are according to the highest aspects of human nature, pleasing to God and in conformity to the will of God rather than in conformity to the behaviour of the world. The adjective is also found in the Vulgate translation of 1 Peter, where the author reminds the community of the meaning of charity. The letter encourages the members of the community, as new born children in the Word, to love each other intensely

---

[33] J. Deshusses – B. Darragon, *Concordances et tableaux pour l'étude des grands sacramentaires*, 3 vol., Éditions universitaires, Fribourg, Suisse 1982-1983. For collects which use *venerari* in this fashion see: *Leon* n° 422, which is also a Gelasian anti-Lupercalia prayer (*Gélase*, ed. Pomarès, 93), and the collect *Leon* n° 877.

[34] ELLEBRACHT, *Remarks*, 150. Note that Ellebracht does not identify any particular missal of Pius V, rather stating that her study is based in the critical edition: P. BRUYLANTS, *Les oraisons du Missel Romain, texte et histoire* (Études liturgiques 2 vol.), Mont César, Louvain 1952; see: ELLEBRACHT, *Remarks*, xxiii.

[35] For further examples of the use of *rationabilis* see: DESHUSSES, *Concordances* 3, 4, 24-25.

[36] C. MOHRMANN, *"Rationabilis - Logikos"*, in *Études sur le latin des chrétiens*, Edizioni di Storia e Letteratura, Rome 1958, 179.

from the heart and to rid themselves of such things as spite and deceit. In this way they seek the spiritual milk (*rationabile lac*) that leads to salvation (1 Pet 1:22-2:2).[37]

In liturgical usage, *rationabilis* retained this biblical sense of 'spiritual', while indicating that it is spiritual because it is in conformity to God's good pleasure. This is indicated in the *Veronense* collect, "Da nobis, domine, rationabilem, quaesumus, actionem; ut te solum sincera mente uenerantes, et fiducialius quae tua sunt postulemus, et facilius adsequamur"[38] an oration which provides a direct parallel with our text.[39] In that collect, as in ours, Christians are called to love all humans with a spiritual love, a love that is in accord with the greatest commandment, and is total (*tota mens*) and sincere (*sincera mens*). Note also that the collect, as quoted above, associates the verb *uenerari* with the worship of God.

In another prayer, meditating on what is spiritual, on what is pleasing to God, leads to following God both in word and deed: "Praesta, quaesumus, omnipotens deus, ut semper rationabilia meditantes quae tibi sunt placita et dictis exequamur et factis".[40]

A similar use is seen in the Roman Canon where *rationabilem* is coupled with *acceptabilem* to describe God's action over the oblation. God is requested to make the oblation blessed, approved, ratified, spiritual and acceptable so that it may become for the community the body and blood of Christ. As approved and ratified, the spiritual and acceptable oblation is right and fitting because it is in line with God's will: "Quam oblationem tu, deus, in omnibus,   quaesumus,   benedictam,   ascriptam   ratam   rationabilem

---

[37] There is some confusion in the Latin Vulgate translation and transliteration of this piece of scripture. One version of the Latin Vulgate (*Biblia Sacra iuxta Vulgatam versionem, editio altera emendata. Tomus II Proverbia-Apocalypsis*, ed. B. Fischer – I. Gribomont – H.F.D. Sparks – W. Theile, Württembergische Bibelanstalt, Stuttgart [2]1975) uses *ratio* in place of *rationabilis*. The 1946 Nova Editio of the Latin Vulgate reads *rationabile* (*Bibliorum Sacrorum iuxta Vulgatam Clementinam*, ed. Gramatica). The Greek text reads "λογικὸν" (*The Greek New Testament*, ed. K. Aland, United Bible Societies – the Institute for the New Testament Textual Research, Biblia-Druck, Stuttgart [3 corrected]1983).

[38] *Leon* n° 877. Author's translation for study purposes: "Give to us, Lord, spiritual worship, so that worshiping you alone with sincere minds, may we both ask confidently for what are your things, and more easily put them into effect".

[39] *Leon* n° 423.

[40] *Gelas V* n° 1521. Author's translation for study purposes: "Grant, we beg all powerful God, that always meditating on spiritual things, we may carry out by words and deeds the things that are pleasing to you". This prayer has been incorporated into the *MR* [1]1970 as the collect for the Seventh Sunday in Ordinary Time (*MR* [1]1970, 346).

acceptabilemquae facere digneris, ut nobis corpus et sanguis fiat dilectissimi filii ...."[41]

As an aside there are perhaps two further points of interest. In liturgical Latin *rationabilis* was later replaced by *purus*, a word avoided by the early Christians because of its association with pagan worship. As well, the adjective gives an added dimension to Gelasius' argument by invoking the scriptural writings of the twin pillars of the Roman church, two powers more potent than any pair of Roman ancestors.

1.4 *Preliminary observations*
Before continuing it is worth summarizing some of the ways in which collects can be said to be suffused by scripture. We have seen prayers that emerge directly from biblical themes and actual passages with a view to applying these to pastoral situations. The pastoral imperatives today are different from those of earlier centuries and so we have classic texts which were not originally fashioned for the challenges and issues of today's communities, yet which have a new force in their new contexts. Other prayers engage in constructive 'play' with the biblical text, challenging the hearers to reinterpret the scriptures for a new situation. There are also examples where there is a 'play' in individual words within the texts, however the sense of these shifts has to be affirmed by the text and context of the oration as a whole and where possible by instances of similar use in other contemporary prayers.

1.5 *Naming God in the collects*
A central feature of the vocabulary of the collects is the way God is named. There are a number of levels at work here. Every collect in the current Missal is framed by its Trinitarian conclusion. This appears to be the case for all ancient orations as well, however the evidence is not as clear-cut. The prayers in the sources end with *per*, though rarely is the concluding formula written out in full.[42] Perhaps the earliest witness to this type of formula can be found in the writings of Fulgentius (d. 533), a North African bishop. In his *Epistola 14*, Fulgentius is faced with a series of questions from the Deacon Ferrandus. The deacon's fourth question, which concerns the expression which closes the presidential prayer, sets out the formula as follows:

---

[41] *GelasV* n° 1248. Author's translation for study purposes: "Grant, Lord, we ask you, to make this offering wholly blessed, approved, ratified, spiritual and accepable so that it may become for us the body and blood of your dearly beloved Son..."; See: *MR* ¹1970, 451.

[42] I am grateful to Daniel McCarthy for pointing up the following references from the critical editions: *Goth* n° 5; *Gellon* n° 623c, 2396; *Liber sacramentorum augustodunensis* n° 1446, ed. O. Heiming (Corpus christianorum series latina 159 B), Brepols, Turnhout 1984. Of these only the text from the *Missale gothicum* is a collect, in this case a prayer *post mysterium*.

Per Iesum Christum Filium tuum Dominum nostrum, qui tecum vivit et regnat in unitate Spiritus sancti.[43] It is reasonable to conclude, then, that in the early Roman Latin liturgy the opening prayer was brought to a close by a formula which invited the mediatorship of Christ and praised the Trinity.

In the main, collects are addressed to God, *Deus, Dominus,* as the first person of the Trinity, but they are addressed through Christ. This is in line with the earliest Roman orations.[44] The overwhelming majority of our current collect style prayers, developed within this patristic framework, address the divinity as God or Lord with or without naming other attributes. Very rarely is God addressed as Father in ancient Latin collects or in the *Missale Romanum* 2002.[45] Referring only to the prayers from the Sundays in Ordinary Time, we can see allusions to the 'fatherhood' of God carried through from the ancient sources. The invocation in the collect for the Nineteenth Sunday in Ordinary Time recalls the name Father without using

---

[43] For the correspondence see: FERRANDUS CARTHAGINENSIS, "Epistula 13 seu epistula Ferrandi diaconi ad sanctum Fulgentium [Ruspensem] episcopum de quique quaestionibus" cap. 2, *Sancti Fulgentii episcopi Ruspensis opera,* ed. J. Fraipont (Corpus christianorum series latina 91), Brepols, Turnhout 1968, 386, lines 34-35; FULGENTIUS RUSPENSIS, "Epistula 14 seu sancti Fulgentii episcopi liber ad Ferrandum diaconum de quinque quaestionibus" cap. 35, ed. Fraipont (CCSL 91), 428-29, lines 1451-53; see also cap. 37, p. 431, lines 1528-29; cap. 38, p. 432, lines 1562-63. Again my appreciation to Daniel McCarthy for updating and expanding this list of references.

[44] See: J.A. JUNGMANN, *The Mass of the Roman Rite: Its Origins and Development,* 2 vol., tr. F.A. Brunner, Christian Classics Inc., Westminster MD, 1992, reimpression of 1951 (of *Missarum Sollemnia, eine genetische Erklärung der römischen Messe,* 2 vol. Herder, Vienna ²1949), 1, 379-380; J.A. JUNGMANN, *The Place of Christ in Liturgical Prayer,* tr., A. Peeler, Alba House, Staten Island NY 1965 (of *Die Stellung Christi im liturgischen Gebet,* Aschendorff, Münster ²1962), 105-123.

[45] To confirm this I examined 1770 collects, prayers over the gifts, post communion prayers, prayers over the people, and the collects within various rites such as those that close the readings for the Easter Vigil contained within the *Missale Romanum* of 2002 (*Missale Romanum ex decreto Sacrosancti Oecumenici Concilii Vaticani II instauratum auctoritate Pauli PP. VI promulgatum Ioannis Pauli PP. II cura recognitum, editio typica tertia,* Typis Vaticanis, Città del Vaticano ³2002 [hereafter *MR* ³2002]). Unavoidably some prayers were counted more than once if they were used for different Masses. Regardless of this inconsistency, the results were overwhelming. Of the 1770 collect style prayers examined, only 18 used the appellation *Pater* (Father). By contrast, 1748 orations used *Deus, Dominus,* or *Domine Deus.* Three collects were found addressed to Jesus (24 Dec, Morning Mass, collect [*MR* ³2002, 149]; 14th Sept, Exalt Holy Cross, post communion [*MR* ³2002, 829]; Votive Mass 4, Myst. Holy Cross, post communion [*MR* ³2002, 1162]). Interestingly a collect in the 1970 Missal addressed to Jesus has since been rewritten with an invocation of God, *Deus* (See: Common BMV 3, alternative collect, *MR* ¹1970, 672, and its revision as Common BMV 7, collect, *MR* ³2002, 903). One prayer had no direct invocation (Masses for various necessities, 39, post communion, *MR* ³2002, 1141).

it directly as a form of address: *Omnipotens, sempiterne Deus, quem paterno nomine invocare praesumimus.*[46] There are also indirect references to the fatherhood of God in those prayers which refer to Christ as *tuus Filius*, as in the collects for the Third[47] and the Fourteenth[48] Sundays in Ordinary Time.

Yet the primary approach to God appears to be based in a theology of the divine 'name'. In collects, the address to God is linked with the invocation of the divine 'name', *nomen*,[49] related back to its manifestation in the scriptures where God names the divine self, enabling the people to name their God. The 'name' of God is a Hebraism transposed into the Vulgate translation of the scriptures and commonly found in liturgical texts, signifying the being, essence, and in some cases presence, of a person or deity.

Apart from addressing all prayers through Christ, the place and redemptive work of the Son is given particular emphasis in the collects for Ordinary Time. In the collect for the Third Sunday in Ordinary Time there is a theology of the 'name' of Christ as the beloved Son of the Father, as seen in the expression *nomen dilecti filii tui*.[50] As seen above, the expression reflects the Vulgate translation of Ephesians 1:19-23, a passage which expresses the community's belief that Christ has been raised by God to the fullness of power, above every name and power. The application of *nomen* also echoes the Vulgate translation of John 17:6, where Jesus declares himself to be the manifestation of God's name to those the Father gave him. From the structure of the collect for the Third Sunday in Ordinary Time, Christ's name as the beloved Son is set in parallel with God's favour, power and salvation.

It is worth recalling that in the collect for the Twenty-third Sunday in Ordinary Time the redemptive matrix of redemption, adoption, freedom and eternal inheritance is ascribed to God's action through Christ.[51] In the collect, those who have been redeemed and become adopted children of God are named as *in Christo credentes*. The Pauline matrix, and especially Paul's understanding of the grace of adoption, presumes faith in the work of Christ and also the work of the Spirit. The redemptive work of Christ is also recalled in the collect for the Fourteenth Sunday in Ordinary Time, where God's raising of the fallen world is said to be in response to the self-

---

[46] *MR* ¹1970, 358; The author's translation for study purposes is: "Almighty, eternal God, whom we presume to invoke by the name father ..."

[47] "Deus ... ut in nomine dilecti filii tui ..." (*MR* ¹1970, 342).

[48] "Deus qui in Filii tui humilitate iacentem mundum erexisti ..." (*MR* ¹1970, 353).

[49]See especially the collects for the Twelfth Sundays in Ordinary Time, "Sancti nominis tui, Domine, timorem partier et amorem fac nos habere perpetuum ..." (*MR* ¹1970, 351) and for the Twenty-second Sunday in Ordinary Time, "Deus virtutum, cuius est totum quod est optimum, insere pectoribus nostris tui nominis amorem ..." (*MR* ¹1970, 361).

[50] *MR* ¹1970, 342.

[51] *MR* ¹1970, 362.

abasement of his Son: "Deus, qui in Filii tui humilitate iacentem mundum erexisti...."[52] As noted in the study of the collect for the Eighth Sunday in Ordinary Time, the Missal of Paul VI gives a more Christological focus to the understanding of God's peaceful order, relating it to the life, work and future coming of Christ.[53]

While the Christology of the prayers in Ordinary Time is well attested, their pneumatology certainly merits further study. The oration for the Nineteenth Sunday in Ordinary Time contains a direct reference to the role of the Spirit in the faithful's invocation of God as Father.[54] Some of the vocabulary of the prayers, such as *procedere*[55] and *adoptio*,[56] infer the presence and work of the Spirit. Similarly, the vocabulary of filial inheritance evokes Ephesians 1:13-14 where the Spirit is described as the pledge of the eternal inheritance (*hereditas*).[57] Here we have picked up a characteristic of the collects, as with Roman euchology and theology in general, that of their implicit, rather than explicit pneumatology. From an ecumenical perspective, therefore, there seems to be at first sight a lack of balance in the theology put forward by the prayers between the place of the Spirit and the redemptive role of Christ. This typical Roman emphasis is only partially softened by the emphasis on the Spirit in the prayers for the vigil and feast of Pentecost.

1.6 *Expressions and attributes of the divine Name*
The collects describe God's being and *nomen* in terms of holiness (*sanctitas*), majesty (*majestas*), love (*dilectio*) and power (*omnipotentia*), which are primarily biblical ascriptions appropriated into Roman euchology. The adjective *sanctum* and the noun *majestas* both express qualities that are practically synonymous with God's name.[58] The collect for the Twelfth

---

[52] *MR* [1]1970, 353.

[53] See: Moore, *Vatican II*, 196. The collect for the Eighth Sunday in Ordinary Time is found in *MR* [1]1970, 347.

[54] *MR* [3]2002, 469. It is interesting to note that the direct reference to the Spirit, present in the ancient oration from Milan found in the *Sacramentarium Bergomense* n° 634, (*Manoscritto del secolo IX della Biblioteca di S. Alessandro in Colonna in Bergamo*, ed. A. PAREDI [Monumenta Bergomensia 6], Fondazione Amministrazione Provinciale, Bergamo, 1962) is no longer present in the text given in the *MR* [1]1970, 358 and *MR* [2]1975, 358. It was it was subsequently restored in *MR* [3]2002, 469, in line with the original Ambrosian prayer. On the other hand, the collect is no longer in use during paschaltide, whereas in the earlier editions of the Missal of Paul VI it also served as the collect for Monday Week 2 in that season (*MR* [1]1970, 315 and *MR* [2]1975, 315).

[55] See, for example, the collect of the Tenth Sunday of Ordinary Time, *MR* [1]1970, 349.

[56] See, for example, the following collects: the Thirteenth Sunday of Ordinary Time, *MR* [1]1970, 352; the Nineteenth Sunday of Ordinary Time, *MR* [1]1970, 358; the Twenty-third Sunday of Ordinary Time, *MR* [1]1970, 362.

[57] See, for example, the following collects: the Nineteenth Sunday of Ordinary Time, *MR* [1]1970, 358; the Twenty-third Sunday of Ordinary Time, *MR* [1]1970, 362.

[58] See: MOORE, *Vatican II*, 622-623.

Sunday in Ordinary Time associates the manifestation of God's *nomen* with the revelation of his love, *dilectio*.[59] The collect for the Twenty-second Sunday in Ordinary Time links the revelation of God's *nomen* to his power.[60] Closely associated with the *nomen* and the titles ascribed to God are the divine attributes to which appeal is made and which express the people's sense of God's attitude towards them, and so ground their confidence that God will respond to their needs. The attributes characteristically appealed to throughout the collects are God's loving kindness, *pietas*, mercy, *misericordia*, and divine strength, *fortitude*, again each of which has strong biblical reference points.[61]

1.7 *Summary remarks*

The preliminary observations above concerning the biblical nature of the prayers can be supplemented with an appeal to the biblical foundation for the theology of God expressed in the prayers, and indeed of the language used to invoke God in the prayers. If the Hebrew theology of the divine '*nomen*' is at the core of the prayers, then this biblical principle informs the possible range of meanings in all vocabulary used to describe God, situated as it always is within a Trinitarian context.

2. A Review of the 'classical' understanding of the collect prayer

The 'collect style' orations not only had a certain shape but were written in a particular style. They are variously described as precise, concise, sober prayers, devoid of overly exuberant, emotive or ostentatious elements, all the while replete with stylistic elements from the rhetorical traditions of Rome. Christine Mohrmann makes the point thus: "In the close-knit, well-composed phrases of the Roman Orations, in which the celebrant resumes, as it were, the prayer of the faithful, we find traces of the style processes of the art of polished speech, taught and practiced for centuries in the schools of Rome".[62]

    In particular, the 'collect style' orations were written in accordance with the rules of the Roman rhetorical device known as the *cursus*.[63] By arranging

---

[59] *MR* [1]1970, 351.

[60] *MR* [1]1970, 361.

[61] An extended discussion of the theology of the divine 'name' in the collects can be found in Moore, *Vatican II*, 621-643.

[62] C. MOHRMANN, *Liturgical Latin: Its Origins and Character, three lectures*, The Catholic University of America Press, Washingtgon DC 1957, 75. For a study of the rhetorical elements in the opening prayers of the Missal of Pius V see: HAESSLY, *Rhetoric*. It is not known which pre-1946 edition of the *Missale Romanum* was used by Haessly in her research.

[63]For a summary description of the three chief forms of cadences in the Roman *cursus* see, JUNGMANN, *The Mass*, 1, 376-377. More complete studies of the *cursus* in litugical

the accents in the last syllables of a literary unit or clause according to a fixed set of rules (the *cursus*), the prayer took on a certain rhythm and harmony.

Even before the origin of collect style prayers (mid fifth century),[64] Latin patristic authors had been turning their attention to the question of the sense and function in Christian writings of the stylistic traditions of classical Roman literature.[65] According to Lactantius (c. 240-320), a polished traditional style could be of service in the conversion of intellectuals to the faith.[66] However, for Hilary of Poitiers (c. 315-367) elegance of style has rich theological connotations in that it showed God reverence and honour.[67] Mohrmann maintained that fifth century Christians were quite at home with the use of highly stylized language in prayer.[68] Though such language could not be easily understood it was felt to ably reflect the sacral style deemed to be appropriate for divine worship. A further consideration is that the collect, as the prayer which took up and gathered the petitions of those present, functioned in and with the prayers of the whole assembly.[69] The faithful did not need to fully understand the presidential oration to know that their prayers, wrought in the collective silence that was perhaps the most important part of the prayer, were being brought to conclusion and placed before God. In a sense all vocabulary falls under this silence-in-prayer.

While these points on style and language are well made they should not be overemphasized. It should not be too quickly concluded that the early prayers were unintelligible, or in fact sought to be somehow elevated in order to be 'above' the grasp of worshippers. We have identified levels and styles in the prayers that show a remarkable degree of biblical sophistication. This could only be aimed at a biblically literate group of hearers, who as Christians desired that their prayer had a biblical sensibility. By grounding prayers in the scriptures, authors could more freely re-appropriate classical styles and pagan vocabulary, placing them at the service of a thoroughly Christian liturgy. The scriptural resonance in orations may well have operated as one of the factors in the retention of prayers in collections and their reuse in later sacramentaries in different countries and diverse contexts.

---

texts are to be found in E. VACANDARD, "Le cursus: son origine, son histoire, son emploi dans la liturgie", *Revue des questions historiques* 78 (1905) 59-102; and H. LECLERCQ, "Cursus", in *DACL* 3, 3193-3205.

[64] For a summary see: MOORE, *Vatican II*, 17-23.

[65] For the following discussion see: MOHRMANN, *Liturgical Latin*, 46-59.

[66] This point is developed further by Mohrmann in her article "Problèmes stylistiques dans la littérature latine chrétienne" *Vigiliae Christianae* 9 (1955) 232-234, drawing upon various sections of his *Divinae institutiones* 1,1,7 and 10.

[67] See: Mohrmann, "Problèmes stylistiques" 234-236, which draws upon various sections of Hilary's *Tractatus super psalmos*, with reference to his commentaries on Psalms 13 and 118.

[68] Mohrmann, *Liturgical Latin*, 60-61.

[69] See: Moore, *Vatican II*, 28-33, 66.

Elements of style could also play a part in rendering the prayers memorable and prayerful, as seen in the attention to the use of the *cursus* in the orations, enabling certain expressions and endings to ring in the minds (and hearts) of the hearers.

Clearly those orations written for special circumstances, such as those composed by Gelasius against the celebration of the Lupercalia by Christians, would have been somewhat pointless if their meaning were unintelligible to the assembly. The same, however, could be said for the collects of major feasts, or prayers devoted to particular pastoral situations. An example is the current collect for the Seventh Sunday in Ordinary Time,[70] first found as an oration in a Mass to be celebrated when there is discord in a monastery (ORATIONES IN CONTENCIONE AD MISSAS. ITEM ALIA MISSA).[71] The content and vocabulary of this prayer are directed clearly towards recovering harmony in the community, and so necessarily implies that it is graspable and understandable, if not also challenging and effective.[72] There is also some basis for positing a degree of correspondence between particular prayers and the readings of the day, as does Chavasse when discussing a set of six Masses for the Sundays after Easter in the *Gelasianum Vetus*.[73]

In summary discussion of the classical rhetorical style of the Roman collects needs to be balanced by closer attention to the accessibility of the prayers themselves. This requires a deeper appreciation of the biblical nature of the vocabulary and construction of the prayers, and a more thorough understanding of the way the pastoral context of the prayers and the context of terms within the text itself are at play in the prayers.

Conclusion

I have argued for a stronger appreciation of the biblical nature of the collect prayers, implying that the first stop for any review of the vocabulary should be a concordance of the Vulgate, much as Blaise has done in his dictionary. Yet a reliance on a supposed biblical resonance is not sufficient to understand the way words are being wrought in the orations. The scriptural basis of the collects can be found in individual words, the structure and content of the prayer, and in various 'plays' within the prayer, and may only become obvious in light of the pastoral or liturgical situation that gave rise to the oration.

---

[70] *MR* ³2002, 457.

[71] *GelasV* n° 1521.

[72] For more complete discussion see: Moore, *Vatican II*, 498-510.

[73] A. CHAVASSE, *Le Sacramentaire Gélasien* (*Vatican Regenensis 316*): *Sacramentaire presbytéral en usage dans les titres Romains au VIIᵉ siècle*, (Bibliothèque de théologie. Série 4: Histoire de la Théologie 1), Desclée, Tournai 1958, 241-44.

Bibliography

A. Holy Scripture

Biblia Sacra iuxta Vulgatam versionem, editio altera emendata. Tomus II Proverbia-Apocalypsis, ed. B. Fischer – I. Gribomont – H.F.D. Sparks – W. Theile, Württembergische Bibelanstalt, Stuttgart ²1975.

Bibliorum Sacrorum iuxta Vulgatam Clementinam, nova editio, ed. A. Gramatica, Typis polyglottis Vaticanis, Città del Vaticano 1946

The Greek New Testament, ed. K. Aland, United Bible Societies – the Institute for the New Testament Textual Research, Biblia-Druck, Stuttgart ³ corrected1983.

B. Research tools

BLAISE, A., *Dictionaire latin-français des auteurs chrétiens*, rev. H. Chirat, Brepols, Turnhout 1954, reprint 1964.

BRUYLANTS, P., *Les oraisons du Missel Romain, texte et histoire* (Études liturgiques 2 vol.), Mont César, Louvain 1952.

Concordances et tableaux pour l'étude des grands sacramentaires, 6 vol., ed. J. Deshusses – B. Darragon, Éditions universitaires, Fribourg, Suisse 1982-1983.

Corpus orationum, 14 vol., ed. E. Moeller – J.-M. Clément – B.C. 't Wallant (Corpus christianorum series latina 160-160 M), Brepols, Turnhout 1992-2004.

C. Patristic sources

FERRANDUS CARTHAGINENSIS, "Epistula 13 seu epistula Ferrandi diaconi ad sanctum Fulgentium [Ruspensem] episcopum de quique quaestionibus", ed. J. Fraipont (Corpus christianorum series latina 91), Brepols, Turnhout 1968, 385-387.

FULGENTIUS RUSPENSIS, "Epistula 14 seu sancti Fulgentii episcopi liber ad Ferrandum diaconum de quinque quaestionibus", ed. Fraipont (Corpus christianorum series latina 91), Brepols, Turnhout 1968, 387-444.

D. Liturgical sources

"Hadrianum ex authentico", *Le Sacramentaire Grégorien: Ses principales formes d'après les plus anciens manuscrits*, 3 vol., ed. J. Deshusses (Spicilegium Friburgense 16), Éditions universitaires, Fribourg ³1992, 1, 83-348 (*Gregor*).

Missale gothicum e codice vaticano reginensi latino 317 editum, ed. E. Rose (Corpus christianorum series latina 159 D), Brepols, Turnhout 2005 (*Goth*).

Liber sacramentorum augustodunensis, ed. O. Heiming (Corpus christianorum series latina 159 B), Brepols, Turnhout 1984 (*Phill*).

Liber sacramentorum engolismensis (Cod. B. N. Lat. 816), ed. P. Saint-Roch (Corpus christianorum series latina 159 C), Brepols, Turnhout 1987 (*Engol*).

Liber sacramentorum gellonensis, textus, ed. A. Dumas (Corpus christianorum series latina 159), Brepols, Turnhout 1981 (*Gellon*).

Liber sacramentorum romanae aeclesiae ordinis anni circuli (*Cod. Vat. Reg. Lat. 316/Paris Bibl. Nat. 7193, 41/56*) (*Sacramentarium Gelasianum*), ed. L.C. Mohlberg – L. Eizenhöfer – P. Siffrin (Rerum ecclesiasticarum documenta. Series maior, Fontes 4), Herder, Rome 1960 (*GelasV*).

Missale Romanum ex decreto Sacrosancti Oecumenici Concilii Vaticani II instauratum auctoritate Pauli PP. IV promulgatum, editio typica, Typis polyglottis Vaticanis, Città del Vaticano 11970 (*MR* 11970).

Missale Romanum ex decreto Sacrosancti Oecumenici Concilii Vaticani II instauratum auctoritate Pauli PP. VI promulgatum Ioannis Pauli PP. II cura recognitum, editio typica tertia, Typis Vaticanis, Città del Vaticano 32002 (*MR* 32002).

Sacramentarium Bergomense, Manoscritto del secolo IX della Biblioteca di S. Alessandro in Colonna in Bergamo, ed. A. Paredi (Monumenta Bergomensia 6), Fondazione Amministrazione Provinciale, Bergamo, 1962.

Sacramentarium veronense, ed. L.C. Mohlberg – L. Eizenhöfer – P. Siffrin (Rerum ecclesiasticarum documenta. Series maior, Fontes 1), Herder, Rome 31978, 58 (*Leon*).

E. Magisterial documents

General Instruction of the Roman Missal, tr. the International Commission on English in the Liturgy (Liturgy Documentary Series 2), United States Conference of Catholic Bishops, Washington DC 32002.

F. Studies

AUVRAY, P., – P. Poulin – A. Blaise, *The Sacred Languages,* tr S.J. Tester (Faith and Fact Books 115), Burns & Oates, London 1961 (of *Les Langues sacrées,* Librairie Arthème Fayard, Paris, undated).

CABROL, F., "Circoncision (Fête de la)", in *Dictionnaire d'archéologie chrétienne et de liturgie,* ed. F. Cabrol – H. Leclercq, Librairie Letouzey et Ané, Paris 1948 (*DACL*), 3, 1717-1727.

CHAVASSE, A., *Le Sacramentaire Gélasien* (*Vaticanus Reginensis 316*): *Sacramentaire presbytéral en usage dans le titres Romains au VIIᵉ siècle* (Bibliothèque de théologie. Série 4: Histoire de la Théologie 1), Desclée, Tournai 1958.

ELLEBRACHT, M.P., *Remarks on the Vocabulary of the Ancient Orations in the Missale Romanum* (Latinitas Christianorum Primaeva 18), Dekker & Van de Vegt, Nijmegen – Utrecht 21966.

GELASIUS PP. I, *Lettre contre les Lupercales et dix-huit messes du Sacramentaire léonien,* ed., tr. G. Pomarès (Sources Chrétiennes 65), Le Cerf, Paris 1959.

GERDES, F., "The Language of the Roman Missal. Part III. Second Sunday after Epiphany to Quinquagesima Sunday", Saint Louis University thesis ad lauream, St Louis MO 1958.

HAESSLY, M.G., *Rhetoric in the Sunday Collects of the Roman Missal,* St Louis Univ. PhD thesis, The Manufacturers Printery, St Louis 1938.

HOLLEMAN, A.W.J., *Pope Gelasius I and the Lupercalia*, Adolf M. Hakkert, Amsterdam 1974.

JUNGMANN, J.A., *The Mass of the Roman Rite: Its Origins and Development*, 2 vol. tr. F.A. Brunner, Christian Classics Inc., Westminster MD, 1992, reimpression of 1951 (of *Missarum Sollemnia, eine genetische Erklärung der römischen Messe*, 2 vol. Herder, Vienna ²1949).

_____, *The Place of Christ in Liturgical Prayer*, tr., A. Peeler, Alba House, Staten Island NY 1965 (of *Die Stellung Christi im liturgischen Gebet*, Aschendorff, Münster ²1962).

KLAUSER, T., *A Short History of the Western Liturgy: An Account and Some Reflections*, tr. J. Halliburton, Oxford UP, Oxford ²1979 (of *Kleine abendländische Liturgiegeschichte. Bericht und Besinnung*, Peter Hanstein, Bonn ⁵1965).

LECLERCQ, H., "Cursus", in *Dictionnaire d'archéologie chrétienne et de liturgie*, ed. F. Cabrol – H. Leclercq, Letouzey et Ané, Paris 1948 (*DACL*), 3, 3193-3205.

MOHRMANN, C., *Liturgical Latin. Its Origins and Character, three lectures*, The Catholic University of America Press, Washington DC 1957,

_____, "Problèmes stylistiques dans la littérature latine chrétienne" *Vigiliae Christianae* 9 (1955) 222-246.

_____, "*Rationabilis - Logikos*", in *Études sur le latin des chrétiens*, Edizioni di Storia e Letteratura, Rome 1958.

MOORE, G., *Vatican II and the Collects for Ordinary Time: A Study in the Roman Missal (1975)*, Catholic Scholars Press, Bethesda 1998.

VACANDARD, E., "Le cursus: son origine, son histoire, son emploi dans la liturgie", *Revue des questions historiques* 78 (1905) 59-102.

CHAPTER 9

Between Memories and Hopes:
Anamnesis and Eschatology in Selected Collects

Daniel P. McCarthy

Introduction

To better understand the anamnetic and eschatological character of the collects, I shall examine four different collects from the current *Missale Romanum* of 2002. After presenting the source of each prayer, I shall examine each according to its literary structure and the times of its verbs. From this structural and verbal analysis, I shall describe the way in which the anamnetic and eschatological character of each prayer is expressed, if at all. After having examined all four prayers, I shall attempt to make an initial statement about the anamnetic and eschatological character of these four prayers.

This study is based on two premises. First, I have decided to consider anamnesis narrowly as the saving deeds of God in Christ. Understanding how these salvific mysteries in human history are understood to have relevance for our day is part of the task of this paper. I have not similarly limited eschatology, however, because the ambiguity of the first subjunctive (present subjunctive) mitigates against this, as will be shown. Thus, I take eschatology to include its partial realization in this life.

1. An example from Ordinary Time: The Third Sunday

Text. A review of the collects assigned to the Sundays of ordinary time in the *Missale Romanum* of 2002 indicates that they typically do not refer explicitly to the saving events of God in the life of Christ. They do, however, have purpose clauses, which are latent of eschatological meaning. Let us take for example the collect assigned to the third Sunday of Ordinary Time, which reads:

Missale Romanum 2002	The Roman Missal
Omnipotens sempiterne Deus, *dirige actus nostros in beneplacito tuo,* *ut in nomine dilecti Filii tui* *mereamur bonis operibus abundare.*[1]	All-powerful and ever-living God, direct your love that is within us, that our efforts in the name of your Son may bring mankind to unity and peace.[2]

The author's literal translation for study purposes is:

> Almighty, ever-living God,
> guide our actions in your gracious purpose
> that in the name of your beloved Son
> we may be worthy to abound in good works.

Source. The collect appears in the *Hadrianum*,[3] a papal sacramentary given by P. Hadrian I to Charlemagne in 785-786,[4] where it is the first of two single prayers given between the octave of Christmas and the feast of Epiphany. It appears under the heading, *oratio alia in dominica*, "another prayer on sunday". This arrangement is also followed in the *Paduense*, a papal sacramentary originally redacted around 670-680 for use with pilgrims to St Peter's basilica.[5] In the *Paduense*, however, the collect is part of a Mass

---

[1] *Missale Romanum ex decreto Sacrosancti Oecumenici Concilii Vaticani II instauratum auctoritate Pauli PP. VI promulgatum Ioannis Pauli PP. II cura recognitum, editio typica tertia*, Typis Vaticanis, Città del Vaticano ³2002, 453 (hereafter *MR* ³2002). See: *Corpus orationum*, 14 vol., ed. E. Moeller – J.-M. Clément – B.C. 't Wallant (Corpus christianorum series latina 160 E), Brepols, Turnhout 1992-2003, 6, n° 3830; P. BRUYLANTS, *Les oraisons du Missel Romain, texte et histoire* (Études liturgiques 2 vol.), Mont César, Louvain 1952, 2, n° 716.

[2] *The Roman Missal, revised by decree of the Second Vatican Council and published by the authority of Paul VI, official English texts*, Collins, London 1974, 290.

[3] "Hadrianum ex authentico" n° 85, *Le Sacramentaire Grégorien: Ses principales formes d'après les plus anciens manuscrits*, 3 vol., ed. J. Deshusses (Spicilegium Friburgense 16), Éditions universitaires, Fribourg ³1992, 1, 83-348 (hereafter *Gregor*).

[4] C. VOGEL, *Medieval Liturgy: An Introduction to the Sources*, tr., rev. W.G. Storey – N.K. Rasmussen (National Association of Pastoral Musicians Studies in Church Music and Liturgy), Pastoral Press, Washington DC 1986 (of *Introduction aux sources de l'histoire du culte Chrétien au moyen âge*, Centro italiano di studi sull'alto medioevo, Spoleto 1981), 80.

[5] VOGEL, *Medieval Liturgy*, 92. The oldest remaining manuscript of the *Paduense* dates to 840-855 and shows Gallican influence. The text of the *Paduense* is found in two recent editions: *Liber sacramentorum paduensis* (*Padova, Biblioteca Capitolare, cod. D 47*), ed. A. Catella – F. dell'Oro – A. Martini (Bibliotheca Ephemerides Liturgicae, Subsidia 131. Monumenta italiae liturgica 3), Centro Liturgico Vincenziano edizioni liturgiche,

formulary.[6] In both the *Hadrianum* and the *Paduense* the formularies assigned to the feast of the Epiphany do not yet evidence the celebration of the baptism of the Lord or of the wedding feast at Cana, which feasts were already celebrated in various ways in Milan, Brescia and in the Christian East.[7] The current text matches that of the critical editions of both sacramentaries, except for the odd phonetic spelling *sempiternae* in the *Hadrianum*.

Thus, although the prayer has rich scriptural allusions,[8] it does not explicitly mention any specific saving event in the life of Christ, and thus has no explicit anamnesis, narrowly understood.

Literary structure. This prayer has a simple literary structure composed of three clauses: an invocation, a petition and a purpose clause.

Invocation. The prayer begins with the complex invocation *Omnipotens sempiterne Deus*, which is rendered in the official English translation literally as, "All-powerful and ever-living God".

Petition. The imperative petition *dirige actus nostros in beneplacito tuo*, "guide our actions in your gracious purpose", is rendered as, "direct your love that is within us".

Purpose. The purpose for which we petition God to guide our actions is expressed classically as, *ut in nomine dilecti Filii tui mereamur bonis operibus abundare*, "that in the name of your beloved Son we may be worthy to abound in good works", and is translated as a purpose clause: "that our efforts in the name of your Son may bring mankind to unity and peace".

Verbal times. Having sketched the clausal structure of the prayer, let us now map out the time sequence of the verbs.

Dirige. The independent verb is the imperative *dirige*, "guide". Its time frame is the present as it continues into the future. We petition God to guide now, to continue guiding, and to guide in the future.

Ut...mereamur. Relative to the imperative *dirige*, the first subjunctive (present subjunctive) *mereamur*, with its complement *abundare*, is contemporaneous, ongoing, incomplete, future and eternal. Thus, we pray that God guide our actions now that we may be worthy to abound now, that God continue to guide our actions that we may continue to be worthy to abound and that God shall guide our actions in the future that in the future we may be worthy to abound in good deeds.

Rome 2005 (hereafter *Pad* 2005); "Gregorianum paduense ad fidem codicis Paduensis D 47, Fragmentis collatis Salisburgensibus", *Le Sacramentaire Grégorien*, 3 vol., ed. J. Deshusses (Spicilegium Friburgense 16), 1, ³1992, 607-684, (hereafter *Pad* 1992).

6 *Pad* 2005, n° 52-54.

7 T. TALLEY, *The Origins of the Liturgical Year*, Liturgical Press (Pueblo Book), Collegeville MN 1986, 141-147.

8 See my commentary on this prayer: D.P. MCCARTHY, "Human Impulse, Divinely Ordered", *The Tablet* 261 (20 January 2007) 17.

Developmental steps. This prayer makes explicit four developmental steps of maturation.

Developmental step one: actus nostros. The prayer affirms that we are acting.

Developmental step two: dirige. We petition God to grant a gift, to guide our actions. This implies our co-operating with the gift of God by being guided in our actions.

Developmental step three: mereamur. We pray that once God directs our actions, God will grant the further gift of making us worthy to abound in good actions. The gift of this developmental step involves more than co-operation on our part, because we pray for an axiological change of status from being unworthy to becoming worthy ourselves to abound in good works.

Developmental step four: bonis operibus abundare. The prayer states that, as we are transformed by God, we do good deeds.

Anamnesis. Although this prayer has rich scriptural allusions, it does not make an explicit reference to any one of the saving mysteries of the life of Christ, and thus lacks an explicit anamnesis. The rich scriptural allusions, however, correlate this prayer to the teachings of Christ as presented in the scriptures.

Eschatology. The eschatological character of this prayer, moreover, is one that is to be realized in this life. Even if we interpret the first subjunctive *mereamur* according to its future significance and correlate it with the last judgement as presented in the gospel of Matthew,[9] when we shall stand before the throne of glory as the Son of Man separates the people as a shepherd separates the sheep from the goats. According to that account the decisive criterion is whether during our lifetimes we abounded in good works. Thus, the good works are to be realized in our lifetimes, and our meriting to abound in good works is to be realized in our lifetimes.

Summary. Typical of the collects assigned to the Sundays *per annum*, the collect for the third Sunday of Lent presents no explicit anamnesis. The eschatological force of this prayer finds its realization in this life. As we mature through the developmental steps presented in the prayer and co-operate with the transforming gift of God, this prayer envisions the mature Christian as one who does good works.

---

[9] Matt 25:31-46; Vulgate, NRSV throughout. Vulgate from *Biblia Sacra: Iuxta vulgatam versionem*, ed. R. Gryson, Deutsche Bibelgesellschaft, Stuttgart 1994. NRSV from *The Holy Bible Containing the Old and New Testaments with the Apocryphal / Deuterocanonical Books, New Revised Standard Version*, Oxford UP, New York – Oxford 1989.

2. **Anamnesis of saving events in the life of Christ**: The collect of Good
   Friday

Text. The collect of Good Friday reads:

Missale Romanum 2002	The Roman Missal
Deus, qui peccati veteris hereditariam mortem, in qua posteritatis genus omne successerat, Christi Filii tui, Domini nostri, passione solvisti, da, ut conformes eidem facti, sicut imaginem terreni hominis naturae necessitate portavimus, ita imaginem caelestis gratiae sanctificatione portemus.[10]	Lord, by the suffering of Christ your Son you have saved us all from the death we inherited from sinful Adam. By the law of nature we have borne the likeness of his manhood. May the sanctifying power of grace help us to put on the likeness of our Lord in heaven.[11]

The author's literal translation for study purposes is:

> O God,
> you who by the passion of Christ your Son, our Lord,
> destroyed the hereditary death of the ancient sin,
> in which the whole race of posterity had followed,
> grant that we, having been made similar to the same one,
> just as we have borne the image of the earthly human
> by the necessity of nature,
> so may bear the image of the heavenly one
> by the sanctification of grace.

The anamnetic character of this collect of Good Friday refers to the definitive and saving action of God in human history. It refers to the passion of Christ as the means by which God acts for our salvation. It also alludes to our sharing in this saving deed of God in Christ sacramentally through baptism. The eschatological character of the prayer will find its fullness in eternity, but is already being realized in our lives, as God grants the gift.

Source. The *Missale Romanum* of 2002 presents a choice of two collects for the liturgy of Good Friday, both originally found in the *Gelasianum*,[12] which was composed between 628-715 for presbyteral use in the titular

---

10 *MR* ³2002, 313. See: *Corpus orationum* n° 1962, ed. Moeller (CCL 160 B); BRUYLANTS, *Les oraisons*, 1, n° 88.

11 *The Roman Missal*, 1974, 157.

12 *Liber sacramentorum romanae aeclesiae ordinis anni circuli (Cod. Vat. Reg. Lat. 316/Paris Bibl. Nat. 7193, 41/56) (Sacramentarium Gelasianum)* n° 398, ed. L.C. Mohlberg – L. Eizenhöfer – P. Siffrin (Rerum ecclesiasticarum documenta. Series maior, Fontes 4), Herder, Rome 1960 (hereafter *GelasV*).

churches of Rome. The first of the two was assigned in the *Gelasianum* to Monday of Holy Week. The second, presented here, was assigned to Good Friday, not as the collect, but after the first reading and psalm response and before the second reading. This prayer was assigned to the same position in three eighth century Gelasian sacramentaries.[13] This prayer was not included in the earliest manuscripts of the *Hadrianum*, although it did appear in certain codices of the *Hadrianum* revised by Gregory of Aniane.[14] It did not appear in the *Missale Romanum* of 1474 or of 1570 or thereafter. Only with the *Missale Romanum* of 1970 was the prayer reclaimed for liturgical use.

Literary structure. This prayer has a literary structure composed of four units. First is a simple invocation. Second, an amplification clause includes the first premise. Third is a simple petition. Fourth, the purpose clause includes the motive and second premise clauses. In examining the clauses of this prayer, I shall also indicate a few biblical allusions.

Invocation. The prayer begins with the simple invocation *Deus*, "God", which is rendered as, "Lord".

Amplification. The invocation *Deus* is amplified by the relative phrase, *qui peccati veteris hereditariam mortem ... Christi Filii tui, Domini nostri, passione solvisti*, "you who by the passion of Christ your Son, our Lord, destroyed the hereditary death of the ancient sin...", which is rendered as, "by the suffering of Christ your Son you have saved us all from the death..." The titles of Christ evoke the confession of the Centurion looking upon the deceased Jesus: *vere homo hic Filius Dei erat*, "Truly this man was God's Son".[15] In Judges 10:6 *peccatis veteribus* refers to idolatry.[16]

First premise. Nestled within the amplification, the premise for Christ's destroying the hereditary death of the ancient sin is given in the relative clause, *qui peccati veteris hereditariam mortem*, "in which the whole race of posterity had followed", which is rendered as, "we inherited from sinful Adam".

Petition. The imperative petition, *da*, "grant", is not translated.

Second premise. The purpose clause has two correlative phrases established by, *sicut ... ita*, "just as ... so". The first correlative gives a second premise, *sicut imaginem terreni hominis naturae necessitate portavimus*, "just as

---

[13] *Liber sacramentorum gellonensis, textus* n° 664, ed. A. Dumas – J. Deshusses (Corpus christianorum series latina 159), Brepols, Turnhout 1981; *Liber sacramentorum engolismensis (Cod. B. N. Lat. 816)* n° 650, ed. P. Saint-Roch (Corpus christianorum series latina 159 C), Brepols, Turnhout 1987; *Liber sacramentorum Augustodunensis* n° 501, ed. O. Heiming (Corpus christianorum series latina 159 B), Brepols, Turnhout 1984.

[14] *Le Sacramentaire Grégorien*, ed. Deshusses (SpicFri 16), n° 118*.

[15] Mark 15:39.

[16] "filii autem Israhel peccatis veteribus iungentes nova fecerunt malum in conspectu Domini et servierunt idolis Baalim et Astharoth" : "The Israelites again did what was evil in the sight of the Lord, worshiping the Baals and the Astartes" (Judg 10:6).

by the necessity of nature we have borne the image of the earthly human", which is rendered as, "by the law of nature we have borne the likeness of his manhood".

Purpose. The second correlative expresses our intention for petitioning and supplies God's intention in granting: *ut ... ita imaginem caelestis gratiae sanctificatione portemus*, "that ... so may we carry the image of the heavenly one by the sanctification of grace", which is refashioned as an exhortative petition, "May the sanctifying power of grace help us to put on the likeness of our Lord in heaven". The correlative is an elaboration on 1 Corinthians 15:49: *sicut portavimus imaginem terreni portemus et imaginem caelestis*, "Just as we have borne the image of the man of dust, we will also bear the image of the man of heaven".

Motive. God's motive for granting that we may carry the image of the heavenly one is expressed in the participial phrase, *conformes eidem facti*, "[we] having been made similar to the same one", which is not translated. The text is an allusion to Romans 8:29: "For those whom he foreknew he also predestined to be conformed to the image of his Son [*conformes fieri imaginis Filii eius*]".

Verbal times. Having sketched the clausal structure of the prayer, let us now sequence the times of the verbal forms.

Da. The independent verb is the imperative *da*, "grant". Its time frame is the present as it continues into the future. We petition God to grant now, to continue granting, and to grant in the future.

Qui ... solvisti. The one form *solvisti* may be understood as expressing Time 4a, (the present perfect) or Time 4b (the historical perfect). Were *solvisti* translated in Time 4a (as a present perfect), meaning, "you have destroyed", it would emphasize the immediacy of God's action in regard to those offering the prayer. I have translated *solvisti*, however, in Time 4b (as a historical perfect), meaning, "you destroyed", because of the idea expressed by the noun *passione*. The passion of our Lord is the historical referent for interpreting the verb *solvisti*. The scriptural passages operative here are those that emphasize that Christ's passion occurred once for all, for example: "But as it is, he has appeared once for all at the end of the age to remove sin by the sacrifice of himself".[17]

Successerat. The time of *successerat* is antecedent to that of *solvisti*. Thus, in this prayer humanity "had followed" or "had been following the hereditary death of the ancient sin", prior to the passion of Christ.

Ut ... portemus. Relative to the imperative *da*, the first subjunctive (present subjunctive) is contemporaneous, ongoing, incomplete, future and eternal. Thus, we pray that God grant now that we may bear now the image

---

[17] Heb 9:26. *Confer*: "And it is by God's will that we have been sanctified through the offering of the body of Jesus Christ once for all" (Heb 10:10), and "For Christ also suffered for sins once for all, the righteous for the unrighteous, in order to bring you to God. He was put to death in the flesh, but made alive in the spirit" (1 Pet 3:18).

of the heavenly one; that God continue to grant that we may continue to bear the image; that God grant at the end of time that we may bear the image at the end of time; and that God grant eternally that we may eternally bear the image of the heavenly one.

Sicut…portavimus. The time of *portavimus* is correlated with that of *portemus*. While the one form *portavimus* may be translated as a Time 4b (a historical perfect), meaning, "we bore" or "we did bear", I have chosen to translate it as a Time 4a (a present perfect), meaning, "we have borne" or "we have been bearing". This means that the time of *portavimus* is considered as antecedent to yet touching upon the whole range of time of *portemus*. Thus, we petition that Grant now that, just as we have been bearing the image of the earthly human, so may we bear (now) the image of the heavenly one". Furthermore, we petition that God continue to grant that, just as we will have continually borne the image of the earthly human, so may we continue to bear the image of the heavenly one". Finally, we petition that God shall grant that, just as we shall ever have borne the image of the earthly human, we may ever bear the image of the heavenly one.

Facti. The antecedent participle *facti*, taken by itself, means, "ones having been made". It is a divine passive, for God is the one who makes us similar to Christ. The participle is antecedent to the first subjunctive *portemus*. But here again we must discern whether *facti* is expressive of Time 4a (the present perfect) or of Time 4b (the historical perfect). Were it interpreted as expressive of Time 4a (the present perfect), then our having been made similar to Christ would be understood as an ongoing process ever antecedent to yet touching upon our bearing the image of the heavenly one. I have translated *facti* as expressive of Time 4b (the historical perfect), however, and see in it an allusion to our baptism when we were made similar to the image of God's Son.[18]

Developmental steps. This prayer presents two events in salvation history and one saving event of God in Christ, all of which is the precondition for the following five developmental steps of our Christian maturation.

Salvation history event one: peccati veteris. Implied is an ancient sin.

Salvation history event two: successerat. Humanity followed the hereditary death of the ancient sin until the passion of Christ.

Saving event: solvisti. God destroyed the hereditary death of the ancient sin by the passion of Christ.

Developmental step one: portavimus. By our birth we bear the image of the earthly human.

---

[18] Rom 8:9. Confer: "Therefore we have been buried with him by baptism into death, so that, just as Christ was raised from the dead by the glory of the Father, so we too might walk in newness of life. For if we have been united with him in a death like his, we will certainly be united with him in a resurrection like his" (Rom 6:4-5).

Developmental step two: facti. We were baptized and so made similar to Christ. This step involves an axiological change in our status, as we are made similar to Christ.

Developmental step three: da. We petition God to grant a gift now and into the future. What God grants, however, is expressed by the entire purpose clause, which involves our cooperation. Part of God's gift, then, is to elicit our cooperation in our very transformation. The way in which God gives is part of the gift.

Developmental step four: portemus. Once God grants the gift, we who were made similar to Christ in baptism and have always borne the image of the earthly human in our humanity, we come to bear the image of the heavenly one. This step involves an axiological change between our status as bearing the image of the human person to one of bearing the image of the heavenly one.

As there can be no difference between the axiological change celebrated in baptism and that mentioned here, these correlative phrases may be seen as an amplification of what it is to be baptized. While Baptism is celebrated only once, the sacrament initiates us into the divine-human exchange in which we mature over the course of our lives by the sanctification of grace. Thus, by sanctification we become ever more who we are by the gift of baptism.

Anamnesis. The anamnetic character of this prayer is established by the time of the verb *solvisti* and the reference to the passion of Christ.

Solvisti. We have already seen that interpreting this verb as Time 4b (the historical perfect) situates the saving action of God in human history. Scriptural allusions suggest God's saving action in Christ was accomplished once and for all.

Passione. The ablative of means indicates that God, the subject of *solvisti*, destroyed the hereditary death of the ancient sin by means of the passion of Christ. Thus, this saving event in the life of Christ is the means by which God acted definitively in our history.

Conformes eidem facti. This phrase alludes to our baptism, when we were buried with Christ by baptism into his death, that we might share in his resurrection.[19] Although this clause does not refer to the saving work of God during the life of Christ, the allusion here is to our sacramental sharing in that saving deed through baptism. Thus, the celebration of the sacraments is the way that in our lives we share in the saving deeds of God in Christ.

Eschatology. The purpose clause, alluding to the full humanity and full divinity of Christ, explicitly expresses our eschatological hope of sharing in the divine-human exchange. This eschatological hope may be sequenced over the entire time frame of the first subjunctive relative to the imperative verb *da*, "Grant", for we hope to bear the image of the heavenly one now and on

---

[19] I follow the Pauline imagery of dying and rising here because of the reference to the passion of Christ in the prayer. See: Rom 6:3-4.

into eternity. Thus, in this prayer our eschatological hope for all eternity is already being realized, as we cooperate with God's gift.

The divine-human exchange, moreover, was first revealed in the incarnation, when "the Word became flesh and lived among us, and we have seen his glory, the glory as of a Father's only son, full of grace and truth".[20] When we were baptized into Christ fully human and fully divine, and made similar to him, we were reborn, according to the Johannine imagery,[21] and came to share in this divine-human exchange.

Summary. What I find interesting in this prayer is that the anamnesis refers to the saving passion of Christ, whereas the eschatological hope refers to the divine-human exchange, which was manifested in the incarnation by Christ's full humanity and full divinity.

The anamnetic character of this prayer refers to the saving passion of Christ by which God acted definitively "once for all" in human history to destroy the hereditary death of the ancient sin. The passion was the means through which God acted in history, who acts in our lives sacramentally. We were made similar to Christ by our baptism, in which we died with Christ to rise with him unto a like resurrection, according to Pauline theology.

While the anamnetic character of this prayer is rooted in the passion and celebrated in baptism, its eschatological hope is that we share in the divine-human exchange, which occurred first and foremost in the person of Christ in the incarnation. Again by our baptism we were reborn unto eternal life, according to Johannine imagery, and came to share in his divine-human exchange.

Christian maturation in this prayer is a two step process. The first step is an axiological change that happens in baptism, when we are made similar to Christ and thereby are initiated into the divine-human exchange. The second step extends what we became in baptism throughout the rest of life, as we who are human by necessity, by sanctification come to share ever more fully in Christ's divinity. According to the divine-human exchange, as we come to receive ever more profoundly the gift of God's self freely given to us in Christ, who taking our humanity brought it to its perfection, so we also mature in our capacity, by the sanctification of grace, to give ourselves freely to God in response. We learn to discern the true gift from its many imposters; we distinguish between self-gift from its many substitutes; we learn not to confuse ourselves with the divine, even as we come to share more deeply in the divinity of him who shares and so perfects our humanity. We may come to a certain mutuality in this exchange not because we are equal to God, but because God is revealed as one of us in Christ where divinity and humanity are united without confusion, distinct without division.

---

[20] John 1:14.
[21] John 3:1-21.

The fullness of our hopes, then, remains in our memories, our eschatology was revealed in our anamnesis. Our access to both memories and hopes, anamnesis and eschatology, is through baptism when we are made similar to Christ. While baptism is celebrated only once, we are called to engage in the divine-human exchange throughout our lives and so into eternity, as God continues to grant.

3. **Anamnesis as celebrating the saving events in the life of Christ:** The collect of Holy Thursday

Text. The collect of Holy Thursday reads:

Missale Romanum 2002	*The Sacramentary*
Sacratissimam, Deus, frequentantibus Cenam,	God our Father,
in qua Unigenitus tuus, morti se traditurus,	we are gathered here to share in the
novum in saecula sacrificium	supper
dilectionisque suae convivium Ecclesiae	which your only Son left to his Church to
commendavit,	reveal his love.
da nobis, quaesumus,	He gave it to us when he was about to die
ut ex tanto mysterio	and commanded us to celebrate it as the
plenitudinem caritatis hauriamus et vitae.[22]	new and eternal sacrifice.
	We pray that in this eucharist
	we may find the fullness of love and life.[23]

The author's literal translation for study purposes is:

> Grant, we pray O God, to us celebrating the most holy Supper,
> at which your Only-begotten,
> about to hand himself over to death,
> entrusted to the Church the new sacrifice for the ages,
> and the banquet of his love,
> that from so great a mystery
> we may draw the fullness of love and life

Source. This prayer is a new composition replacing a prayer in the 1962 Missal ,[24] which appears 103 times in the ancient manuscripts in both the presbyteral tradition (*Gelasianum*; Good Friday)[25] and the Papal tradition (*Hadrianum*; Holy Thursday).[26]

---

[22] *MR* 32002, 300.

[23] *The Roman Missal*, 1974, 149.

[24] *MR* 1962, 150. See: *Corpus orationum* n° 1086 a, ed. Moeller (CCL 160 A); BRUYLANTS, *Les oraisons*, 2, n° 200.

[25] *Gelas V* n° 396.

[26] *Gregor* n° 328.

The source of the new composition is the Constitution on the Sacred Liturgy, *Sacrosanctum Concilium*. The chapter on "The Most-holy Mystery of the Eucharist" begins by saying: "Salvator noster, in Cena novissima, qua nocte tradebatur, Sacrificium Eucharisticum Corporis et Sanguinis sui instituit, quo Sacrificium Crucis in saecula, donec veniret, perpetuaret, atque adeo Ecclesiae dilectae Sponsae memoriale concrederet Mortis et Resurrectionis suae".[27]

Literary structure. This prayer has a literary structure composed of a complex petition, a parenthetical petition and a purpose clause. Nestled within the complex petition is the invocation and an amplification of the petition.

First petition. The imperative petition, *Sacratissimam ... frequentantibus Cenam ... da nobis*, "grant to us celebrating the most holy Supper", is translated as, "we are gathered here to share in the supper". The participle *frequentantibus* refers not only "to ones frequenting", referring to our faithfulness over time to the Lord's supper, but also "to ones gathering in great numbers", referring to the assembly, and "to ones celebrating", referring to the supper.

Invocation. Included within the first petition, the simple invocation *Deus*, "God", is elaborated in translation as, "God our Father".

Amplification. Normally amplifying the invocation, here the relative clause amplifies the word *Cenam*, "Supper": *in qua Unigenitus tuus, morti se traditurus, novum in saecula sacrificium dilectionisque suae convivium Ecclesiae commendavit*, "at which your Only-begotten, about to hand himself over to death, entrusted to the Church the new sacrifice for the ages and the banquet of his love", which is rendered as, "which your only Son left to his Church to reveal his love. He gave it to us when he was about to die and commanded us to celebrate it as the new and eternal sacrifice".

Second petition. The parenthetical *quaesumus* is translated literally as, "We pray".

Purpose. Our purpose for praying and God's intent in granting is *ut ex tanto mysterio plenitudinem caritatis hauriamus et vitae*, "that from so great a mystery we may draw the fullness of love and life", which is rendered as, "that in this eucharist we may find the fullness of love and life". There is a parallel between the fullness of love (*caritatis*) and the banquet of his love (*dilectionis*), and a contrast between the fullness of life (*vitae*) and the new sacrifice (*sacrificium*) suggesting a life-giving sacrifice.

---

[27] "Our saviour inaugurated the eucharistic sacrifice of his body and blood at the last supper on the night he was betrayed, in order to make his sacrifice of the cross last throughout time until he should return; and indeed to entrust a token to the church, his beloved wife, by which to remember his death and resurrection" (CONCILIUM OECUMENICUM VATICANUM II, Constitutio de sacra Liturgia *Sacrosanctum concilium*, 4 decembris 1963, n° 47, in *Acta Apostolicae Sedis* 56 [1964] 113).

Verbal times. Having sketched the clausal structure of the prayer, let us now map out the time sequence of the verbs.

da. The independent verb is the imperative *da*, "grant". Its time frame is the present as it continues into the future. We petition God to grant now, to continue granting, and to grant in the future.

frequentantibus. All alone this contemporaneous active participle is contemporaneous with *da*. It agrees with *nobis* and describes our activity.

in qua ... commendavit. The one form *commendavit* may be understood as expressing Time 4a, (the present perfect) or Time 4b (the historical perfect). Were *commendavit* translated in Time 4a (as a present perfect), meaning, "you have entrusted", it would emphasize the immediacy of Christ's entrusting to the Church the meal we are celebrating. I have translated it as a Time 4b (as a historical perfect), meaning "you entrusted", to refer historically to the last supper when Christ entrusted this meal to the church. The presence of the following participle is concurrent with this decision.

traditurus. All alone this future active participle means "one about to hand over". It refers to Christ at the last Supper about to hand himself over to death.

hauriamus. Relative to the imperative *da*, the first subjunctive (present subjunctive) is contemporaneous, ongoing, incomplete, future and eternal. Thus, we pray that God grant now that we may draw now the fullness of love and life, that God continue to grant that we may draw, that God grant at the end of time that we may draw at the end of time, and that God grant eternally that we may eternally draw the fullness of love and life.

Developmental steps. This prayer first presents two saving events as historical, as the precondition for the following four developmental steps of our Christian maturation.

Saving event one: commendavit. At the last supper Christ entrusted to the church the new sacrifice for the ages and the banquet of his love. The Church cooperated with the divine intent by receiving this gift.

Saving event two: traditurus. During that supper Christ was about to hand himself over to death, thus completing the sacrifice of his self.

Developmental step one: frequentantibus Cenam. We celebrate the meal. The full valence of the participle *frequentantibus* involves not only our celebrating the meal over the centuries in continuity with what Christ once entrusted to the Church, but also our celebrating the meal in numbers, as the assembly of those called out by God, the Church.

Developmental step two: novum in saecula sacrificium. Celebrating the meal we share in the new sacrifice, which, although accomplished once, is for the ages.

Developmental step three: da. God grants yet a further gift to us who celebrate the meal that Christ entrusted to the Church. What God grants, however, is expressed by the entire purpose clause, which involves our cooperation. Part of God's gift, then, is to elicit our cooperation in our self-transformation. The way in which God gives is part of the gift.

Developmental step four: hauriamus. When we cooperate with God's gift, we then draw from so great a mystery. That the mystery from which we draw is both the meal and the sacrifice is indicated by the parallelism. As Christ entrusted to the Church the meal of his love, so we draw from this mystery the fullness of love; as Christ entrusted to the Church the new sacrifice for the ages, so we draw from this mystery the fullness of life, according to the divine-human exchange whereby he took our death that we might share divine life.

Anamnesis. The anamnetic character of this prayer is established by the following expressions.

in qua ... commendavit. Interpreting this term as Time 4b (the historical perfect) situates the saving action of God in human history precisely at the last supper.

Unigenitus tuus. While the anamnetic character of this prayer centres on the saving deeds of God in Christ at the last supper, the only way in which the prayer refers to Christ is as *Unigenitus tuus*. That Christ is God's Only-begotten, stretches the anamnetic character of this prayer to include the incarnation.

morti se traditurus. At the last supper Christ anticipated his handing himself over to death. The near juxtaposition of *Unigenitus* and *morti* emphasizes that while the anamnetic character of this prayer and the celebration on Holy Thursday centres on the last supper, every Eucharist celebrates the whole mystery.

novum in saecula sacrificium ... Ecclesiae commendavit. What Christ entrusted to the Church is the two-fold gift of both sacrifice and banquet. First, Christ entrusted the new sacrifice for the ages. Because the sacrifice occurs but once for all time, it is not repeated.

dilectionisque suae convivium Ecclesiae commendavit. Secondly, Christ entrusted to the Church the banquet of his love. This banquet is the repeatable element of the two-fold gift of Christ to the church.

Sacratissimam ... frequentantibus Cenam. Here the anamnetic character of the prayer refers not to the saving event in the life of Christ, but to the saving event in its sacramental celebration.

ex tanto mysterio ... hauriamus. Once again the anamnetic character of the prayer refers not to the saving event in the life of Christ, but to our access to the saving event from which we draw the fullness of love and life, as God grants the gift to those celebrating the meal.

plenitudinem caritatis ... et vitae. The effect of our drawing from so great a mystery is that we draw the fullness of love and life. While these two are not properly anamnetic, these effects in our lives witness to the anamnetic character of our celebrating the meal of his love, who took our death that we might share divine life.

Eschatology. Yet, if the fullness of love and life witnesses to the anamnetic character of the meal we celebrate, they are also the foretaste of the prayer's eschatological force. The purpose clause of this prayer draws together anamnesis and eschatology in the present realization of both.

ex tanto mysterio. The anamnetic force of the purpose clause comes from our drawing from the mystery of the two-fold gift entrusted to the Church by Christ.

plenitudinem caritatis ... et vitae. What we draw from so great a mystery is the fullness of love and life, which are themselves witnesses to the anamnetic character of our celebration even as they are foretastes of eschatological joy.

hauriamus. Yet, the church prays that God grant now that today and continually we may draw the fullness of our hopes from the mystery we celebrate sacramentally. The praying church stands between memories and hopes, between anamnesis and eschatology, drawing the fullness of what we hope for from our sacramental celebration of the saving deeds of God in Jesus Christ.

Summary. The anamnetic character of this prayer centres on the saving work of God in Christ at the last supper and in his sacrificial death, which the Church celebrates in this most holy meal as the repeatable element of a two-fold gift, perpetuating the sacrifice of Christ offered once and for all. As God grants the further gift, we come to draw from this saving mystery the fullness of love and life, themselves partial realizations of our eschatological hopes.

4. **Anamnesis as lived by the faithful**: The collect of the Fourth Sunday of Advent

Text. The collect for the fourth Sunday in Advent reads:

Missale Romanum 2002	*The Roman Missal*
Gratiam tuam, quaesumus, Domine,	Lord, fill our hearts with your love,
mentibus nostris infunde,	and as you revealed to us by an angel
ut qui, Angelo nuntiante,	the coming of your Son as man,
Christi Filii tui incarnationem cognovimus,	so lead us through his suffering and death
per passionem eius et crucem	to the glory of his resurrection.[29]
ad resurrectionis gloriam perducamur.[28]	

The author's literal translation for study purposes is:

> Pour forth your grace, we ask, Lord, into our hearts,

---

[28] *MR* ³2002, 141. See: *Corpus orationum* nº 2748, ed. Moeller (CCL 160 C); BRUYLANTS, *Les oraisons*, 2, nº 575.

[29] *The Roman Missal*, 1974, 25.

that we, who came to know the incarnation of Christ your Son,
as the angel was announcing,
may be led through his passion and cross
unto the glory of the resurrection.[30]

Source. This prayer first appears in the *Hadrianum*,[31] the papal sacramentary given by Pope Hadrian I to Charlemagne in 785-786, in which it served as a post communion prayer of a Mass formulary titled, VIII KALENDAS APRILES ID EST XXV DIE MENSIS MARTII ADNUNTIATIO SANCTAE MARIAE, "the eighth day before the calends of april, that is the 25th day of the month of march, the annunciation to holy mary". The prayer also appears in a later redaction of an earlier source, the *Paduense*,[32] an adaptation of the papal sacramentary compiled around 670-680 for presbyteral use for pilgrims to St Peter's, in which it served as the collect of a mass formulary titled, VIII KALENDAS APRILIS ADNUNTIATIO SANCTAE DEI GENITRICIS ET PASSIO EIUSDEM DOMINI, "The eighth day before the calends of april, the Annunciation of the holy Mother of God and the passion of the same lord". The phrase *eiusdem Domini*, "of the same Lord", agrees with *Dei*, "of God", and refers to the passion of our Lord, born of Mary.

In the *Missale Romanum* of 1962[33] this prayer is given as the post-communion prayer for the feast of the Annunciation. In the *Missale Romanum* of 1970[34] this prayer was transferred to the fourth Sunday of Advent, and another prayer was assigned to the Annunciation. The text of the prayer in the *Missale Romanum* of 1970 and in subsequent missals is the same as that given in the *Paduense*, and differs from that given in the *Hadrianum* only by the addition of the parenthetical petition *quaesumus*.

Assigning this prayer to the Sunday before Christmas warrants fuller explanation according to the currently most-developed theory presented by Thomas Talley, who refutes the attribution of Christmas as a Christianization of the pagan feast of the unconquered sun (*sol invictus*). I summarize Talley's account in the following.[35]

The original Christian feast is Sunday, the Lord's day, on which we celebrate the entire mystery of salvation. By the end of the first century an annual celebration of the passion was celebrated on 14 Nisan, the day in the Jewish lunar calendar on which Christ died according to John (but not

---

[30] Translation by author for study purposes only.

[31] *Gregor* n° 143.

[32] *Pad* 2005, n° 385.

[33] *Missale Romanum ex decreto sacrosancti Concilii Tridentini restitutum summorum pontificum cura recognitum, editio typica*, Typis polyglottis Vaticanis, Città del Vaticano 1962, 496.

[34] *Missale Romanum ex decreto sacrosancti Oecumenici Concilii Vaticani II instauratum auctoritate Pauli PP. IV promulgatum, editio typica*, Typis polyglottis Vaticanis, Città del Vaticano ¹1970, 132.

[35] TALLEY, *The Origins of the Liturgical Year*.

Matthew, Mark and Luke). By the beginning of the second century the nascent Christian community could no longer look to the Jewish leaders to determine when to add an extra month to their lunar calendar to keep it in synchronization with the solar calendar, so they decided to calculate back to the year of our Lord's passion to reckon its exact date according to the solar calendar. In Rome they decided that this fell on 25 March, but in Asia Minor the same day was reckoned as 6 April, because their respective calendars were twelve days off.

This annual feast celebrated in one day the whole mystery of the Lord's dying and rising, to which *passio* in the *Paduense* refers. Furthermore, the idea was then current that a holy person's birth was to be celebrated on the day of one's death so that one's life makes a unity. Thus the incarnation was added to the celebration of the passion. This accounts for the title in the *Paduense*, which unites the annunciation to the passion. As the mystery of the incarnation was apportioned different feasts, the Annunciation remains to this very day on 25 March, but the nativity was assigned to 25 December, nine months later. Similarly, nine months after 6 April is 6 January, the feast of the Epiphany, thus creating the twelve days of Christmas. As Easter has since been transferred to Sunday, so has the Epiphany; of these only the Annunciation and Christmas remain on fixed dates. Thus, we see the genius of offering the prayer originally commemorating the passion and annunciation on the Sunday, the fundamental Christian feast, before the Nativity.

Literary structure. The literary structure of this prayer is composed of two complex units. First a complex petition clause includes a parenthetical petition and a simple invocation. Second, a purpose clause includes a motive and a premise clause as well as a phrase expressing instrumentality.

First petition. The prayer begins with the imperative petition, *Gratiam tuam, quaesumus ... mentibus nostris infunde*, "pour forth your grace, we ask, into our hearts", which is translated as, "fill our hearts with your love". The noun *mentibus* refers to the internal life and thus the mind, heart, conscience, intention.

Second petition. Nestled within the first petition is the parenthetical petition *quaesumus*, "we ask, please", which is translated in the concluding doxology as, "we ask this".

Invocation. Also nestled within the petition is the simple invocation *Domine*, which is translated literally as, "Lord".

Purpose. The prayer then states the purpose for which we petition, and the Lord's intention in pouring forth grace, *ut ... per passionem eius et crucem ad resurrectionis gloriam perducamur*, "that we may be led through his passion and cross unto the glory of the resurrection", which is translated as, "so lead us through his suffering and death to the glory of his resurrection".

Motive. God's motive for leading us through the passion and cross to the glory of the resurrection, is expressed by the relative clause nestled within the purpose clause, *qui … Christi Filii tui incarnationem cognovimus*, "we who came to know the incarnation of Christ your Son", which is translated by, "as you revealed to us… the coming of your Son as man".

Premise. Nestled within the motive clause is an ablative absolute expressing the premise of our coming to know, *Angelo nuntiante*, "as the angel announces", which is translated as an ablative of instrument, "by an angel". The participle *nuntiante* is contemporaneous with *cognovimus*. One of the subtleties of this prayer is that the Angel's announcing could refer to the annunciation to Mary (Luke 1:26-38), or the proclamation of the nativity to the shepherds (Luke 2:8-14).

Verbal times. Having sketched the clausal structure of the prayer, let us now map out the time sequence of the verbs.

infunde. The independent verb is the imperative *infunde*, "pour forth". Its time frame is the present as it continues into the future. We petition God to pour forth now, to continue pouring forth, and to pour forth in the future.

perducamur. Relative to the imperative *infunde*, the first subjunctive (present subjunctive) *perducamur* is contemporaneous, ongoing, incomplete, future and eternal. Thus, we pray that God pour forth grace into our hearts now that we may be led now, that we may continue to be led and that at the end of time we may be led finally.

Qui … cognovimus. The one form *cognovimus* may be understood as expressing Time 4a, (the present perfect) or Time 4b (the historical perfect). Were *cognovimus* Time 4a (a present perfect), meaning, "we have come to know", its subject "we" would be identified specifically as the ones offering the prayer, as in "we who are praying have come to know of the incarnation of Christ, your Son". Because *cognovimus* is dependent upon *perducamur*, its time frame would be determined by the full range of time that *perducamur* has in the prayer; as a present perfect *cognovimus*, would refer to a time before but touching upon the time of *perducamur*. I have translated *cognovimus*, however, as expressive of Time 4b (a historical perfect), meaning, "we came to know". Such a translation is reinforced by the idea expressed in the ablative absolute, so let us first consider the ablative absolute.

Angelo nuntiante. The participle *nuntiante* is contemporaneous with *cognovimus*. The idea expressed in the ablative absolute, however, refers to two saving mysteries in the history of salvation, both the annunciation of the Angel unto Mary and the proclamation of the nativity to the shepherds keeping watch over their flocks. These referents in the history of salvation suggest translating *cognovimus* as Time 4b (a historical perfect), meaning, "we came to know", as in the translation: "we who came to know the incarnation of Christ your Son, as the Angel was announcing".

Translating *cognovimus* as Time 4b (a historical perfect), and anchoring it to the time of the annunciation and incarnation means that the subject "we" must refer to those who first came to know of the incarnation, whether Mary in the annunciation, the shepherds of the nativity, or even believers or the world in general. Yet, the ones offering the prayer understand themselves in some way connected with those who first came to know of the incarnation.

Developmental steps. This prayer presents two saving events as historical, as the precondition for the following five developmental steps of our Christian maturation.

Saving events one: nuntiante. The angel announces the incarnation.

Saving events two: cognovimus. Humanity receives this announcement in the person of Mary, and in the shepherds. Thus, the initiative is the Lord's, while Mary cooperates, and the shepherds respond.

Developmental step one: cognovimus. We who offer this prayer see ourselves in some way part of the "we" who first came to know of the incarnation.

Developmental step two: infunde. We pray that the Lord grant the gift of pouring forth grace into our hearts. This implies on our part an active receptivity of the Lord's grace.

Developmental step three: perducamur. We are led. As *perducamur* is a divine passive, it implies that the Lord leads us, and we cooperate by being led.

Developmental step four: per passionem eius et crucem. We are led through the passion and cross of Christ, as we take up our crosses daily and follow Christ.

Developmental step five: ad resurrectionis gloriam. We are led unto the glory of the resurrection, which we come to enjoy, if only partially, as we pass through the previous four steps.

Anamnesis. The saving deeds of God in Christ as mentioned directly or indirectly in this prayer are the incarnation, the passion, the cross and the resurrection. Let us look at each one of these individually.

incarnationem cognovimus. If one defines anamnesis narrowly to refer to the saving deeds of God in Christ, then the Angel's announcing is not properly part of the anamnetic character of this prayer. But, the Angel does announce the saving mystery of the incarnation, be it the annunciation or the nativity. Furthermore, the incarnation is not presented in this prayer as a verb, but as the object of our coming to know. Thus, the saving mystery in the life of Christ is presented in its quality as known by us, even if by our association with those who first came to know of the incarnation.

per passionem eius et crucem. Similarly Christ's passion and cross are not considered in their quality as historical events. Rather, they are the means through which we are led unto the glory of the resurrection. In this regard, the use of the word *crucem* instead of *mortem* allows a subtlety of interpretation. Were the purpose clause to state, "that we may be led through his passion and death unto the resurrection", then one could more easily establish a one to one correspondence between Christ's passion and our suffering, Christ's death and our death, Christ's resurrection and our hope for the after-life. The allusion to the death of Christ, I suggest, however, does not correspond directly with our own death, because in the Gospels Christ tells us to take up our cross and follow him. The cross corresponds, then, to our lives lived in the light of his cross. Viewed in this light the reference to the passion of Christ does not correspond simply with the struggle of our last hours before death, but is also patient of our way of living as well.

Eschatology. *Ad resurrectionis gloriam*. Similarly, this prayer does not refer to the resurrection in its quality as a past event. Were the prayer to petition that we may be led unto the resurrection, it would easily correspond to our hope for the after-life. I suggest that the phrase "glory of the resurrection" is patient of a present realization, if only partially. Such an interpretation is permitted grammatically because *perducamur* may be interpreted as contemporaneous to *infunde*. In the appearances of the risen Lord to the disciples, moreover, we see our future fulfilment, our eschatological fullness, revealed to the first disciples in history.

Summary. On this Sunday before the feast of the nativity of the Lord, the prayer states that we have come to know the incarnation. Thus, the incarnation, although a saving event of salvation history, is not referred to in its quality as a historical event, but as a reality that we share in through knowing. Even more, the passion and cross of Christ, however historical, are not presented in their quality as historical events, but as realities through which we are led to arrive at the glory of the resurrection. Thus, the passion and cross of Christ are the means through which we are led to the glory of the resurrection. Our hope in this prayer is that we may be so led to share in the glory of the resurrection even now as God pours forth grace into our hearts.

There is a lovely inversion in this prayer between our memories and our hopes. First, all references to the mysteries of the life of Christ in salvation history are situated within the purpose clause, and thus our memories are situated within our hopes: *anamnesis* is part of *eschatology*.

Second, because our future glory has already been revealed in salvation history in the appearances of the risen Christ to the disciples, our hopes are already fulfilled in our memory: *eschatology* is part of *anamnesis*.

Third, all the references to the saving mysteries of the life of Christ are made in regard to our experiencing them now. The incarnation, although situated in salvation history, is not referred to in its quality as a historical event, but as a reality that we came to know through Mary and the shepherds. Furthermore, the passion and cross are not referred to in their quality as historical events, nor do they correspond simply with our own suffering and death, but are presented as the means through which the Lord is working in our lives now. Finally, the glory of the resurrection is not presented as a historical event, or as corresponding to our after-life, but as a glory unto which we are led even now, if only partially, as the Lord pours forth grace into our hearts. Thus, our memories and hopes all impinge upon the present moment and are at work in us even now: *anamnesis* is active and *eschatology* is being realized, even if inchoately. The present moment is not static, for both our memories and hopes play a dynamic role as we progress through the developmental steps of Christian maturation.

Conclusion

This examination of four collects allows us to make some initial comments on the anamnetic and eschatological character of the collects.

Anamnesis. Concerning anamnesis we can say first of all that many collects do not have an explicit reference to the saving deeds of God in Christ.

Second, we have examined the collect of Good Friday, which mentions the saving work of God in Christ, whose passion was the means by which God destroyed the hereditary death of the ancient sin. Furthermore, through the sacrament of baptism we are made similar to Christ, and thus come to share in God's saving work in Christ.

Third, we examined the collect for Holy Thursday, The Mass of the Lord's Supper. While the anamnetic character of this collect focuses upon the Last Supper, it also alludes to the incarnation and the death of Christ, providing a broader reference to the saving work of God in Christ. At the Last Supper, the Only-begotten entrusted a two-fold gift to the church. He entrusted both the new sacrifice for the ages and the banquet of his love. The banquet is the repeatable element of this two-fold gift of Christ. We come to share in this saving work through our sacramental celebration of the most-holy supper. The mystery from which we draw is not only the saving events in the life of Christ but is also our sharing in them through the sacramental meal. From this mystery, we draw the fullness of love because we draw from the banquet of the Only-begotten's love, and we draw the fullness of life from the new sacrifice of him who once took our death that we might share his life.

Fourth, we examined the collect for the fourth Sunday of Advent, previously assigned to the feast of the Annunciation on 25 March. Only part of the anamnetic character of this collect is set in the past; it concerns our coming to know the incarnation through Mary and the Shepherds. The passion and cross of Christ are presented not in their quality as historical events, but as the means through which God leads us unto the glory of the resurrection.

Thus, the anamnetic character of these prayers involves both the narration of the saving work of God in Christ and their ritual celebration in baptism and in the meal we share. Furthermore, the specific mysteries in the life of Christ were the means by which God worked in Christ and remain the means by which God continues the saving work of Christ in our lives.

Eschatology. Lest it be presumed that these collects need to reclaim their eschatological dimension, the full range of time of the first subjunctive (present subjunctive) relative to the imperative verb, allows not only a future eschatology, but admits its present, even if partial, realization in the lives of those praying. Each collect presents the eschatological element in a proper way.

First, the collect for the third Sunday of Ordinary Time presents an eschatology that is realized only while on earth, for our good works now pertain to the final judgment.

Second, the eschatological hope expressed in the collect of Good Friday is our desire to share in the divine-human exchange by coming to share in the divinity of him who shared in our mortality. Yet, the very idea of the union between God and humanity speaks not only to the death of Christ, but also to the incarnation and life of Christ now seated at the right hand of the Father. Thus, our sharing in the divine-human exchange finds its referent not simply in the death of Christ, but in his person. We pray that this hope be realized now, continuously, in the future, and eternally, for at present we hope to share if only partially in the divine-human exchange, which we hope to enjoy in its fullness eternally.

Third, the collect for Holy Thursday presents an eschatological hope that we may draw the fullness of love and life. Yet, we draw both of these from the mystery of Christ's entrusting to the church the new sacrifice for the ages and the banquet of his love, which meal we share. In sharing this meal, we already draw from the fullness of the love and life of God.

Fourth, the collect for the fourth Sunday of Advent presents an eschatological hope, which we come to share in this life as we are ever drawn toward its fullness already revealed in the risen Lord's appearances to the disciples.

Between memories and hopes. The praying church, standing in the present, is called to her future eschatological fullness, which was already revealed in her past. The praying church, standing in the present, recalls the memories of saving deeds of God in Christ in salvation history, which reveal the eschatological hopes to which she is called. Not only is her future revealed in her past and her memories reveal her hopes, but both past and future impinge upon the present moment of prayer in that the saving deeds of God in Christ in salvation history remain the means through which God works our salvation today, which is to say that already in the present God brings us to share even if only partially in that fullness to which we are called. Thus, to say that the saving deeds of God in Christ are active today is to say that the eschatological fullness is already being realized, even if partially, in the praying church: anamnesis, then, is active and eschatology is being realized. Thus, the praying church, standing in the present, projects herself into her own hopes, already realized in her memories and sees that her memories are actively transforming her at present.

This transformation, furthermore, comes about *per ritus et preces*, "through rites and prayers",[36] through word and sacrament, through proclamation and ritual. The praying church both narrates her memory of the saving deeds of the life of Christ, and ritualizes them, but not as two successive steps, for her narration is ritualized, and her ritual is narrative. The collect for Holy Thursday indicates that through the church's celebration of the banquet of Christ's love the saving deed of his sacrifice, made once and for all, is perpetuated. So too, even the proclamation of simple collects involves a ritual, for we gather, stand, raise our hands and proclaim the saving deeds of Christ in the ritual context. Thus, the anamnetic force of even these brief collects comes from their ritual narration of the saving mysteries of the life of Christ, and the narrative ritual of the church at prayer.

---

[36] *Sacrosanctum concilium* n° 48, in *AAS* 56 (1964) 113.

Bibliography

A. Holy Scripture

Biblia Sacra: Iuxta vulgatam versionem, ed. R. Gryson, Deutsche Bibelgesellschaft, Stuttgart 1994.
The Holy Bible Containing the Old and New Testaments with the Apocryphal / Deuterocanonical Books, New Revised Standard Version, Oxford UP, New York – Oxford 1989.

B. Research tools

BRUYLANTS, P., *Les oraisons du Missel Romain, texte et histoire* (Études liturgiques 2 vol.), Mont César, Louvain 1952.
Corpus orationum, 14 vol., ed. E. Moeller – J.-M. Clément – B.C. 't Wallant (Corpus christianorum series latina 160-160 M), Brepols, Turnhout 1992-2004.

C. Liturgical sources

"Gregorianum paduense ad fidem codicis Paduensis D 47, Fragmentis collatis Salisburgensibus", *Le Sacramentaire Grégorien*, 3 vol., ed. J. Deshusses (Spicilegium Friburgense 16), Éditions universitaires, Fribourg ³1992, 1, 607-684 (*Pad* 1992).
"Hadrianum ex authentico", *Le Sacramentaire Grégorien: Ses principales formes d'après les plus anciens manuscrits*, 3 vol., ed. J. Deshusses (Spicilegium Friburgense 16), Éditions universitaires, Fribourg ³1992, 1, 83-348 (*Gregor*).
Liber sacramentorum paduensis (*Padova, Biblioteca Capitolare, cod. D 47*), ed. A. Catella – F. dell'Oro – A. Martini (Bibliotheca Ephemerides Liturgicae, Subsidia 131. Monumenta italiae liturgica 3), Centro Liturgico Vincenziano edizioni liturgiche, Rome 2005 (*Pad* 2005).
Liber sacramentorum augustodunensis, ed. O. Heiming (Corpus christianorum series latina 159 B), Brepols, Turnhout 1984.
Liber sacramentorum engolismensis (*Cod. B. N. Lat. 816*) n° 650, ed. P. Saint-Roch (Corpus christianorum series latina 159 C), Brepols, Turnhout 1987.
Liber sacramentorum gellonensis, textus n° 664, ed. A. Dumas – J. Deshusses (Corpus christianorum series latina 159), Brepols, Turnhout 1981.
Liber sacramentorum romanae aeclesiae ordinis anni circuli (*Cod. Vat. Reg. Lat. 316/Paris Bibl. Nat. 7193, 41/56*) (*Sacramentarium Gelasianum*), ed. L.C. Mohlberg – L. Eizenhöfer – P. Siffrin (Rerum ecclesiasticarum documenta. Series maior, Fontes 4), Herder, Rome 1960 (*GelasV*).
Missale Romanum ex decreto SS. Concilii Tridentini restitutum summorum pontificum cura recognitum, editio typica, Typis polyglottis Vaticanis, Città del Vaticano 1962.
Missale Romanum ex decreto sacrosancti Oecumenici Concilii Vaticani II instauratum auctoritate Pauli PP. IV promulgatum, editio typica, Typis polyglottis Vaticanis, Città del Vaticano ¹1970.

Missale Romanum ex decreto Sacrosancti Oecumenici Concilii Vaticani II instauratum auctoritate Pauli PP. VI promulgatum Ioannis Pauli PP. II cura recognitum, editio typica tertia, Typis Vaticanis, Città del Vaticano ³2002 (*MR* ³2002).

Le Sacramentaire Grégorien: Ses principales formes d'après les plus anciens manuscrits, 3 vol., ed. J. Deshusses (Spicilegium Friburgense 16), Éditions universitaires, Fribourg, 1 ³1992, 2 ²1988, 3 ²1992.

D. Translations of liturgical sources

The Roman Missal, revised by decree of the Second Vatican Council and published by the authority of Paul VI, official English texts, Collins, London 1974.

E. Magisterial sources

CONCILIUM OECUMENICUM VATICANUM II, Constitutio de sacra Liturgia *Sacrosanctum concilium*, 4 decembris 1963, in *Acta Apostolicae Sedis* 56 (1964) 97-138.

F. Studies

MCCARTHY, D.P., "Human Impulse, Divinely Ordered", *The Tablet* 261 (20 January 2007) 17.

TALLEY, T., *The Origins of the Liturgical Year*, Liturgical Press (Pueblo Book), Collegeville MN ²1991.

VOGEL, C., *Medieval Liturgy: An Introduction to the Sources*, tr., rev. W.G. Storey – N.K. Rasmussen (National Association of Pastoral Musicians Studies in Church Music and Liturgy), Pastoral Press, Washington DC 1986 (of *Introduction aux sources de l'histoire du culte Chrétien au moyen âge*, Centro italiano di studi sull'alto medioevo, Spoleto 1981).

CHAPTER 10

Concluding Synthesis

Ephrem Carr

What is a collect? From different fields and approaches the essays in the present volume reflect on the question and offer insights that may help toward an ever more satisfactory answer to the question. Four papers were prepared for a colloquium held at the Pontifical Athenaeum of Sant'Anselmo, Rome, in May 2008, the first in a series of colloquia, which form part of the *Documenta Rerum Ecclesiasticarum Instaurata* project. The idea for such an undertaking sprang from an informal discussion at the Societas Liturgica meeting at Palermo in 2007. As a result of discussions at the colloquium, the four papers were revised, and others already commissioned were added to complete this volume.

Dom James Leachman began the colloquium with a historical presentation on collect studies from the sixteenth century to the present to give a context for the methodology of studying and interpreting liturgical sources. This methodology has been built upon critical editions of historically important liturgical texts and is currently used at the Pontifical Institute of Liturgy of Sant'Anselmo. The sixteenth century saw the first collection and publication of sources, often in the context of controversy between Reformers and Roman Catholics. The following two centuries witnessed the publication of other important medieval liturgical books and commentaries. The first scientific studies on collects come from Anglican and Roman circles in the nineteenth century.

During the twentieth century the first truly critical editions of the texts were produced and the scientific methodology was developed for liturgical studies upon the basis of source and form criticism. The historical critical method in liturgy was borrowed from biblical and historical studies and applied to liturgical texts. The research into the origins and forms of Christian Latin became an important auxiliary science. Decisive for the methodology developed at Sant'Anselmo was the insistence of the early generation of professors that the program concentrate on the method used to attain a truly academic approach to the study of liturgy. The method developed and applied today represents the successive efforts of M. Augé, A.M. Triacca with R. Farina, and R. De Zan.

One should note also the amazing development of on-line tools for research, and the increasing knowledge of medieval Latin with the aid of specialized dictionaries and studies of the Latin language by scholars like E. Rose in the recent critical edition of the *Missale gothicum*.

Father Reginald Foster has contributed a study on the Latin of the Roman collects. He explains the importance of the clausal structure of the Latin language, which he illustrates with many Latin collects of the Roman Missal of Paul VI. After enumerating the times of Latin verbs, he places special emphasis on the distinction and sense of times 4a and 4b. Their forms are identical, but their meanings quite distinct, which he compares to a video and a snapshot. He goes on to treat the principles for using the subjunctives and the sequence of tenses – also important for an accurate sense of the verb used in its clausal structure. Again of note is the clear distinction he introduces between purpose and result clauses. Finally he explains the Latin gerund and gerundive. A correct understanding of the Latin usage is the surest way to arrive at the true meaning of the collect. It is to be regretted that he did not go into the other areas he mentioned at the end of his article: participles and the accusative and infinitive, for example. We await his further contributions to complete his comprehensive study of the Latin language of the collects.

Don Renato De Zan applies his work on the method of interpreting liturgical texts to the specific case of the collects. First he researches the words used for this first presidential prayer of the Eucharist. After the question of the vocabulary he turns to the character or genre of the prayer, then its place within the rite. The essay reviews the search for a systematic and integral method that takes into consideration the stylistic features within the use of the historical-critical method and with a sense for the ritual context of the prayer and the help of the human sciences.

After a brief introduction to the history of collect studies, the author first considers the role of textual criticism, then of philological analysis of the Latin words and constructions. A detailed presentation of semasiological analysis and of semantic analysis follows with examples from Mass collects. The study turns to the fabric of meaning by illustrating the methods of Bremond and Greimas. Because the sense of a prayer in its original context may differ significantly from that of its "new" context, the author then considers the question of the historical-geographical epoch and the subsequent development of the text; this raises the question of the "authenticity" of the prayer in regard to its historical period. The literary identity of the text includes a presentation of the literary structure of a collect used in all the studies of this present volume. This literary structure is composed of various arrangements of five basic elements: invocation, amplification, petition, purpose and motive (or cause). The article closes with a treatment of pragmatic analysis; this addresses the difficult question of what the collect does in its ritual position. De Zan's aim is to combine the essential elements from the historical-critical methodologies with linguistic and anthropological approaches. He deliberately does not consider in this article the theology of the collect nor its translation.

Dom Patrick Regan places the collect in its literary and ritual context. He first covers the history of naming the prayer in Roman and non-Roman liturgical documents. The use of the name "collect" began North of the Alps in the Carolingian epoch but became official for the Roman rite only in the Missal of Paul VI (1970), though it was used earlier, especially in the twentieth century. Its earlier denomination was simply "*Oratio*" (prayer).

A collect is a succinct, carefully drafted formula. The Roman Missal of Paul VI calls it a "presidential prayer" that expresses "the character of the celebration". It is a prayer of petition that "collects" the sentiments, needs, desires, and aspirations of all present. Its purpose is to gather and synthesize the prayers made silently by the assembled faithful. Its theological import comes from the fact that it is a "corporate prayer" giving climactic utterance to the silent petitions of the faithful with their response "Amen" that confirms, approves, corroborates, ratifies the "common prayer". As to its function, the collect concludes everything which precedes it and so becomes the pinnacle of the entrance rites of the Eucharist. It concludes one ritual unit but is also a link to the next, the Liturgy of the Word. The collect also has a place in the Liturgy of the Hours and other ceremonies.

Each of the studies establishes the source of its prayer and offers a linguistic analysis, though not all follow the presentation of the Latin Language by Foster. With the exception of the contribution of Gerard Moore, the papers that follow consider specific collects. Each follows the method of De Zan, though none use to the full extent the detailed methodology expounded by him. All follow his outline of the collect's literary structure, though some add elements not noted by him, for example, expressions of means or instrumentality, premise clauses and the divine passive.

The collect for the Easter Vigil is considered in the contribution of Dom James Leachman, which includes a history of the prayer from the Old Gelasian through all the centuries of the Roman liturgy, and there follows a presentation of its literary or stylistic structure. The immediate context in the Easter Vigil and its surrounding texts and the larger context in the *Order of Christian Initiation of Adults* and in the liturgical year are all important for the theological sense of this collect. The prayer has been altered to fit its new position in the Vigil after the Gloria and before the celebration of Baptism. There is an interesting verbal parallel with the collect of the Midnight Mass of Christmas and, less so, with the Pentecost Vigil Mass. The allusions bring together the Incarnation, Easter and Baptism.

Leachman's article introduces the use of theological interpretative keys drawn from other writings of E. Lodi and De Zan. Leachman concludes that the contexts and interpretative keys situate the liturgical-theological core of the prayer in the divine–human exchange, which results from God's initiative and calls forth the openness of our human cooperation. Our human-divine development runs through all our life to the end.

The Easter Sunday collect for Holy Communion in the first *Prayer Book* of Edward VI (1549), a classic example of an Anglican collect, is considered in the contribution of Bridget Nichols. Although it is derived from an original Latin text in the Sarum Missal (a descendant of the *Hadrianum*), this English prayer is more an adaptation from the hand of Thomas Cranmer than a translation. To the original the English collect adds emphasis, color and feeling, all part of the distinctiveness of an Anglican collect. More than anything else the prayer vividly expresses the Reformation mindset of Cranmer who eliminated any suggestion of merit or good works from the collects of the *Prayer Book* (1549). The new doctrinal approach reveals Cranmer's evangelical interpretation of justification, grace and works and salvation by faith alone. Cranmer embraces the notion of "convergent wills", the will that desires to work in harmonious obedience to the will of God who wills good for his creation.

In discussion Nichols asked whether the method outlined by De Zan can be applied as it stands to English language collects. In terms of liturgical structure and language she noted the problem of "committee revision" to produce modern collects. How does that influence the interpretation of the text?

The opening prayer for the Epiphany is the subject of the presentation of Rev. Anthony Igbekele. The collect is first found in the *Hadrianum* and may have been written by the hand of Gregory the Great. The collect interprets the visit of the Magi according to Matthew (2:2) in a liturgical-theological manner to express the core idea of the manifestation of Christ to the nations. The vocabulary of the prayer shows numerous other biblical parallels, of which 2 Corinthians 5:7 is of particular note. Igbekele uses philological analysis, historical identity and contextual identity to arrive at the meaning and theology of the prayer. The text puts especial theological emphasis on the necessity of faith and hope in the eschatological vision of the glory of God. The Father's saving work in Christ is stressed as well. The author finds that the collect presents salvation history according to six stages, yet, here, it seems to me rather forced.

Gerard Moore examines the vocabulary of the Roman collects as a Biblical heritage. Contrary to the position of Theodor Klauser, Moore insists with the *General Instruction of the Roman Missal* (391)[1] that these prayers draw upon the inspiration and spirit of the Sacred Scriptures. The question is not just whether their vocabulary is found in Scripture, rather it concerns how

---

[1] "Ex sacra Scriptura enim ... atque ex eius afflatu instinctuque preces, orationes et carmina liturgica effusa sunt, ut ex ea significationem suam actiones et signa accipiunt" (*Missale Romanum, ex decreto Sacrosancti Oecumenici Concilii Vaticani II instauratum auctoritate Pauli PP. VI promulgatum Ioannis Pauli PP. II cura recognitum, Insituttio Generalis, ex editione typica tertia cura et studio Congregationis de Cultu Divino et Disciplina Sacramentorum excerpta, editio prae-typica tertia*, Libreria editrice Vaticana, Città del Vaticano 2000, n° 391.

the collects reflect a Biblical basis. While some collects clearly derive from Scriptural passages often applied to pastoral situations, others contain a "play" on a Scriptural text or on particular Biblical words, and so challenge the faithful to hear the words of the Scriptures in a different context. Collects are faithful to Biblical usage even when their meaning is enriched through allusions to the Scriptures. The text of the collect alone is not enough; the historical and liturgical context of the prayer is important for understanding its Biblical content.

Moore insists on the importance of the vocabulary of naming God in the collects. The Hebrew theology of the divine 'Name' is at its core and informs the range of meanings when speaking of God. 'Name' expresses the divine being or essence. Although the doxology that concludes the collect at Mass clearly names the Trinity, Roman collects as a whole exhibit an implicit rather than explicit pneumatology. The Biblical foundation for the theology of God is expressed in the prayers' characterize of God as holiness, majesty, love and power, as well as by loving kindness, mercy and divine strength.

The second major theme of Moore's article is the characteristic style of a collect. The author is skeptical of the need for a "high" style in vocabulary and grammatical structure. Is a priestly and holy style that avoids familiarity the sole style fitting for prayer? Collects are often characterized by a precise, concise, sober style without exuberant, emotive or ostentatious elements. But is a highly stylized form and elegant language uniquely appropriate for divine worship? The influence of the rhetorical traditions of Rome is certainly felt, in particular in the use of *cursus* – rhythm and harmony of units or clauses – that ring in the ears and minds of the hearers. The prayer's accessibility to the faithful and the grasp of familiar Biblical texts were not above the "sophistication" of worshippers in the early Latin church. Incomprehensibility is not necessary to reverence and honor God, as some would claim.

Dom Daniel McCarthy chooses to study two interpretative keys in four collects of two Sundays, Holy Thursday and Good Friday. They represent both traditional Roman prayers and new compositions. His method is especially structural and verbal analysis. A study of this sort is valuable for the comparison and contrast of prayers following a certain theological theme or themes. Each collect is analyzed in terms of its historical source, its literary structure, the verbal times (according to Foster's scheme), developmental steps of Christian maturation and then in terms of anamnesis and eschatology.

An important discovery is that many collects do not have explicit reference to the saving deeds of God in Christ. The collect for Holy Thursday, on the other hand, posits the whole 'mystery' from the incarnation to the death of Christ. It also presents the Eucharist as both sacrifice (once for all) and banquet (repeated in each celebration). The collect for the fourth Sunday of Advent covers all the saving deeds of God in Christ from the incarnation to the general resurrection on the final day.

The definition of anamnesis that is chosen – the saving deeds of God in Christ – is neither typical nor complete. Normally anamnesis is of all the variable *mirabilia Dei*. For the study, eschatology can be both present (being realized in this world) and future. In the selected collects eschatology covers the full range of time from realization in the present in the lives of those praying to future eschatological fullness. Thus the title of the paper: "Between memories and hopes".

The essays gathered in this volume show a great amount of convergence, but also divergence in some particulars of approach. The volume shows the value of such a colloquium on the subject and should encourage further such efforts. Some further clarity in terminology and perhaps a discussion about the 'why' of the divergences, in my opinion, would be useful. Were the full program of methodology as outlined by De Zan to have been used by each participant, it might have provided a more fruitful comparison of results for the interpretation of collects; yet one of the strengths of this collection of essays is its diversity of voices. May the good work begun with the grace of God continue to bear fruit in a greater appreciation of the liturgy!

List of Participants at the First Colloquium
31st May 2008

Rt Rev. Cuthbert Brogan OSB (St Michael's Abbey, Farnborough, UK)

Fr Ephrem Carr OSB (St Meinrad's Archabbey, Indiana, USA)

Fr Reginaldus Thomas Foster OSD (Secretariat of State, Vatican City)

Rev. Dr. Anthony Igbekele (Diocese of Ondo, Nigeria)

Rev Dr. John Lampard (Methodist, London, UK)

Fr James G. Leachman OSB (St Benedict's Abbey, Ealing, London, UK)

Fr Daniel P. McCarthy OSB (St Benedict's Abbey, Atchison, Kansas, USA)

Dr Bridget Nichols (Diocese of Ely, Church of England, UK)

Fr Patrick Regan OSB (abbot emeritus, St Joseph's Abbey, Louisiana, USA)

Index of Names

Index of Biblical Sources

Index of Liturgical Sources

Index of Incipits of Prayer and Hymn Texts